KING ALFRED'S COLLEGE
WINCHESTER

To be returned on or before the day marked
below :—

19. MAY 1978		
0 1 OCT 2001		

GEORGIAN OXFORD

Oxford University Press, Amen House, London E.C.4

GLASGOW NEW YORK TORONTO MELBOURNE WELLINGTON
BOMBAY CALCUTTA MADRAS KARACHI KUALA LUMPUR
CAPE TOWN IBADAN NAIROBI ACCRA

GEORGIAN OXFORD

University Politics in the
Eighteenth Century

BY

W. R. WARD

OXFORD
AT THE CLARENDON PRESS
1958

Pedantry is perhaps a thing, more or less, inseparable from all Universities, I say, from a mixture of old recluses, and unexperienced striplings, as the getting rid of it, is one advantage a man has by coming abroad in the world. . . .

J. TOLAND, *The State Anatomy of Great Britain* (1717)

PRINTED IN GREAT BRITAIN
AT THE UNIVERSITY PRESS, OXFORD
BY CHARLES BATEY, PRINTER TO THE UNIVERSITY

PREFACE

THIS study aims to cast light on certain aspects of Oxford life in one of its less esteemed and less understood periods, and on one of the many varieties of eighteenth-century Toryism of which much remains to be learned. It is not a tract for the times, though not a few of the issues raised in it have become painfully familiar of late years. I cannot hope to have successfully surmounted all the hazards of college history, but must plead that progress in the writing of college history waits upon a fuller knowledge of university affairs. My obligations are legion. To Sir Lewis Namier I owe my first introduction to the Newdigate MSS. from which this study grew; his patience with young students grows no less with the years, and the archive of the *History of Parliament* has become a bottomless well of information for all who will make use of it. I am particularly indebted to him for permission to use his transcripts of the Bute MSS., and to Lord Lansdowne and the Trustees of the *History of Parliament* for access to transcripts of the Bowood MSS. My best thanks are due to Mr. Humphrey Fitzroy Newdegate for permission to use the papers of Sir Roger Newdigate, to the Earl of Aylesford for hospitality and access to his family papers, and to the Earl of Harrowby for the loan of a typescript copy of the MS. Diary of Sir Dudley Ryder. Through the kindness of the Wake Trustees and Librarian of Christ Church I was able to make use of the valuable papers of Archbishop Wake, and the Trustees of Dr. William's Library admitted me to their collections of Lindsey MSS., Blackburne MSS., and Disney Papers. For permission to examine the rest of the Lindsey MSS. I am indebted to the late Principal of the Unitarian College, Manchester. My obligations to authorities of the University and colleges of Oxford are too numerous to record in full, but I am particularly grateful to Mr. W. A. Pantin for access to the university archives and Provost Carter's Memorandum Book, and to the Warden and Librarian of All Souls, the Librarian of Balliol, the Custos Archivorum of Exeter, the President of Magdalen, and the Librarian of Queen's for access to manuscripts in their charge. The county archivists at Warwick and Lamport Hall dealt helpfully with inconvenient requests, and whatever

v

else may fail in the Bodleian, the milk of human kindness always abounds; especially am I obliged to Messrs. Cordeaux and Merry who have made available to me their monumental bibliography of works on the University which is now in progress. To Mr. I. G. Philip I owe the information received after this book was in print that some Blackstone correspondence in his charge suggests that Blackstone's missing pamphlets referred to in Note T, p. 284, may be identified with papers in Bodl. G.A. Oxon. b. 19. The Master and fellows of Trinity College, Cambridge, granted permission to refer to two transcripts from their Browne MSS. kindly lent me by Dr. J. F. A. Mason of Christ Church. Mr. W. C. Costin supplied me with useful information relating to St. John's, and Mr. M. G. Brock made some valuable suggestions as the book went through the press. The whole work was greatly facilitated by a generous research grant made by the Leverhulme Trustees.

W. R. W.

Manchester
5 November 1957

CONTENTS

CONTENTS

PART IV

THE COURT TRIES AGAIN
1751–68

PART V

THE RECONCILIATION OF COURT AND UNIVERSITY, 1768–80

ABBREVIATIONS

All Souls Archives	C. T. Martin, *Catalogue of the Archives of All Souls College* (London, 1877).
All Souls MSS.	MSS. in the archives of All Souls College, Oxford: MSS. of Warden of All Souls College are MSS. in possession of the Warden not deposited in the College archives.
Balliol College MSS.	MSS. in the Library of Balliol College, Oxford.
B.M.	MSS. in the British Museum, London.
Bowood MSS.	MSS. of Lord Lansdowne at Bowood.
Browne MSS.	MSS. at Trinity College, Cambridge.
Cal. S.P. Dom.	*Calendar of State Papers Domestic.*
Christ Church MS. Arch. W. Epist.	MS. Letters of Archbishop Wake at Christ Church, Oxford.[1]
C.J.	*Journals of the House of Commons.*
Cobbett	*Cobbett's Parliamentary History of England*, ed. W. Cobbett (London, 1806–24).
Coxe, *Walpole*	W. Coxe, *Memoirs of Sir Robert Walpole* (London, 1798).
D.N.B.	*Dictionary of National Biography* (London, 1885–1900).
E.H.R.	*English Historical Review.*
Exeter College MSS.	MS. College Register, and bundle of MS. correspondence of Thomas Bray in the archives of Exeter College, Oxford.
Halkett & Laing	S. Halkett and J. Laing, *Dictionary of Anonymous and Pseudonymous English Literature*, ed. J. Kennedy, W. A. Smith, and A. F. Jackson (London, 1926–34).
Hearne's Collections	*Remarks and Collections* of Thomas Hearne published by the Oxford Historical Society in 11 vols. (Oxford, 1885–1921).
Hist. MSS. Comm.	*Historical Manuscripts Commission.*
J.O.J.	*Jackson's Oxford Journal.*
Lamport Hall	MSS. in Northamptonshire County Record Office, Lamport Hall, Northampton.
Nichols, *Anecdotes*	J. Nichols, *Literary Anecdotes of the Eighteenth Century* (London, 1812–15).
Nichols, *Illustrations*	J. Nichols, *Illustrations of the Literary History of the Eighteenth Century* (London, 1817–58).

[1] In vol. 16 MS. no. 210 is succeeded by a second no. 111 and all the numbers thereafter are 100 in arrear. The true number to references to subsequent documents in this volume is therefore appended in square brackets.

Oriel College MS.	MS. Provost's Memorandum Book in the archives of Oriel College, Oxford.
Packington Hall MSS.	MSS. of the Earl of Aylesford at Packington Hall, Warwickshire.
MSS. of President of Magdalen College	President Bloxam's MS. Collections in possession of the President of Magdalen College, Oxford.
P.R.O. SP	MS. State Papers Domestic in the Public Record Office, London.
Queen's College MSS.	MSS. in the Library of Queen's College, Oxford.
Rashleigh MSS.	MSS. at Cornwall County Record Office, Truro.
Sandon Hall	Typescript of the Earl of Harrowby's MS. Diary of Sir Dudley Ryder at Sandon Hall, Staffs.
Unitarian College, Manchester	Lindsey MSS. at Unitarian College, Victoria Park, Manchester 14.
University Archives	MSS. in the archives of the University of Oxford.
Warwick C.R.O.	MS. Newdigate Letters and Diaries deposited at the County Record Office, Shire Hall, Warwick.
Dr. Williams's Library	Lindsey MSS., Blackburne MSS, and Disney Papers in Dr. Williams's Library, Gordon square, London S.W. 1.

PROLOGUE

Eighteenth-century Oxford

To the universities in the century following the Revolution, politics were a field of activity rather than of study, and were among the important activities of academic life. There were those, with Oxford in mind, who proclaimed shrilly enough that "'tis not their province to meddle with government and titles of crowned heads, or worldly kingdoms, Christ nor his Apostles never showed them that way',[1] but that was because they were opposed to both the cause and the doctrine to which Oxford had pledged herself: events revealed plainly enough that they also would have exploited her prestige and influence had they been able to seize control of the machinery of the University. Oxford was still a school of the Church, and the Church, its privileges, its property, and its doctrines, all became bitter political issues. To the dominant high-church school in Oxford, Church and University were inseparable members of a political organism whose authority derived from God Himself; the mechanistic doctrines of the Whigs were a betrayal of all things sacred. Neither the University nor its opponents could easily break off the battle.

So far as political issues turned on ideas, the universities, and especially Oxford, were of particular importance. At the beginning there were academic pronouncements upon the origin of government and the doctrine of the Trinity, together with pressure upon tradesmen's votes; at the end there were definitions of predestination and active development of canals and turnpikes. Throughout, the political life of Oxford had a double reference, and it is the intermingling of disputes about first principles with the issues of the parish pump, the interaction of the high politics of London with collegiate squabbles, and not least the University's long period in the political wilderness, which make this study in local politics of unique interest. Even the University of Cambridge, for much of the period, was a much more familiar type of constituency, where ministerial influence reigned supreme.

[1] *An Answer to the Address of Oxford University* (London, 1710), p. 21.

Eighteenth-century political life was never confined within the closed circle of Parliament. The opposition tended constantly to look for support among the political public, and most especially in those great strongholds of opposition, the City of London and the University of Oxford. By the same token electoral success in a 'popular' constituency, be it London, Westminster, or Oxford University, was sought as a matter of prestige by the government. Early in the Hanoverian era, with parties approximating to the factions in a civil war, much more was at stake. For the alumni of the University filled the parishes and the bench, and from the House of Lords down to the charity school were the most powerful propagandist force in the country. Academic addresses to the Crown gave an important lead to public opinion, which, whether in the lobbies of the House of Commons or in mob violence, was a concern to the insecure ministries of these years; inevitably addresses were courted by those who could court them, and savagely assailed by those who could not. Expressions even of undergraduate opinion mattered then as do student riots in the East to this day. For all these reasons, the academic standing of Oxford was rarely temperately debated; it was an object of veneration to her friends, and of scorn and disgust to her enemies.

Neither in theology nor in politics was the University ever unanimous, and the ultimate issues of the political debate were confused repeatedly by the manœuvres of factions, the rivalries of individuals and colleges, by the the powerful pressure of patronage in a church where too many clergy were pursuing too few comfortable benefices. Particularly in the early years the University viewed with favour the connexions of the great clans which made up the high-church faction in politics, even if they had no local roots; but the neighbouring families of the county soon established an interest in the University as in other constituencies.

These varied political influences raise acutely the vexed question of Tory terminology in the eighteenth century. High-church Toryism in Anne's reign was the politics of a group of powerful families who could on party issues carry with them other sympathizers of two quite different kinds, court politicians whose loyalty was primarily to the government irrespective of its party complexion, and country politicians who, by contrast, were primarily opposition men. The church Tories were, of course, far from insensible to the fruits of office, and by office the Hydes, Seymours, and Finches, the core of the church Tory connexion, all profited handsomely. In Anne's reign majority opinion at Oxford hoped for both security for the Church and the gains of politics by power at Court. Before 1714, therefore, there were court and country wings to the Tory connexions, with the Church interests, lay and clerical, never without hope of becoming a court interest in the full sense. After 1714 the court interest fell exclusively into Whig hands, and gradually court Toryism crumbled. Among those with a following in Oxford, Harcourt came to terms with a Whig ministry, while the Harley family reverted to a 'country line', followed by the majority of clerical Tories and Oxford dons. Henceforth both at Oxford and Westminster, Toryism approximated increasingly to 'independent', 'country' politics. How this painful change took place is analysed in Part II.

This process took place in reverse for the Whigs, who before 1714 had also boasted a court and a country wing, but now gradually alienated their old 'country' sympathizers. Seventeenth-century traditions of theological and ecclesiastical opposition, however, left their mark upon the Whig mind as surely as Anglican high churchmanship was imprinted upon the Tory mind; in Oxford as elsewhere heterodox Liberals rallied to the Whig cause, but their disillusionment at the efforts of Bishop Gibson to create that unnatural monster, a high-church Whig connexion, swelled the bitterness of the independent Whigs at the wholesale transformation of Whiggism into court politics. Nevertheless, heterodoxy in the Whig camp out-lived Edmund Gibson, and Liberal arguments against Oxford orthodoxy provided regular ministerial ammunition for half a century after the Hanoverian accession.

All, Whig or Tory, great magnate or local squire, had to reckon with the complex machinery of the University itself, the very complexity of which powerfully aided the dons to keep the initiative in their affairs in their own hands. By long tradition not only the parliamentary burgesses but also the Chancellor were elected by Convocation from the outside world. The Oxford Chancellor, unlike his counterpart at Cambridge, appointed the High Steward, another magnate from the outside. Again, unlike the Cambridge Chancellor, he annually nominated that potent dignitary the

Vice-Chancellor, who named his own deputies, was chairman of the Hebdomadal Board and all its committees, and had a veto on all measures brought into Convocation. The Chancellor appointed heads of halls (other than St. Edmund Hall); he was the chief channel through which favours in the granting of degrees, so frequently essential to church preferment, were sought, and was consulted by the Crown on important academic matters, such as the proposal to transform Gloucester Hall into a college.[2] In recent times the Chancellor had generally been a political magnate, and his election was more than a declaration of political faith, it was the establishment of an important influence in the University. If by virtue of his position in the state the Chancellor had ecclesiastical patronage or other favours to confer in Oxford, his influence might be extensive indeed. In return for his favours he gained the prestige of the freely conferred favour of a large and learned body, a prestige hardly to be contested by even the most respectable knight of a shire.

In daily business the University was ruled by a narrow oligarchy of comparatively recent origin, the Hebdomadal Board. This body consisted of the Vice-Chancellor (himself the head of a house), the twenty-four other heads, and the two proctors who were nominated annually by the colleges according to a fixed cycle. The Hebdomadal Board had the sole initiative in university legislation and the chief share in its administration. The Oxford heads were thus a more powerful body than their Cambridge brethren, for there was no Oxford counterpart to the Caput, and they alone could prepare legislation for submission to Convocation. In the domestic affairs of their societies the authority and patronage of the heads was also extensive; there were even some who claimed a right of veto in the election of fellows. And the heads shared with the canons of Christ Church the privilege of being able to marry. It is this combination of constitutional power with social privilege which makes the heads of houses the chief figures in the history of eighteenth-century Oxford.

Yet they were not often elected on account of their merits as rulers of the University. Most of the heads of colleges were elected by the fellows (or the senior fellows) from among their own number—though the Deanery of Christ Church was in the gift of the Crown, and the Archbishop of Canterbury chose the Warden of

2 B.M. Add. MS. 28880, fo. 18.

Merton from three names submitted by the senior fellows—and apart altogether from some cases of astounding jobbery, fellows considered their own convenience in making their choice. A potential benefactor like Charlett (whose benefactions remained potential), a member of the college who would vacate a valuable living or other office, a political sympathizer, a boon companion who promised lax discipline for the future—of such were the Oxford heads. Merit did not go altogether unrewarded even in this period, but more often than among the college heads it was to be found among the Chancellor's nominees to those financially unattractive places, the headships of halls. So great was the power of the heads, however, that in times of greatest political excitement, elections to the headship were most likely to degenerate into a political fracas, with all who could pull a wire, members of other colleges, politicians, bishops, taking a hand.

The other members of the Hebdomadal Board, the proctors, bore responsibility for university discipline, possessed a joint veto upon legislation, and had to be present in person or by deputy at all meetings of the Hebdomadal Board; in times of excitement, therefore, they more than once earned great notoriety, but on the whole they were of small consequence. Appointed simply for a year, and usually chosen by seniority within their colleges, they could not often hope to rival the importance of those pillars of academic society, the heads.

The great corporate organ of the University was Convocation, the precise membership of which was a matter of frequent dispute in the eighteenth century; but which was normally assumed to consist of all Masters of Arts and Doctors who had taken out their regency and were members of a college or hall. It might reject, though it never amended, legislation proposed by the Hebdomadal Board; measures it accepted became statutes. Convocation might debate such measures, but debates in Latin gravely restricted serious discussion. To Convocation belonged the right of conferring degrees out of the usual course, a matter of periodical acrimony, but its most exciting functions were electoral. Convocation elected not only the Chancellor and burgesses, but many of the professors and university officers such as the bedels (or beadles as they were commonly called at this time) and verger, and exercised the ecclesiastical patronage of the University. The university politicians, therefore, had ample room for the exercise of their talents;

no connexion need wilt for lack of practice in acting together, or in whipping in non-resident voters. From an academic viewpoint no worse method of appointing to places of learning could be conceived; the Crown did not always nominate wisely to the regius chairs in this period, but only once, during the tenure of Thomas Randolph (1768–83), did Convocation elect a more distinguished man to the Margaret chair of divinity than the Crown appointed to the regius chair in that faculty.

Especially in the elections of burgesses interested parties brought personal pressure from relatives, parents of pupils, and patrons lay and ecclesiastical, to bear upon the electors, as will be abundantly illustrated in the narrative; but in no constituency of more than 500 voters was it easy for an outside influence to establish a secure interest, still less in Oxford where an unusual proportion of the active electorate consisted of non-residents scattered across the country. The most important influence upon the voters was undoubtedly college pressure. A society that could poll unanimously whether for a professor or a burgess put a premium on its importance, and especially on that of its head, in a narrow university community where corporate jealousies were rife. Moreover, although Christ Church and Magdalen outshone all other houses in size and magnificence, much poorer societies, such as Balliol, could maintain a respectable place in the academic firmament by virtue of a consistently substantial and united poll; in the reign of George II their importance even increased, as for political reasons Christ Church and Magdalen came to counterbalance each other. Some societies, such as Jesus, never attained this desirable unanimity, but most colleges acted together with great consistency.

No doubt this solidarity sometimes sprang from the intense *esprit de corps* of men who lived a close communal life, and owed whatever significance they would ever attain to the college which elected them into their fellowships. Yet, as will become abundantly clear in Part II, the unanimity of many colleges in the eighteenth century was the result of pitched battles rather than natural harmony, and fierce college contests arose not only from the sense that in times of bitter political division men of the opposing party were intolerable, but from experience of university life which bore out the scriptural assertion that a house divided against itself cannot stand.

It was to the colleges, therefore, that politicians from the county or capital must turn if they were to build up a political interest. There were some 500 fellowships in the University, but the twenty colleges among which they were divided were of manageable size. The head often had the authority to decide when, and how many, elections should be made, and he might be won for the ministry by a prebend, a royal chaplaincy, appointment as a Whitehall preacher, even a deanery; the opposition exploited lively fears of the Whig menace to the *status quo* in Church and University. Not only was there influence at the head of a college, but there was a restricted inlet at the bottom, as hardly any of the fellowships were open. Thus it was that early in the Hanoverian era there were tremendous struggles in the politically divided colleges, and thus also it was difficult to upset an interest once it was firmly established. After this the maintenance of an interest might proceed as quietly as in a corporation borough, as the regular lists of connexions of the fellows of Merton maintained by the ministers bear witness. Here, as in a corporation borough, there could be no absolute security, for discipline collapsed even in Merton in the middle of the century. Nevertheless, the academic parties which formed in the first two decades of the century lasted long after their *raison d'être* had been forgotten. It was not, of course, that the fellows themselves went on for ever, even though their fellowships were for life. College purchases of advowsons were restricted by Act of Parliament in 1736, but already there was more than one college living for every two fellows, and dons leaked away steadily into country parishes; the average tenure of a fellowship then was probably much shorter than it is now, perhaps no more than ten or a dozen years.

This continuous renewal only emphasized the importance of the University and college statutes which maintained Oxford's Anglican and clerical character. At matriculation all swore to maintain the university statutes, and there was powerful support for the opinion that the University could not, without royal licence, alter the important body of statutes which comprised the Caroline Code. Further oaths, including those of Allegiance and Supremacy, were imposed on graduation. All over the age of sixteen must subscribe the XXXIX Articles on matriculation, and all must subscribe at graduation. Apart from those elected to a few faculty fellowships reserved for the study of law and medicine,

7

all fellows must proceed to holy orders within a limited period from their election. All heads and fellows took an oath, sometimes of astonishing length and complexity, inviolably to observe the college statutes; by the eighteenth century this obligation was impossible to fulfil, but it prohibited alterations in the statutes, and prevented college life from changing nearly as fast as the governing body. Certainly all were aware that if by some means the obligations upon fellows to enter holy orders were relaxed (as was demanded at the beginning of the eighteenth century), or there was a general abolition of subscription to the articles (as was demanded in the seventies), there must be a rapid upheaval in Oxford owing to the rate at which those elected under the old order might be expected to ebb away in pursuit of ecclesiastical preferment and connubial bliss.

The main bait which might be held out to individual dons by both the Crown and the private politicians consisted of preferment outside Oxford, but the Crown was not without resource within the walls. Its chief patronage in Oxford consisted of the five regius chairs founded by Henry VIII (of Divinity, Civil Law, Medicine, Hebrew, and Greek) and the sixth (of Modern History) established by George I; their main bearing upon the political balance among the colleges was to confirm the ministerial interest at Christ Church. In Stuart times canonries of the cathedral had been annexed to the chairs of divinity and Hebrew, and for almost the entire eighteenth century the chair of Greek was a perquisite of Students of the House, one of whom also became the first regius professor of modern history. The Deanery and other canonries were also in the gift of the Crown, and were bestowed with political intent by both Harley and Newcastle. The latter's influence at Westminster School was also the means of pouring into the House a steady stream of young court politicians. As will later transpire, the close link between Winchester and New College afforded the ministry a means of altering the political complexion of that society, but New College proved a good deal more restive than Christ Church, the political loyalties of which changed steadily with those of the ministry.

Yet, in conclusion as at the beginning, it must be stressed that Oxford societies were not so isolated from the general current of national politics as to be occupied by the tactics of common room and Convocation to the exclusion of all else, and the narrative of academic affairs must be set against that of English political and ecclesiastical history. This narrative is carried forward in the five books which follow, each of which has a unity of its own. Particularly in Part II it is impossible to make the chapters strictly chronological, but as the books show clearly, time never stood still, even in eighteenth-century Oxford.

PART I

OXFORD UNDER WILLIAM AND ANNE
1689–1714

'We your Majesties most dutifull and loyall subjects . . . of the University of Oxford . . . most humbly beg leave in this public and solemn manner . . . to assure your Majestie of the continuance of Or inviolable duty and allegiance to your sacred person and Government. . . . We most humbly pray your Majestie to believe that We do and will always use Or utmost endeavours to promote the peace and quiet of your reign, by teaching and encouraging such principles as may lead to true virtue, piety and loyalty.'

Humble Address of the University of Oxford to the Queen, 1 April 1710

'. . . Knowing that education has the great sway in our humane depraved judgements, we can attribute all this commotion to nothing so much as the principles imbibed at the Universities, and which are apparently opposite to our constitution as they are contained in some parts of the Oxford Decree.'

University Loyalty (London, 1710)

CHAPTER I

Oxford and King William

'WHOEVER considers well the short reigne of King James', wrote old Sir John Bramston with sick heart and stumbling pen, 'he will see what havock he was making in the Church and Vniversities, the nursaries of our relligion, what hast he made to settle Popery, [and] must thinck all these were in danger.'[1] Oxford had pledged herself to the most extravagant support of the royal prerogative in 1683, only to be forced into vigorous opposition to the Romanizing policies of James II which culminated in the purge at Magdalen. True, the king had finally permitted the restoration of the President and fellows, and given favours to the University Chancellor, the Duke of Ormonde, but Oxford would not trust again. When

---

[1] *The Autobiography of Sir John Bramston*, ed. Lord Braybrooke, Camden Soc. xxxii (London, 1845), 356.

in December 1688 the Princess Anne, who had deserted her father, arrived with a splendid cortège led by the Earl of Northampton and the Bishop of London and preceded by a cornet bearing the inscription in golden letters on his standard *Nolumus Leges Angliae mutari*, she was received 'with all possible demonstrations of love and affection'.[2] For some time past Oxford had been disturbed by parties of troops manœuvring in the rival interests, and by gownsmen breaking the windows of papists;[3] the Vice-Chancellor now offered William of Orange the University's loyalty and their plate, and looked forward eagerly to a visit from a prince[4] who could be no more than a usurper by the principles of divine hereditary right thundered forth by Convocation only five years before.

The events of those years were sufficient to guarantee Oxford's loyalty to the new régime for many years to come. Heads and fellows flocked to take the new oaths of obedience; Henry Fleming believed 'the whole university will not afford above six dissenters',[5] and non-jurors were much less numerous at Oxford than at Cambridge. In 1690 the University resolved to raise a regiment of horse,[6] and, mightier with the pen than with the sword, poured forth laudatory addresses and verses on every possible occasion and in every tongue then known at Oxford.[7] While Queen Mary lived university patriotism could avoid hyperbole in music no more than in prose and verse, and in 1693 the public act 'ended with a fine consort of musick, wherein the word Maria was so sett it took up halfe an hour in singing, and Brittannia an hour'.[8] When in 1696 the University publicly abhorred the attempt on the king's life, the Chancellor refused to present the university address, as it did not equal the loyal professions of a Whiggish Parliament, but in a stormy meeting of Convocation the Vice-Chancellor, Dr. Adams, Rector of Lincoln, procured a new fulsome document acknowledging 'to all the world' the king's legal title to his crown, and promising to defend it against every foe and

---

[2] *Original Letters Illustrative of English History*, ed. H. Ellis, 2nd series, iv. 177–8.   [3] *Wood's Life and Times*, ed. A. Clark, iii. 287.

[4] *Hist. MSS. Comm. Le Fleming MSS.*, p. 234.

[5] Ibid., p. 252, cf. Bodl. MS. Ballard 3, fo. 18.

[6] *Hist. MSS. Comm. Le Fleming MSS.*, p. 283.

[7] To some of these the king gave special attention. *Wood's Life and Times*, iii. 477.

[8] N. Luttrell, *A Brief Historical Relation of State Affairs* (Oxford, 1857), iii. 134.

'particularly against ye late King James [and] all his adherents'.[9] Further addresses in 1697 and 1701 were reported to be particularly acceptable, and there were loyal celebrations with bells, bonfire, and illuminations.[10]

Jacobitism fell on lean days. A pessimistic correspondent of Charlett in 1689 had little foundation for his fear that 'University politicks are going down the wind', for the overwhelming majority in Oxford had already concluded that 'passive obedience is a doctrine and lesson only for privat Xtians, not for whole Kingdoms or their Representative Conventions. If Kings will abdicate, we may take them at their word'.[11] The non-juror, Dr. Hickes, refused an invitation to Oxford, where he could enjoy neither respect nor security, and cried out against the University for indulging in 'unchristian slander' and 'grosse flatteries'.[12] Members of the University were indeed titillated by stories that William Bromley, their future M.P., and now knight of the shire for Warwick, had been dining with the king over the water,[13] and amused by the government's suspicions of a large chest carried into St. John's,[14] but even in 1696 after the University had had to alter its address to comply with the wishes of the Junto, Smalridge could testify confidently that he knew of 'no persons that either are, or ever were, disaffected to the government, but some very few who have suffered for their non-compliance with it', and related how the Vice-Chancellor had even held up publications of the University Press which might give offence to those in authority, if only by reflecting on their favourite, the great Bentley of Cambridge.[15]

The University, moreover, like the Church, was among the beneficiaries of the Revolution. Their first move in 1689/90 to secure a Bill for the 'confirmation of the Charters and Privileges of the Universities, and the several colleges there', twice failed to get through the House of Commons, and was finally defeated by

[9] University Archives: MS. Conv. Reg. Bc 30, fos. 79–80; Bodl. MS. Rawlinson D 912, fo. 61; Hist. MSS. Comm. Downshire MSS. I, pt. ii, 650.
[10] Cal. S.P. Dom. 1697, p. 479; Hist. MSS. Comm. Downshire MSS. I, pt. ii. 770–1.
[11] Bodl. MS. Ballard 30, fo. 31.
[12] Ibid. 12, fo. 90.
[13] Nichols, Illustrations, iii. 242.
[14] Cal. S.P. Dom. 1690/1, p. 47.
[15] Nichols, Illustrations, iii. 255–7, 261.

pressure from the city corporation of Oxford,[16] but there was
room for both to bask in the sun which now shone upon vested
interests of all kinds. In 1702 the University quarrelled with the
city again because on Queen Anne's visit a number of academic
dignitaries were jostled and forced 'to ride promiscuously with
the body of the townsmen through the High Street to the dis-
creditt of the procession (together with some particular indignities
offered the Vice Chancellor and other Doctors not proper to be
here recited)', but after innumerable exchanges of papers, and
twenty-three meetings of delegates, the order of precedence for
the next royal visit (which did not occur for eighty years) was
agreed upon.[17] Although there was some discontent among townsmen at the University's repeated interference in city politics in
support of the Earl of Abingdon's interest and at the extension of
university buildings at the expense of the town,[18] the two parties
agreed to bury the hatchet.

One of the firstfruits of the Revolution, moreover, was an Act
'to vest in the two universities the presentations of benefices
belonging to Papists',[19] and further preferment was assured by the
royal favour on which the University complacently congratulated
itself in its addresses. The expulsion of a popish king reopened the
way to royal chaplaincies to orthodox Oxford men, among them
Arthur Charlett, Master of University College, an aspiring
Maecenas, prolific correspondent, and one of the most important
moderate court politicians in the University in the next twenty-
five years.[20] Nor were royal chaplaincies the only way by which
Oxford men sought the lusher pastures of church preferment.
There were, of course, those like Dr. Jane, the regius professor
of divinity, whose violence against the king's government was
ascribed by his enemies to his being refused the See of Exeter
when, in the uncertain days of 1688, he had come with the Vice-
Chancellor to offer the king the university plate. But hope sprang
eternal even in Dr. Jane, for confident reports that he had sur-

---

[16] C.J. x. 112, 274, 343; Wood's Life and Times, iii. 317, 322, 323.
[17] University Archives: MS. Conv. Reg. Bc 30, fos. 256, 280, 28 seq. at back of
volume. See also M. G. Hobson, Oxford Council Acts 1701–52 (Oxford, 1952),
App. II, pp. 289–307; also pp. 14–29 passim.
[18] Bodl. MS. Ballard 31, fo. 34; Hearne's Collections, vii. 224; Hist. MSS.
Comm. Portland MSS. vii. 293, 442.
[19] 1 W. & M. s. 1, c. 26.
[20] Luttrell, Brief Relation, ii. 355, iv. 142.

rendered his chair by refusal to sign the Association in 1696 proved unfounded.[21] William sought further to ingratiate himself by grants in aid of Arabic studies, but his greatest and most popular act of grace was his visit to Oxford in November 1695.

In the second half of 1695 the royal favour set steadily towards the Whigs, and in response the University chose as its burgess not the usual court or church Tory but the new Whiggish Secretary of State, Sir William Trumbull. Trumbull immediately sought to prove the strength of the new interest by urging the king to visit the University as he had promised when passing by at Abingdon in 1688. Somewhat reluctantly the king agreed. Trumbull fussed busily to drill him and his constituents in proper etiquette. He urged the king to tour the colleges but, preoccupied by the new session of Parliament, William made only a brief appearance in the Theatre.[22] This visit was nevertheless a great success, but the enemies of the University averred that the king had departed hastily without dining because he had been warned he was to be poisoned, and that there was hissing in the Theatre in his presence.[23]

Trumbull differed from the other university burgesses of this reign. In 1688 the University had chosen Sir Thomas Clarges and Heneage Finch. Clarges, as brother-in-law of General Monk, had been instrumental in bringing about the Restoration, and in subsequent years had been a staunch friend of the Court, except when the Court endangered the interests of the Church. He had adhered to William as early as December 1688, thus endearing himself to the University which had been active in the same cause. Possessed of a long parliamentary memory and a great thirst for business in the House, he was one of the most active members the University ever had, and his scruples in recognizing the new sovereign he had helped to introduce were doubtless characteristic of many of his constituents.

His fellow member, Heneage Finch, was a lawyer whose father had represented the University in the Cavalier Parliament, and who had himself sat for Oxford in 1679. He was a member of a

[21] *The Life of Humphrey Prideaux* (London, 1748), p. 55; Luttrell, *Brief Relation*, iv. 150.

[22] *Hist. MSS. Comm. Buccleugh and Queensberry (Montagu House)*, II, pt. i. 242–55 *passim*; *Cal. S.P. Dom. 1695: 1689–95*, pp. 86–96 *passim*.

[23] *The Diary of Abraham de la Pryme*, ed. C. Jackson, Surtees Soc. liv (1870), 74–76.

powerful clan led by the Earl of Nottingham which were the steadiest friends of the Established Church. He, too, met trouble by his support of a regency,[24] but in the next generation his personal and family record disproved charges that he would sacrifice the Church by dealings with the Stuarts. The Finches were firmer in their principles than the Hydes, another great church Tory family with intimate Oxford associations, yet Heneage had the family gift of advancing himself at Court; he was made Solicitor General by Charles II, created Lord Guernsey by Anne, and Earl of Aylesford by George I. Through his elder brother, the second Earl of Nottingham, who held high office in the three reigns following the Revolution, Oxford was linked with the inmost councils of politics. Within the University was Heneage's kinsman, Leopold William Finch, a member of the elder branch of the family; in his youth a boon companion of the disorderly fellows of All Souls, he was appointed Warden by James II in 1687 and was legally installed in 1698.

In 1695 Clarges died and, fortified by the victory of Namur, William resolved to give a fresh impulse to his flagging government by calling a new Parliament and electioneering vigorously himself. Among his rewards was the election of Sir William Trumbull with Finch for Oxford. Trumbull, who had married into the family of Cotterell of Rousham near Oxford, was invited to stand by the court Tory George Clarke, and though he was acting with the Whigs, his friends denied the 'malicious story that [he was] Whiggish, that is an intimate crony of Wharton . . . now soliciting for [him] in Buckinghamshire'. His choice was approved even by the non-juring Earl of Clarendon,[25] whose blessing on the election is characteristic of the perplexing confusion of these years; for though elected unanimously, Trumbull had in fact defeated Sir Christopher Musgrave (who declined a poll), a long-standing ally of the Hydes and Seymours,[26] who with the Finches and Granvilles formed the backbone of the church Tory party. Musgrave was himself a political power in Cumberland and Westmorland, but he now lost his seat for the latter county because of the failure of his entente with Lowther; Musgrave refused

---

[24] M. B. Rex, *University Representation in England* (London, 1954), pp. 313–18.
[25] *Hist. MSS. Comm. Downshire MSS.* I, pt. ii. 559, 561; Bodl. MS. Rawlinson Letters 91, fo. 284.
[26] *The Flemings in Oxford*, ed. J. R. Magrath, iii. 246, 250; *Hist. MSS. Comm. Downshire MSS.* I, pt. ii. 564–5.

to promise Lowther to vote for any supplies required for the war, and his rejection at Oxford could therefore be represented by the ministry as an academic vote of confidence in the king's war policy. All the resources of the Court had been brought to bear, however. Henry Compton, Bishop of London, rallied St. John's, Balliol, and All Souls. The Vice-Chancellor, Fitzherbert Adams, Rector of Lincoln, was won over; Magdalen and New College were solid for the Secretary. The Bishop of Rochester worked for Trumbull from without, while Charlett, who preferred to labour for those in office, and Dr. Hayley were active within. The two societies of which the Secretary had doubt were All Souls (which flirted with the notion of putting up Codrington) and Christ Church, but when both were secured Trumbull's cause was safe.[27]

Before the next election in July 1698 the political situation had changed. The war over, the Junto was reeling before the attacks of the new country opposition of mixed Whig and Tory origin; they now needed such a Secretary of State 'as has more of the buckler in him than the sword' and concluded that 'some Jonah or another must be thrown overboard, if the storm cannot otherwise be laid'. Trumbull had become querulous at being 'treated more like a footman than a secretary'[28] and resigned. With Finch too ill to attend the House,[29] the attractiveness of both the sitting members was tarnished; the foreign policy pursued by Trumbull could be represented as obsolete, and the University had every inducement to support the new Tory party which Musgrave and Harley, supported by the rising Oxfordshire magnate Harcourt, were trying to forge by furious assaults upon government expenditure.

Suspecting perhaps that Trumbull's prospects of re-election were diminishing, the University Chancellor, the Duke of Ormonde, introduced another Whiggish candidate, John Ellis, an undersecretary of state.[30] Wisely reluctant 'to intrude upon the privileges and liberties of the University', Ormonde commended Ellis's services to his family, and his distinction as a son of the University.

---

[27] Ibid. 560–5. Codrington had been lately honoured by William, and delivered the university oration at his reception.
[28] *Letters Illustrative of the Reign of William III* (cited below as *Vernon Corr.*), ed. G. P. R. James (London, 1841), i. 391, 404, 432. For a different interpretation of the resignation, Bodl. MS. Ballard 9, fo. 129.
[29] *Vernon Corr.* ii. 148.
[30] B.M. Egerton MS. 2618, fo. 182.

Ellis had been a student of Christ Church, was a friend of Humphrey Prideaux (who was now perhaps too disgruntled with Oxford to be of much assistance),[31] had accompanied that Oxford worthy, Sir Leoline Jenkins, to the Nimeguen conference, and had gained his own successes in diplomacy before becoming under-secretary in 1695. He had contributed to the cost of Peckwater buildings then being erected at Christ Church. Ormonde claimed support for Ellis in Oxford, but though not averse to private wire-pulling, the University always resented public interference in its elections; the general political tide, from which Oxford was never insulated, was running strongly against candidates of his connexions; and in the event his campaign never began.

The voting in Convocation as finally declared was:[32]

Sir William Trumbull .	. 120
Heneage Finch .	. 183
Sir William Glynne .	. 205
Sir Christopher Musgrave .	207

Musgrave, aggressively championed by Christ Church, not only triumphed but carried with him Sir William Glynne, an Oxfordshire baronet and a protégé of the Earl of Abingdon.[33] The political excitement in Oxford, however, was not yet over. There were rumours that Musgrave would resign as university burgess to serve elsewhere,[34] and that not only Finch and Trumbull, but the eloquent Harcourt, whose seat at Abingdon was in jeopardy, would contest the vacancy. Finally, Musgrave kept his seat for the whole Parliament, the disillusioned Trumbull, whose friends ascribed his defeat to the total failure of his influential friends to apply for him,[35] retired into private life, and Finch and Harcourt, the old and the new generation of political churchmen, bided their time.

The violence of this conflict was not soon forgotten in the University. Royal bounty had long provided university dignitaries

---

[31] *Hist. MSS. Comm. R5, Pine-Coffin MSS.*, pp. 374, 376.

[32] University Archives: MS. Conv. Reg. Bc 30, fo. 186.

[33] R. Walcott, *English Politics in the Early Eighteenth Century* (Oxford, 1956), pp. 221, 232.

[34] *Vernon Corr.* ii. 148. It was also rumoured that he would not qualify himself by signing the Association.

[35] *Hist. MSS. Comm. Downshire MSS.* I, pt. ii. 781.

with '8 brace of bucks out of Woodstock park'[36] and other per-
quisites, but in 1698 Charlett and the Dean of Christ Church (who
had encouraged Boyle and the other wits in their controversy with
the Whig favourite Bentley) found their 'New-Years-Gift . . . stopt
by ye club at O[rie]l', which in a few years was to become a
notorious nursery of political weathercocks.[37] Roger Altham had
been turned out of his Hebrew professorship for political unreliability the year before, and months after the election Charlett
was striving to allay the animosities which it had created.[38] More
than twenty years hence, this election served the ruling clique of
heads as an example of the evils to be expected from allowing the
peace of the University to be rudely disturbed.

The next election, of January 1701, proved no more encouraging to the Junto, and Oxford once again sent up Sir Christopher
Musgrave, who had been considered for Speaker and had played
a strenuous role in the last Parliament, and Heneage Finch, who
had taken 'it amiss that he was left out last time'.[39] Another election was necessary in March, however, Musgrave having chosen
to serve for Westmorland, and now William Bromley, a Warwickshire squire and alumnus of Christ Church, defeated Sir George
Beaumont by 197 votes to 164.[40] Once again there was great agitation. In January Musgrave had been championed by Harley and
Harcourt, who both built up a considerable interest in Oxford in
the next reign, but the opposition to him was spurred by suspicions
that he would desert the University for Westmorland if the opportunity arose, a discourtesy which Harcourt affirmed would 'be
taken most heinously', and a possibility which he urged Harley
to deny. Dr. Aldrich, Dean of Christ Church, and Leopold Finch,
Warden of All Souls, came out confidently for Musgrave and
Heneage Finch. Sir William Glynne was, however, still in the
field, and Sir George Beaumont, a high-church Leicestershire
baronet who was a fellow of New College, was also put forward.

The old church party stalwarts, Finch and Musgrave, finally
triumphed, acknowledging their indebtedness to Harley, and
Musgrave's own son had no doubts that he would continue to

---

[36] Luttrell, *Brief Relation*, iii. 129.
[37] Ibid. iv. 221; Bodl. MS. Ballard 31, fo. 16.
[38] Ibid. 20, fo. 59.
[39] The poll read: Sir William Glynne 132; Heneage Finch 205; Sir Christopher
Musgrave 275. University Archives: MS. Conv. Reg. Bc 30, fo. 225.
[40] Ibid., fo. 226.

serve the University.[41] Musgrave's choice proved otherwise, and in March Sir William Whitelock, Sir Thomas Dyke, William Bromley, Sir William Glynne, Dr. Edisbury (a university burgess in 1679), and Sir George Beaumont were all actively canvassed for the vacancy. It soon became apparent that some candidates would have to pool their interest, and, finally, with the Vice-Chancellor aiming mainly 'to free ourselves from ye suspicion of chusing for tubs of ale etc.', Charlett, the peacemaker of 1698, took the lead in securing the election of Bromley.[42] In November 1701 there was a fresh general election, but the academic peace was preserved by the unanimous re-election of the sitting members.[43]

Bromley, 'the darling of one if not of both' the universities, remained burgess for Oxford till his death. He was a distinguished member of that large undistinguished class of midland squires which supplied most of Oxford's representatives in the eighteenth century. Of Staffordshire origin, his family had been settled in Warwickshire for three generations, and he himself had been knight of that shire since 1689. Though unconnected with the great aristocratic clans of which the high-church party was mainly composed, he soon stood out as one of their younger leaders in the Commons, where his rigidity of character helped to compensate for a certain rigidity of mind. 'Tho', perhaps of noe very shining parts, [he] hath a character of great integrity.'[44] Already the tours abroad, which he commemorated in boring books of reminiscences, had occasioned malicious gossip that he was flirting with the Pretender.[45] By 1695 he had adumbrated the alliance between his friends and the Harley–Foley connexion which he was to cement in 1708, and was elected on the opposition list to the Commission of Accounts above his Oxford rival of 1700, Sir Thomas Dyke.[46] Despite Harley's pressure, however, Dyke and Bromley refused to sign the Association, which they regarded as a Whig party manœuvre.[47] For the moment Bromley must be

[41] *Hist. MSS. Comm. Portland MSS.* iv. 9–10, 12, 14.
[42] Bodl. MS. Ballard 21, fos. 166, 168; 30, fo. 54.
[43] University Archives: MS. Conv. Reg. Bc 30, fo. 239.
[44] *Hist. MSS. Comm. Portland MSS.* iv. 292; *The Wentworth Papers*, ed. J. J. Cartwright (London, 1883), p. 429.
[45] Nichols, *Illustrations*, iii. 242. He was attacked in this way in the press in 1707. *Observator*, vi, no. 15.
[46] K. Feiling, *A History of the Tory Party 1640–1714* (Oxford, 1924), p. 310.
[47] Ibid., p. 321; Luttrell, *Brief Relation*, iv. 74.

reckoned an opposition man, but within a few months the death of William III, and the accession of Anne, encouraged him to exploit royal favour for an aggressive high-church policy.

Thus, for the University as for the Church, William's reign ended less auspiciously than it began. For a number of years the government had left corporations, Oxford included, alone, and even in 1695 the University had been willing to endorse the king's foreign policy by the election of Trumbull. But the Revolution had reinvigorated party, and opened the way to faction fights which compelled the government to intervene in local affairs as in pre-Revolution days. The University, moreover, was intimately concerned in the theological conflicts which broke out in the nineties and continued unabated for more than a generation. Dr. Bury, the Rector of Exeter, and a number of the fellows, were expelled by Sir Jonathan Trelawney, the college Visitor, for resisting his visitation in 1690, when 'ye opposite parties went to fisty-cuffs for about 3 or 4 minutes, wch ended in ye utter ruin of a great many caps & periwiggs'. This dispute went to the King's Bench and the House of Lords. The truth about Bury's conduct is obscure, but college discipline was certainly bad, Exeter being, according to Humphrey Prideaux, 'totally spoyld' by 'drinking and duncery'.[48] The sinister feature of Bury's case, however, was that he had published a tract of Socinian tendencies, *The Naked Gospel*, urging that Christian union could be promoted on the basis of the clear and simple ideas which were of the essence of the faith, as distinct from the tangled barbarism of orthodox theology, the unhappy heritage of an unenlightened past.[49] With the two divinity professors refusing to act, Convocation condemned this tract as impugning the chief mysteries of the faith, to the great annoyance of the press.[50] Since Liberal theological opinion was Whig in politics, Exeter already appeared a political pariah in Oxford, persecuted both by Visitor and Convocation.

The political implications of theological controversy were further underlined in December 1695 when the University condemned heretical propositions of William Sherlock, who, confident in the support of the Court, made an insolent reply. William

---

[48] *Hist. MSS. Comm. R5, Pine-Coffin MSS.*, pp. 374, 376. Bodl. MS. Smith 48, fos. 333–9.

[49] On this case C. N. Boase, *Registrum Collegii Exonensis* (Oxford, 1894), pp. cxxix seq.

[50] J. Parkinson, *The Fire's continued at Oxford* (n. pl., 1690).

Lancaster, who later became Provost of Queen's and a connexion of Marlborough, assured Charlett that provided the University avoided the word 'heresy' they might 'call the doctrine impious, the reasoning scandalous, & the language Billingsgate (where the author had most of his breeding) without being in danger of a reprimand from the Court';[51] in fact William consulted his judges who declared that the University's condemnation was 'a high usurpation upon his Majesty's prerogative, and manifest violation of the laws of this realm', and he commanded Archbishop Tenison to rebuke the Vice-Chancellor. It was only seven years since the Magdalen College case, and only a month since the king had been triumphantly received in the Sheldonian Theatre, and he promised to take no further action.[52] But dons must wonder what might happen if in future they opposed the theological line of a less inhibited court.

The University already had enemies in London, ready to represent it as a seditious body[53] (and to threaten double land tax if they did not take special oaths),[54] and even before Atterbury and the Christ Church circle launched the Convocation controversy in 1697, the dominant faction in the University tended to regard the Whig minority as a dangerous fifth column anxious to discredit their *alma mater* with the Court in the hope of private advancement. Since the Convocation controversy[55] turned largely on the attempt of Tory presbyters to throw off the control of a Whiggish bench of bishops under court influence; and since the propagandists on both sides were Oxford men—the Tory Atterbury being created D.D. by the University for his services,[56] and Wake, Gibson, and White Kennet establishing a claim on the gratitude of the Whigs for theirs—the political cleavage in the University could hardly but be deepened. Again, after the Peace of Ryswick not only the theological deviations of the Court, but also its foreign policy, were suspect in Oxford, and the conscience of the conventional church Tory was torn once more between the

[51] Bodl. MS. Ballard 21, fo. 62.

[52] B.M. Stowe MS. 799, fos. 149, 151.

[53] *Original letters of Eminent Literary Men*, ed. Sir H. Ellis, Camden Soc. xxiii (London, 1843), 224.

[54] *Wood's Life and Times*, iii. 380.

[55] On this question see N. Sykes, *Church and State in England in the 18th Century* (Cambridge, 1934), pp. 297 seq.

[56] University Archives: MS. Conv. Reg. Bc 30, fo. 229.

desire to venerate the offices and the urge to revile the persons of both king and bishops. Small wonder that between 1698 and 1710 there was a series of contested elections of parliamentary burgesses, each with its heritage of intrigue and acrimony. Small wonder, too, that about this time Lord Somers urged the king to undertake a visitation of the universities, a violent project from which William was deterred by Holt's doubts of its legality and Shrewsbury's doubts as to its policy.[57] And all the forces which had made themselves felt under William III were to grow in importance in the next reign.

[57] *The Life of Humphrey Prideaux*, p. 192; B.M. Egerton MS. 2618, fo. 219.

CHAPTER II

Oxford and the Political Factions

THE reign of Anne opened with the brightest prospects. The queen was the idol of the high-church party, the grand-daughter of the first Earl of Clarendon, the University's old Chancellor, the niece of the second earl, its present High Steward, and of the Earl of Rochester, the political head of the powerful and expectant Hyde connexion. Surely now Oxford orthodoxy, whether in theology or politics, would be secure, and its adherents would regain that access to ecclesiastical preferment for which they had looked at the Revolution. The University began the reign by returning its sitting members to swell the Finch connexion, and celebrated with two grand 'Philological Exercises' in which students of approved social standing presented odes and essays on courtly themes. Excitement reached its peak in August 1702, when the queen herself visited the University on her tour of the west to be received, despite the disconcerting jostling of the townsmen, with boundless enthusiasm, more 'fine musick and Inglish versis'.[1]

The University sustained its enthusiasm by addressing Her Majesty with unexampled frequency throughout her reign, sending up its deputations almost every year. Even in 1702 an address might cause embarrassment, for (as so often in later reigns) 'that scurvy word Restor'd [would] not go down with ye Bps',[2] but the widely disseminated press reports of the addresses enabled the University to capture the political limelight, to further the cause favoured by the majority of its resident members, and to call their enemies to task; thus, during the Sacheverell crisis in 1710, the University assailed both Whigs and Jacobites in abhorring 'that Popish Republican Doctrine of Resistance of Princes',[3] an attack made more explicit in 1713 when Oxford besought Almighty God to defeat those 'who are such enemies to their country as to desire a popish, or to be in hast for any successor'.[4]

---

[1] *Verney Letters of the 18th Century*, ed. M. M. Lady Verney (London, 1930), i. 113.   [2] Bodl. MS. Ballard 21, fo. 189.
[3] University Archives: MS. Conv. Reg. Bd 31, fo. 62.   [4] Ibid., fo. 96.

Indeed, there was much to convince Oxford that deity, royalty, and University were working together for good. In 1704 the University acknowledged the queen's generosity 'in so freely parting with a branch of [her] own revenue for the more comfortable subsistence of the poor clergy of the Church of England', a grant fittingly remembered as Queen Anne's Bounty.[5] The queen made a grant towards the building of the University Observatory,[6] agreed to legislation confirming letters patent by which the Rectory of Ewelme and a Christ Church canonry were annexed to the regius professorship of divinity, and annexing prebends to the headships of Pembroke and Oriel.[7] So many Oxford Tories were raised to the bench of bishops that even by 1710 the possibilities of a revival of the Church–Whig alliance seemed remote; after 1710 the dominant Oxford school virtually monopolized all the higher church patronage. And in 1713 the University publicly congratulated itself 'that one of the sacred order, bred amongst us', the Bishop of Bristol, was treating for peace on terms dictated by an army under the command of their Chancellor, Ormonde.[8] At a lower level Oxford men were invited almost exclusively to preach before the Commons at the Commemoration of King Charles the Martyr, and on other special days, except during the years 1708–9 when the Whigs turned in revenge to Cambridge; and Tory majorities were more avid for sermons than Whig.

The ascendancy of the present court and church Toryism in Oxford was so great that in its parliamentary elections the University enjoyed a period of comparative peace. At the end of 1703 Heneage Finch joined his elder brother in the upper house as Lord Guernsey, and at the by-election Sir William Whitelock of Henley defeated Francis Clarke, an Oxfordshire squire from Weston, by 174 votes to 111. Whitelock, 'old shoe strings',[9] was not an altogether surprising choice, although his father was a notorious regicide and his enemies affirmed that 'he looks as if . . . for fear of being hang'd, [he] had stole into a Sanctuary'.[10] His family had long been influential in Oxfordshire, his father had

---

[5] Ibid., fo. 7.
[6] Hist. MSS. Comm. Portland MSS. iv. 197.
[7] 10 Ann. c. 45 and 13 Ann. c. 6.
[8] University Archives: MS. Conv. Reg. Bd 31, fo. 89.
[9] Hist. MSS. Comm. Portland MSS. vii. 231 and many references elsewhere.
[10] Observator, vi, no. 15, 19–23 April 1707.

at one time been a friend of the young Clarendon, his brother had been killed at Woodstock defending Lovelace in the cause of the Revolution in 1688,[11] while he himself had forfeited Lovelace's patronage by voting against the Bill of Abjuration in 1690,[12] and been deprived of the silk by the Junto in 1696.[13] Whitelock had worked his passage, and well before the election he was championed for the succession to Finch by Arthur Charlett, for his 'integrity, and warm zeal for ye true interest of the nation and church, as also against all opposers, [which have] long made him very deare to our friends of the highest rank'; Charlett set Thomas Turner, the President of Corpus, Whitelock's oldest friend in the University, to organize his interest.[14] Both Whitelock and Bromley were honest toilers in the cause of the University and of high-church politics, and both retained their seats for life.

Yet for the University as for the Church, the glory of Anne's reign proved less golden than her gracious accession. What more fitting for the University than to exploit the queen's known sympathies by striking a blow for Church and party by abolishing occasional conformity, the practice by which, in the Oxford view, dissenters sapped the foundations of both Church and State? There is no need to re-tell here the familiar story of the agitation against occasional conformity which was defeated three times between 1702 and 1705. It is sufficient to say that the head and front of this campaign throughout was William Bromley,[15] that he was followed at a respectful distance by Whitelock, and that the signal for the attack was given in a characteristically violent sermon at Oxford by Dr. Sacheverell, who dared to 'hang out the bloody flag of defiance' to occasional conformists, those 'insidious persons who ... creep to our altars'.

The manner of the failure in this campaign was as disconcerting as the failure itself for it showed that the queen would not become the tool of the church Tories with whom she was linked both by blood and religious sympathy. She told the Duchess of Marlborough that 'Mr. Bromley will be disappointed', kept her hus-

---

[11] *Wood's Life and Times*, iii. 282.
[12] Bodl. MS. Ballard 22, fo. 51.
[13] Luttrell, *Brief Relation*, iv. 27.
[14] Bodl. MS. Rawlinson Letters 92, fos. 153, 188, 192.
[15] Bromley, with Oxford backing, had planned this campaign against what he regarded as 'abominable hypocrisie' and 'inexcusable immorality' before the first session began. Bodl. MS. Ballard 38, fo. 137.

band away from the House of Lords, and though sympathetic to the policy of the Bill, regretted its introduction to the Commons because she 'would not have any pretence given for quarrelling'.[16] Anne herself was present at the debate in the Lords at which the Bill was defeated in December 1704, and it was with some desperation that Whitelock wrote to Oxford that 'she heard that said which (one would think) should make her trust her reall . . . friends and not her occasional ones'.[17] Bromley's next campaign to declare the Church in danger also failed in both houses, and his suspicions that the Whig bench abandoned the defence of the Church to Tory laymen were confirmed by the discovery that two bishops had primed a member of the lower house with information about Parker's Academy in Oxford to discredit his fulminations about dissenting schools.[18]

These defeats led in the autumn of 1704 to an attack by the Tory extremists upon the non-partisan supporters of the government, and an attempt by Sir Humphrey Mackworth, a Magdalen man, a founder member of the S.P.C.K. and a celebrated mining speculator and pamphleteer, to oust Harley from the Speaker's chair in favour of Bromley[19] or that other Oxford politician, Harcourt. Harcourt was finally rejected by the Tory managers, and, after much earnest speculation in Oxford, in October 1705 Bromley was narrowly defeated in a packed house.[20] This bitter severance between the church Tory and Harleyite connexions had a twofold repercussion in Oxford. In the first place, hostility grew towards Marlborough and the Whigs whose parliamentary votes he was seeking to obtain at the cheapest possible price. George Clarke, fellow of All Souls and a benefactor of the University, was rudely ejected from his private secretaryship to Prince George and all his public offices for voting for Bromley, and in the debate there were attacks upon an assize sermon denouncing occasional conformity preached at St. Mary's by Mr. Tilly of Corpus, a sermon which had already annoyed the judges.[21] The University, Corpus Christi, and Tilly in particular, had been

[16] W. S. Churchill, *Marlborough. His Life and Times* (London, 1933–8), ii. 272.
[17] Bodl. MS. Rawlinson Letters 92, fo. 292.
[18] *Hearne's Collections*, i. 132.
[19] It was understood that the university politicians were scheming to put forward Bromley as Speaker as early as April 1704. Bodl. MS. Ballard 6, fo. 93.
[20] *Hearne's Collections*, i. 58–60; *Hist. MSS. Comm. Portland MSS.* iv. 269.
[21] *Hearne's Collections*, i. 10, 12, 27, 70.

attacked in the Lords by Bishop Burnet in 1704.[22] These incidents were not trivial, for the Bishop of Ely called for a royal visitation of the universities,[23] and in Oxford there were the first symptoms of the apocalyptic fears which haunted the University in the next reign.[24]

The Tory agitation against Harley was felt, secondly, in a contested election in Oxford in 1705. Whitelock inspired little enthusiasm, and in 1704 Dean Aldrich began to recommend George Clarke; others talked again of Dr. Edisbury, a master in Chancery, and an influential party championed Sir Humphrey Mackworth. The latter did not scruple to claim the support of the high-church magnates Nottingham, Guernsey, and Rochester (who were in fact friends of Whitelock), nor disdain the assistance of Bacchus, but Whitelock, with Magdalen support, enlarged his following of 1703 at the poll, which read:[25]

Sir Humphrey Mackworth .   110
Sir William Whitelock .   . 214
William Bromley .   .   . 325

Although in 1710 Bernard Gardiner, Warden of All Souls, was arguing that 'his age, and ye compliments already payd him by ye university' ought to convince Whitelock that it was time to retire,[26] neither member was disturbed again in this reign.

Other incidents exacerbated ill feeling between the majority in Oxford and the Whigs both within the University and without. In the summer of 1702 came the notorious affair of Bishop Nicolson.[27] Nicolson was made Bishop of Carlisle through the influence of Sir Christopher Musgrave,[28] and applied to the University for the degree of D.D. by diploma. In the Convocation controversy, however, he had opposed Atterbury, who had received the same degree for his efforts. A number of M.A.s immediately signed a protest that the bishop's opposition to Atterbury implied 'a severe

[22] Bodl. MS. Rawlinson Letters 92, fos. 181, 196, 245.
[23] *Hearne's Collections*, i. 124.
[24] Ibid. 61, 64.
[25] *Hist. MSS. Comm. Portland MSS.*, iv. 105; *Hist. MSS. Comm. Downshire MSS.* I, pt. ii. 874; Bodl. MS. Rawlinson Letters 92, fos. 292, 300; University Archives: MS. Conv. Reg. Bd 31, fo. 15.
[26] Bodl. MS. Ballard 20, fo. 21.
[27] This is related fully in N. Sykes, *Edmund Gibson* (London, 1926), pp. 56 seq.
[28] *Hearne's Collections*, ix. 384.

and indecent reflection upon the proceedings of the University', and demanded satisfaction. The Vice-Chancellor communicated the protest to the furious new bishop and the outcome was that Bentley arranged for Nicolson, together with Kennet and Gibson, two of the outstanding Oxford Whigs, to take honorary doctorates at Cambridge. Nicolson believed that Bromley and the Vice-Chancellor had staged the M.A.s' protest themselves, and that Atterbury, a man of ungovernable temper, 'upbraid[ed] the Queen with her giving a Bishoprick where the University had refused a degree'.

It was poetic justice that as Dean of Carlisle Atterbury had soon to contend openly against Nicolson, but the University was the immediate sufferer, her enemies in London representing the affair as 'a direct affront to . . . the Queen, the whole Bench of Bishops and the present Establishment', and a claim by Oxford to veto episcopal appointments.[29] Moreover Charlett and the heads of Christ Church and Magdalen, who seem honestly to have recommended Convocation to yield, were accused of helping the Vice-Chancellor to block any concession. Nicolson himself attacked the University for abandoning her doctrine of prerogative: 'Will not the *Muses sons* (who now find their *long desponding hopes revived* in her present Majesty) renounce the fanatical and republican notion of the Supremacy's being seated in Parliament?'[30]

Such incidents were worse when they concerned preferment in the University itself. Great heart-ache was caused by Crown nominations to the regius chairs. It was said that Archbishop Tenison secured Hody's appointment as regius professor of Greek in 1698 because he could stand him no longer at Lambeth, and required that he should reside and lecture,[31] a condition notoriously unfulfilled. His successor and former deputy, Thomas Milles, was equally unwelcome to Hearne who regarded his qualifications as 'all banter';[32] his decisive asset was doubtless being chaplain to the Earl of Pembroke, one of the heroes of the university Whigs. Dr. Hoy, who was put into the regius chair of physick in 1698 by the interest of Lord Somers, also caused dissatisfaction by his

[29] *Letters of William Nicolson D.D.*, ed. J. Nichols (London, 1809), ii. 647–9.
[30] Ibid. 640.
[31] Bodl. MS. Rawlinson Letters 91, fo. 428.
[32] *Hearne's Collections*, i. 326.

political connexions and his non-residence; even Hoy's deputy appointed a deputy, appointments which aroused public controversy well into the next reign.[33] Swift groaned for 'this exploded custom of rewarding merit'.[34]

The most important regius chair, that of divinity, became vacant at a most unhappy moment by the death in 1707 of Dr. Jane, who had been appointed in the high noon of divine right in 1680, had drafted the decrees on passive obedience in 1683, and helped to defeat the comprehension scheme in Convocation in 1689. The University was still licking the wounds incurred in the struggle against occasional conformity and had run into fresh trouble from political preaching. In April 1706 even the steady nerves of Dr. Stratford had been shaken by fear of the consequences of a sermon in Christ Church by Read, 'the most silly and worthless person of the whole society'. His text—'As then, he who was born of the flesh persecuted him who was born of the spirit, even so it is now'—permitted him to fulminate against the dangers of Presbyterianism to episcopalians in both Scotland and England, and in his peroration 'he bid them arm against the fiery trial that was now approaching', the fiery trial presumably being union with Scotland. It was said that 'Sacheverell has been outdone by one of Christ Church'.[35]

This incident passed over quietly, but in the following July the government took action against a sermon in St. Mary's by Mr. Hart of Magdalen. Hart's case was that 'he had no manner of Reflection upon ye Union, nor anything in his sermon yt insinuated ye Church was in any danger from ye Government; but only yt some danger seemed to threaten it from ye Growth of Atheism & Prophaneness & ye prevailing of faction & Schism in ye Nation'. The secretaries of state insisted that Hart be examined repeatedly before the Vice-Chancellor and heads, but he prudently burnt his sermon notes and refused to be questioned under oath until an accuser with a precise charge should appear. Delaune, the Vice-Chancellor, claimed that the statutes forbade him to do more, and was accused by the government of wilful evasion of the queen's commands. Dean Aldrich suspected that the charge was a by-

[33] *Hearne's Collections*, i. 230, ii. 380–2.
[34] *The Correspondence of Jonathan Swift*, ed. F. E. Ball (London, 1910–14), i. 287.
[35] *Hist. MSS. Comm. Portland MSS.* iv. 295.

product of the notorious political divisions within Magdalen,[36] while Dr. Lancaster wished to oblige his patron the Duke of Marlborough by procuring a submissive address to the queen. Luttrell reported that Ormonde had expelled Hart,[37] but in fact the University seems to have left the ministers to settle the matter as best they could.

Marlborough, who was in the background of the whole dispute, was already 'highly offended' with the University for presenting an address to the queen early in 1705 in which the war-time services of Admiral Rooke were rated as highly as his own.[38] Installed now at Woodstock it was natural for him to cultivate an interest in the University, like that of other Oxfordshire magnates and especially Harcourt. But the matter was the more urgent, since in the autumn of 1707 it was clear that a breach between the Marlborough–Godolphin and the Harleyite connexions in the government could not be delayed much longer, and, for some months past, the Whig party in the Church had been clamouring for an unusual crop of vacant ecclesiastical preferments of which the regius chair was the least. Committed to gratifying the Junto by their strained relations with the Harleyites, Marlborough and Godolphin found the queen determined on the personal exercise of her ecclesiastical prerogatives.[39] The succession to Dr. Jane therefore attained a significance in the politics of the University, county, and nation out of all proportion to its intrinsic worth, and occasioned a contest behind the scenes which lasted for almost a year, a year of miserable uncertainty in Oxford.

In March 1707 there was speculation 'whether the C[ou]rt is turning to High Ch[ur]ch, or them to the C[ou]rt', and Dr. Lancaster, the Provost of Queen's, whose name was canvassed for the bishopric of Chichester, could not decide whether to exploit the apparently favourable turn in court opinion to accept Marlborough's hint to address in favour of the Union.

The men who made the Union Act, and refused the two Universitys

[36] In fact the informer seems to have been Rye, one of the weathercocks of Oriel. *Hearne's Collections*, ii. 109 n. 3.
[37] Ibid. i. 282, 284, 286; *Hist. MSS. Comm. R7, Ormonde MSS.* 781; Luttrell, *Brief Relation*, vi. 83.
[38] A. Boyer, *The History of the Life and Reign of Queen Anne* (London, 1722), pp. 168–9.
[39] On this whole question, N. Sykes, 'Queen Anne and the Episcopate', *E.H.R.* l. 440 seq.

the same conditions that were granted to those in Scotland, are the men who hate us, and [yet] all our friends in Parliament dislike the Act as it now stands, and may be offended with us and forsake us upon our address, and so we may be forsaked upon all hands.[40]

There was the same difficulty in knowing how to construe the Court's failure to appoint a successor to Jane. For over a year before Jane's death in February 1707, Marlborough had been pressing at Court for the appointment to go to Dr. Potter, chaplain to Archbishop Tenison, who in January 1707 refused Harley's offer of the regius chair of Greek on the grounds that he had 'turned his study wholly to divinity'. Marlborough declared 'that if he has not the Professor's place, I will never more meddle with anything that may concern Oxford'. For months, however, he doubted his ability to carry the appointment with the queen.

For an equal period the Christ Church interest had been pressing the claims of Dr. Smalridge, Dr. Jane's deputy for several years past, and the favoured candidate in Oxford. Smalridge was a lifelong friend of Atterbury, whose politics he combined with an equable temper, and had obtained some notoriety for a ferocious sermon on Gen. xlix. 6 before the House of Commons on 30 January 1702.[41] It was now said that Dr. Lancaster, the Vice-Chancellor, and Dean Aldrich had gone over to the Court, promising a free hand for Marlborough and Godolphin if Smalridge should have the chair; Lancaster's kinsman, the Bishop of London, the Archbishop of York, and Robert Harley, were also strongly in his favour. Yet the necessities of Marlborough, Godolphin, and their Whig allies were great: their pressure finally told; Potter received his chair and, to the disgust of majority opinion in the University, turned it into a sinecure. Smalridge professed no disappointment, his financial loss was assuaged by the lectureship of St. Dunstan's-in-the-West, and his future importance in the University was probably enhanced by martyrdom in the cause.[42] The ecclesiastical appointments announced in January

---

[40] Finally only Cambridge addressed on the Union.

[41] G. Smalridge, *Sermon preached before the Honourable House of Commons* (London, 1702). This occasioned a reply in *Animadversions on the Two Last 30th of January Sermons* (London, 1702).

[42] *Hearne's Collections*, i. 233, ii. 88, 90, 91, 448; *Hist. MSS. Comm. Portland MSS.* iv. 320, 386, 473, vii. 24; Bodl. MS. Ballard 21, fo. 67: 31, fo. 61; Wm. Coxe, *Memoirs of the Duke of Marlborough* (London, 1907), ii. 101, 161; A. T. Hart, *Life and Times of John Sharp, Archbishop of York* (London, 1949), p. 243; Nichols, *Illustrations*, iii. 272–3.

1708 were on the whole a disappointment to the Oxford Tories, for despite his flirtation with Marlborough, Lancaster lost his bishopric through his kinship to Bishop Compton who had turned Tory, and the See of Norwich went to Sunderland's tutor Trimnell who in 1701 had failed by one vote to be elected Warden of New College.[43]

Public reports followed that

the Oxonians do extremely resent the late affronts put upon them by ye Court, & do very much blame ye Bps of [the other] University for interesting themselves in the promotion of unworthy men to places in their University. They stick not to say that you endeavour to raise the reputation of Cambridge by sinking that of Oxon.

Nevertheless, the display of strength achieved by the old court connexion and the Whigs in the recent church preferments had its effect, and when canvassing for the next election began early in 1710, the Earl of Abingdon accused Charlett and other court politicians in the University of shifting to the low-church interest. 'They smile in coffee houses and say now, since the great dons in O[xfor]d are turned about, ye small ones they hope will follow their example. ... Interest is at the bottom, & safe is ye word now with these new converts.'[44] Two events, however, helped to maintain the old interest in the University.

The first was a recrudescence of the controversy about the obligation of college fellows to take holy orders. Early in 1709 a pamphlet was printed urging the repeal of such college statutes in Oxford and Cambridge as compelled 'the taking of orders under a penalty', and 'given out only to such persons as are favourers of the proiect conteyned in it'. This suspicious wire-pulling was followed by an attempt to introduce legislation in Parliament. Bromley opposed the Bill, Sir William Whitelock ridiculed the whole idea, 'letting ye chief promoters of it knowe that when the saints themselves had the absolute dominion the same proiect had been ... three several times attempted and as often baffled', and as all the bishops and the Speaker of the House of Commons declared against it, the Bill was dropped.[45] The opposition to the measure was remarkably unanimous: Bishop

---

[43] *Hearne's Collections*, i. 219.
[44] Bodl. MS. Ballard 31, fos. 78, 80.
[45] Ibid. 49, fos. 164, 166; Nichols, *Illustrations*, iii. 280; *Hist. MSS. Comm. Downshire MSS*. I, pt. ii. 871.

Trelawney, the former scourge of Exeter, thought the Bill would turn the colleges into 'nurserys of lawyers & attorneys' and expose them to litigation 'in Westminster Hall, where atheism, socinianism & a proper detestation of ye principles & government of ye universitys is allowed and justifyd', while the Whig White Kennet trembled at the thought of meddling with college constitutions and the intentions of benefactors, and thought the policy of the Bill must 'tend . . . to the breeding up Sparks and Beaux instead of grave divines', which in eighteenth-century circumstances was doubtless true.[46]

All parties in Oxford united therefore against legislation which could only have been promulgated with the sympathy of the Whig ministry, and which was revived in similar circumstances in 1716. The trouble had begun in All Souls where the Warden, Bernard Gardiner, was trying to compel William Blencowe[47] (and, it was falsely rumoured, his friend Matthew Tindal the deist) to take orders as required by the college statutes. Legislation promoted by himself, Meredith, Littleton, Dalton, and other fellows having failed, Blencowe applied for a dispensation to Lord Sunderland who wrote to Archbishop Tenison (the college Visitor), that since Blencowe was employed in deciphering letters, it was the queen's pleasure that Gardiner should no longer require 'him to take a new profession which would hinder him from attending her Majesty's service'—a strange construction of the obligation to enter holy orders. Tenison acted accordingly, but could have met no more resolute defender of the legal rights of his office than Gardiner. To ask the Visitor to break the statutes he was pledged to maintain was a revolutionary innovation, and Dr. Stratford of Christ Church epitomized the general feeling in taking 'the case to be altogether as arbitrary as anything done by the late Lord Sunderland at Magdalen College'.

The Blencowe case drove the waverers in Oxford back to the old interest the more effectively because Gardiner was a friend of the Vice-Chancellor, Lancaster, who was sympathetic to the government. This friendship had availed him nothing. Gardiner, with characteristic obstinacy, rallied the Bishop of London, Brom-

[46] Bodl. MS. Ballard 9, fos. 69, 73; B.M. Lansdowne MS. 1013, fo. 120; *Catalogue of the Archives of All Souls College*, ed. C. T. Martin (cited below as *All Souls Archives*) (London, 1877), pp. 342–5.

[47] Blencowe owed his fellowship to the favour of Archbishop Tenison M. Burrows, *Worthies of All Souls* (London, 1874), p. 356.

34

ley, Whitelock, Lord Digby, Lord Dartmouth, the Duke of Buckingham, and others, and by 1711 the queen agreed not to press
the case. The affair concluded melodramatically when Blencowe
shot himself in bed in the following year 'because [so Hearne
moralized] the Whiggs were turn'd out, as they deserv'd, & by
that means he lost the Hopes he had conceiv'd of Prefermt'.[48]

The government's blunderings in the Blencowe case, however,
were as nothing to their sins against Sacheverell. The celebrated
sermon on the perils amongst false brethren which he preached
before the Lord Mayor on 5 November 1709, and for which he
was impeached, was not new; he had preached it with complete
impunity at St. Mary's in December 1705 in support of the campaign to declare the Church in danger.[49] In 1707 and 1708 the
University had been sharply attacked in the Whig press, and
there had been threats of burning all the books in which non-
resistance was taught—'I wish the Bible itself may escape', declared Smalridge;[50] now by impeaching the author of a sermon
too violent for the city to dare to print, the government seized a
golden opportunity to proclaim the principles of the Revolution,
to restrict political sniping from the pulpit, and to discredit the
University which inspired the propaganda of its opponents. The
House of Commons condemned his sermon and another preached
at Derby, and exacerbated their offence by addressing the queen
to prefer the Whiggish and Liberal Hoadly for his services to
Revolution principles. These resolutions were put through a thin
house in which the minority of five for Sacheverell included both
the Oxford and one of the Cambridge burgesses.

There is no need to recount here the story of Sacheverell's trial
and condemnation. No shade of opinion in Oxford respected
Sacheverell or his unbridled venom in the pulpit of St. Paul's, and
there was much resentment when he tried to use his new notoriety
to become proctor of the diocese in Convocation. But, as Stratford
told Harley, 'so solemn a prosecution for such a scribble will make
the Doctor and his performance much more considerable then
either of them could have been on any other account', and scenting that decisive changes in the political world were imminent,

[48] Bodl. MS. Ballard 10, fo. 77; *Hist. MSS. Comm. Portland MSS.* iv. 529–31;
Hist. MSS. Comm. Dartmouth MSS. i. 299; *Hearne's Collections*, ii. 313, iii. 439;
All Souls Archives, pp. 346–50; *Hist. MSS. Comm. R7, Ormonde MSS.*, p. 782.
[49] *Hearne's Collections*, i. 138–9, cf. 312.
[50] *Observator*, vi, nos. 15, 27; Nichols, *Illustrations*, iii. 277.

orthodox Oxford politicians strained every nerve in his cause. The Vice-Chancellor went bail for him,[51] Harcourt defended him, and it was coffee-house gossip that the University had composed his speech. Though the penalties were moderate, Sacheverell's condemnation was a foregone conclusion, and the Lords consigned not only his sermons but the Oxford decrees of 1683 and a mass of other offending literature to the bonfire. Oxford orthodoxy as well as Sacheverell was under judgement, for the majority amended Bromley's motion to address the queen for 'a general fast to implore God's blessing, and avert his Judgements wch are to be fear'd upon account of ye horrid Blasphemies, irreligion and profaneness' of recent publications, to the effect that these were the publications of Dr. Sacheverell.[52]

The burnings over, in April 1710 the University addressed the queen again in inflammatory terms. University loyalty would never suffer them to 'question any title by which your Majestie holds your Crown, particularly that which is hereditary'; they would labour for social tranquillity and regretted that 'ill men [e.g. Hoadly] have found means to propagate so many blasphemous and heretical doctrines among us which tend not more to the undermining of religion, than they do to the disturbance of the civil peace'; and since the Anglican Church was 'framed most exactly according to the primitive and apostolical model we cannot but with the deepest sorrow bewail the danger of so many deluded souls as are misled into the damnable sin of schism'. Hearne regarded this address as a shameful lapse from the grace of 1683, but Whig pamphleteers naturally read it as an insult to queen and parliament by maintaining propositions so recently condemned, and by giving 'countenance to the rebellious mob, rais'd in favour of their dear Sacheverell, by pulling down the Meeting-House'.

On a text soon to be expounded even more ominously by Bishop Hoadly—'My kingdom is not of this world'—Oxford men were told that it was 'not their province to meddle with government and titles of crowned heads', and that 'whenever the minister or priest hath the least of power, the more religion and the nation flourish'. Another pamphlet pointed out that the University's

[51] See note A, p. 280.
[52] *Hearne's Collections*, ii. 229, 306, 320, 361, iii. 36; *Hist. MSS. Comm. Portland MSS.* iv. 530, vii. 7, 17; Bodl. MS. Ballard 31, fo. 82.

36

behaviour during the Revolution belied the decrees of 1683, that it was evading the parliamentary basis of the queen's title, and concluded that the faith of the University was worthless, and that its object was to twist scripture in the cause of absolute power.[53] The recriminations which followed the Sacheverell crisis and the subsequent Tory triumph seriously widened the breach between Whig and Tory in Oxford, and reunited the latter with the weathercock court politicians. The next few years were to see the testing of this alliance in Oxford as at Westminster.

[53] University Archives: MS. Conv. Reg. Bd 31, fo. 62; *Hearne's Collections*, ii. 374–5; *An Answer to the Address of Oxford University* (London, 1710); *University Loyalty, or the Genuine Explanation of the Principles and Practices of the English Clergy* (London, 1710).

CHAPTER III

Tory Hey-day

THE Tory landslide in the elections of 1710 occasioned great satisfaction in Oxford, not least because it had been accomplished without any general change in the lords lieutenancies and benches of justices;[1] it must therefore strengthen the hand of the high-church interest *vis-à-vis* the Court. The new government was formed of a coalition of the Harleyites with the church Tories— the very coalition which Bromley under university pressure had taken the lead in breaking in 1704 and 1705, and which he had been labouring mightily to revive since 1708. 'I do not take Mr. Bromley for a great negotiator', Marlborough had concluded, 'but a less able man than himself will reconcile Lord Rochester and Mr. Harley at this time.'[2] They resolved to contest the Speaker-ship in 1708; Harley championed Bromley, and Bromley rallied all his friends in the hope of dividing the government party. This contest was abandoned because of the death of Prince George, the queen's husband, but Bromley became Speaker after the Tory victory at the polls in 1710. From the beginning the strains in the coalition, which developed finally into the great duel between Harley and St. John, made themselves felt, but Bromley kept loyally to the agreement. He wrote highly of Harley to his constituents:

I look upon it that we are embarked in the same bottom, engaged in the same interests, . . . and shall do my utmost . . . to support his ministry, and I do hope that such reasonable care will be taken to satisfy and make our friends easy, that I may be able to serve him.[3]

The crowning disappointment of Anne's reign in Oxford arose from the efforts of rival interests to satisfy and make their friends

---

[1] *Hist. MSS. Comm. Portland MSS.* vii. 23.

[2] St. John was putting the strongest pressure upon Harley to effect a reconciliation from his side. *Hist. MSS. Comm. Bath MSS.* i. 191–2.

[3] W. Coxe, *Marlborough*, ii. 291; Lamport Hall: Isham MS. IC 1705; *The Correspondence of Jonathan Swift*, ed. F. E. Ball (cited below as *Swift Corr.*), i. 117; *Hist. MSS. Comm. Portland MSS.* vii. 50.

easy, in which it became apparent that even confessing friends of
the Church had not put off the old man. But the church Tories
were not the only connexion in Oxford. At the time Marlborough
had been contending for the preferment of Dr. Potter, it had been
said that 'it would be policy in the Duke of Marlborough to oblige
the university' by making Aldrich Bishop of Exeter and Atterbury Dean of Christ Church, but such patronage had never been
at his disposal, and although in 1711 Dr. Stratford declared that
'Blenheim is a curse upon this place' and talked jovially of burning it down, Marlborough never created a solid following in the
University.[4] Among his friends was Benjamin Woodroffe, Principal of Gloucester Hall, a man, according to Humphrey Prideaux,
'of a maggoty brain', and of no great consequence in the University.[5] Much more significant was Dr. Lancaster, who had become
Provost of Queen's after a disputed election in 1704. An early
protégé of Sir Joseph Williamson, he had preached in Oxford on
William's coronation day, and had always been orthodox in theology and a court Whig in politics. Vice-Chancellor from 1706
to 1710, Lancaster had the opportunity of serving the Court by
procuring favourable addresses against Jacobitism and of defending Woodroffe who was being sued for debt by the Treasurer of
Christ Church. He tried to get satisfaction for the Court in the
case of Mr. Hart's sermon, 'always express'd a most passionate
honour for the D[uke] of M[arlborough]', and from the time he
was Vice-Chancellor could reckon on the support of the Whig
heads of Wadham and Merton as well as connexions of his own
such as Warden Gardiner of All Souls. Lancaster was not a good
foundation for a political connexion, however, since like Marlborough himself he was primarily a court politician or, as Hearne
put it, 'a person who drives at nothing but self-interest, and . . . of
no steddy principles'; when convenient 'he spoke much in praise
of the Doctrine of Passive Obedience in the University', and in
1710 procured the university address in favour of Sacheverell's
principles at the very moment he was working for the Whig
interest in the county election.[6] Less of a faction Whig than his

[4] Ibid. viii. 280, vii. 55.

[5] *Hearne's Collections*, i. 282; *Hist. MSS. Comm. R5, Pine-Coffin MSS.*, p. 377.

[6] F. Thompson, *A True State of the Case concerning the Election of a Provost
of Queen's College in Oxford* (Oxford, 1704); *Hearne's Collections*, i. 216, ii. 98–
99, 101, 137, 279–81, 296, 348, 384; B.M. Add. MS. 6116, fo. 34; *Hist. MSS.
Comm. Portland MSS.*, v. 206; Ellis, *Letters of Eminent Men*, p. 234.

friend and fellow-collegian, Edmund Gibson, Lancaster was not of the stuff of which parties could be made by politicians with the limited ecclesiastical patronage of Marlborough.

Faction Whiggism had never been without its witnesses in Oxford, despite the discouragement they received from the irresponsibility of the lay leadership of the party in matters of church preferment. The chief strongholds of the Whigs were Merton and Wadham; Exeter had not yet attained political importance, but there were active Whigs also in Jesus and New College. When new Wardens were elected at Merton the senior fellows selected three candidates, from whom the Visitor, the Archbishop of Canterbury, made the final choice. With Tenison at Canterbury the way was open to Whig influences. In 1693, indeed, Merton had narrowly escaped having the notorious Dr. Radcliffe imposed upon it as Warden, from the king's gratitude for his having cured the Earl of Portland. As it was, the fellows refused to elect Tenison's favourite, Dr. Huntingdon, and to ensure that Tenison selected their choice, Dr. Conant, they submitted the names of Dr. Bateman, a potential non-juror, and the aged and uninfluential Dr. Lydall. Tenison gained his revenge, however, by choosing Lydall, and subsequently Whig pressure was brought to bear on elections to fellowships. But it was not till 1709 that a known Whig was made Warden, in John Holland, reputed 'Loe Church enough' even in the hottest days of Toryism.[7]

The steadily increasing power of the heads of houses at the time, which even Whigs like White Kennet considered good for the proper government of the University,[8] gave them unrivalled power in the politics of college and University, and ever since the Revolution Wadham had been governed by a well-known Whig, Dr. Dunster, abused by the university Tories as 'Dunstar ye lowsy', and 'one of ye violentest Whiggs and most rascally lowchurch men of ye age'.[9] One of the fellows and benefactors of the college, moreover, had been Dr. Hody, the unpopular regius professor of Greek installed by William in 1698. Neither Wadham nor Merton, however, could do more than hope for the future during the Indian summer of Tory glory, 1710–14.

[7] B.M. Lansdowne MS. 1013, fos. 55, 57; Bodl. MS. Ballard 5, fo. 148; *Verney Letters*, i. 313.
[8] Bodl. MS. Ballard 6, fo. 98.
[9] *Hearne's Collections*, i. 291, ii. 109.

The delight of the Oxford majority in the impotence of the Whigs in those years lost its sweetness as it became apparent that neither in Oxford nor in Westminster were the triumphant Tories to enjoy the fruits of power in harmony, nor finally could they solve the succession problem in the party interest. The oldest of the Tory interests in Oxford had been that created by the great contriver of the Restoration, the Earl of Clarendon, Lord Chancellor of England and Chancellor of the University. This interest was now on the wane, but eighteenth-century politics (not least in Oxford), Whig, Tory, and Radical, was generally backward-looking, and the Hyde interest did not become a mere memory for nearly a century after the greatness of the first earl. The second earl was appointed High Steward of the University in 1686, the first vacancy after his father's death, but he weakened the family following in the University by refusing to take the oaths and abandoning the leadership of connexion to his younger brother, the egotistical Earl of Rochester. He, too, was a disappointment in Oxford as a politician who never quite arrived;[10] nevertheless, the Duke of Ormonde installed him High Steward on his brother's death in 1709, and two years later, on his death, installed his son. It was significant, however, that on this occasion, only a few months after the return of the Tories to power, the Countess of Rochester appealed to Robert Harley not to take the place for himself, for, since bickering in the ministerial coalition was already common knowledge, the University would 'turn it as if you intended to conquer from us'.[11]

It is a measure of the strength of court politics in Oxford that Robert Harley, the son of a Whig, the alumnus of a dissenting academy, and in religion (according to Dean Aldrich) 'that spawn of a presbyterian', should by virtue of the queen's favour and traffic in crown patronage already have a party in Oxford. In 1711 he took the title of Earl of Oxford because of a distant connexion with the former earls of the Vere family, but Harcourt emphasized its university associations, claiming that 'the encouragement of those who excel in [letters], is one distinguishing part of your character'.[12] Harley's services to the Tory cause

[10] The University acknowledged Rochester's appointment as Viceroy in Ireland in 1700 by creating him and his son D.C.L. Luttrell, *Brief Relation*, iv. 695.

[11] *Hist. MSS. Comm. Portland MSS.* iv. 687–8.

[12] A. Collins, *Peerage* (London, 1735), II, pt. ii. 593; printed also in *Harcourt Papers*, ed. E. W. Harcourt (Oxford, n.d.), ii. 38.

enabled him even in 1701 materially to assist Sir Christopher Musgrave's election for the University, and in 1705 he was receiving the compliments of Dr. Charlett, who was always sensitive to the political breeze.[13] In the same year he secured a canonry at Christ Church for his chaplain, William Stratford, an appointment which the apostles of the high-church interest, Bromley and Dean Aldrich (who at this date acknowledged his indebtedness to the new Secretary) professed to approve. He also strove to secure the regius chair of divinity for Smalridge, and his coalition with the high-church party in 1708 provided them much-needed access to the queen, and with a leadership more skilful than scrupulous. In 1711 Harley made Smalridge a canon of Christ Church and dean of Carlisle, and another canon indebted to him, Francis Gastrell, preferred in 1702, now became a chaplain to the queen.

Harley's patronage had so far created an interest in Oxford that when in 1710 he wanted the University to confer a degree upon Samuel Palmer, a clergyman who had been so rash as to 'reflect . . . upon the universities' in print, Stratford could write:

I hope I have secured Magdalen an account of our late merits on Dr. Sa[cheverell]'s account. I reckon too upon Jesus, Corpus Christi, most of New College and Lincoln and St. John's. And should any peevish men persevere to oppose it, I hear we shall have some friends too in other colleges.[14]

Harley's friends, in short, could rally societies such as St. John's and Lincoln where there were court Tories, New College and Jesus where there were court Whigs, and Corpus, the President of which was the enigmatic Thomas Turner, the brother of the deprived Bishop of Ely who was persistently reported to have non-juring tendencies, but in fact was 'too wary a man to enter into an open opposition of anyone unless the occasion should be very extraordinary'.[15]

Nevertheless, it was a weakness in Harley's position that, having no roots of his own in Oxford, he had to depend excessively upon the power of Christ Church, the society most open to royal influence. The wealth, prestige, and voting power of Christ Church

---

[13] *Hist. MSS. Comm. Portland MSS.* iv. 14, 197.
[14] Ibid. 203, 473, vii. 4–5.
[15] Ibid., p. 53; Luttrell, *Brief Relation*, v. 201; cf. *D.N.B.* and Feiling, *Tory Party*, p. 302.

created a certain animosity in the rest of the University, and in 1709 when Stratford, the Treasurer of the House, sued Woodroffe for debt outside the Vice-Chancellor's court, Dr. Lancaster made 'a most scandalous and uncharitable Reflection upon Christ Church, as if they were bitter and inexorable enemies to the University'; Hearne, who was out of sympathy with so much in Oxford life, had a characteristically perverse fondness for Christ Church.[16]

Still worse, on the death of Aldrich in 1710 Harley made a false move in translating Atterbury from the deanery of Carlisle to that of Christ Church. To Atterbury's disgust the preferment was kept vacant for months, while politicians jostled behind the scenes, the Bishop of London tottered at the edge of the grave, and Oxford men hoped that Smalridge, who finally became a canon, would get the deanery. The probability is that Harley was coerced into translating Atterbury by his high-church allies, who wished to use the first substantial preferment to end Atterbury's misery as dean of Carlisle, though it is possible that, like Swift, he underestimated the restless dean's capacity for creating trouble.[17] Atterbury arranged a reception in the splendid style he loved, being 'met on Shotover Hill by some 400 or . . . 500 horse, and all the coaches that belong to this town. 'Twas the greatest appearance that has been known', but though he professed never to 'ask for anything more, [and to] . . . employ all the interest he has in the Lord Treasurer for others', it soon transpired that his great fanfare was on behalf of the Harcourt connexion, of which something must now be said.[18]

The rise of Simon Harcourt of Stanton Harcourt was one of the wonders of the day in Oxfordshire. Of Harley's generation, he was early allied with the younger St. John, and, like Hardwicke later, won the glittering prizes within the grasp of those who could succeed simultaneously at the professions of law and politics. From the beginning a strong Tory, Harcourt conducted the prosecution of Somers and Defoe and the defence of Sacheverell; he was made Solicitor-General, knighted, and created D.C.L. at Oxford in 1702, became Attorney-General 1707 and drafted the Act of Union, and

---

[16] *Hearne's Collections*, ii. 281, 296.
[17] Ibid. iii. 112; Jonathan Swift, *Journal to Stella*, ed. H. Williams (Oxford, 1948), i. 153, 298, 346.
[18] *Hist. MSS. Comm. Portland MSS.* v. 93, vii. 62.

succeeded as Lord Keeper 1710, but until 1713 refused all offers of the Great Seal, while he increased his fortune at the Bar. His new wealth was surmised from his great purchases of real estate and his building at Nuneham Courtenay, Cokethorpe, and elsewhere in the county; Harcourt was the great parvenu of Oxfordshire Tory society as Marlborough was of the Whig. This status alone would have been sufficient to interest Harcourt in university politics, but he also coveted one of the university seats in Parliament. It was already recognized that 'those who have ye honor to serve ye University escape both the trouble & expense other gent[lemen] meet with', and enjoyed unusual security as well.[19] Harcourt's tenure of Abingdon was insecure and finally failed him altogether; and although he entered the upper house in 1711 he was still ambitious to establish his son, 'young Sim', a Christ Church man, as a university burgess.

Already in 1695 Harcourt was warning Dr. Charlett of the imminent death of Sir Thomas Clarges, and negotiating with Trumbull to stand for the vacancy; in 1698 he was himself talked of as a member; in 1700 he and Harley helped Charlett through the difficulties created by Musgrave's decision to stand for Westmorland—he was always ready to further the University's business in Parliament.[20] His chief friend within the University, a court Tory like himself, was Dr. Delaune, the President of St. John's, during the Vice-Chancellorship of whom (1702–6) Harcourt procured a satisfactory address of thanks for Queen Anne's Bounty.

Delaune had been elected in 1698 'to ye great satisfaction of ye most worthy part of ye university' in a sharply contested election over a confident opponent, Torriano, who had even contracted for the late President's housekeeper; and though highly disreputable in character Delaune continued to enjoy considerable popularity in the University. A confirmed gambler—his habits were attacked in 1703 by Terrae Filius, the licensed buffoon of the Public Act, in a speech beginning 'jacta est alea'—Delaune was financially unscrupulous. It is well known that during his Vice-Chancellorship he defrauded the University of more than £2,000 derived

[19] Bodl. MSS. Ballard 10, fo. 72: 38, fo. 116; Lord Aylesford to Lord Guernsey, 14 Aug. 1717, Packington Hall MSS.
[20] Bodl. MS. Ballard 10, fos. 92, 93, 113, 115; *Vernon Corr.* ii. 148; *Hist. MSS. Comm. Portland MSS.* iv. 9–10.

from sales of Clarendon's *History of the Rebellion* and else-where,[21] and although the University reimbursed itself by seques-trating the profits of his church livings, individuals who suffered from his dishonesty were not all so fortunate.

From at least 1705 Delaune was a financially embarrassed man, and sought to escape from his difficulties by ecclesiastical prefer-ment of which only the government disposed. This was probably the explanation of reports in February 1710 that he was among the Oxford court politicians who were flirting with the Whigs, though he had lately stood bail for Dr. Sacheverell. After the election of 1710, however, he set his hopes on an Irish bishopric to be obtained through Harcourt—first Raphoe, then London-derry. These proposals only inflamed the conflict between the two Tory interests in the University, and Bromley, who loyally sup-ported Harley, was primed to insist that Delaune's debts to the University be made a first claim on any episcopal revenues he might receive. When therefore Atterbury became Dean of Christ Church, with the intention of developing the Oxford interest of Harcourt and St. John, Delaune became his right-hand man, the more useful because his erratic finances had not destroyed his popularity as a preacher nor his reputation among the midland clergy and gentry.[22]

Atterbury's stormy history as Dean of Christ Church has been well known since the publication of Dr. Stratford's correspon-dence with Edward Harley, and need be recounted only briefly here. Atterbury's contest with the college, and especially with the canons of the Harleyite connexion, was unique only in its ferocity; Dr. Trevelyan noted its resemblance to the Bentley affair in Cam-bridge,[23] and similar incidents, which were mostly political in origin, occurred in other Oxford societies. Atterbury's objects were two. To increase the power of the head of the House would enable

---

[21] For this squalid transaction see *The First Minute Book of the Delegates of the Oxford University Press 1668–1756*, ed. S. Gibson and J. Johnson (Oxford, 1943), pp. xxvi, 25, 28–33. Delaune was again appointed a Delegate of the Press in 1724.

[22] *Hearne's Collections*, i. 100, 193, ii. 89, 115, 280, iv. 315, v. 371; Nichols, *Illustrations*, i. 411; Bodl. MS. Rawlinson Letters 91, fo. 428; MS. Ballard 31, fos. 78, 80; *Hist. MSS. Comm. Portland MSS.* iv. 105, v. 239, 359, vii. 113, 172, 175; *Verney Letters*, ii. 69.

[23] Bentley indeed was advised that the confusion of Christ Church had created an atmosphere favourable to the settlement of his own conflict. *The Correspon-dence of Richard Bentley*, ed. C. Wordsworth (London, 1842), ii. 455.

him to guarantee the great strength of Christ Church to his friends in the government, and he sought secondly to develop the Harcourt interest in the University, and to forward young Simon Harcourt's ambitions to be a university burgess. Atterbury made a parade of improving the state of learning in the college, but most of the conflicts in the chapter broke out over his attempts to control college business. Any dispute over the meaning of the statutes must be settled by the Crown as college Visitor, and the powers of the Crown would probably be deputed to Harcourt, or at least to Harcourt and Harley. Atterbury enjoyed the political sympathies of Smalridge from his youth, and to discredit Stratford and Gastrell, the other two Harleian canons, and to alienate them from the rest of the college, would further his domination. He was even accused of arranging the results of college competitions to suit his ends, and the charge is not wholly implausible.[24]

One of Atterbury's first claims as head of the House was 'to dispose of all the college curacies by his sole authority', an invaluable means of building up a following both in the college and in the University. He formed a connexion not only with Delaune but with Jonathan Edwards, the Principal of Jesus, who was too near the grave to be of much assistance, and hoped to rally Magdalen by courting Sacheverell. Atterbury's other chief hope was Robert Shippen who had been elected Principal of Brasenose in 1710.[25] The only favourable remarks about Shippen appear to be those of the latter-day historians of his college; for a couple of years he had certainly been employing corrupt means to create a party among the fellows which would ensure his election as head. More than a year before old Dr. Meare's death the disorder in Brasenose occasioned rumours which Wake, the college Visitor, denied, that he 'design[ed] to turn out the old principall merely from the infirmities of his age, & this to serve Dr. Smith,[26] a man of many ill qualities, especially drinking; that for this purpose [he had] . . . continued the Vice-Principal, a sot & gambler, besides a Block[h]e[a]d & Illiterate'. Shippen's high-flying views were attacked in a pamphlet on his presentation to the rectory of Whitechapel,[27] proved by his manipulation of college admissions,

[24] *Hist. MSS. Comm. Portland MSS.* vii. 49, 52, 63, 66, 77, 80, 110–12, 115–16.
[25] Ibid. 53, 72, 140.
[26] Principal of Hart Hall; Shippen defeated him by one vote in the election for Principal of B.N.C. in 1710.
[27] *The Spiritual Intruder Unmasked.*

and guaranteed by his brother, the celebrated William Shippen.[28] No one, however, seems to have credited Robert with William's reputed incorruptibility, and he was an obvious ally for one as clearly on the rise as Atterbury after 1710.

The intrusion of so restless a force into the University inevitably created opposition. Thomas Turner, the respected and non-committal President of Corpus, was by nature hostile to such violent ways; Lancaster and Atterbury were virtually committed by their political connexions to the contest for which the Dean was spoiling from the beginning, and even the Vice-Chancellor, Thomas Brathwaite, Warden of New College, was not exempt from the Dean's animosity when it came to the election of a beadle of beggars in 1711.[29] Yet Atterbury and Harcourt were not without resources to attract the wavering, for Charlett and other heads who were queen's chaplains were complaining that they were being neglected 'which is discouraging to them and to the University, and exposed them to some contempt'. At the end of 1711 the scheme for annexing some of the prebends in the Crown's gift to certain college headships was revived, apparently at Harcourt's request, and, it was feared, with Atterbury to have the choice of the fortunate colleges. An unseemly struggle for the crumbs of preferment followed; as Stratford remarked later, 'since it was perceived that votes were valued, everyone was for getting something, a promise at least', and everyone who could gain by giving promises gave them. It was rumoured that it was in fact the Earl of Oxford who had obtained the loaves and fishes. Bishop Wake was urged to exert his influence; Bromley and political connexions of Bolingbroke actually did so.

In the end prebends were annexed to the headships of Oriel and Pembroke, John Baron, Master of Balliol, was given a prebend not annexed to his office, and there were rumours, apparently unfulfilled, that Charlett was to get a prebend of Worcester on the same terms.[30] Of the fortunate recipients, Brickenden, Master of Pembroke, was the undistinguished successor of Dr. Hall,

[28] *Hearne's Collections*, ii. 295; iii. 8; Bodl. MSS. Ballard 3, fos. 76, 93, 95; 35, fo. 117; Christ Church MS. Arch. W. Epist. 16, no. 216 [316]; *Hist. MSS. Comm. Kenyon MSS.*, p. 447.

[29] *Hist. MSS. Comm. Portland MSS.* vii. 53, 68, 75.

[30] Ibid. 75, 77, 171, v. 240; Christ Church MS. Arch. W. Epist. 17: Dr. Potter to Bp. Wake, 15 May 1712; Oriel College MS. Memorandum Book of the Provost of Oriel, pp. 12–13; 13 Ann. c. 6.

one of William's Whig bishops, while Carter, the Provost of Oriel, was a court politician of the crudest sort with a dubious record after 1714. In 1708 he was approved by Hearne as 'a worthy, ingenious, sober Gentleman, and a good scholar', he wrote flatteringly to Bromley, and sought a royal chaplaincy through Bolingbroke; but having cultivated every shade of Tory opinion, he revealed the truth about his politics by becoming a cringing Whig after the Hanoverian accession.[31] Dr. Baron of Balliol, though described by the college historian as 'a stalwart Whig', bears all the marks of a court Tory; he had preached in favour of the campaign against occasional conformity, was an enemy of Hearne, and studiously 'moderate' after 1714 (though affecting Jacobitism outside Oxford), and commended as 'one of the honestest men we have here' by Stratford in 1721.[32] Charlett's character and aspirations to a prebend have already been described. A handful of prebends were a powerful bait by which the Harcourt interest might recruit a party amongst heads whom they had been hitherto unable to influence.

A further head was secured at the foundation of Worcester College. The settlement of Sir Thomas Cookes's benefaction (which all thought destined for Magdalen Hall) had been delayed by the committee of heads, and even in 1710 Dr. Clarke had urged Ormonde to insist on a settlement. At the end of 1712 Harcourt as Lord Keeper set aside their award, and the benefaction was settled on Gloucester Hall, which after many disputes was established as Worcester College in 1714. The object of this manœuvre was plain enough, since in 1712 the Chancellor had appointed the last head of the old foundation, who became the first head of the new, Richard Blechynden, Harcourt's chaplain, who had already received canonries of Rochester and Gloucester from the government, and the rectory of Nuneham Courtenay from Harcourt himself.[33]

At the end of 1712, therefore, Harcourt had reasonable hopes in testing the prospects of his son's election; he argued that Sir

[31] *Hearne's Collections*, ii. 105; *Letters and Correspondence of Lord Bolingbroke*, ed. G. Parke (London, 1798), iv. 465; Oriel College MS. Memorandum Book of the Provost of Oriel, p. 4.

[32] *Hearne's Collections*, ii. 130, vi. 232; *Hist. MSS. Comm. Portland MSS.* vii. 307. Cf. *Verney Letters*, ii. 68.

[33] *Hist. MSS. Comm. Portland MSS.* vii. 110, 115, 126, 139, 170, 175, 305, 365, 386; *Hist. MSS. Comm. R7, Ormonde MS.*, p. 782; *Hearne's Collections*, iii. 155.

William Whitelock was too old to stand again, and acquainted the University with young 'Simkin' by having him made M.A. and taken around in the wake of Atterbury. The latter, however, had gone out of his way to alienate the Harleyite and other connexions, Harcourt was on the worst possible terms with the Vice-Chancellor, Bernard Gardiner, and the plan to dislodge a sitting member when the political situation was as favourable as in 1713 smacked of breach of faith by the University. Like the alternative plan of running young Simon for the county, the scheme had to be dropped as quietly as possible.[34]

The power of the faction led by Bolingbroke and Harcourt was demonstrated again in June 1713 upon Atterbury's preferment as Bishop of Rochester and Dean of Westminster. Harleyite perplexities were revealed by Dr. Stratford who affirmed

that nothing that has been done since [Oxford's] . . . ministry has struck such a damp upon the hearts of all that have honour or honesty, as this promotion. All of any weight here . . . wondered that such a one should be permitted so long to act as he did here, but they lift up their hands to see him preferred for it.[35]

With Atterbury's departure to sow dissension in the Chapter of Westminster, university affairs became more tranquil, and as the queen appointed prelates more congenial than the high-church fanatics, the Harleyites reaped their reward. Smalridge, who in Christ Church politics was prepared to act against Atterbury, succeeded him as Dean, and became not only Bishop of Bristol but Lord Almoner to the queen. Gastrell, who had waited longest,[36] became Bishop of Chester, and Dr. Terry, Lord Harley's tutor,[37] obtained a canonry at Christ Church.

Thus when it was already becoming clear that Lord Oxford could not solve the succession question in the Tory interest, his connexion in the University received the public testimony to its strength which Stratford had always urged.[38] On matters of clerical preferment, which touched Oxford hearts deeply, the two Tory factions continued to clash. In October 1713 Atterbury, Harcourt, and the commissioners of the public accounts recommended Mr. Hinton as Speaker's chaplain; the University as

---

[34] *Hist. MSS. Comm. Portland MSS.* vii. 118, 121, 126, 139, 151.
[35] Ibid. 140.   [36] Ibid. 163.
[37] Ibid. v. 296, vii. 162.   [38] Ibid. 47.

represented by the Duke of Ormonde and William Bromley con-
tended for Dr. Pelling and succeeded.[39] Both Harcourt's attempts
to secure an Irish bishopric for Delaune failed, and he was furious
when the university delegates of accounts wrote to Bromley and
Ormonde to 'represent to the Queen the debt due to the University, and beg the grant may be stopped till security is given to the
university for it'.

As the divisions in the Tory ranks grew more bitter, and as the
queen's life ebbed away with the Tories reconciled to neither of
the claimants to the throne, Oxford men pored over their London
correspondence in bewilderment. The official Oxford politicians,
especially Ormonde and Bromley, increased in importance as the
crisis drew nearer. At the beginning of the ministry Bromley had
been well disposed to St. John and Harcourt,[40] and he had continued to pursue the policy they desired for political reasons. He
took a leading part in the October Club, promoted the attack on
Walpole, and launched the Occasional Conformity and Schism
Acts. Yet Bromley remained loyal to the alliance with Harley, to
whom he owed his appointment as Secretary of State in 1713. In
Parliament he stood above the contest between the latter and the
Tory group led by Bolingbroke, Harcourt, and Atterbury, and
generally opposed them in the University. Ormonde also had
worked strenuously to keep the coalition together, and there were
some fears amongst Harleyites that if he and Anglesey joined
Bolingbroke's ministry when at the last Oxford was dislodged
from office, Bromley might accompany him.[41]

In fact neither joined, and in the last week of Anne's reign the
situation in Oxford was as tantalizing as that at Westminster.
The two chief Tory interests in the University had long been at
loggerheads and a prey to fluctuating hopes and fears. Delaune
affected the complete court politician. Called on by the President
of Trinity to toast the Earl of Oxford he replied: 'He is out, what
do you toast him for? What have we to do with him?', and being
reproached on the day of Anne's death for ordering prayers for
King George in the college chapel when it was not certain that
the queen was dead, 'Dead', says he, 'she is as dead as Julius

[39] Hist. MSS. Comm. Portland MSS. vii. 170, 181, 183.
[40] Epistolary Correspondence of F. Atterbury (London, 1783), i. 27.
[41] Hist. MSS. Comm. Portland MSS. vii. 192–3; Swift Corr. ii. 170. Cf. Bolingbroke, A Letter to Sir William Wyndham (London, 1753), pp. 63, 66.

Caesar', as politically she was.[42] Oxford men must fend for themselves until those who had dabbled in university affairs for so long gave a clearer lead. The one cause which no one of consequence in the University, any more than Oxford, Bolingbroke, or Harcourt, considered in the summer of 1714 was that of the Pretender. At that moment, as *Hearne's Collections* witnesses eloquently, Jacobitism was a forgotten creed among those who counted.[43]

[42] *Hist. MSS. Comm. Portland MSS.* vii. 197, 198.
[43] It is interesting that Steele, who in Nov. 1715 was representing the University as an apostle of indefeasible hereditary right, described her in Dec. 1713 as a pillar not only of the Church but also of civil liberty. R. Steele, *The Englishman*, ed. R. Blanchard (Oxford, 1955), pp. 140, 394.

PART II

THE HANOVERIAN SUCCESSION
1714–25

Oxford, that English Avignon, or independent ecclesiastical state in the heart of the Kingdom of Britain.

St. James's Post, 7–10 December 1716

> When Rakes Reforming Tracts compose,
> And sober Blockheads read 'em,
> Oxford! beware of Godly Foes,
> And doubly guard thy Freedom.

From the frontispiece to the reprint of John Allibond's
A Seasonable Sketch of an Oxford Reformation. 1717

CHAPTER IV

Oxford under suspicion

THE death of Anne left the Oxford politicians in confusion, but not in despair. White Kennet related that 'none to all appearance [were] more sanguine than they who would still be called Tories'. Although the foreign policy of the late government had driven the king to the Whigs, no one yet knew how far he was committed to them. Few had been in the secret of the ministers' intrigues with the Pretender, which in any case had ended several months before Anne's decease, and prudence and honesty alike counselled the Tories to make the best terms possible with the new dynasty. Atterbury acknowledged George's title with nauseating fulsomeness, and recommended Harcourt to write to Hanover 'not merely as a single person, but in some measure as the head of an interest'.[1]

---

[1] *Original Letters Illustrative of English History,* ed. H. Ellis, 2nd series (London, 1827), iv. 286–8; F. Williams, *Memoirs and Correspondence of Francis Atterbury* (London, 1869), i. 278.

The Harleyites in Oxford had no desire to be included in this interest, and scorned his professions that 'old quarrels must be forgotten, we must unite again' in the knowledge that the Earl of Oxford was flirting with the Whigs. Stratford revealed his prescience declaring that he 'always thought the possession would be quiet. The struggle if any will be some time hence, when we see what we are to expect upon the revival and animosities of parties', a forecast remarkably like that of Bolingbroke.

Meanwhile the Vice-Chancellor, Dr. Gardiner, was 'very zealous to pay his duty to the King', and produced an address giving the king every possible pledge, and claiming for Oxford as great a share of the royal favour as she had enjoyed in any previous reign. Verses followed, including a poem 'To the King' by Smalridge, in which he praised his sovereign's 'mighty mind' and invited him to visit Christ Church to hear

> this Loyal House proclaim
> What Reverence she paid to Anna's Name

now paid to George himself. Vice-Chancellor, heads, and proctors offered £100 for the discovery of the author of a letter to the mayor ordering him to proclaim King James. Bromley moved the voting of the Civil List and lent his weight to the other Tory leaders who were urging the rank and file to welcome the new reign with an appearance of enthusiasm. In October 1714 he was offered the place of Teller of the Exchequer, but refused it when he could not have it for life. Oxford men, in short, pledged their loyalty willingly and, in Stratford's phrase, waited to see what they were to expect.[2]

As late as January 1716 the Vice-Chancellor and heads of houses agreed unanimously 'to embrace this happy opportunity of expressing our duty to his Ma^ty by paying the utmost respect to [the] . . . Prince [of Anhalt], who we understood had the honour of being well known to his Ma^ty, & much favour'd by him'. By that time, however, the University was already under an official

---

[2] *Hist. MSS. Comm. Portland MSS.* vii. 199–203; University Archives: MS. Conv. Reg. Bd 31, fos. 112–13; G. Smalridge, *Miscellanies* (London, 1715); *Hearne's Collections*, iv. 389–90; *Wentworth Papers*, pp. 411, 423, 429; *The Jacobite Memorial* (London, 1714); J. Toland, *The State Anatomy of Great Britain* (London, 1717), p. 91. In his account of the transaction Horatio Walpole seems to have confused the offers made to Bromley and Hanmer. W. Coxe, *Memoirs of Sir Robert Walpole* (London, 1798), ii. 48.

cloud, it was guilty of a degree of disaffection, and its disillusionment with the new system was well expressed by Smalridge who
'heartily wish[ed] that no occasion had been given for ye least
abatement of that warmth and zeal, wch those of this place
amongst ye rest of his Ma^{tie's} subjects profess'd at his first happy
accession to the Throne'. The calamity feared in the middle of
the last reign had now come to pass; a Whig government, supported by a partisan king, was making a party issue of every place
and every policy, and the fact that friends of Oxford in the October Club had recently demanded similar measures in the Tory
interest made the pill no less bitter to swallow.[3]

Oxford opinion was reflected in the university sermons which
in the circumstances were often political in character. As long
as Hearne kept a full account, many of the sermons were remarkably favourable to the government, or no more unfavourable than
to dwell tactlessly upon the glories of the previous reign, and the
Vice-Chancellor took care to publish sermons which denounced
non-jurors or were otherwise pleasing to those in authority.[4] But
in September 1715 Abel Evans of St. John's, an unstable man who
had served both the Marlborough and Harcourt interests and
had a chequered future before him, preached on Matt. vi. 10 and
hinted 'at some of our modern tyrants and usurpers . . . meaning
particularly ye present Elector of Brunswick', as Hearne still
described George I. In March 1716 Dr. Haywood, of the same
college, was reported by an enemy to have asserted that 'K. George
had suspended his favours at present from ye University by some
misrepresentations', and in July, Jones of Balliol was attacked in
the London press for offending the judges in his assize sermon in
which he affirmed 'that our constitution was broke, that the nation
groan'd under a load of oaths; and that it was a very hard case
for honest men to be oblig'd to swear against their inclinations or
loose their bread'.[5]

The expression of university opinion most characteristic and
most damaging to its reputation were the political celebrations

[3] Christ Church MS. Arch. W. Epist. 20: Bp. of Bristol to Abp. Wake, 26 Jan.
1715/16: David Wilkins to Abp. Wake, 26 Jan. 1715/16: 15, Bp. of Bristol to Abp.
Wake, 9 Jan. 1715/16; *Hearne's Collections*, iv. 409, v. 95.

[4] Ibid. v. 19, 62, 236, vi. 32–33, 76.

[5] Ibid. ii. 359, v. 121; Christ Church MS. Arch. W. Epist. 20: D. Wilkins to
Abp. Wake, 15 March 1715/16; *Dawkes's News Letter*, 26 July 1716; *The Flying
Post*, 24–26 July 1716.

and the disorder that sometimes accompanied them; these gave the greatest opportunity to the enemies of the University, and have been the chief evidence for the wholly unwarranted opinion that the University was a hot-bed of Jacobitism for more than half a century after the Revolution. Unfortunately, King George's birthday (28 May), Restoration day (29 May), and the Pretender's birthday (10 June) were inconveniently close together, and by the time they were first celebrated under the new dynasty the Whigs' intentions of butchering their opponents to make a party holiday were abundantly clear.

On 28 May 1715 the Constitution Club, an aggressive body of Whig graduates recently formed by some New College men, which the Tory majority in the University soon learned to detest and distrust, met at the King's Head Tavern to celebrate the king's birthday and induct the Marquis of Hartington as president. Having arranged for a gigantic bonfire to be lit and the windows to be illuminated, they attracted the attention of a mob of townsmen unhappily swollen by the crowd that had come into market. According to the Whig account

all the time the mob was thus employ'd, the disaffected scholars, who had crowded the houses and streets near the tavern, continued throwing up their caps, scattering money amongst the rabble, and crying down with the constitutioners: down with the Whigs: No G[eorg]e; Ja[me]s for ever, Ormonde, Bolingbroke &c.

As soon as the Constitutioners were found to have escaped from the tavern, the mob broke all the illuminated windows in the town, sacked the Presbyterian meeting-house, and carried off the pulpit for another bonfire at Carfax. Thomas Hamilton, a Constitutioner of Oriel and son of the late queen's physician, took refuge in New College and fired a pistol at the mob. The next night the mob appeared in the streets again, this time to break windows which were not illuminated in honour of the Restoration; they sacked the Quaker meeting-house and came to Oriel to seek out the Constitutioners who had been kept in college by their tutors. One of the Constitutioners, probably Ingram, Lord Irwin's brother, repelled an assault upon the windows of the college by firing a shot which wounded a Brasenose man, and finally the mob dispersed.[6]

[6] See note B, p. 280.

55

The immediate consequence of the riots was to give the government the hold upon Oxford which some Whigs had always desired. Townshend, the Secretary of State, sent down 'rattling letters' to Charlett, as Pro-Vice-Chancellor, and to the mayor, which induced the university authorities to issue a programma deploring the whole incident, threatening dire punishment on the guilty, and admonishing 'all persons whatsoever to avoid all odious and contumelious words of reproach and distinction which may tend to create discords and animositys'. The disturbances (and those which followed at Cambridge) also occasioned an important alteration in constitutional law, for they led to the passing of the Riot Act. The printer and publisher of *The Evening Post* were taken into custody by order of the House of Commons for printing a letter purporting to have been written by Walpole to Sunderland demanding forcible measures against the University. Though extremely plausible, the letter was resolved to be 'a false, scandalous and traitorous libel'. The situation in Oxford and in the country as a whole became very tense. Bromley wrote anxiously to the Vice-Chancellor to suppress the trouble and provide him with material to counter the University's enemies. It was feared that the riots would remove the government's last scruples against taking the life of the Duke of Ormonde, the most prominent of the new recruits to Jacobitism, and the Whig Ingram prepared to withdraw from Oxford to a commission in his brother's regiment, that being 'the only thing that can secure a man's life' for 'officers nowadays are the safest'.[7]

Oxford remained quiet on the Pretender's birthday, and before the anniversary of the king's accession on 1 August the Vice-Chancellor and heads took measures to prevent any further disturbances. Yet the government was being plied with highly coloured stories of Oxford's preparations for treason, and the tension was intensified by a succession of minor incidents as troops went about recruiting and by the scholars' rescue of a publican taken up by Roger Hutton, Student of Christ Church, for alleged treasonable utterances. The government required the Oxford J.P.s to search for weapons and gunpowder, but they produced little

---

[7] *Hearne's Collections*, v. 64; *University Notices 1662–1821*, 4 June 1715 (Bodl. G.A. Oxon. b 19); A. Boyer, *Political State of Great Britain* (cited below as *Political State*), x. 55–58; Bodl. MSS. Ballard 38, fos. 168, 170: 36, fo. 174; *Hist. MSS. Comm. Various MSS.* viii. 91.

besides 'birding guns' and 'fowling pieces'. Hearne began to expect a Jacobite invasion, but there were few resources in Oxford with which to support it.[8]

The immediate question, however, was how the University was to manage without a Chancellor. Ormonde, who had cultivated popularity in Oxford by lavish entertainment and had been savagely calumniated by the Whigs as a Jacobite for supporting Lord Treasurer Oxford as his ministry foundered, had finally, to the incredulity of Swift, been goaded into actual treason, and in August left the country to join the Pretender, never to return. Attainted by Act of Parliament Ormonde was given till 10 September to surrender, and on 9 September, despite feverish attempts to get in touch, no one in Oxford had any news of him. Nerves were the worse frayed by memories of Ormonde's own election in July 1688. The news of the old duke's death had reached the Vice-Chancellor at 2 p.m. on a Sunday, and under the statute requiring a new election as soon as possible, he had the late Chancellor's grandson elected next morning, just before the arrival of letters mandatory from James II for the election of Lord Chancellor Jefferies. Despite the king's displeasure, the Earl of Clarendon had also rushed on Ormonde's election as High Steward of Westminster.[9] In 1715 as in 1688 it was essential for the Tory factions in the University to keep the election in their own hands, for the Chancellor's office carried extensive powers which made it desirable to leading politicians throughout the century. A Chancellor pledged to the present government might contrive a complete political upheaval in the University.

The Vice-Chancellor, Gardiner, now wanted to declare the office vacant and have a fresh election, but despite the legal opinions of Sir Constantine Phipps the constitutional situation was obscure, and any move

was warmly oppos'd by some of the friends of the D. of Ormond, who out of zeal to him would not suffer him to be divested of the honour till the expiration of his civil no more than of his natural life and

[8] *Hearne's Collections*, v. 68, 87, 97, 99, 103; P.R.O. SP 35/2, fos. 45–46, 125: /3, fo. 252 (misdated 1716): /4, fos. 42–45; *Miscellanies*, no. 9 (Bodl. 4 Δ 260); *Hist. MSS. Comm. Townshend MSS.*, p. 157.
[9] *Hist. MSS. Comm. R5, Sutherland MSS.*, p. 187; *Wood's Life and Times*, iii. 494; *Prose Works of Jonathan Swift*, v. 334, 452–3; *Swift Corr.* ii. 295; *Correspondence of Henry Hyde, Earl of Clarendon*, ed. S. W. Singer (London, 1828), ii. 182–3, 187, 490–2; *The Flemings in Oxford*, ii. 220.

apprehended that such a proceeding . . . might for the future . . . make the office precarious.

At the eleventh hour, however, Lord Arran, Ormonde's brother, returned the patent and a letter of resignation; at 9 a.m. on 10 September he defeated Lord Pembroke in the election by 140 votes to 3.[10] By rejecting Pembroke, a court politician who had held office with the Whigs but had supported Sacheverell and who had long been concerned in university business, the University committed itself to the old order;[11] but it could hardly avoid making an immediate choice of a candidate known to be willing to accept election.

The Vice-Chancellor planned Arran's installation as a quiet occasion, but it proved to be a boisterous success. Hearne noted with approval that he was 'in all respects much like the Duke', and he seems to have won some of the popularity which Ormonde had attracted. Swift agreed with Macky's estimate of him as a man 'of very good sense, though [he] seldom shows it', adding that 'he is the most negligent of his own affairs', an estimate not borne out by Arran's successful parliamentary campaign to regain his brother's confiscated estates. The Earl of Mar in his Jacobite days respected him highly 'for his known honesty, honour and worth', and William Bromley 'would as soon take the word of Lord A[rran] as of any man alive'. At his death in 1758 he had outlived his political generation, but Horace Walpole, always good for a sneer, summed him up comparatively kindly as 'an inoffensive old man'.[12]

In personal character Arran was not unworthy of his office; the University, however, might tremble at his politics. Arran had been a member of Swift's 'Club', but, like other Tories, his present politics were settled less by his past connexions than by his reactions to the goading of the Whigs; when he was installed Chancellor he was threatened with the total loss of his property. A story was circulated in Cambridge in 1716 that he had outlived his usefulness, was to be deprived and replaced by the Prince of

[10] *Hearne's Collections*, v. 110 seq.; Bodl. MSS. Ballard 38, fos. 224–7: 21, fo. 198; *Hist. MSS. Comm. Townshend MSS.*, p. 233 (misdated 1716).

[11] *Hearne's Collections*, i. 40, ii. 93, iii. 453, iv. 105; Coxe's *Marlborough*, iii. 27: he was a benefactor of Lincoln College; Lamport Hall: Isham MS. IC 2625.

[12] *Hearne's Collections*, v. 116–19; *Swift's Prose Works*, x. 281; *C.J.* xix. 299, 304, 608; *Hist. MSS. Comm. Stuart MSS.* iv. 414; Lamport Hall: Isham MS. IC 1869; H. Walpole, *Memoirs of the Reign of George II* (London, 1822), ii. 332.

Wales, a charge which is interesting in view of Oxford's flirtation with the Hanoverian reversionary interest at that time; but in fact Arran served the ruling heads well. During his term of office (and until the very end of the century) none of the heads of the original Whig colleges was invited to serve as Vice-Chancellor; no Dean of Christ Church, the society penetrated most rapidly by ministerial influence, served till 1870. Even in Oxford, however, there was murmuring when he kept Robert Shippen Vice-Chancellor for five of the most crucial years in the University's history, 1718–23.

Arran's brother being one of the few disinterested friends of consequence the Pretender had, it was inevitable that he should be drawn into the Jacobite circle of which Atterbury, no friend of Ormonde in 1714, was the moving spirit. Upon Ormonde's flight Arran was reckoned with Wyndham and Lansdowne among the chief friends of the Pretender in London and in July 1716 was appointed Commander-in-Chief of all the Pretender's land and sea forces in England, an empty honour indeed. Arran stuck to the Pretender longer than Wyndham, for his name was prominent in Jacobite correspondence until the attempt of 1719, but he was of little practical assistance. In quest of the family estates, Arran had to tread very delicately; nothing would have delighted the government more than to take him in the act as they finally took Atterbury, but Arran was never fatally committed.[13]

The flight of Ormonde deepened the bitterness felt in Oxford, and the election of Arran, whose equivocal position could not but be suspected, only increased the ministers' distrust of the University. Still plied with alarming fantasies 'that there was several thousands lying in & about Oxford ready to rise', the government sent a spy, Cornet Vissouse, and found that in fact there was a handful of disaffected officers (the most notable of whom was Colonel Owen) who had been dismissed on account of their political opinions. Colonel Pepper's regiment, which was apparently on its way to suppress disorder in the west of England, turned aside at Banbury and, marching all night, aroused the authorities of Oxford at 4 a.m. on 9 October and established a

[13] *Swift Corr.* ii. 331; Bodl. MS. Ballard 6, fo. 137; *Hist. MSS. Comm. Stuart MSS.*, *passim*, e.g. ii. 305, iii. 557 (misdated 1716); W. K. Dickson, *The Jacobite Attempt of 1719*, Scottish History Society, xix (Edinburgh, 1895), 51, 123.

complete blockade of the town. The mayor and Vice-Chancellor offered every assistance, and were accordingly convicted in the Whig press of 'guilt by dissociation'. 'Nothing is either more *insolent* or *abject* in the various vicissitudes of *prosperity* and adversity than either a *divine*, or a country magistrate.' The Vice-Chancellor, Abel Boyer asserted, had behaved like a Jacobite at the installation of Arran, but 'now trembling with a downcast look, in a broken speech, made large professions of loyalty and affection to his Majesty'.

Pepper then made a search and captured the ten or eleven men whom he had come to apprehend, with the exception of Owen who escaped over Magdalen wall in his night-gown. To point the moral Pepper produced a warrant from the Secretary of State appointing Caleb Colston, the Whiggish keeper of the Star Inn, as postmaster. Wild stories were pressed on the government that all the postmasters in the district were Jacobites, and now Oxford dons could only suffer in silence as their letters were pilfered, and score a point by electing Pottle, the dispossessed postmaster, as university verger. When the prisoners were tried, it proved that there had been no conspiracy worth the name, that the discontented officers had attracted one or two followers by stories that there were 10,000 scholars ready to rise at Oxford (four or five times the entire strength of the University), and that their failure had been ridiculous rather than tragic.[14]

Meanwhile, at the outset of the '15, James had dispatched a declaration dated 20 October to Oxford and Cambridge asserting that the government, 'not content with imposing on them a necessity of renouncing their principles or preferments', proposed to filch their endowments, and 'to reduce them to the compass of some foreign universities composed only of a few professors with precarious salaries', and, on this low estimate of academic ideals, offering to guarantee Church and universities in their existing rights. For the Pretender himself to be silent about divine right was acute psychology indeed,[15] but there seems no evidence that

---

[14] *The Muses' Fountain Clear* (London, 1717), p. 35; Bodl. MS. Top. Oxon. C 164, fo. 4; MS. Ballard 38, fo. 215; Boyer, *Political State*, x. 342–6, 535–6, 595; *Hearne's Collections*, v. 125; P.R.O. SP 35/3, fo. 253; Christ Church MS. Arch. W. Epist. 20: D. Wilkins to Abp. Wake, 1 April 1716; cf. Bodl. MS. Ballard 21, fo. 62.

[15] The declaration was nevertheless too niggardly for Bolingbroke: *Letter to Wyndham*, p. 281.

Hearne, at least, saw the declaration, expectant though he was. The Whigs, however, alleged that on 27 October the Pretender was proclaimed in Oxford, and that a regiment of students had been formed to rise under disaffected officers, though the most incriminating evidence was only a box found in November on a barge from London containing 'twelve dozen swords, and about the like number of bayonets'. On 28 October Brigadier Handasyde's regiment was quartered in Oxford, and the military occupation of the city began.[16]

What Whig writers described as the 'courteous, benign violence' of the garrison was sufficient to keep order in the town and University for a year; the political festivals of the Hanoverian order were dutifully observed, and 29 May and 10 June passed off quietly. Inevitably the Tory connexions in the University felt themselves singled out for political humiliation, chafed against the garrison, and became involved in a series of petty incidents with the troops, both parties being provocative. In Christ Church at least the college authorities dealt hardly with undergraduates who uttered treason in their cups, but mutual irritation was unavoidable, especially as the Whigs of the Constitution Club took advantage of military protection to stage public exhibitions of their principles both in Oxford and in the London press.

'The Gentlemen of Merton College take all opportunities of distinguishing themselves from the factions in the University', announced the *St. James's Evening Post*, 'and of proving to the world that they are sincerely in the interest of his Majesty', and on the king's birthday, 28 May 1716, they had a great celebration. They gave the soldiers 24 guineas to drink the king's health, entertained the officers, and 'invited all the honest gentlemen in the University to repair to the Three Tuns'; with the aid of bonfires, illuminations, drummers, and a barrel of Merton beer, a demonstration of popular loyalty was put on, and the proceedings closed peaceably at the tolling of Great Tom. Charlett and other heads, knowing the risks, kept their colleges closed, and were assailed in the Whig press as Jacobites. The next day, Restoration day, the Tories appeared quietly with 'boughs of oak in their breasts and caps', so the Whigs staged a rival celebration in the evening and

---

[16] *Hist. MSS. Comm. Stuart MSS.* i. 438; Boyer, *Political State*, x. 536; *Hearne's Collections*, v. 122. Hearne, an enthusiast for disaffection, is silent about the alleged events of 27 Oct.

drank publicly to 'the Reformation of the University'. The demonstration of the Constitution Club involved some of their members in a protracted quarrel with the Proctors to be discussed later, but for the moment peace was preserved, though the aggressiveness of the Whig dons and press was an ominous sign.[17]

In July 1716 the judges on assize warned undergraduates by sentencing Frank Nichols, a commoner of Exeter, to a fine of £5 and six months' imprisonment for crying out 'An Ormonde for ever' in the streets. His tutors begged the remission of half the sentence, but he had to make an apology before Convocation.[18] This warning was so far effectual that when serious disorder broke out again on 30 October, the Prince of Wales's birthday, the university Tories took no part. On that day the Constitution Club repeated its celebrations of 28–29 May, and entertained the officers of the garrison at the Star Inn. According to the unanimous testimony of Tories of all shades, the Major of the regiment, without provocation, ordered his men to break all unilluminated windows, saying, 'Come in, Boys, and drink, and then go out and at it again'. The Whigs alleged that the loyal celebrations at the inn were interrupted by stones from the mob of townsmen; but whoever moved first, it is clear that relations between troops and townsmen had reached breaking point, and in the scuffle which ensued the Mayor of Oxford was roughly handled, the windows of his house were broken, and a soldier's bullet passed through his macebearer's hat.

Tom Rowney, M.P. for the city, immediately protested to the Secretary of State that the troops sent to keep the peace were not only the ruin of the ale-house keepers, but created disturbances, damaged property, and abused the magistrates; the Vice-Chancellor and mayor collected depositions from thirty-six witnesses very unfavourable to the soldiers. These were laid before Lord Townshend and the Privy Council by the earls of Arran, Rochester, and Abingdon (High Steward of the city) with the request that the offenders might be punished. The affair, however, did not end so simply, for, as in May, the Whig press resumed its clamour against

---

[17] *Reasons for Visiting the Universities* (London, 1717), p. 46; *Hearne's Collections*, v. 229, 234–5, 237, 260; *Hist. MSS. Comm. Portland MSS.* vii. 216; Bodl. MS. Ballard 6, fo. 47; *The Weekly Journal*, 31 March 1716; *St. James's Evening Post*, 31 May–2 June 1716; *Original Weekly Journal*, 26 May–2 June 1716.
[18] *Hearne's Collections*, v. 268; Boyer, *Political State*, xii. 124; *The Flying Post*, 24–26 July, 1716; University Archives: Conv. Reg. Bd 31, fo. 135.

Oxford, dismissing the depositions as the vapourings of a high-church faction, and insisting that the initiative had been taken by the town mob. This campaign went on with little respite until the end of the year. The ministers were given a broad hint by their supporters that it was 'very hard that men who have all along acted with zeal, and suffer'd for their stedfast adherence to the Protestant Succession, should be hated by the malice of the high church faction', and that it was time something was done for them.

Besides trying to discredit the affidavits collected by the Oxford authorities, they seized on Paris reports of the riot as evidence that 'our British Jacobites' were encouraging the Pretender and discrediting the army. Having formerly abused Marlborough for beating the French, Oxford politicians were now seeking to disgrace the inferior ranks. No scrap of evidence from the past eighteen months which might suggest that the University was guilty of active treachery was disdained, not even barber's gossip. The University's reply to this stream of abuse was to publish the affidavits, whereupon the 'loyal collegians' began to collect depositions of their own.[19]

It was suspected that the city of Oxford's protest against the conduct of the soldiers was drawn up by Sir William Gifford and Lord Harcourt, and the bold reactions of Tory dons and newspapers to the riot suggest real confidence that they at last had a stick with which to beat the government. Subsequently the Privy Council reported in favour of the soldiers and condemned the publication of the affidavits as 'irregular, disrespectful . . . and tending to sedition', but when the Mutiny Bill was being discussed in the Lords on 23 March 1717, one Tory peer demanded that before they passed the Bill they should inquire into the troops' behaviour in the Oxford riot. The ministers required the Bill to be passed immediately, but won the initiative by promising a whole debate on the Oxford issue, doubtless rejoicing at the opportunity to belabour the University with their majority. Thus

[19] *Hearne's Collections*, v. 333; *Hist. MSS. Comm. Portland MSS.* vii. 218; *The Several Depositions concerning the Late Riot in Oxford* (London, 1716); *The Several Papers laid before . . . the Lords . . . relating to the Riots at Oxford . . .* (London, 1717); Boyer, *Political State*, xii. 505–33; Bodl. Nichols Newspapers, vols. 30B, 30C, especially *St. James's Evening Post*, 5–7 Nov. 1716, 24–27 Nov. 1716; *The Weekly Packet*, 3–10 Nov. 1716; *The Flying Post*, 22–24 Nov., 24–27 Nov., 29 Nov.–1 Dec. 1716; *The Evening General Post*, 4–6 Dec. 1716.

the manœuvre which led to the debate on 30 March began ineptly and ended in a fiasco for the University.

Instead of emphasizing the fact that the allegedly disloyal members of the University had taken no part in the riots, Smalridge, Gastrell, and Atterbury who conducted the defence, allowed themselves to be misled by a tendentious resolution of the Privy Council ascribing the troops' misconduct to the neglect of the University to arrange any public celebrations into attempting a patently tendentious explanation of the University's lack of enthusiasm, and moving for the debate to be postponed until further affidavits were collected. Coningsby and other Whig speakers had an ideal opportunity to contrast the loyalty of the University under the later Stuarts with its present sullen acquiescence which, however irrelevant to the issue, was splendid party propaganda. The day ended with resolutions hostile to the University passed by 65 votes to 33. Twenty-seven Tory peers replied with a spirited protest, but the second round of the battle of words begun by the Whig journalists was won by the Whig peers. As one correspondent remarked, 'Lds Ab[ingdo]n & Harc[our]t had a bite put on them, [and] . . . 6 or 7 out of 13 Bps. were agst the University', and as Archbishop Wake bantered Bernard Gardiner—'If there be no disaffection in ye Universityes to the present government... I may truly say you are very unfortunate in the reports wch everywhere spread abroad.'[20]

Meanwhile in the middle of January 1717 an amusing episode had occurred which further illustrated the relations of garrison and University. The king was shortly expected to return from Hanover, an occasion which the officers proposed to celebrate by a procession bearing effigies of the Duke of Ormonde, the Pope, the Pretender, and others, lately imported from London, which should finally be consigned to a bonfire. The heads naturally expected disorder; the commander of the garrison agreed, but pleaded insufficient 'authority to restrain them from diverting themselves in such a manner as they lik'd best'. The heads therefore appealed to the Secretary of State to prohibit the procession, and to Wake to intercede for them. The Secretary of War gave

[20] Bodl. MSS. Ballard 6, fo. 141: 32, fo. 17; Cobbett, vii. 430 seq.; *The Several Papers laid before the Lords*; *The Weekly Journal*, 6 April 1717; Christ Church MS. Arch. W. Epist. 20: D. Wilkins to Abp. Wake, 28 April 1717: 15, Abp. Wake to (? Dr. Gardiner), n.d.

the necessary orders on condition 'that upon the first notice of his Majesty's happy arrival, they set all their Bells a-ringing', and the day finally passed off satisfactorily with every window illuminated and with the soldiers providing fireworks and the largest bonfire ever seen outside the Angel Inn, and making a profit by exhibiting their effigies for money in the guard room.

More serious was the fact that the Warden of Wadham, seconded by two other Whig heads, the Bishop of St. Asaph (Principal of Jesus) and the Warden of Merton, moved the heads to present a loyal address on the king's return, but Gardiner, Charlett, and Hudson, who was Bodley's Librarian and Principal of St. Mary Hall, were now in a petulant mood and defeated the motion. The most private meetings in Oxford were no longer sacred, and this transaction at once leaked to the Whig press.[21]

Although at the Revolution the non-jurors had been a much stronger force in Cambridge than in Oxford, Whig propaganda had always made Oxford loyalty the particular subject of attack; now, as on other occasions, the circumstantial evidence seemed to prove the Whigs right. In October 1716 Cambridge addressed the Prince of Wales (in his father's absence) with fulsome congratulations on the suppression of rebellion; even the king's unpopular visit to Hanover was condoned, for Cambridge could 'scarce esteem it absence while you only cross your own seas to visit your own hereditary countries'. This address was Bentley's pledge of political reliability to Lord Townshend, and evidence for his bland assurance that preferment for himself and Waterland would enable him to complete the rout of the anti-ministerial interest in that place. According to Jacobite information, which other circumstances make credible,

there was an address . . . framed by the University of Oxford to be presented to the Prince, in which they magnified his wise administration, but took no notice of the father. The Prince, being pre-advertised of the contents, gave them to understand that he would accept of no addresses but such as gave due respect to his father.

In short, Oxford's failure to address in October 1716 was due not to disloyalty but to an abortive attempt to exploit the reversionary interest of the dynasty the bulk of Oxford men had always accepted, and a typical manœuvre of the court Tories, who had been influential in Oxford for so long.

[21] See note C, p. 280.

That opportunity had nevertheless been let slip, and in January 1717 an occasion which the Whig heads considered suitable for an address had been refused, and the ministerial press could hardly fail to put an appropriate gloss on the publicly known facts.[22] Another unpleasant episode widely reported and embroidered to the discredit of the whole University occurred in Oriel in July 1717, where one Eves, 'making too free with His Majesty's character in a way very unbecoming to him', was alleged to have been reproved by another undergraduate, Stafford, and to have replied by stabbing him to death with a pen-knife. Whig papers had no scruple in clamouring for 'the just reward of his bloody crime'. He was in fact acquitted for lack of evidence.[23]

The Oxford authorities moreover were somewhat prone to tactlessness. On the very day of the king's coronation they conferred a doctorate upon Sir Constantine Phipps, one of the barristers who had defended Sacheverell, and who had been rewarded by the Tory ministry with a knighthood and the Lord Chancellorship of Ireland. Acting as leader of the Irish Council during Ormonde's absence he had aroused a fervent Whig reaction, and fervent support from Bolingbroke. On the Hanoverian accession he was disgraced by the king and attacked by the Irish House of Commons for 'having acted contrary to the Protestant Interest of that Kingdom'. Tories approved of the honour bestowed by Oxford on their Chancellor's Deputy in Ireland and Bishop Nicolson merely teased the University for emulating the king's coronation clemency—'conferring a degree upon a certain notorious delinquent was only a respectful mimicking of [their] Anointed Lord in the pardoning of that month's malefactors'—but the ministerial journalists took the incident very solemnly as an insult to His Majesty, and ground out their refrain against it with the monotony of juke-boxes for seven years or more.[24]

[22] London Gazette, 20–23 Oct. 1716 (for the politics behind the address, Evening General Post, 20–23 Oct. 1716); Bentley Corr. ii. 526–9; Hist. MSS. Comm. Stuart MSS. iii. 50.
[23] The Weekly Journal, 20 July 1717; The Original Weekly Journal, 13–20 July 1717; Boyer, Political State, xiv. 87; The Original Weekly Journal, 15–22 March 1718.
[24] B.M. Add. MS. 6116, fo. 33; Bodl. MS. Ballard 31, fo. 133; The Conduct of the Purse of Ireland (London, 1714); Toland, State Anatomy, pp. 52, 72; Amhurst, Terrae Filius, i. 32. Phipps was among the legal counsel consulted by the University on the flight of Ormonde a year later (MS. Ballard 38, fo. 225), was joint trustee with Lord Arran for the young Lord Wharton, who became

Thus in the early years of George I Oxford politics were characterized by some gaucherie as well as some disaffection. Smalridge,
stout high churchman as he was, did not deny to the Whig Archbishop Wake that there were some grounds for the imputation
of disloyalty; the alcoholic outbursts in the streets and the equivocations of the Chancellor could not be gainsaid. Yet it is hard to
challenge Smalridge's considered opinion that the 'disaffection is
neither of so early a date, nor in the measure and degree of it so
vehement as hath been represented', nor that in part the government had only itself to thank for it. It is impossible to date the
beginnings of disaffection in Oxford much earlier than the end of
1714, and it is also impossible to overlook the provocation to which
the University was exposed.

Like other clergymen Oxford dons wished to succeed in their
profession, and their loyalty to Anne had not blinded them to the
place-hunting ability of the various connexions. The church Tory
and the court Tory were often as difficult to distinguish in Oxford
as at Westminster, and Stanhope's relief to dissenters in 1718
caused less heart-ache in the University than the avowed intention of the Whigs to treat patronage as a purely party matter.
Despite the promptings of Gibson they organized their ecclesiastical less thoroughly than their political patronage, but the results
were sufficiently devastating. Oxford men were still preferred, but
they were either time-serving court politicians or members of the
Whig minority, and the old brigade, whether of the Harcourt or
Harleyite factions, fell on hard times. Smalridge, who made his
peace most successfully with the new king and Prince of Wales,
lost his place as Lord Almoner for refusing to sign the declaration
of the bishops against the Jacobite rebellion; Charlett, who could
make himself agreeable to most governments, and Stratford, the
Harleyite, were dismissed as chaplains to the king early in 1717,
and to aggravate the offence the latter was replaced by Carter, the
cringing Provost of Oriel. Still worse, during a general purge of
the bench of justices in 1718, Charlett and Gardiner, who had so
often acted with the Oxford court Whigs, but now was proving
truculent at All Souls, were erased from the Commission of the
Peace. To sit on the bench was one of the marks of a gentleman,

a Jacobite and a benefactor of All Souls (*Hist. MSS. Comm. Stuart MSS.* iii. 356;
Christ Church MS. Arch. W. Epist. 16, no. 162), and was considered as a parliamentary candidate for Oxford in 1717 (MS. Ballard 32, fo. 37).

a mark which, it appeared, the government would reserve for only its most abject followers.

Apart from the promotion of leading clerical Whigs such as Wake, Nicolson, White Kennet, and Edmund Gibson who had not resided in Oxford for some time, Potter the Whig canon of Christ Church was removed to Cuddesdon, while John Wynne, Principal of Jesus, and something of a trimmer, became Bishop of St. Asaph in 1715, keeping his headship till he married in 1720, and Robert Clavering, fellow of University College, obtained a canonry of Christ Church and the regius chair of Hebrew in 1715. The decisive influence in Wynne's appointment seems to have been that of Sir Roger Mostyn, the Flintshire political magnate, but Clavering, who was a chaplain and protégé of Archbishop Tenison, was a ministerial nominee appointed over the heads of other candidates. Dr. Pelling, who had been recently made Speaker's Chaplain by Bromley and the Harley interest, 'would have the best title to the canonry', declared Kennet blandly, 'if he understood Hebrew', but he took a canonry at Windsor instead. Simon Ockley, Lord Oxford's chaplain, was hopeful; Christ Church recommended Dr. Wells, Browne Willis's tutor; John Knight of St. John's also had a claim. To all these places the government made perfectly reputable appointments, and Clavering in particular was the best scholar in the field, but no one doubted that it was politics rather than scholarship or piety which had carried the day, and the subsequent behaviour of Wynne and Clavering in university affairs showed that they understood what was expected of them. The experience of power was still so recent a memory among Oxford's leaders that such appointments, and the threat they bore to established connexions, were gall and wormwood.[25] Yet there was worse in store.

[25] Christ Church MS. Arch. W. Epist. 15: Bp. of Bristol to Abp. Wake, 9 Jan. 1715/16; Boyer, *Political State*, xviii. 234; *Hearne's Collections*, i. 114, iii. 299, vi. 27, 392; *Hist. MSS. Comm. Portland MSS.* vii. 239, 207; Ellis, *Original Letters*, 2nd series, iv. 288.

CHAPTER V

Oxford under Attack

T HE feature of the new reign most provoking to the majority of heads was not the loss of spoils but a violent campaign waged against the universities, especially Oxford, by Whig pamphleteers and journalists. This verbal battle has been curiously neglected by historians, yet there have been few occasions when Oxford affairs have been reported more widely and in more intimate detail or discussed with more uninhibited spleen in the national press. This campaign began in 1714 and some of its features have already been noted. The honorary degree conferred upon Sir Constantine Phipps was the first offence, and served the pamphleteers for many years. Other favourite themes were ground out within a few months of the Hanoverian accession, many of them exploiting the religious liberalism and anticlericalism which, for a time at least, rallied to the Whig cause. Traditional Whig suspicions of Oxford preaching were given full vent, and Oxford dons were warned not to 'prostitute their sacred functions, their abilities and their pulpits' in political causes, though they were still remarkably complacent towards the government; in 1717 Toland, who had been a known enemy of the University for many years,[1] demanded that the pulpit be curbed for the clergy were inveterate bunglers in politics.

The present conduct of the University was said to reveal the falsity of their loyal professions in the previous reign,[2] but much more frequent was the old[3] and implausible accusation that Oxford dons acted contrary to their oaths. Few Oxford men had refused the oath to George I—a clear proof to the Whig press that they had forsworn themselves, since it was axiomatic that they were mostly Jacobites. That Oxford was taking to the politics of the 'country' party, to what became familiar as the 'patriot' line, was not always to be denied, but made no difference to the charges: '. . . A swearing Jacobite . . .—that very honest fellow—

[1] Bodl. MS. Ballard 31, fo. 17.
[2] *The Conduct of the Purse of Ireland*, pp. 8–9, 41, 44; Toland, *State Anatomy*, p. 75.   [3] Swift, *Prose Works*, v. 35.

that curls like a Vine, and struts and looks big as if a thing of importance—that sets itself off as a Patriot—as in the Country Interest—as above corruption—is really—a creature without Christ.'

There were ingenious explanations of the alleged scandalous laxity of academic consciences. Serjeant Miller, engaged in his own contest with Bentley at Cambridge, demanded the reformation of the oaths and statutes of both universities as they were obsolete, and led other pamphleteers to the discovery that the reason why 'our Jacobite or High-flying clergy' played 'legerdemain . . . both with God and the King' was that they were plied with 'oaths, which . . . they cannot keep, even from their matriculation oath, to that of Fellows of a College; and that the whole body of students live in a constant breach of every oath they take without the least reflection or regret'. Gordon and Trenchard embroidered this point with the further charges that college oaths were 'in some respects impertinent or ridiculous, in others wicked', and that at Oxford 'open and black perjury is justified, and it is held to be lawful to defy Almighty Vengeance for a morsel of bread'.

In the two great repositories of second-hand arguments against Oxford, Toland's *State Anatomy* of 1717 and Amhurst's *Terrae Filius* of 1721, the charge was repeated, the latter even alleging that Oxford had played off William of Orange against James, and James against William, as well as the Pretender against Anne; and newspapers published letters purporting to come from undergraduates who were being educated out of their moral principles. When the circumstances of Colonel Pepper's occupation of the city had been forgotten, the theme of Oxford's perjury was illustrated by fanciful stories that Owen, the leader of the forlorn handful, had been the toast of heads of houses.[4]

For some years after 1715 events in Oxford were meat and drink to pamphleteers, journalists, and even poetasters, for George Waldron, a former gentleman commoner of Queen's, attacked Ormonde, called, in terms reminiscent of Sacheverell, for the

---

[4] *A Case of Conscience Humbly put to the . . . University of Oxford* (London, n.d.), p. 14; E. Miller, *An Account of the University of Cambridge* (London, 1717), pp. 11–12; *Reasons for Visiting the Universities* (London, 1717), pp. 16, 22; T. Gordon and J. Trenchard, *The Independent Whig* (London, 1721), p. 124; Id., *The Character of an Independent Whig* (London, 1719), p. 11; N. Amhurst, *Terrae Filius* (London, 1726), i. 31; *The Flying Post*, 13–15 Dec., 20–22 Dec. 1716.

'removal of all false brethren from places of trust', and assailed the University for harbouring traitors.[5] Abel Boyer, the best-known of the Whig journalists, made copious and unfavourable reports of events in Oxford throughout 1715. At the time of Ormonde's flight he reported the king as insisting that Oxford men 'should convince him of their loyalty by *Actions* and not by *Words*', a rebuke he held to be well merited by students' affronts to recruiting officers. The election of Arran as Chancellor gave him an obvious opening, though his main evidence of its treasonable implications came from an undelivered letter of an anonymous undergraduate which stated that 'the Prince [of Wales] thought to have been made *Chancellor*, and by that to have been a Bishop, but thank God he was disappointed'. In this there may have been some truth, for the prince succeeded Ormonde as Chancellor of Trinity College, Dublin, soon afterwards. The willingness of university officials to co-operate with Colonel Pepper was to Boyer proof of their duplicity, though he accepted the professions of loyalty made by the Whig dons.[6]

1716 proved an even richer year for the press, and two pamphlets were published by the Whigs of the University. The first concerned the case of Dr. Ayliffe, a Whig of New College, who produced a treatise entitled *The Ancient and Present State of the University of Oxford* in 1714. For statements hostile to the Stuart kings he was condemned in the Chancellor's Court to be deprived of his degrees and banished. Early in 1716 he made his case public in a pamphlet, and was championed by an Oxford Whig in the *St. James's Post*, who declared that the public sale of his pamphlet was prohibited in Oxford; this correspondent affirmed that Ayliffe had been unjustly condemned, and that 'many of us are ready to attest the same at the time of the Royal Visitation', for which Ayliffe himself had called. This pamphlet is important chiefly for its declaration of war by the university Whigs on the existing order, since for some reason Ayliffe never became a hero with contemporary Whig journalists as with later historians of the University.

The Constitution Club attracted more favourable notice, and

---

[5] *An Ode on the Birthday of King George I* and *A Persuasive Oration to the People of Great Britain* (1715), pp. 20, 58, reprinted in *The Compleat Works of George Waldron* (n. pl., 1731).
[6] Boyer, *Political State*, ix. 453, x. 55–58, 121, 341–6.

followed Ayliffe's lead in publishing the speech of one of their members in the Chancellor's Court upon charges arising from the club's celebrations on the king's birthday, 28 May 1715. This speech attacked the whole process by which the charges were brought, and although the defendant was acquitted on all the main heads, the pamphlet abused the university authorities and their justice. There was widespread favourable comment in the press on the manœuvre by which the Warden and Whig fellows of Merton managed to carry their whole list of six Whigs in the elections to fellowships in March 1716, a true exertion of the 'English Spirit' in the view of *The Flying Post*. On the other hand, the University was said to have considered only Jacobite candidates in its elections of a beadle and a verger. Meanwhile Mr. Justice Blencow, the father of the former agitator of All Souls, had reproved disorder in the University at the Assizes, but Oxford correspondents coupled reports of his remarks with coffee-house gossip designed to convict the University of disloyalty, and sharp reflections on a sermon preached in St. Mary's before the judges.[7]

As under Queen Anne, crown patronage to regius chairs caused much discontent in the University, but the London press did not now disdain even a trivial dispute over the appointment of a deputy to the regius professor of physick. Dr. Hoy, the present professor, had been put in by Lord Somers, and had systematically neglected his duties, leaving the work to a deputy, who in turn had appointed a deputy. According to Hearne, and to other evidence, the professor had the right to nominate a deputy, and the Vice-Chancellor and proctors the right to approve the nomination, and to appoint if the deputy was not qualified. In 1716 Dr. Tadlow, Hoy's deputy, died, and the Vice-Chancellor nominated Dr. Code to succeed him, Hoy being in Jamaica. The government, however, notwithstanding that Code was a trimmer reported in the press to be acceptable to the ministers, nominated Dr. Lasher of St. John's by virtue of its patronage to the chair. The University resisted this incursion of ministerial influence, and the Whig press turned up with the usual charges of effrontery and disloyalty, claiming (falsely) that Queen Anne had nominated Tadlow.

<hr />

[7] *St. James's Post*, 9–12 March 1715/16; *The Speech of a Member of the Constitution Club* . . . (London, 1716); *The Flying Post*, 12 March 1715/16, 5–7 April 1716; *The Weekly Journal*, 31 March 1716; *The Original Weekly Journal*, 24–31 March 1716.

Lasher admitted privately that Tadlow had never had 'a Royal Deputation, Dispensation or commendatory letter from ye Government', but pleaded with Sunderland to send 'a peremptory, sharp & commanding letter from ye Government to ye Vice-Chan. to admit me without any further delay . . . yt ye Government may have a Professor to serve ym with a constant fidelity'. The University appeared to have acted according to the statutes and had nominated Code only when Hoy had failed to answer an invitation to nominate personally. None of these or subsequent transactions was reported in the press which had abused the Vice-Chancellor as a 'surly fellow' resisting a clear prerogative of the Crown. Finally, Hoy was given a royal dispensation of absence, and Lasher appointed his deputy; in fact he was not installed till after Code's death, and to secure himself began to agitate that Hoy should resign the chair to him. Lasher had many trials ahead, for Marten of Merton tried to defeat his interest at Court, and when, finally, Lasher had approved himself to the king as 'the only person of eminence in that profession at Oxford, whom one should chuse to distinguish', Hoy's resignation did not come in proper form. But at some time in 1722 or thereafter he obtained his prize.[8]

1716 closed with two events already discussed which aroused a violent reaction from the ministerial press—the riot on the birthday of the Prince of Wales on 30 October, and the failure of the University to send up a loyal address on the king's return from Hanover. Throughout this period the Whig papers sought to incriminate the majority in the University for disturbances in which only the Whig minority had taken part, arguing that the true attitude of Oxonians could be judged by the riot which had taken place on the king's birthday on 28 May, and that the University was in some way guilty of treason because the Paris papers carried full reports of the riot which reflected severely upon the troops. *The Flying Post* considered this as proof 'that our British Jacobites continue to furnish the French Gazeteer with such news as they think may tend to keep the Pretender and his friends in heart, and to make them believe that the Army . . . is now become

[8] *Hearne's Collections*, i. 230, ii. 380, vi. 74, 200, 249; *The Weekly General Post*, 20–26 April 1716; *St. James's Post*, 9–11 May 1716; *The Weekly Observator*, 12 May 1716; P.R.O. SP 35/9, fos. 243, 300, 432, 434; /15, fo. 229; /16, fos. 161, 186; /30, fo. 144. The *D.N.B.* misdates Lasher's death, which took place in 1729. *Hearne's Collections*, x. 114.

hateful to the nation', and romanced at length upon the propaganda value of such news to Jesuits and Jacobites. Subsequent Paris reports convinced the same paper that the University was seeking to let in the Pretender. The Whig papers also sneered at the honesty of depositions which concealed the alleged fact that the Oxford mob had begun the disorder. No sufferings of individual Whigs were too trivial to adduce as evidence that Oxford was organizing a plot against 'the honest, victorious, and therefore never-to-be-forgiven soldiery from Dublin South to the Northern Orcades'.[9]

The most sinister feature of the press reports of the autumn of 1716 was their steadily increasing clamour for a royal visitation of the universities, inspired doubtless by the knowledge that the ministers' thoughts were already moving in this direction. Pamphlets in 1717 devoted themselves to the same subject at great length. Serjeant Miller, who, in Bentley, had encountered the astutest opponent of all, urged a radical upheaval. Miller began from the assumption that the universities were too disaffected for favours either individual or corporate to be of any avail. Even the advancement of the government's friends would accomplish little as they were in such a tiny minority, though with an eye to his own prospects Miller conceded that 'a steady perseverance in that, may do some good'. Even a visitation would accomplish little if confined to academic personnel; there must be a remodelling of the statutes on lines 'more suitable to the present times and government'. His two chief proposals bore directly upon the controversies of the last decade. Firstly, fellows should not be compelled to enter holy orders and should be encouraged to pursue secular studies, for (he declared in emphatic capitals) 'A LAYMAN ENDOW'D WITH GOOD SENSE OR LEARNING, IS TEN TIMES MORE UNLIKELY TO BE A HIGH-CHURCHMAN, THAN A CLERGYMAN IS WITH THE SAME SHARE'. Then, as a further safeguard against the academic church Tory interest, there should be an appeal from the university courts, which might no longer defy the friends of the government with impunity.[10]

Others took up the same cause. One writer declared that the

[9] e.g. St. James's Evening Post, 22–24 Nov., 24–27 Nov. 1716; The Flying Post, 24–27 Nov., 29 Nov.–1 Dec., 13–15 Dec., 29 Dec. 1716–1 Jan. 1717; St. James's Post, 7–10 Dec. 1716.

[10] E. Miller, An Account of the University of Cambridge, pp. 141–5, 148 seq., 170, 176 seq.

nation (and especially the clergy) was suffering from moral in-discipline, and 'that the great original ... cause of the immorality, and scandalous lives of those [clerical] wretches, [was] the present degenerate state of the Universities'. Again the remedy lay in a wholesale revision of the statutes, which he declared, against strongly held convictions to the contrary, to be within the com-petence of Parliament. He wished not merely to expel the political opponents of the government but also Socinians, Arians, Armi-nians, and deists; but the most famous champion of a visitation was a deist, John Toland. When urging the government to inter-vene in the universities, Toland paradoxically ascribed to educa-tion a providential power to settle the destinies of state, yet he scoffed at any confidence Oxonians might derive from the notion 'that they can at any time turn the nation as they please, and that therefore no King dares disoblige 'em'. He also made short work of the idea that the ministers had no authority to bring about such an upheaval. 'Why may not Oxford ... be reform'd or purg'd by a Royal Visitation tomorrow, as Aberdeen was the other day, or as Oxford itself was at the Reformation?' He recommended that the Statute of Mortmain be put into full force, a proposal of which much more was to be heard, and while despairing of abol-ishing pedantry from academic life, looked forward to the time

when Barbarism and Ignorance, Turbulency and Sedition, are banish'd out of that delicious spot, when public lectures in all faculties are frequented (as elsewhere) under pain of expulsion, when the fruits of private lectures are seen in publick exercises, and that instead of the bare Editors of old books, they become the authors of new ones.[11]

Ignorance, immorality, and treason did not exhaust the charges made against the University in 1717. The old accusation was revived that the high-church party were concealed Papists, and when Townshend, Walpole, and their connexion broke with the government, they were accused of coming every day nearer to Popery and to the universities which taught it. *The Flying Post* wished 'some clear pen would furnish out an epistle of thanks as from the Pope to his reverend friends here [in Oxford], for stick-ing so hard for him', while elsewhere the 'Hieroglyphical Figures' in the Oxford Almanack which gave trouble at intervals down the century, were interpreted to mean that since the University

[11] *Reasons for Visiting the Universities*; Toland, *State Anatomy*, pp. 69–76.

could not have the Church of England 'protected by *papists* & *Turkish Tories* (for they care not who had the governing of it so that a Protestant did not) they have put the Christian church under the protection of *Infidels*'. No university men should be admitted to Parnassus, wrote another correspondent, till they 'publickly renounce[d] all principles of Tyranny, Slavery and Bigottry' which were then considered to be of the essence of Popery.[12]

Towards the end of 1717 the Whig papers found new charges by ascribing to an Oxford origin a short-lived and extremely scurrilous high-church paper, *The Scourge*. No precise evidence for this charge was ever produced, but the paper was boldly described as 'usher'd into the world as if it were approv'd by the better part of the University of Oxon'. The *St. James's Weekly Journal* published a letter reported to have been written to *The Scourge* from an Oxford college, declaring it 'full of that true spirit of religion, which is for our purpose, and cannot fail of making people mad. *Church* is the Word and . . . if well follow'd, it will do our business', that is, to rouse public opinion in press and pulpit to give a fresh chance to the Jacobites. Within a few weeks *The Scourge* was presented by the Grand Jury of Middlesex, and the year 1717 ebbed to the hackneyed refrains of press attacks upon the hieroglyphics in the Oxford Almanack, which seemed always patient of a treasonable interpretation.[13]

The next year witnessed the familiar mixture of highly coloured allegations from the ministerial press and provocative letters from the university Whigs. There were a fresh cry for a visitation; an attack from St. John's on Nathaniel Mist as 'a well-meaning man to the faction', i.e. the majority of the University; and crude verses from Wadham satirizing 'the Perils of *False-Brethren*'. The latter writer's address to Bishop Hoadly began

> Hail! Sacred Prelate! thro whose righteous lines
> Truth's glorious light in bright description shines;

but his brethren of Christ Church and Magdalen were

---

[12] *The Defection consider'd*, summarized in Boyer, *Political State*, xiv. 546 553; *The Flying Post*, 17–19 Jan., 26–29 Jan. 1717; *The Weekly Journal*, 12 Jan. 1717.

[13] *St. James's Weekly Journal*, 28 Sept., 9 Nov. 1717; *The Flying Post*, 1–3 Oct. 12–14 Dec. 1717; *The Weekly Packet*, 30 Nov.–7 Dec. 1717; *The Weekly Journal* 4 Jan. 1718.

> Ye spawn of Jesuits, that profanely teach
> Treason in Schools, and from the pulpit preach.

So the charges continued with little fresh invention for the first
half of the year, while the friends of the universities rehearsed
trite references to the fact that in the previous century attacks on
the University were the prelude to the downfall of Crown and
Constitution in a light-weight sheet called *Heraclitus Ridens*.[14]
By the middle of 1718, however, the public must have tired of
such a repetitive debate, and apart from continued reporting of
political manœuvres in fellowship elections, Oxford affairs disappeared from the press.

By 1719 a visitation of the University was again a political issue
and produced a fresh crop of pamphlets though few new arguments. It was doubtless Warton's notorious sermon which provoked verses like the following:

> Faction at Oxford is the Test,
>   To which each author must submit,
> Ev'n Dulness, in Treason drest,
>   Clears up and brightens into Wit.
>
>   .   .   .   .   .
>
> The Bard reigns darling of the Crowd
>   Who dares the government abuse;
> But Quarter never is allow'd,
>   To a vile, flattering, Whiggish Muse.

A more serious campaign against the universities was begun by
Gordon and Trenchard, in the name of the current anti-clericalism
and an extreme liberal-rationalist version of the faith. To them
Oxford was guilty not merely of 'a popish, impious and rebellious
spirit', but of sins rivalling those of Anti-Christ. They declared
that William III had intended 'a regulation' of the universities,
but had been deterred by the dishonest advice of the Duke of
Shrewsbury, and that

the same spirit which leads us to lessen our taxes and clear the publick,
and enlarge the bottom of liberty and the Protestant Faith by un-
yoking of Dissenters, will carry us also to remove the corruption from
our Seminaries, and their disaffected spawn in too many parishes.

---

[14] *The Weekly Journal*, 11 Jan., 25 Jan., 19 April, 10 May 1718; *The Flying
Post*, 11–13 Feb., 27 Feb.–1 March, 3–5 April, 8–10 May, 7–10 June, 12–14 June
1718; *Heraclitus Ridens*, 27 March 1718.

Already, however, Trenchard and Gordon foreshadowed the long Radical tradition of the eighteenth century in their disillusionment with the official Whigs, admitting that they had been 'deluded with many prophecies and promises' of a visitation which had remained unfulfilled. Against such opponents Oxford might be assisted even by Abel Boyer, who scoffed at the 'Independent Whigs' for wanting to demolish 'the Bishops, the Clergy, the Ministers of State, the Universities, and the soldiers, and when they have set us together by the ears on these points, they very seasonably propose, that a general peace be made throughout Europe'.[15]

When in 1720 Trenchard and Gordon resumed their attack upon clergy and universities in a periodical called *The Independent Whig*, their campaign was based less on the exigencies of party interest which earlier preoccupied the scribblers of the ministry than on an extreme modernist simplicity in theology very inconvenient to the government. It was at the universities that recruits to the clergy were 'hamstringed and manacled with early oaths and subscriptions, and obliged to swear to notions before they know what they are'. Thereafter

not only their present revenues and subsistence but all their expectations are annexed to certain opinions, established for the most part by popes and synods, in corrupt and ignorant ages, and even then often carried by faction and bribery, in concert with the designs and intrigues of statesmen.

The essence of the Reformation was that 'the laity were resolved to be no longer hoodwink'd', and the great error of the Reformers had been not 'to retrieve the education of youth out of the hands of the Priesthood, and to reform the Universities'. In another periodical, *Cato's Letters*, Trenchard and Gordon continued their hearty iconoclasm in a more political vein, asserting that 'the fate of millions, and the being of states must not stand and fall by the distinctions of monks, coined in Colleges', and challenged the universities to deny the title of a dynasty towards which they had begun by being almost offensively complacent.

The brash rationalism of *The Independent Whig* was paradoxically a hopeful sign for Oxford, for it showed that her opponents

<hr />

[15] *The Oxford Criticks* (London, 1719), pp. 11, 13; Trenchard and Gordon *The Character of an Independent Whig*, pp. 11-13; Boyer, *Political State*, xix. 9

were becoming divided, and revealed, as Charlett assured Wake, 'how much the enemys of the Universities are not lesse [hostile] to your Grace's order and person and the Christian Religion'. Propaganda of the old sort still appeared, however, and 'a very scurrilous, heavy scandalously abusive pamphlet [was] shewed about and sold publickly in the Court of Request[s] agst. Dr. Delaun[e]'. Neither the private nor public morality of the President of St. John's was spared, and he was said to have become a flaming Jacobite since the disappointment of his hopes of a bishopric in the previous reign. Within the college 'he always keeps the majority of his senior fellows in his interest, by disposing of all the places of profit in the college among them only, so that they are as sure votes to him, upon any emergence, as the most servile Court pensioners of 'em all'—an interesting comment on political management by Oxford heads.[16]

This pamphlet was probably written by Delaune's great enemy Nicholas Amhurst who had lately been expelled from St. John's, and who in 1721 launched the last and most famous of the press attacks upon the University in his periodical *Terrae Filius*. So far as Oxford was concerned, this was almost pamphleteering to end pamphlets. It was unlikely that a periodical could sustain itself for long on so narrow a basis as attacks upon Oxford alone, at a time when Parliament and government were preoccupied by the aftermath of the South Sea crisis; but in the few months of its existence *Terrae Filius* rehearsed all the old arguments against the University in sparkling style and with an abundance of circumstantial detail well calculated to disguise innuendoes and liberties with the truth.

Amhurst claimed that he need 'not use any arguments or produce any vouchers to prove' the existence of treason in Oxford, attacked the programme of studies followed in the University, though admitting 'that Locke, Clarke and Sir Isaac Newton begin to find countenance in the schools, and that Aristotle seems to totter on his antient throne', adduced the usual charges of perjury, and compared the Oxford heads with the directors of the South Sea Company, whose fundamental crime had been to betray the

[16] *The Independent Whig* (reprinted London, 1721), pp. 29–30, 219–20; *Cato's Letters* (3rd edn., London, 1733), i. 75, 95; Bodl. MS. Ballard 32, fo. 114; *Letter from a Student in Grub Street to a Head of a College in Oxford* (London, 1720), pp. 16, 19.

trust reposed in them by the government and nation. Amhurst published letters probably written by John Russell, fellow of Merton, attacking the subscription required at matriculation to the XXXIX Articles, which related 'to subtil and abstruse points, in which it is not easy for the clergy themselves to form a judgement'. The panacea lay of course in a visitation, and Amhurst found himself hard pressed to explain why the government he championed had delayed the visitation so long.

Dr. Shippen of Brasenose regarded the whole publication as very idle and scandalous and hoped it would die soon, and, indeed, Amhurst now found the government as ungrateful as he later found the opposition. The government now contemplated drastic action against neither University and the press campaign naturally ceased. Trenchard and Gordon, however, delivered themselves of another onslaught on the occasion of Atterbury's conspiracy in 1723, Boyer attacked the Oxford heads who had subscribed to a new edition of Prior's works which he described as 'one of the lewdest books, that ever was openly published in any Christian country', and before making his terms with the political friends of Oxford, Amhurst wrote *Oculus Britanniae; an Heroi-Panegyrical Poem on the University of Oxford* in 1724, containing some well-calculated thrusts at the leading heads.[17]

A decade of bitter press attacks together with loss of preferment provoked much petulance amongst those influential at Oxford, and in the constitutional circumstances of the period the University could not readily attack the ministers it loathed without disloyalty to the king who appointed them. Fair commentators like Rapin could point out the 'rancourous party spirit' which underlay many of the ecclesiastical scruples of the high-church party, while denying the Whig fantasies that they 'desire to live under a Popish King', but the University had to look to its defence. Its cause was stated in three pamphlets. For popular consumption there was John Allibond's *Seasonable Sketch of an Oxford Reformation*

written originally in Latin . . . (on the occasion of the Oxford visitation of 1648) and now reprinted, with an English Version, that the world

---

[17] N. Amhurst, *Terrae Filius* (reprinted London, 1726), pp. iv, xvii, vol. i. 31, 67–68, 94–97, vol. ii. 8–9; Bodl. MS. Ballard 21: Robert Shippen to A. Charlett, 3 Feb. 1720/1; *Cato's Letters*, iv. 184; Boyer, *Political State*, xxviii. 204; *Oculus Britanniae* (London, 1724).

may see what a hopeful regulation of the two Universities, the republican author of *The Anatomy of the State* and his atheistical abettors are driving at.

Thus the Whig fiction that Oxonians were indistinguishable from Papists was countered by a Tory fiction that the Whigs were indistinguishable from the men of 1648.

Another writer attempted a candid and reasoned defence of the University. Oxford was bound to support monarchy, for monarchy and episcopacy were inseparable; they approved the Revolution, for even Dr. Sacheverell had allowed that the doctrine of non-resistance was subject to some extraordinary exceptions among which had been the Revolution. The decrees of 1683 had never been repealed, but that they had in fact been abandoned was apparent from the University's whole conduct over a generation. The new régime in 1714 had been proclaimed with almost extravagant 'transports of joy', and 'those who are now call'd *Jacobite Heads*, appear'd with the foremost in their healths and good wishes'; that Oxford had been irritated by the subsequent turn of events and that treasonable cries were heard in the streets did not prove the existence of conspiracy. 'The loss of our old Chancellor (who was very well belov'd here) gave us a distaste to some in the government', but this did not extend to the king. Smalridge, who had suffered bitter attacks, had served the king well and charged the clergy of his diocese to 'be steadfast to . . . principles of loyalty'. The pamphlet ended with the frank confession that many in Oxford longed for nothing more than to reveal their aspirations as court politicians: 'And as for our divisions, murmuring, aversions, and political feuds, there is one infallible cure . . . viz. A convenient sphere in Church or State wherein we might gloriously display our most loyal and truly Protestant affections.'

At the same time Bernard Gardiner published a justification of his conduct in his last year as Vice-Chancellor, covering the disorders of the summer of 1715. Never averse to a contest, Gardiner placed the blame squarely upon the aggressiveness of the troops in Oxford and of the Constitutioners who fraternized with them. If this was too one-sided to be the whole truth, Gardiner scored a good point by publishing excerpts from the University's addresses to Anne professing zeal for the House of Hanover and letters from the Lords Justices acknowledging Oxford's 'zeal and affection' at the beginning of the present reign. For the rest, the University had to rely on occasional favourable press reports of their transactions, such as when the scholars of Corpus contributed for 'a curious picture' of the Prince of Wales to be painted and erected in a gold frame in their hall.[18] In the end Oxford men might reflect that hard words from the ministerial press could break no bones, but it was impossible to be so philosophical before another threat, that of a visitation.

[18] P. de Rapin, *An Historical Dissertation upon Whig and Tory* (London, 1717), pp. 72–73, 81; J. Allibond, *A Seasonable Sketch of an Oxford Reformation* (London, 1717); *The Muses' Fountain Clear, or the Dutiful Oxonian's Defence of his Mother's Loyalty to His Present Majesty King George* (London, 1717); [B. Gardiner] *A Plain Relation of Some Late Passages at Oxford* (Oxford, 1717); *The Original Weekly Journal*, 15–22 June 1717.

CHAPTER VI

Oxford under Visitation?

To reply to taunts of disaffection was difficult without aggravating
the offence, and hence the Oxford pamphlets appeared only in
1717 when the government seemed likely to take decisive action.
The leading Whigs had been genuinely convinced that on the
eve of Anne's death their opponents had made serious arrangements to bring over the Pretender, and in any case would not now
surrender the party advantage of branding them and their friends
in Oxford as Jacobites. How quickly real danger to the universities materialized was revealed in July 1715 when, as we have
seen, *The Evening Post* paid the penalty for publishing an alleged
letter from Walpole to Sunderland threatening dire measures to
suppress disorder and disaffection in Oxford. The academic
friends of the ministry quickly sensed the direction of the prevailing breeze, and in October Edmund Miller and his friends at
Trinity College, Cambridge, petitioned for a royal visitation to
restrain Dr. Bentley, while John Russell, one of the Constitutioners, wrote hysterically to Wake from Oxford that 'the King
must lose his Crown, or this university must be reform'd'. Russell's
immediate object was to bring about an intervention in the forthcoming fellowship elections at Merton, for though he did not
scruple to affirm that he had 'not the least relation to Merton
College, & . . . [his] circumstances [were] much above one of their
Fellowships', he was in fact one of the successful candidates at the
next election. Wake was already urging upon Smalridge that the
public reputation of the University must be salvaged somehow, to
which the latter replied in terms reminiscent of those of that
excellent Whig, Gibson, at the time of his breach with Walpole
twenty years later, that certain policies of the lay Whigs could
hardly fail to distress the clergy.[1]

Lord Townshend, the Secretary of State, was seriously afraid of

[1] Boyer, *Political State*, x. 55–58; P.R.O. SP 35/4, fo. 133; Christ Church MS.
Arch. W. Epist. xv: J. R. to ?, 27 Nov. 1715 (partly printed in B. Williams, *Stan-
hope* (Oxford, 1930), pp. 399–400): Abp. Wake to Bp. of Bristol, 31 Dec. 1715:
Bp. of Bristol to Abp. Wake, 9 Jan. 1715/16.

the universities' politics, and had been persuaded by Humphrey
Prideaux, dean of Norwich, to accept a plan of university reform
which, with new regulations for ordination, was essential in
Prideaux's view for a reform of the Church. Action was postponed
by the changes in the government, but in November 1715 Townshend took up the matter in earnest. Prideaux wanted a complete
reformation of university studies and discipline and the establishment of a visitatorial authority sufficient to deal with any trouble
that arose. His recommendations were nothing if not far-reaching.
Improvident marriages among upper-class undergraduates were
to be made felonious, servant maids were to be licensed, fellows
who failed to pass a merit bar twenty years after matriculation
were to be pensioned off in an institution called Drone Hall.
Prideaux insisted that for a reformation to be pushed through
unchallenged special legislation was essential, but the core of his
recommendations was to advance the growth of oligarchy in the
University by increasing the power, patronage, and emoluments
of the heads, and to provide for a political visitation at the beginning of every parliament by a commission composed of members
of both Houses, archbishops, the Lord Chancellor, and other
officials. Prideaux was also convinced that it would be impossible
to raise the standards of the parish clergy without a similar exercise of dictatorial authority by the bishops, and for the next four
months he pressed his plans on a somewhat reluctant Wake.[2]

The archbishop feared what might be in store for Oxford and
told Prideaux that there was to be no visitation. The lay Whigs
had nevertheless got the bit between their teeth, and the private
discussions among those in authority were the signal for the first
campaign for a visitation in the press. Many of the clergy were
frankly alarmed at the situation, and at an archidiaconal visitation at Derby

it was told among them that there was a design on foot to have all the
revenues of the clergy brought into the Exchequer, and payments
made to them from thence of 100 lib. per ann, and no more to any of
them in order to keep them under the . . . direction of the Court.

Wake, however, was working for peace and besought Oxford men

    [2] W. Coxe, *Memoirs of Sir Robert Walpole* (London, 1798), ii. 52; *The Life of
Rev. Humphrey Prideaux, D.D.* (London, 1748), pp. 188–276; Christ Church MS.
Arch. W. Epist. 20: H. Prideaux to Abp. Wake, 10 Feb., 23 Feb., 8 March
1715/16.

to 'put an end to the unhappy heats abt. politicall matters ... wch are not yr. concern'.

He also commended the University for mollifying the government by putting 'some stop to Mr. Hearn's treasonable zeale'. Hearne, the celebrated chronicler of Oxford affairs, had imbibed non-juring principles from his earliest patron, Francis Cherry of Shottesbrook, at whose expense he had been educated. Through the influence of Hudson, Bodley's librarian, he had gained a place on the library staff, which enabled him to acquire immense antiquarian erudition. In 1715 he was elected architypographus and esquire bedel in civil law, two offices which had long been combined, but which the Vice-Chancellor and others now sought to separate. Hudson tried to get him out of the library, and persuaded the Visitor to declare that the offices of under-librarian and bedel were inconsistent. Hearne at once resigned the bedelship, and on 23 January 1716, the last day fixed by the new act for taking the oaths to the new dynasty, he was excluded from the library and later formally deprived of his place for neglect of duty. Later, innumerable obstacles were placed in the way of the publication of his work.

Hearne, completely preoccupied with personalities, did not realize that his martyrdom was a public pledge of Oxford loyalty to the dynasty, but Smalridge made no bones in asserting that his prosecution would 'be for the honour and interest of the University'. In the summer of 1716 there seemed a prospect of academic peace, for not only did Wake urge Oxford to acts of peace and duty, but in Cambridge Edmund Miller, whose motives, like those of so many of the Oxford Whigs, were largely political, assured Townshend that 'if I did but know yt this prosecution was disagreeable to yr Lordship, or any considerable friends of [the government] ..., I would immediately let it drop'.[3]

At that moment, however, the ministry was not to be deterred, for it appointed commissioners to visit the University of Aberdeen, who were soon reported in the press to be exposing numerous non-juring episcopalians. By the next session of Parliament the riot on the Prince of Wales's birthday had taken place, the

---

[3] Bodl. MS. Ballard 3, fos. 110, 118, 122: 6, fo. 66; Christ Church. MS. Arch. W. Epist. 20: John Tatam to Abp. Wake, 12 May 1716; *Hearne's Collections*, v. *passim*; *Letters of Wm. Nicolson, D.D.*, ed. J. Nichols, ii. 438; P.R.O. SP 35/5, fo. 270.

inquiries into which, as Wake remarked, must 'be either very much to [Oxford's] advantage, or to [her] prejudice'. The university Whigs strained every nerve to discredit the University and advance themselves. In December David Wilkins, Wake's Prussian-born protégé, was urging a royal visitation as the sole means to 'bring 'em to obedience', the Whig press thundered more ferociously than ever for the government to take action, and in January 1717 Abel Boyer disclosed that the ministers proposed to repeal the Occasional Conformity Act and 'to bring the Universities, particularly Oxford, to a more decent behaviour towards the present Government', and barely concealed his disappointment that neither had been mentioned in the king's speech.

In fact Walpole had presented the government in November with a scheme for gagging the universities. Parker, himself an Oxfordshire magnate, was preparing a Bill in consultation with the Lord Chancellor and Archbishop Wake, and the rumour having spread at Court 'that 15 Bps. had thought it reasonable that the King should have disposall of all offices, Headships & Scholarships within the 2 Universities, for seven years', the Bishop of Ely pressed Wake to prevent any mention of the scheme in the king's speech, 'since whatever odium may (as indeed much may) arise on this occasion, it must all be laid upon us, if we are represented as the movers and advisers to this proceeding, originally'.[4]

Parker and someone unknown had indeed drawn up large memoranda stating the extreme Whig case against the universities. The majority of dons they claimed were irreconcilable, and while any device to encourage the University to be 'more diligent . . . in their studies, in the pursuit of usefull knowledge' would make them 'more sensible . . . of the great happiness they enjoy under the present government', some quicker and more drastic methods were needed. Like Prideaux he considered that the autonomy of the University was the great asset which enabled the dominant connexions to keep together and triumph over the Whigs. There must be some appeal from university jurisdiction. Ecclesiastical patronage should be used ruthlessly for the encouragement of government supporters. Heads of houses should be

    [4] *Original Weekly Journal*, 21–26 July 1716; *The Weekly General Post*, 15–22 Sept. 1716; Christ Church MS. Arch. W. Epist. 20: D. Wilkins to Abp. Wake, 20 Dec. 1716; *The Flying Post*, 17–19 Jan. 1717; Boyer, *Political State*, xiii. 233; Coxe, *Walpole*, ii. 122; Christ Church MS. Arch. W. Epist. 15: Bp. of Ely to Abp. Wake, n.d.: Parker to Wake, 21 March [1717].

chosen by a commission of officers of state, archbishops, bishops, and the Visitor; fellowships should be limited to twenty years, with two tutors in each college elected for life after fifteen years' service. The right of election to scholarships, exhibitions, and fellowships should also be vested in a commission, and modern studies should be encouraged. These proposals, which clearly bore the stamp of Prideaux's influence, were embodied in a simple and ruthless Bill which vested the nomination to every university and college place in the king, and empowered him to exercise his authority through a nominated commission.[5]

The crisis came to a head in March 1717. The intentions of the government were now common knowledge, and the Oxford heads not only appealed to public opinion in pamphlets but sent a joint letter to Wake to exert his interest against the storm threatened by Serjeant Miller and others, and affirming that they were all strictly bound by their oaths not only to the dynasty but to their statutes. Gardiner put in a personal plea against Miller's hostility to the fellows' obligation to enter holy orders, and Charlett besought the university Chancellor as chief Visitor of his house to protect them against any alteration in their statutes, and assuring him 'of the steady and most sincere loyalty to King George' of every member of the society. The University faced powerful foes, however, for Sunderland, Stanhope, and Bernstorff, and most of all the king, were hot for the Bill, and David Wilkins was trying to bring Oxford's old opponent Bishop Nicolson into the fray again.

Finally, the University was fortuitously saved by the split in the Whig party. Cowper advised the ministry that they would never carry the repeal of the Occasional Conformity Act and the University Bill at the same time; indeed, Sunderland and Stanhope proved unable to carry even the former. Devonshire (who was promptly deprived of office), Newcastle (doubtless swayed by Bishop Trelawney who was celebrating his marriage at this time), and Wake (who nevertheless insisted that Oxford must mend her ways), also worked to prevent the introduction of the University Bill. Not till May 1717 was the danger past and even then it was

[5] B.M. Stowe MS. 799, fos. 2–12; J. Gutch, *Collectanea Curiosa* (Oxford, 1781), ii. 53–73 (summarized in C. Wordsworth, *Social Life at the English Universities in the 18th Century* (Cambridge, 1874), p. 568); Christ Church MS. Arch. W. Epist. 15: Parker to Abp. Wake, Monday, n.d. (printed in B. Williams, *Stanhope*, 456–8).

known that the University had only a temporary reprieve.[6] For the moment the ministry must rest content with the victory in the House of Lords in the debate on the Oxford riots.

The factor which alarmed the Oxford heads, and accounts for much of their intolerance towards the university Whigs, was that they were confronted not merely by enemies within the ministry and press but by an organized minority of 'loyal collegians' bent on exploiting their distress. The Constitution Club, which throughout its history was a storm-centre in Oxford, was formed early in the reign by a New College connexion led by Captain Thomas and George Lavington, whose services were rewarded by rapid ecclesiastical preferment, and who in the next reign became a chaplain to the king and Bishop of Exeter.[7] The determination of the Constitutioners to mark themselves out from the rest of the University as the sole friends of the Constitution inevitably aroused the hostility of the university governors. Members of the club were summoned before the Vice-Chancellor's Court on charges arising from their celebrations on 28 May 1715, the burden of which was that though warned that their display of loyalty would cause disorder, they would not be deterred. The only charge on which there was a conviction was that of their 'voluntary presence in a Tavern', so nominal an infraction of the statutes as to call for no penalty.

Meanwhile the grand jury of Oxfordshire presented 'the Constitutioners, as a set of factious men, who, shrouding themselves under the specious name of the constitution club, were enemies to monarchy, and all good government' and were responsible for all the disorder. Defending themselves by a pamphlet, and relying on the protection of the garrison, the club were again provocative on the next Restoration day, 29 May 1716, by which time their methods of denouncing the University in the press and in private letters to those in authority were well known. On this occasion their proceedings were interrupted first by squibs from

[6] *Hearne's Collections*, vi. 30; Christ Church MS. Arch. W. Epist. 15: B. Gardiner to Abp. Wake, 17, 27 March 1717: Abp. Wake to B. Gardiner, 21 March, n.d. [1717]: J. Baron to Abp. Wake, 18 March 1716/17; Bodl. MS. Top. Oxon. B 48, fo. 53. Cf. *Hearne's Collections*, vi. 75–76; Christ Church MS. Arch. W. Epist. 20: Lord Cowper to Abp. Wake, 14 March 1716/17: D. Wilkins to Abp. Wake, 30 March 1717; *Nicolson Letters*, ii. 457; Bodl. MS. Ballard 32, fos. 22–24.

[7] Lavington was supported by Hoadly and pushed on by Harley's inveterate enemy Lord Coningsby to whom he was chaplain, and whose daughter's maid he married. *Hist. MSS. Comm. Portland MSS.* vii. 367.

the crowd, and then by the junior proctor, Holt of Magdalen. Meadowcourt of Merton, the club steward, though not quite sober, forestalled any proctorial rebuke by requiring Holt to join them in drinking the king's health; but he had still to deal with the senior proctor, a vindictive lawyer of Christ Church, John White. By him Meadowcourt was fined 40s. and put in the Black Book, a stigma by which he was prevented from proceeding to his Master's degree until he had given the proctor satisfaction. It took Meadowcourt two years to discover the charges made against him, although he brought pressure to bear from two peers. Finally, he found that he and Carty of University College had been charged with various offences from defying proctorial authority to causing disorder. Carty went down without his M.A. and Meadowcourt refused to read a paper before Convocation, denying the current story that he was punished for his loyalty to King George, and graduated only in 1718 when he was included in a royal act of grace.

Amongst the others on whom White inflicted similar penalties were Costard, fellow of Wadham, Scurlock, fellow of Jesus, and Russell, Cowper, and Bearcroft, fellows of Merton. It was perhaps poetic justice that in 1720, despite the Christ Church poll, White fared miserably as a candidate for the Camden chair.[8] The Constitutioners were now thoroughly unpopular; David Wilkins helped to destroy his chances of obtaining an Oxford degree by associating with them; and in the winter of 1716–17 they completed their isolation by trying to discredit the affidavits collected by the Vice-Chancellor relating to the riots on the Prince of Wales's birthday, by their continued fraternization with the garrison, and by their open campaigns in the press.[9]

The affairs of the club came to a crisis over two controversial sermons. In 1717 and 1718 the controversy aroused by Bishop Hoadly's extreme glorification of private judgement and extreme depreciation of catholic church order was at its height, and on 30 November 1718 Peter Maurice preached at St. Mary's 'in commendation of the Bangorian doctrine, and it was brought very oddly from his text, which was "Let no man despise thee". But he

---

[8] University Archives: MS. Conv. Reg. Bd 31, fo. 163.
[9] *Speech of a Member of the Constitution Club*; Amhurst, *Terrae Filius*, i. 123–41, ii. 118–26; Christ Church MS. Arch. W. Epist. 16, no. 51: 20, D. Wilkins to Abp. Wake, 4 July 1716.

said the exorbitant claims of the clergy were the only reasons of the contempt they met with.' Maurice, a young Whig fellow of Jesus, was believed by his enemies to be of immoral character, 'and yet amongst other things he said no ministration from an ill clergyman could be of any validity'. This sermon had already given offence when preached at a visitation held by the Bishop of Gloucester, and now the Vice-Chancellor demanded his sermon notes, which he produced with no fear of being unable to justify himself. Nevertheless, he was censured before the heads by the two divinity professors, the Whig Potter and the Tory Delaune, and convicted of preaching against the XXVIth Article which affirms that 'the unworthiness of the ministers . . . hinders not the effect of the Sacrament'.

Maurice read a grovelling recantation before Convocation, but neither University nor press failed to note that he published his sermon with a vindication in the next year, was rapidly advanced in the diocese of Bangor, and became finally a chaplain to the king. Maurice's condemnation coincided unhappily with a triumphant peal of Merton bells in honour of Meadowcourt's ultimate graduation, and the Constitutioners could hardly but feel themselves implicated in the censure of Maurice, who was more than a political sympathizer—for Meadowcourt himself was suspect of theological unorthodoxy.[10]

With Meadowcourt and the others held back from their degrees, the flow of new B.A.s into the club dried up; the royal visitation for which the Whigs hoped still tarried, and it became apparent that the club's survival depended on forcing the ministers' hand. Their opportunity seemed to have arrived when the sermon on Restoration day, 29 May 1719, was preached by Thomas Warton, the poetry professor. Warton had succeeded Joseph Trapp, formerly chaplain to Sir Constantine Phipps, in the chair of poetry, and was also a violent Tory. In the circumstances of 1717–18 he did not scruple to curry favour among the junior electors by circulating a ballad called *The Turnip Hoer*, satirizing the king who 'when he first came into England talk'd of turning St. James's Park into Turnip Ground, & to employ

<hr/>

[10] *Hearne's Collections*, vi. 255, 261, 262–3; *Hist. MSS. Comm. Portland MSS.* vii. 246–7; Bodl. MS. Ballard 20, fo. 117; University Archives: Conv. Reg. Bd 31, fo. viii; Boyer, *Political State*, xix. 245; Christ Church MS. Arch. W. Epist. 16, no. 156 [256]; P. Maurice, *The True Causes of the Contempt of Christian Ministers* (London, 1719).

Turnip Hoers', and also circulated verses on the Pretender's picture.[11] Warton, in short, like William King who thoroughly
approved of his equivocal conduct, belonged to the lunatic fringe
of younger men who were as dissatisfied as the Constitutioners
with the efforts of the reigning heads to keep the ministry out of
Oxford.

On Restoration day he preached on Hos. xiii. 39, 'Oh Israel,
thou hast destroyed thyself; but in me is thine help', and developing the theme of the nation's self destruction, he forced

all the events and circumstances of King George's reign . . . into a
description of the miserable state of the nation during the usurpation
of Cromwell. And the case of the Pretender was set forth and represented under partial and strained allusions to the sufferings of
King Charles the second. The most odious reflexions, and most
groundless calumnies were thrown upon the King and his administration.

The ministers' policy of extending toleration and suppressing
Convocation came in for especial attack. Charity, he thundered
in the apostle's words, hopeth all things, *restoreth* all things.
Meadowcourt, after a prudent interval, calculated that he might
secure satisfaction for the censure of Maurice, and perhaps bring
in the ministry. He complained to the Vice-Chancellor that the
sermon was seditious; the latter demanded particular charges in
writing, and Meadowcourt insisted that the sermon notes be sent
for: the Vice-Chancellor refused to proceed on charges which he
insisted were still too general, though the statute did not forbid
general charges, so Meadowcourt appealed to the Lords Justices.

They ordered the Vice-Chancellor to send for the sermon notes,
and proceed at once, but Warton professed to have lost his sermon.
The remainder of the episode did little credit to any of the parties.
Meadowcourt and his Whig friends (including two who soon
became well known, John Conybeare of Exeter and Nicholas Amhurst of St. John's) bombarded the Lords Justices with memorials
of circumstances, including the dinner-table conversation of
bishops, prejudicial to Warton. The Lords Justices chastised the
Vice-Chancellor mercilessly, but he put up so successful a passive

[11] No copy of *The Turnip Hoer* is known to be extant, but the verses by
Warton on James's picture dedicated to William Cleland are to be found in
P.R.O. SP 35/68, fo. 1. A paean to the Pretender's virtues concludes:
> How would great James increase each muse's fire,
> When even the royal image can inspire.

resistance that in the end nothing was done. There were interesting reactions from moderate academic opinion, Charlett blandly denying that the sermon contained any *double-entendre*, while Edward Harley feared the consequences to the University and called Warton 'as great a coxcomb as ever Magdalen College bred though Sacheverell himself was one of her Fellows'. The Whigs did not forgive Warton and waged a great campaign against him when he stood for re-election to his chair in 1723.

Meanwhile Meadowcourt, who had begun with the purest professions of patriotism and had been summoned to London to prosecute the case, informed the ministry that after all the injuries he had received, he could not 'return to Oxford without some mark of approbation from the government' (such as a prebend of Canterbury), and began a wearisome series of begging letters. At the beginning of the next academic year the Vice-Chancellor spoke proudly of his handling of the Maurice and Warton cases, and denounced Meadowcourt as an informer who had taken a case out of the University contrary to his oath. Even during the case, Pearse, the Whig Vice-Principal of St. Edmund Hall, had excoriated the politics of many of the university Whigs: 'One's afraid of disobliging ye Head of his House; another of losing pupils; and a third that he shall not act like a cunning man, be *utrique paratus*, and pitch upon his leggs wch ever way he's thrown, & wtever comes of it.' And with no 'marks of approbation' for Meadowcourt forthcoming, the Constitution Club broke up in confusion.[12]

This was neither the first nor the last time that the lay Whigs abandoned their clerical allies, but they had their own motives for intervening in the universities, and they had kept the question of a visitation alive. In February 1718 it was learned that the Hanoverian connexion was still anxious for the project, and in May the Attorney General was at work upon it. The issue seemed to be coming to a head at the end of the year. In November Wake was collecting legal material bearing on a university visitation. By December Bentley's disputes had reached a crisis which everyone expected would involve both universities. It was rumoured

[12] *Hearne's Collections*, vi. 134–5, vii. 14, 24, 25, 32, viii. 96–97; Amhurst, *Terrae Filius*, i. 81–92, ii. 47; P.R.O. SP 35/16, fos. 170, 322–32, 356: /17, fos. 102, 103, 108–14, 139, 143–60, 196–7, 219–21: /18, fos. 14, 90–91, 254: /19, fos. 346–7: /21, fo. 342; *Hist. MSS. Comm. Portland MSS.* v. 587; Christ Church MS. Arch. W. Epist. 16, no. 60.

that 'a certain great d[u]ke, captain of the m[o]b [said] ... yt tho'
Bentley was not to be valued of sixpence, yet haveing given them
an handle to humble the universities, it must not be delayed'.
The Attorney General was consulted by the Cabinet how far the
king's powers extended in this matter, and George Clarke, now
M.P. for Oxford University, urged on Charlett that the University as a lay corporation was not subject to ecclesiastical jurisdiction, and that the colleges, having local visitors, were subject to
no outside jurisdiction whatever. The government itself concluded that no more was possible without a special Act, and once
again the universities were saved by Walpole who would exploit
any issue to assail his former colleagues.[13]

Before the king went abroad in May 1719 there was a Privy
Council meeting in which a commission was appointed to prepare
for a visitation of Cambridge, and, it was feared, measures against
Oxford were discussed also. Not only was the king enthusiastic
for action against the universities, but Sunderland hoped to re-
unite the Whig factions on the basis of extreme partisan legislation. 'The King is more determin'd than ever', he wrote to
Newcastle in October 1719, 'to persist with vigour in the measures
you & yr. friends wish. He is resolv'd to push the Peerage Bill,
the University Bill, & the repeal of the Septennial Bill. If this
wont unite the W[h]igs nothing will.' Newcastle urged Stanhope
to introduce the Peerage Bill, and commended the University
Bill 'as being agreeable to ye party, & a solid advantage to ye publick'. In fact the obviously partisan character of the programme
merely strengthened Walpole's hand against the ministry, and
the defeat of the Peerage Bill killed the whole plan. There were
those in Oxford who put on a bold face throughout these proceedings and owned to no fears, but the memory of the threatened
special act was not soon erased, and in 1729 when Bishop Peploe,
who had caused trouble for Oxford ever since his connexion with
the collegiate church of Manchester, promoted a Bill against the
power of that body, Stratford concluded that it was a precedent
from which university foundations would suffer.[14]

Agitations in the press and reforming legislation were not the

[13] Bodl. MS. Ballard 32, fos. 50, 61, 71, 79: 20, fos. 114, 115; Christ Church
MS. Arch. W. Epist. 16, no. 3; B.M. Egerton MS. 2618, fo. 219; Hist. MSS. Comm.
Portland MSS. v. 574, 576.
[14] Bodl. MS. Ballard 32, fo. 190; Christ Church MS. Arch. W. Epist. 16, no. 26
et passim; Hist. MSS. Comm. Portland MSS. vii. 474-7.

only threats which hung over the University in these years. In February 1717 Sir Jonathan Trelawney, Bishop of Winchester, reacted strongly to Wake's request for his vote for the University Bill. His immediate stumbling-block was that he had a son standing for election to Christ Church, but as he professed the view that 'both universitys ought to be scourg'd into perfect duty, & better manners to ye King & His family', he had to produce an alternative policy; finally he remembered his expulsion of Rector Bury of Exeter a quarter of a century earlier. 'Ye heads of houses have trembled ever since', he declared, and asserted that a determined exercise of visitatorial power would silence the government's critics in Oxford and would permit all alumni of the University to honour their undertakings to maintain the statutes. Those who wished to promote a wholesale upheaval in the universities denied that the local Visitors could effect root-and-branch reformation, but Trelawney matched the action to the word in a very characteristic current case.

Dr. Lombard, fellow of St. John's, denounced Thomas Tooley, a brother fellow, for 'lewdness and disloyalty' and giving a 'villainous character' of the whole royal family. Trelawney thirsted to expel him as an example. He had now been convinced by Dr. Mather, President of Corpus, that members of the University were bound by oath to resist the University Bill. 'If a bill should pass requiring ym to go out of yr statu[t]able method of electing yr prest. fellows scholars & disposing of yir preferments, they will by yt bill no doubt be expell'd if they doe not, & if they doe, they are expell'd and perjur'd too.' Wake might become 'a greater founder yn Wickam or Chicheley by keeping ye colleges firm on ye foot they left 'em'. The St. John's case, however, illustrated the difficulty of methods which made any concessions to justice.

Lombard, the son of a Huguenot pastor, had been chaplain to the Princess Sophia and the embassy at Hanover since 1701, and in 1714 became chaplain to the Princess of Wales. He was therefore a long-standing adherent of the Hanoverian Court, and his denunciation of Tooley as a Jacobite is an interesting example of the aggressive methods of the university Whigs, for Trelawney found the whole charge to spring from 'ye rancour of a lying phanatig parson there, & ye belief of designing men yt they make yir court by 't'.[15] Trelawney considered the effect of the visitation

[15] See note D, p. 280.

to have been salutary, however, and made his intentions plain to the heads of New College and Magdalen. Things remained unquiet, even though Lombard accepted a Cornish living in 1718.

In 1719 Nicholas Amhurst, scholar, instead of proceeding to a fellowship, was expelled on charges of libertinism and misconduct. Amhurst gloried in suffering for his politics in Church and State, 'for believing that steeples and organs are not necessary to salvation . . . for preaching without orders and praying without a commission, for lampooning priest-craft and petticoat-craft', and so forth. Lampooning was probably his chief offence, for he had defended Hoadly, guyed university morality in *The Oxford Toasts*, and commended himself in print to both Addison and Stanhope. He had also assisted in Meadowcourt's agitation against Thomas Warton. Amhurst's press campaigns against the University were not the only consequences of his expulsion, for in December 1721 Tooley was at last expelled from the college on charges of abusing the President and fellows and assisting Amhurst in writing *Terrae Filius*. He was promised pardon if he would sign an acknowledgement of his offences, but refused and appealed to the Visitor, now the Whig Trimnell, who had succeeded Trelawney at Winchester. According to Hearne, 'the Statute being express against him, the Visitor . . . confirm'd the expulsion'.

Thus Tooley, who was in trouble as an alleged Jacobite in 1717, was finally expelled for Whig activities, the sentence being confirmed by a Whig bishop. The truth probably is that Tooley was in opposition to the court interest throughout, opposed to court Whigs like Lombard and Trimnell, and to an aspiring court Tory like the President Delaune as well.[16] By the time *Terrae Filius* was written the campaign against the universities had already been abandoned by the government, and the radicalism of pamphleteers like Amhurst, Trenchard, and Gordon was not welcome to the ministers' clerical advisers such as Gibson. Amhurst had taken the first steps on the road which was to lead to his emergence as a great Tory journalist, and in supporting him Tooley won no sympathy from court politicians.[17]

[16] It is possible also that Delaune was hoping to work his passage to the Court as successfully as did his patron at this moment.
[17] *Reasons for Visiting the Universities*, p. 51; Christ Church MS. Arch. W. Epist. 15: Bp. of Winchester to Abp. Wake, 17 Feb., 13 March, n.d. [1716/17], 29 March, 1 April, n.d. [1717]: 16, no. 176; *Hist. MSS. Comm. Portland MSS.* vii. 257; *Hearne's Collections*, vii. 307, 336; Bodl. MS. Top. Oxon. e 54.

The example of active visitatorial intervention set by Trelawney was not lost upon other Visitors, who at a time of great turbulence in the domestic affairs of the colleges had abundant opportunities. In 1720, for example, Gibson, Bishop of Lincoln, restored a Whig to Brasenose who had been expelled on a charge of heterodoxy. Shippen, the Principal, was then Vice-Chancellor also, and in that capacity considered expelling the offending exhibitioner from the University, but finally desisted from such a challenge to authority. Archbishop Wake also, in concluding his visitation of All Souls, sent down a set of injunctions in 1720 which were intended to be a model for the University, were disseminated amongst the heads, and won the approval not only of Whigs but of court politicians like Charlett and former Harleyites like the Canons of Christ Church. To insist upon the requirement to take holy orders, to put down faction, and to increase the power of the heads, seemed the way to peace, and the trimmer Clavering insisted that if all Visitors would follow Wake's example 'we should not then be afraid of any extraordinary visitations'. Even Clarke and Gardiner reluctantly approved Wake's settlement, but so deeply had the relations of many colleges with their visitors been vitiated by politics that the latter, with the support of Delaune and other heads, sought to limit visitatorial authority. In 1710-11 Bromley had deterred Gardiner from promoting a special Bill for this purpose, and now, a decade later, it became 'a fashionable doctrine among the Heads of Houses to deny a right of appealing to the Visitor' by an interpretation of a common clause in college statutes regarding 'amotion'. Delaune's attempt by this means to prevent Trimnell's hearing the appeal of Tooley against his expulsion failed, however, and the issue of the rights and powers of visitors continued to vex the University for another decade. For although the Whig threat to take the University by storm had proved hollow, their attempts to seize power in individual colleges continued, and provoked a Tory reaction.[18]

[18] *Hearne's Collections*, vii. 131; Christ Church MS. Arch. W. Epist. 16, nos 72, 73, 78, 154, 155, 157, 176, 177, 189; *All Souls Archives*, pp. 321, 350-1; Burrows *Worthies*, p. 379.

CHAPTER VII

The Battle in the Colleges

EVEN without a visitation, general or local, the supporters of the ministry could carry on the contest through the normal college machinery. There was no college in 1714 in which the Whigs reigned unchallenged, and even in Anne's time they were struggling hard in several societies. The death of Principal Jonathan Edwards of Jesus in 1712 robbed Harcourt and Atterbury of an ally in university affairs, a sufficient reason (even if there was no family tie between the Lord Keeper and James Harcourt of Breconshire, one of the candidates for the succession) for them to be concerned about the ensuing election. Dr. Wynne, the other candidate—Vice-Principal and Margaret professor, a disciple of Locke and a friend of the Harleyites—could raise exactly half the votes, but in the opposite party were the senior fellow, Tremallier, who had a casting vote, and another influential senior man, John Ellis. However, after the old Principal's death, Wynne began proceedings against Ellis for holding a living above the value permitted by the statutes, and on the day of the election deprived Tremallier of his fellowship for not proceeding to his doctor's degree and for marrying during his long absence from Oxford. Both appeared to vote, however, and each party polling six votes, Harcourt and his friends seized the Principal's lodgings while Wynne kept the Register and was declared Principal by his party.

The dispute now came before the Visitor, the Earl of Pembroke, who was subjected to much pressure by the Lord Keeper, by Wright, the Oxford Recorder, and by Dr. Bouchier, the regius professor of law. Pembroke nevertheless declared as expected for Wynne (whose patron he was), a decision which probably caused him to be nominated in the election for Chancellor in 1715, and which was loudly trumpeted by Whig journalists raking over the crimes of academic Tories in 1716. Wynne, as we have seen, made very successful terms with the new dynasty; his Whig fellows had no fear in expressing their views, and when he resigned on his marriage in 1720 there was no difficulty in the election of

William Jones, who, like Wynne, was acceptable to both Whigs and Harleyites.

The political balance in Jesus was still precarious, however, the more so as in 1725 the college petitioned to create two new scholarships and two new fellowships in law and medicine under the will of Sir Leoline Jenkins. The organizer of the court interest in Oxford was now Bradshaw, Dean of Christ Church and Bishop of Bristol. He was doubly concerned in Jesus College politics, as he wished to carry the election of another friend of the government when Principal Jones should die, and also to secure one of the new fellowships for his nephew William Bradshaw, who had failed to be elected fellow in the ordinary way. Moreover, Thomas Price, for whom the college had petitioned to fill one of the new fellowships, was a sure vote on the side of the Tories and an associate of 'Oldesworth, who wrote the Examiner in Qn. Anne's reign, & lives now at St. Mary Hall, a non-juror yt does a great deal of mischief by corrupting the principles of young gentlemen'. Price had moreover been expelled from his fellowship for refusing to enter holy orders, and the Bishop of Bristol claimed that the college was creating faculty fellowships contrary to Sir Leoline's will solely to reinstate him. If the government could get the licence of mortmain through before Principal Jones died, it could nominate the first fellows to the vacancies and so influence the next election of a Principal.

Archbishop Wake held up the business to prevent Price's nomination, Jones died before the licence of mortmain was granted, and the Attorney General advised that until the college had a head no further progress could be made. The court interest led by Thomas Pardo did not therefore have Bradshaw's vote. Two Tory interests in the college led by Eubule Thelwall and Humphrey Lloyd, the latter backed by Shippen of Brasenose, the Earl of Abingdon, Lord Craven, and others, canvassed actively against Pardo. Pardo's calculations of victory by one vote were upset by the defection of Wynne, chaplain to the former Principal, the Bishop of St. Asaph, who defied extreme episcopal pressure, to join Lloyd. Unable to raise a majority at the last, Pardo's friends defeated Lloyd and his powerful supporters by uniting their interest with that of Thelwall whom 'they thought not so violent a party man as the other'. Thelwall was an old friend of Hearne, 'a modest, good natur'd Man', who fortunately for the

Whig interest in the college 'used little or no exercise, wch shortened his life', and little more than eighteen months after his election in December 1725 he died. Supported now by the new fellows appointed by the Crown, Pardo triumphed without opposition. But before the ultimate Whig victory, even the execution of Sir Leoline's will had been a matter of party conflict.[1]

Merton, as a college of greater wealth and numbers, was even more important to the Whigs than Jesus. John Russell, an unhappy Whig of Brasenose, seeking a haven in Merton, sought to bring the Archbishop of Canterbury into the fray in November 1715.[2] 'There are but three Houses, viz. Wadham, Jesus and Merton whose heads are not violent Tories or Jacobites. Merton stands fairest for a cure, as having yet several sound members left among them.' Elections of fellows were in the hands of the Warden (with two votes) and thirteen seniors; an election of up to eight fellows was pending, and however the political allegiances of the fellows were calculated there were only seven Whig to eight Tory votes. Moreover, although no Whig doubted Warden Holland's essential soundness, he was suspected of being unable 'to stem the Tyde that runs violently against him', and to be willing to compound with the Tories in order to secure the election of his nephew Meadowcourt to one of the vacancies. 'But if a little opposition of persons in power were made . . . the College would be entirely gained to his Majty's interest, & begin a reformation among us.' Byne and Marten, the leaders of the Tory interest, agreed with the Warden to elect three of his candidates and five of their own, their influence being strengthened by his dislike of 'every relation of the late Archbishop' Tenison, one of whom, Thomas Hearne, was standing with the support of Lord Somers and the bishops of Gloucester, Oxford, and Meath.

---

[1] *Hearne's Collections*, iii. 453–4, iv. 105, ix. 59, 66–67, 318–19, 326; B.M. Loan 29/106: Wm. Stratford to Edw. Harley, 28 July, 5 Aug. 1712, Portland MSS.; E.G. Hardy, *Jesus College* (London, 1899), pp. 163–6; *St. James's Post*, 7–10 Dec. 1716; *Hist. MSS. Comm. Portland MSS.* v. 210, vii. 276; Christ Church MS. Arch. W. Epist. 16, nos. 229 [329]–245 [345]; P.R.O. SP 35/14, fo. 45: /14, fos. 323 seq.: /58, no. 24b, fos. 72, 113, 133: /59, fos. 103, 105, 109, 121, 123–33, 134, 138–47, 148, 152, 160, 162, 164, 166, 171, 174.

[2] Russell's part in this transaction was commemorated in an epitaph produced by a member of the Oxford Poetical Club.

> Here lies Count R[u]ssell
> Who made a damn'd bustle.
>
> Amhurst, *Terrae Filius*, i. 150.

Governmental pressure told, however, and Holland secured the election of six Whig candidates including Hearne, Russell, Meadowcourt, and John Cowper, nephew of the Lord Chancellor and father of the poet, by methods which occasioned a legal inquiry. The Warden and thirteen seniors having completed the examination of the candidates, 'ye Warden instead of proposing wt numbers shd be elected, declared six places void, & six of ye fellows [i.e. the entire Whig strength] concurring did actually elect six gentlemen into those vacant fellowships'. The Warden thus evaded the Tory majority among the seniors by appeal to irrelevant statutes which affirmed that 'the fellows to be concerned are ye 13 senrs. only & if they disagree, ye Warden & six of the said 13 may elect'. The Dean of Arches concluded that although the college ought to have elected more than six fellows, the existing fellows for their own profit having allowed their numbers to fall seriously below strength, the election was valid. By these underhand proceedings the Whig interest was secured and six fellows elected whose adherence to Revolution principles gladdened *The Flying Post*, which in a splendid euphemism declared the public indebtedness 'to the steady probity of the Reverend Dr. Holland . . . and several of the Fellows'.[3]

After such a public conflict the new fellows naturally commended themselves in the London press for taking 'all opportunities of distinguishing themselves from the factions in the University', and the outmanœuvred Tory connexions took revenge for their provocation by severe penalties on the Constitution Club's celebrations on the next Restoration day. Meadowcourt, Russell, Bearcroft, and Cowper were all withheld from their degrees, though undeterred from their activities in the club. A year later, encouraged by Wyntle,[4] who had been the most militant Whig fellow in the last election, Warden Holland began to prepare for another election as soon as a favourable result could be assured.

The difficulty was that the triumphant Whig connexion of 1716 was becoming disrupted by personal and theological differences.

---

[3] Christ Church MS. Arch. W. Epist. 15: J. R[ussell] to ? [Edward Tenison], 27 Nov. 1715: Bp. of Meath to Abp. Wake, 10 Feb. [1715/16] and six subsequent documents concluding with 'Statement by Dr. Bettesworth May 2, 1716'; *The Flying Post*, 12 March 1715/16; cf. *The London Post*, 17 March; *The Weekly Journal*, 17 March; *The British Weekly Mercury*, 14–21 March 1715/16.

[4] Who succeeded Holland as Warden in 1734.

Thomas Hearne, who had been stoutly backed by Wake on his election, became alarmed at reports that the archbishop intended to expel him for heresy on the suspicion that he had written anti-Trinitarian papers under the pseudonym of *Phileleutherus Cantabrigiensis*, and without actually confessing to the charge pleaded hard with his Grace not to hold a visitation. Wake was certainly concerned at the 'great increase of loose principles' in matters theological at Merton, and John Russell came forward with an unsolicited profession of innocence. Hearne, indeed, was surreptitiously organizing a party of alleged Bangorian fellows[5] which should have so secure a majority at the next election that they could disregard the wishes of the Warden, between whom and Hearne there had never been any love lost. Hearne died before the election came on in January 1721, but the Warden's party suffered a set-back in the loss of one of the candidates they wished to elect. White Kennet, son of the Bishop of Peterborough, applied to Congregation for leave (by privilege of being a bishop's son) to proceed to the degree of B.A. although he was of only three years' standing. Knowing that he required the degree to stand for a Merton fellowship, and that refusal to grant it would aggravate the University's difficulties in opposing the Lambeth degree granted to Peploe, Warden of Manchester, Charlett and Gardiner supported the application but were defeated by the senior proctor Robert Brynker, one of the Tory fire-brands of Jesus, and the majority in Congregation.

On the eve of the Merton election the Warden's party, consisting of Hartop, Russell, Meadowcourt, and Cowper, were outnumbered by the late Thomas Hearne's faction, consisting of Marten, Streat, Allen, Breton, and Gilbert (all Whigs), and Thomas Cox, 'a bigotted Tory'. The Warden's men therefore coalesced with 'Trowe, Tovey & Moseley 3 Hannover Tories' and carried the election for five fellows celebrated equally for their scholarship and their reliability in politics and theology: Stillingfleet (grandson of the bishop), Gardiner (nephew of the Warden of All Souls and son to Sir Brocas Gardiner, a Commissioner of

---

[5] i.e. they were said to follow Bishop Hoadly of Bangor in holding that since Christ's kingdom was not of this world it was improper to protect the Anglican ascendancy by temporal penalties upon dissenters, and that Church and Chapel were alike voluntary societies, whose respective value to God depended solely on the sincerity with which their adherents held the different faiths which they enshrined.

Stamps and persecutor of the opposition press), Robinson (the protégé of Clavering, the Hebrew professor, and apostle of the court interest), White (son of an alderman and nephew of the Recorder of Oxford), and Woolley ('son to a very useful and honest man of the City of Worcester' and supported by the bishops of Salisbury, Lichfield, and Coventry).

At the last moment, finding their situation desperate, the dissident faction sent two men to London 'that Secretary Craggs should know . . . what a game . . . Meadowcourt was playing at Oxford', and came back armed with intimidating letters from Secretary Craggs, Under-Secretary Delafaye, the Lord Chancellor, Cowper's father, the Lord Justice of Chester, and the Bishop of Salisbury. After the election they appealed to Archbishop Wake, but it was too late; the Warden's party had kept out their candidates Makepeace and Lewin, 'the first for his ill principles or immorality, the other for his ignorance in all useful learning', had promised nothing to the Tories beyond 'protection from hardships', and were full of professions of doctrinal orthodoxy.[6]

Even now the struggle in Merton was not over, for the rival connexions held together. In 1723 a fresh election was to be held, and the dissident faction assembled all their forces unexpectedly at a college scrutiny to compel the Warden to agree to hold the election during the year of grace allowed to Breton, the leader of the dissidents, before resignation to accept a living. Threatened with a complaint to the Visitor, the Warden agreed. Russell and Meadowcourt now objected that Breton had accepted his living six months earlier than anyone had suspected, and that his fellowship was already void. Thereupon Cox, whose enemies avowed he would have been a non-juror could he have afforded to resign his fellowship, sent evidence to Archbishop Wake that in the last election Russell and Meadowcourt had bought the late Dr. Hartop's vote by a bribe levied upon the successful candidates. Meadowcourt admitted the notorious fact 'that Dr. Hartop was a person of a mercenary spirit', and that at the election he had claimed 30 guineas to cover his expenses and loss of earnings as a medical practitioner in Nottingham. He insisted that it was not

[6] St. James's Evening Post, 31 May–2 June 1716; Amhurst, Terrae Filius, ii. 126; Christ Church MS. Arch. W. Epist. 20: J. Holland to Abp. Wake, 29 March 1717: 16, nos. 123 [223]–150 [250]; Hearne's Collections, vii. 190–2; P.R.O. SP 35/22, fo. 37: /25, fos. 10, 22; Bodl. MSS. Ballard 20, fo. 29: 38, fo. 217; Hist. MSS. Comm. Portland MSS. vii. 287.

corrupt to levy this from White, Woolley, and Robinson whose election had depended on Hartop's vote, and that Woolley, who had refused to pay, had passed the information to Breton's faction to help them deter Russell and him from objecting to Breton's vote. All parties offered specious reasons to explain their actions, and the election finally passed quietly with the choice of four men acceptable to the Warden and ministry.

The Warden's interest had thus twice survived the challenge of the Merton 'Bangorians' and their alleged Jacobite ally. Russell was duly rewarded, for he had earlier become chaplain to Bishop Kennet who made him a canon of Peterborough in 1720; he received a living in Lincolnshire in 1722 and a canonry of Lincoln in 1724. Meadowcourt's first patron, Lord Cowper, to whom he was chaplain, fell from office in 1718; his next hope, Craggs, died too soon, and he then backed a loser in Lord Carteret. Though professing in March 1722 that he would 'never be wanting to oppose all innovations in religious matters, and to discountenance the authors of them', Meadowcourt was none the less a notorious preacher of the doctrines of Maurice and Hoadly. White Kennet obtained the royal presentation to the rectory of Passenham in his diocese for him, but the private patron successfully maintained his disposal of the living against the Crown. Meadowcourt continued to serve the ministers in acquiring places at Merton for their friends, to apply tirelessly for preferment, and complain of the straitened circumstances of college life. Not till 1727 did he obtain a living in Buckinghamshire; in 1734 the archbishop passed over his nomination as Warden of Merton, but in 1735 as a lackey of Newcastle he obtained a canonry in his native city of Worcester, acquiring livings and political influence in that diocese thereafter. Blossoming in his place in the sun, he won some distinction for studies on Milton and other poets, and 'undisturbed by ambition and envy' (though expecting 'a Deanery at least for his good works') died in September 1760, just before a change of court interest which would have taxed his agility as much as any at the beginning of the Hanoverian era.[7]

The third of Russell's Whig colleges was Wadham, a society with an excellent academic reputation at the end of the previous century, which under the Whig rule of Dr. Dunster had been the only house to hang portraits of William III and George I in the

[7] See note E, p. 281.

hall. On his death in May 1719 the general opinion in the University was that he would be succeeded by a Tory fellow, Thomas Girdler, who was nevertheless melodramatically defeated by another 'stinking Whigg' William Baker. The election took place in the chapel after morning prayers, and was turned by the vote of John Leaves, who had firmly pledged himself to Girdler and had just been rescued from imprisonment in Exeter by the Wadham Tories.

While they were at prayers, a paper being put into his hand (a Bank Bill it is supposed, or promise of preferment), the promises vanished, and he immediately voted for Baker. But what is more extraordinary, within six hours after the election this fellow's conscience turned upon him so violently that before night he grew distracted, and is now so raving mad that there are two keepers upon him in his own chambers.

One report dated Leaves's insanity from the next day after he had been refused the living of Marsh Gibbon, and Hearne collected the circumstantial detail that Leaves had received 50 guineas during prayers. Mist's *Weekly Journal* flayed him in indignant verse:

> Transcendent Knave! who could have closer trod
> Thy Friend Iscariot's steps, who sold his God?
> Transcript of Judas! Go, refund the Pelf,
> Then like thy great Exemplar, hang thyself!

The Tory poet, however, had tragically hit the wrong target, for a fortnight later came the suicide not of Leaves but of John Evans, whom Harley credited with delivering the bribe during prayers, and who shot himself to avoid arrest for debt.[8]

Dr. Baker, the new Warden, had long been known as a determined Whig, and like his predecessor was a friend of the Duke of Marlborough who presented him to the living of Bladon and Woodstock. Under the new dynasty he became archdeacon of Oxford and rector of St. Giles-in-the-Fields. His election cost the college a great endowment promised by the Primate of Ireland if Girdler was elected, and his influence was soon felt, for on the day

---

[8] *Hist. MSS. Comm. R5, Pine-Coffin MSS.*, p. 374; *Hearne's Collections*, vii. 11, 13, 18, 19–20, 21, 28–29; *Hist. MSS. Comm. Portland MSS.* v. 583, 588, vii. 251; B.M. Loan 29/106: Wm. Stratford to Edw. Harley, 20 May 1719, Portland MSS. Leaves later recovered sufficiently to hold two livings.

Amhurst was expelled from St. John's, Baker ejected a Tory probationer fellow from Wadham, and on the king's coronation day
ordered 'more than ordinary rejoycings . . . thinking by that
means to gain a Bpprick or a Deanery'. As the king's chaplain
appointed to accompany him to Hanover, Baker was on the sure
road to advancement, and was fancied to become Dean of Christ
Church. In fact in 1723 he became Bishop of Bangor, being translated to Norwich in 1727, and leaving a reputation for nepotism in
both sees. On resigning, Baker tried to secure the election of Nash
who had voted for him in 1719, but Thistlethwayte, his junior, who
had also supported Baker, carried the day. 'Both these gentlemen
are Whigs', declared Hearne, 'but Nash being look'd upon as the
cunninger man, and more able than the other to do mischief in
the college, they unanimously struck in for Thistlethwayt, especially since the Tory side could not carry it for one of themselves.'
Thistlethwayte proved sufficiently mischievous, however, for
under him Wadham lapsed steadily into political insignificance,
and (a scandal which delighted the Oxford rhymers) he was
expelled in 1739 for offences against a student, and resigning his
Prebend at Westminster, 'he retired beyond the seas where he
died [at Boulogne] and being brought over about the year 1743,
was buried at Dover'.[9]

Exeter College had long harboured a phalanx of Whig fellows
and had seen stirring events after the Revolution when the Visitor,
Sir Jonathan Trelawney, had been driven to the House of Lords
to defeat the Socinian Rector Bury. Under his successor Paynter
the college was of small political consequence, but under the new
dynasty the Whig fellows stirred again, and when Paynter died in
1716 a fierce contest ensued. Whig and Tory in the college were
equally balanced, and as neither side could carry its point, and
Exeter had had its fill of appeals to the Visitor, they compromised
by the election of Matthew Hole, who had resigned his fellowship
some years previously in favour of church preferment obtained
by his friend Henry Godolphin.

Hole's chief characteristics were an enthusiasm for preaching

---

[9] *Hearne's Collections*, ii. 18, 26, vii. 57, viii. 148; *Verney Letters*, i. 388;
P.R.O. SP 35/15, fo. 229; *Hist. MSS. Comm. Portland MSS.* vii. 257, 321, 330;
B.M. Add. MS. 32686, fo. 312. There are serious errors in the entry on Thistle-
thwayte in the *Alumni Oxonienses* which should be corrected by reference to
Gutch's edition of Wood's *History*, i. 597 and R. B. Gardiner, *The Registers of
Wadham College, Oxford*, Part I (London, 1889), p. 433.

and a universally noted miserliness. He was a politician no more than Paynter, and in 1718, to the delight of *The Flying Post*,[10] was outmanœuvred by the Whig faction in the fellowship elections; when, however, the next election came on in July 1719, during a smallpox epidemic, the deadlock of 1716 recurred.

The Whigs presumed they should have had a majority, because one of the Tories, who had never had the smallpox, was absent; but he lay two miles out of town, and appeared at the election. The votes were equal. Their statutes direct in such a case to call in the Vice-Chancellor [who being Shippen of Brasenose] turned the election on the Tory side.

The Whig interest was not yet submerged, however, for a year later two of the three probationary fellows, Bartlett and Eastway, were denied their actuality, according to the College Register 'for disaffection and drinking the Pretender's health', according to scandalized Tory opinion 'for nothing . . . but that they were Torys'. There being no appeal from this decision, the Whig cause was kept alive and was able to re-enter the field of university politics in 1730 by electing, as Rector, the most active and most successful social climber of their number, John Conybeare.[11]

Two societies in which court politics were strong were Christ Church and Oriel. On the accession of the new dynasty, Smalridge, to his friends 'the greatest saint upon earth', employed all his skill to keep the University out of conflict with the government and to prepare for better times which seemed deceptively near. In the House of Lords Smalridge commonly acted with his friend Atterbury. He voted against the first address of thanks for the king's speech, refused to sign the declaration of the bishops against the '15, voted for the Earl of Oxford in the debates about his impeachment, and strongly opposed the repeal of the Occasional Conformity and Schism Acts. Yet Smalridge was not merely the Tory fire-brand suggested by his parliamentary record. At the accession he kept his place as Lord Almoner, was popular with the royal family as a preacher, and, entrenching himself in the affections of the Prince of Wales, was one of the pioneers of the attempt to exploit the Hanoverian reversionary interest in the

---

[10] *The Flying Post*, 5–8 July 1718.

[11] *D.N.B.*, article on 'Matthew Hole'; *Hearne's Collections*, v. 267, x. 310; Amhurst, *Terrae Filius*, i. 173; *Oculus Britanniae*, p. 23; *Hist. MSS. Comm. Portland MSS.* vii. 256; Lamport Hall: Isham MS. IC 3899; C. W. Boase, *Registrum Collegii Exonensis*, pp. cxxxiv, cxxxviii.

University's favour. Lady Cowper was 'told for a certainty that he and my Lord Nottingham are the hopes of the Tories, and that the one in the church, and the other in the state, had undertaken to set all things upon the right foot as they call it'. For a high-churchman Smalridge was very complacent to the ladies of the princess's heterodox circle gossiping their way through the mysteries of the Trinity, and affirmed 'that every private Christian was not obliged to believe every part of the Athanasian Creed'.

Striving to avoid the academic tactlessness so irritating to the government, Smalridge urged the University to yield on inessentials, and laboured vainly to secure a degree for Wake's librarian Wilkins, who had acquired a well-merited notoriety as a spy in university affairs. He set forth the University's grievances against the garrison, assured Townshend that the riots of 1715 were not as bad as they were painted, and severely punished treasonable cries in his own house. In 1716 he insisted at length to Wake that the political character of the University had suffered gross calumny, and he led the deputation of heads to His Grace with the petition against a visitation. It was characteristic of Smalridge that in the last university crisis before his death he was very hostile to Warton's sermon on Restoration day, for it was an exemplar of the overt provocation which he had always deplored. Characteristic, too, was his ability to avoid the domestic contests which had disrupted Christ Church in Atterbury's time, although among his canons was Clavering, the new regius professor of Hebrew, an active organizer of the ministerial interest. Even when he advised against an address to the Crown in January 1717, Smalridge found reasonable defenders.[12]

On Smalridge's death in 1719 the government knew well that his successor would require integrity and courage. Lord Chancellor Macclesfield, his purse-bearer Sir John D'Oyley, Archbishop Wake, the canons of Christ Church, and even Atterbury, Bishop of Rochester, strenuously advocated the claims of Potter, the Whig Bishop of Oxford, to the Deanery also, but he pleaded to be excused on financial and valetudinarian grounds. The canons' second choice was Dr. Egerton, son of the Earl of Bridgwater, who had joined their number in 1716, but his interest was not sufficient. As embodying the Earl of Sunderland's notion of a strong

[12] See note F, p. 281.

man, Hugh Boulter outstripped all other candidates, 'being ye best able to stem ye torrent of ye university'. But Boulter cut no great figure as Dean, and by 1722 was reported as anxious to leave, though in 1724 he hesitated before accepting the primacy in Ireland to stem another torrent there. Before long Boulter was being abused by Townshend as a 'beast and wretched fellow . . . and a blockhead', who 'being made Dean in order to strengthen the Whig interest . . . did nothing but laze away his time, and suffered the Tories to increase their power and numbers in that University', but he opened the floodgates to the ministerial interest in Christ Church which evolved from a seed plot of Harleyites into a Whig society. William Bradshaw, a chaplain to the king and Christ Church canon of a year's standing, succeeded Boulter as Dean and Bishop of Bristol on the same day as Clavering was promoted to the deanery of Hereford and See of Llandaff. Stratford's expectation that Bradshaw would 'make a little more bustle' than his predecessor and 'attend the meetings of his brother Pates, be pressing or opposing things which he may think will recommend him above, and possibly raise some intestine broils amongst the Heads, and inform against them to the ministers' proved amply justified by his intervention in the affairs of Jesus and New College. Within the college he ejected Dr. Terry from his office as sub-dean, he having enraged all the Whigs by seeking the deanery for himself, and raised college disputes on party lines second only to those of Atterbury.[13]

In Oriel the personal animosities which complicated politics in every Oxford society blossomed in their full rancour, but the outlines of the contest are clear enough. Dr. Carter, the Provost, was a time-server, cringing towards those in authority and dictatorial towards those whom he regarded as his juniors. Having fawned upon (and profited by) the Tory government of Queen Anne's last years, he fawned again upon the Hanoverians, and in 1716 assured Wake that he had entire confidence in the political reliability of the newly elected fellows

inasmuch as those persons on whom they depend chiefly, as well as they themselves are wholly devoted to King George. The young men

---

[13] Christ Church MS. Arch. W. Epist. 16, nos. 63–65: 21, Earl of Sunderland to Abp. Wake, 27 Oct. 1719; *Hist. MSS. Comm. Egmont Diary*, i. 225; *Hist. MSS Comm. Portland MSS.* v. 588, vii. 263–4, 321, 381–3, 441; B.M. Add. MS. 32686 fo. 153.

chosen Fellows are Mr. Ingram [who had shot the Brasenose man in
the riot of 1715], brother to the Lord Irwin, Mr. Evans nephew to ye
Bp. of Llandaff, a Mr. Hodges whose relations live in Wiltshire. In all
elections . . . I shall have a particular regard to men's principles and
loyalty as well as learning.

Before the end of this year Carter, who had Atterbury's capacity
for antagonizing his college, was consulting with Wake how to
outmanœuvre a block of fellows united against him, and how long
to delay elections in order to carry suitable candidates. He delayed
finally until 1718, praising his candidates for their Whiggism, and
one especially, Hearne's great aversion, Joseph Bowles, because
'he will allways vote with me'.

    The personal and domestic aspects of Oriel politics came out
in the way Carter contrived to incur the hostility of fellows on
whose election he had spent considerable pains, but the political
aspect of the struggle was duly noted at the time. Carter's own
court politics were quite clear; he supplanted Smalridge as a royal
chaplain (a place which he had earlier sought through Bolingbroke) and supported Wilkins's claim to a degree. Trouble arose
over the fellowship elections in 1721, 1723, and 1724, in which the
Provost, having failed altogether to break up the clique of fellows
opposed to him, and supported only by the obsequious Bowles,
claimed to overrule the majority vote by 'a negative voice'. Gibson
and Reynolds, who as bishops of Lincoln were successively
Visitors, supported Carter, who thus obtained almost complete
authority in college elections.

    The Tory reaction to this situation was expressed by Dr.
Gastrell, Bishop of Chester, who regarded this exercise of visitatorial power 'as a specimen of that oppressive scheme which was
to have been brought into Parliament if the lay-lords had no more
regard to rights and properties than the spiritual', and set to work
to organize the injured fellows. Under his inspiration the case
went to the Court of Common Pleas, which not only declared in
favour of the fellows chosen by the majority but pronounced the
Crown, not the Bishop of Lincoln, to be the Visitor, and the
operative statutes to be those of January, not those of May, 1326,
as had been assumed for four centuries. This decision heartened
the university Tories, not least as a hopeful precedent for the
great struggle being waged over the visitation of University College, but it left one loophole to Carter. Since the Crown, in whose

service he had spared nothing, was now the Visitor, perhaps the new Visitor might reject the fellows whose admission the Court of Common Pleas had required. Carter therefore prepared a petition to the king to be presented by the Bishop of Lincoln. The government, however, could not afford to slight the Court, and the bishop wisely refused to present the petition. Thus, through identifying the ministerial cause too closely with his personal self-assertion, Carter lost a battle which had been won in other colleges.[14]

New College had a chequered political history, partly because of its uncertain relationship to the Crown. The later Stuarts, and William III after the Revolution, had frequently issued letters mandatory in college elections, by which means the society had lately received repeated infusions of Whig blood. Dr. Traffles, Warden 1701-3, nevertheless 'obtain'd a promise from ye Court that no more mandatory letters should be sent, for Winchester College or New College', an achievement recorded in his epitaph. He was succeeded by Thomas Brathwaite, a man of Tory inclinations, who resigned in 1712 while Vice-Chancellor to become Warden of Winchester at more than twice the salary. John Cobb, the next Warden, was chosen in a hotly contested election in which he barely defeated two candidates, a Whig and a Tory with more pronounced political connexions than his own. The Tory sympathies of the Wardens, and the persisting Whig connexion in the college were revealed in some celebrated events after 1714.

One of the Whig fellows, John Ayliffe, was attacked in 1714 by the Vice-Chancellor, Bernard Gardiner, for laying open the privileges of the University, abusing its heroes, and dedicating his offending treatise *The Ancient and Present State of the University of Oxford* to Lord Somers instead of the Duke of Ormonde. An aggressive Whig who sought the protection of the Duke of Marlborough, Ayliffe was prosecuted in the Vice-Chancellor's Court by Gardiner and Brathwaite, the former Warden of New College, and was finally condemned as contumacious while in London trying to stop the proceedings, deprived of his degree, and banished. The case now went down to New College where the Warden and five fellows decided that he had incurred expulsion, and nine fellows that he had not incurred expulsion but deserved to be punished. The Warden's party then referred the matter to the Visitor, Sir Jonathan Trelawney, who offered Ayliffe the choice of expulsion or a public recantation of his 'unjust reflections'; Ayliffe forestalled expulsion by resigning, and, to the applause of the Whig press, was rewarded by the government with a Commissionership of Hawkers and Pedlars. The strength of the Whig interest in New College was demonstrated not only in the nine votes against Ayliffe's expulsion but in the initiative of New College men in founding the Constitution Club, and providing, it is said, ten members. Ayliffe intended to seek redress in Chancery but, deterred by the cost, published his case in a pamphlet, and joined the clamour for royal visitation. But Ayliffe had not been simply a victim of the university magnates, and his general unpopularity with the Tory rank and file was not to be diminished by public agitation; his fate remained the stock-in-trade of the Whig journalists.[15]

In 1717 Cobb was among the heads who opposed the address to the Crown, and in 1720 he was elected Warden of Winchester, whither his successor, John Dobson, son of the President of Trinity, followed him in 1725. The ministerial interest was now in the hands of the bustling Bishop Bradshaw, himself a former fellow of New College, and with a connexion there still in Reynell his chaplain. The outcome was that in another three-cornered election the bishop's candidate, Henry Bigg, carried the day by an absolute majority. The next step in the advance of the ministerial interest is obscure, but in the next year the wardens and fellows of New College and Winchester College petitioned the Crown against the issue of letters mandatory in elections on the grounds that William III had agreed to abandon the practice. It is probable that the immediate trouble was at Winchester, where John Bromfield, who had been a member of the grand jury which in 1716 presented Winchester College for disaffection, had been persistently thwarted in securing a place for his son; but both foundations stood together, and Gibson, Bishop of London, advised the ministry that no more could be done unless the Attorney General should find a new opening in their charters and statutes. New College, which in 1715 had had a head and a minority of

---

[15] Cf. *St. James's Post*, 24–27 Oct. 1718. In Jan. 1719 he sought election to the professorship of civil law at Gresham College on the grounds of 'having suffered much for his principles to the late Revolution and the present Government from the University of Oxford'. *Whitehall Evening Post*, 29–31 Jan. 1719.

fellows ready to persecute the friends of the ministry, had a decade later a head and majority who favoured the ministry, but were still prepared to resist court pressure.[16]

It is unnecessary to recount here the story of the great visitations of All Souls which embittered the reign of Warden Gardiner[17] and had serious effects upon his society. The influence of events upon Gardiner himself is nevertheless of interest, not only because of his personal importance in the University in these years but as illustrating the difficulties of politicians whose inclinations were to keep to the middle of the road. By nature Gardiner was a court Whig, who associated with Lancaster before 1710, and whose brother, Sir Brocas, under the new dynasty, was a Whig placeman who hunted down anti-ministerial publications. Gardiner, there-fore, might have been expected to be among the favourites of the ministry after 1714. In fact his history was very different. The agitation against the obligation to enter holy orders, 1709–11, was conducted by partisan Whig fellows, and Gardiner's defence of the college statutes was assisted and congratulated by the Tory member for the University, Sir William Whitelock. Moreover, Gardiner's chief ally in the perennial struggles at the election of fellows was his relative by marriage George Clarke, fellow and benefactor of the college, a Tory whom Gardiner came to cham-pion as M.P. for the University. If any further experience was needed to loosen Gardiner from his old moorings it was the fact that both the archbishops whose visitations proved so costly to the college and to his own prerogatives were Whig nominees.

As a court politician Gardiner was hostile to Jacobitism, and for the first year of the new reign tried as Vice-Chancellor to see that the University kept up appearances satisfactorily, only to find that it was the policy of the new ministry and its scribblers to brand the universities and rank and file of the clergy as Jacob-ites, and that he himself was a target. Finally, in 1717 Gardiner was stung by attacks on his rule as Vice-Chancellor, which had

---

[16] B.M. Add. MS. 36136, fos. 75, 104–5, 109, 111, and other papers 65–11: passim; Wood's History of the Colleges of Oxford, ed. J. Gutch (Oxford, 1786) i. 210–11; Hearne's Collections, iii. 331–2, viii. 314–15; Verney Letters, i. 313 Bodl. MSS. Ballard 1, fos. 87–89: 21, fo. 197; Boyer, Political State, xiii. 236; R Rashdall and R. S. Rait, New College (London, 1901), pp. 198–203; St. James' Post, 12 March 1715/16, 10 Dec. 1716.

[17] He was also hostile to the kind of opposition promoted by Terrae Filiu whose performance he suppressed in 1713.

ended in 1715, into replying in a pamphlet. That he was one of the heads who opposed an address to the king in 1717 did not improve his reputation with factious Whigs, and in the following year, just as fresh trouble with the Whig Visitor was brewing up, he was one of the heads humiliated by being removed from the Commission of the Peace. The object of uninhibited Whig abuse, Gardiner was provoked into writing (though he did not publish) another pamphlet denying the charge that the money which Barzillai Jones embezzled from the college was sent abroad to the Pretender with his connivance.

Gardiner's efforts to give satisfaction to the government without slandering the University, as required by the more vocal Whigs, exposed him to equally savage attacks from the wilder spirits among the Tories. Among them were a number of the younger dons, who, unable to see any benefit accruing from the statesmanship of the ruling heads, succumbed to demagogy, to occasional flirtation with the Pretender, and to co-operation in several elections with the Constitutioners. Dr. King, Principal of St. Mary Hall, a bitter enemy of Gardiner, became the leader of this faction in the University, and his right-hand man, Sedgwick Harrison, after proving the strength of his position by winning election as Camden Professor, became a thorn in the Warden's side by 'fomenting disturbances' among his brethren, the fellows of All Souls.[18] It was true to Gardiner's character that in 1723 he opposed the re-election of Thomas Warton as poetry professor for having rocked the boat so dangerously by his sermon in 1719. Characteristic, too, was the tribute paid Gardiner when he died in 1726 by Dr. Stratford, a member of another court connexion now out of favour; they recognized their common ground in their distaste of the demagogic methods of the party extremists.[19]

Such was the force of personal and other animosities in Oxford

[18] One of the first results of Wake's visitation of the college was that Gardiner failed to prevent Harrison from holding his fellowship along with the chair (M. Burrows, *Worthies*, p. 379). A little earlier Harrison had openly laughed at the Warden during a fellowship election, and Littleton, another member of the college, declared: 'ye King was to come bef[ore] Xmas' (All Souls College MS. Appeals, 401 gg.).

[19] *Hearne's Collections*, ii. 297–8, iii. 121, v. 79, 83, vii. 250, viii. 96–97; Bodl. MS. Ballard 21, fo. 134; *Hist. MSS. Comm. Portland MSS.* vii. 67, 239, 434; Christ Church MS. Arch. W. Epist. 16, nos. 78, 127, 160. A good account of the visitations is to be found in MSS. of Warden of All Souls College: Thomas Wenman's History, i, fos. 69–76: ii, fos. 140–1 *et passim*.

that there was one important episode, the disputed election of the Master of University College, in which Stratford acted with the vociferous democracy which he commonly deplored. The events which followed the death of Arthur Charlett in November 1722 have never been fully explained, and perhaps cannot now be interpreted completely. In brief, Thomas Cockman received five votes at the election and William Denison four. Denison's party claimed that the election was not canonical on the grounds that Cockman did not have an absolute majority of the ten qualified voters, and held a new meeting at which they elected Denison Master. He appealed to the Vice-Chancellor and doctors of divinity as Visitors of the college, and they decided in his favour. Cockman's party appealed to the Crown as Visitor and in 1727 the Court of King's Bench determined that King Alfred was the college founder, that the Vice-Chancellor, masters, and scholars had no visitatorial jurisdiction, and that Cockman was duly elected Master. Under this decision also a new set of statutes for the college was approved by the Privy Council in 1735.

By the college historians this episode is explained as a dispute between North and South among the fellows, but this circumstance does not account for the passionate differences which the conflict aroused in the University at large, nor the fact that a dispute, like that of Oriel, on the extent and location of visitatorial power, should provoke such different reactions. Amhurst analysed the situation in sarcastic verse:

> Pert upstart patriots with rebellious pride,
> Spurn at the *Heads*, and Golgotha deride,
> In bold confederate clubs and plots engage,
> And youthful whims oppose to thoughtful age,
> Each day the hoary sages sink in pow'r
> And Presidents and Provosts sway no more,
> With grumbling tories factious whigs combine,
> And against D[e]n[iso]n perversely join. . . .

Gardiner's misfortune in arousing the animosity of rabid Tories as well as Whigs has already been discussed. The alliance of these two forces, which had been adumbrated in the election of Delaune as Margaret professor, was confirmed by the disillusionment of the extreme Whigs that the government had not openly intervened in the University, and shown forth both in the election of Harrison as Camden professor in 1720 and in the odd mixture of

Whig and Tory votes for the Jacobite Dr. King in the parliamentary election of 1722.

In 1722 Charlett brought the fellows of University to vote solidly against King, but in 1720 the candidate unsuccessfully run by the 'moderate' heads against King's intimate, Harrison, had been none other than Denison, who had then been defeated partly by the popular revulsion against the political management of the heads and partly by the fact that Christ Church supported a third candidate of their own. Denison was faced once more by this combination of forces and supported by the same allies. Denison was tutor to the Duke of Beaufort, a relative of Ormonde and Arran, who as late as 1728 was urging the heads to take the case of the University's visitatorial right to the courts, and whose agent in the University, Dr. Shippen, the Vice-Chancellor, was the chief stickler for Denison throughout.[20] Shippen's extreme unpopularity, and his part in turning the Earl of Arran against his quondam secretary, Dr. King, sufficed to rally the friends of King and Harrison to Cockman, and produced the extraordinary circumstance that Hearne, who normally referred to His Majesty as the Duke of Brunswick, insisted throughout that the Visitor of University College was George I. Cockman's propaganda stressed that he was defending the rights of the college and Crown against 'some unstatutable invasions . . . [of] the Vice Chancellor and some few Drs.' Likewise many Whigs who also wished to break up the present political connexions supported Cockman also.

Finally, there was a factor overlooked by Amhurst: Shippen belonged to the Harcourt interest led by Delaune, and old enmity swung Harleyites such as Stratford in favour of Cockman. With both Harleyites and Whigs hostile, Denison found as in 1720 that he had Christ Church solidly against him and now openly allied with his most powerful enemies. Hence when the university Visitors assembled to discuss Denison's appeal they were staunchly opposed by Hammond, Burton, Stratford, Terry, and Clavering (canons of Christ Church), Carter, the Provost of Oriel, and Moulden of Pembroke. The Warden of Merton soon dropped out

[20] Denison's election to a fellowship at University had been decided on appeal to the Vice-Chancellor and doctors; in due course the Chancellor rewarded him by appointing him Principal of Magdalen Hall at the next vacancy, which occurred in 1745. The alliance between Shippen and Arran was sealed by the appointment of the former's nephew, Leybourne, as chaplain to the Chancellor. *Hearne's Collections*, viii. 10; Lamport Hall: Isham MS. IC 1866.

of the commission of Visitors, of which Delaune and a group of doctors from St. John's formed the backbone. Even so Delaune could not bring Dr. Evans with him, and Dr. Haywood eventually rebelled against his pressure. The Vice-Chancellor put about that Cockman's friends were trying to bring a royal visitation upon the University (the traditional Whig offence) and abused them to the ministers as Jacobites, thus acknowledging the combination of forces against authority. The paradox was complete when, to the applause of Jacobites, Hanoverian authority triumphed, and to the satisfaction of Whigs and Harleyites a Master of University was confirmed in office who a few years before had been recommended to Lord Rochester, the church Tory magnate, as a tutor to Lord Cornbury. It was indeed the Whig heads who finally blocked the Chancellor's attempt to revive the matter in Convocation in 1728.[21]

Shippen's connexion regained some lost ground in 1726. At first the Vice-Chancellor had inveigled Dr. Hunt, Master of Balliol, into his crusade against Cockman. However, the Dean of Christ Church reported to Wake that not long before his death Hunt 'join'd heartily with the King's Friends ... deserted Shippen and his party, and ... promis'd me that he will steadily adhere to his Majesty's Friends and interest, and do all that he can to promote it in the College and University'. By promoting a court interest in Balliol Hunt could not fail to divide the college (which had been the chief support for King in 1722), and to raise a party against William Best, whom he and his surviving brother, the Archdeacon of Bath, openly designated as his successor as Master. The leader of the opposition to Best was Joseph Sanford, who had been in the bad books of the previous Master, Dr. Baron; his party urged Dr. Brydges, the Archdeacon of Rochester (who had been elected Visitor of Balliol because he was a friend of Atterbury, his bishop), to stand for election, and on his refusal put up Brydges's nephew, Theophilus Leigh, a young fellow of Corpus. The story of this highly coloured election has been well told by

²¹ N. Amhurst, *Oculus Britanniae*, p. 33; *Hearne's Collections*, vii. 312, viii. 19–32, 52–53, 57–58, 62–64, 70–71, 89, 204, 304, 370, 372; *Hist. MSS. Comm. Portland MSS.* vii. 340, 342 seq., 369, 436, 462 seq.; B.M. Add. MSS. 35584, fo. 310: 36137, fo. 63; Bodl. MS. Rawlinson Letters 92, fo. 419; MS. Top. Oxon. d 5, fos. 2–9; University Archives: MS. Conv. Reg. Bd 31, fo. 163; Christ Church MS. Arch. W. Epist. 16, nos. 103–12; P.R.O. SP 35/42, fo. 166.

the college historian. The two factions being equal, Lux, the senior fellow of Best's party, was picketed in his rooms by his friends to save him from the other side, who stuck at nothing to get him brought out and declared insane; while Best's friends strove to have Quick, the junior fellow of the opposite side, deprived as a non-juror because he had failed to subscribe the Act of Uniformity on his election. Each side brought pressure from parents to bear and threats that pupils would be removed. There was a dreadful scene in the chapel as Best's party were convinced that Lux, who must act as a scrutator, would be frightened into imbecility. The election ending in a tie, Best was carried in triumph by his friends to the Master's Lodgings, since in their view, if Quick had been entitled to vote at all he should as junior fellow have crossed according to the statutes to Best's party to make a majority. Leigh's party remained in the chapel, declared the election void, and unanimously chose Leigh as Master. The election devolving to the Visitor, Leigh's uncle, Dr. Brydges, the result was a foregone conclusion.

Organizing an opposition to Hunt's favoured candidate was not solely a college matter; the first to invite Leigh's intervention was Sedgwick Harrison, Dr. King's ally, and active from the beginning were Delaune, the ally of the late Vice-Chancellor, and Dr. Morley, Rector of Lincoln, who was of the same kidney as Shippen. In short the contested election marked the attempt of Shippen's connexion, still fighting tooth and nail against Cockman, to re-establish the grip on Balliol which they had lost by the defection of Hunt to the court interest. To this end they did not scruple to champion Leigh who had voted for their enemy King in 1721, nor to employ an interest led by Sanford and Jones who had 'plumped' for him and were morally supported by Hearne. Such a factious policy could hardly conduce to a simple result. In 1728 Leigh helped to defeat the Chancellor's efforts to continue the struggle against Cockman. Moreover, although he looked a safe enough Tory at the time, Leigh was the nephew not only of the Tory archdeacon but also of the Whig Duke of Chandos. This connexion enabled the Master over the years to drift from his old political moorings, till by the middle of the century he was more than half a court politician.[22]

[22] Christ Church MS. Arch. W. Epist. 16, no. 234 [334]; *Hist MSS. Comm. Portland MSS.* vii. 346, 387; *Hearne's Collections,* ix. 131, 206, 287, xi. 41;

A final case which aroused controversy in press and pamphlet is interesting as showing that despite the unprincipled manœuvrings of the University and Balliol cases, some of the political factors at work in 1715 were still operative in 1730. In 1729 Francis Ayscough, a probationer fellow of Corpus, was expelled and was reinstated the following year by the Visitor, the Bishop of Winchester. Neither party attempted to disguise that the dispute was mostly political in origin. Ayscough, whose fortunes turned on his being tutor to George Lyttelton, whose sister he eventually married, affirmed that his loyalty to the dynasty was never in question, but that he was 'represented as disaffected to the Church of England', that is, he 'suffered . . . as a Whig and Hoadleian'. The college claimed that he had abused a senior fellow, crying 'I dont fear you, I know where to have redress'. The technical issue was whether the President and fellows were the 'Denier judges' in approving or denying the probationer fellows their actuality, and, like most others, this appeal to the Visitor succeeded, 'Old Ephraim, as [the Visitor] was called, giving the President and Fellows to understand . . . that if they did not admit Ayscough in a quarter of an hour, . . . he would *out* every man of them in the next quarter'. However, Ayscough crossed Bishop Potter, and went into opposition with the reversionary interest, for in 1740 he became clerk of the closet to Prince Frederick; in the next decade he became preceptor to Prince George, who as George III brought Ayscough finally into the promised land as dean of Bristol in 1761.[23] Ayscough's personal triumph did not, however, alter the fact that the tide of Whig advance had been checked, a fact which led to some strange manœuvres in the election of university burgesses.

D3, D3.18b, D3.19; Bodl. MS. Dep. b 48, fo. 1. See also B.M. Add. MS. 29601, fos. 32, 91, 125.

[23] *The Proceedings of Corpus Christi College, Oxon, in the Case of Mr. Ayscough Vindicated* (London, 1730); *A Vindication of the Proceedings in the Case of Mr. Ayscough, of Corpus Christi College, Oxon.* (London, 1731); *Whitehall Evening Post*, 24–26 March 1730; *Memoirs of a Royal Chaplain 1729–63*, ed. A. Hartshorne (London, 1905), p. 282; *Hearne's Collections*, ix. 266, x. 243, 261.

CHAPTER VIII

The Battle at the Polls

VEXED by factious politics in these years, the University could hardly hope for peace in its constitutional functions of electing parliamentary burgesses. Bromley, as we have seen, spared no effort to ingratiate himself with the new king, though Hanmer failed to get him continued as Secretary and he refused the place of Teller of the Exchequer—political self-abnegation which won the commendation of Atterbury in the hysterical pamphlet he wrote for the next election, *English Advice to the Freeholders of England*. It was Whitelock, however, who acted as a mouthpiece of the bishop in the Commons. At the end of March 1715 he was the only one who made any demur to Walpole's motion for an address of thanks for the king's speech, and though both he and Bromley opposed the terms of an address, it was he who blurted out Atterbury's abuse 'that the Whigs design'd to involve the nation in a new war, and lay six shillings in the pound [on land]'. A fortnight later, on a motion to consider the king's proclamation summoning a new parliament, he 'made exceptions to the said Proclamation as *unprecedented* and *unwarrantable*, [and] . . . was call'd upon by some members of the court party to explain himself'. Whitelock like Wyndham was much provoked by the king's partisan leanings to the other side, but after these unhappy outbursts seems to have kept silent for the rest of his parliamentary career.

In August 1714 Bromley and Sir William Wyndham had been very forward in moving for the civil list, but by the following May, when the king's income was to be put on a permanent footing, they were less enthusiastic, and hinted that they should first be given details of the royal expenses. A year later Bromley was denouncing the Septennial Bill as an open encroachment of the Crown and Lords upon the rights of the Commons, and smiting the Whigs hip and thigh for emulating the later Stuarts in depriving the people of frequent elections. Bromley was now in opposition; Mar and other Jacobite conspirators began to have hopes of him, and in 1717 to praise him highly to the Pretender.

Yet as even the Jacobites had to recognize, Bromley was not faced by a simple choice between George or James. In September 1716, when the University was trying to exploit the reversionary interest in an address to the Prince of Wales and Smalridge was currying favour with the princess, Bromley was working for an address to the prince, now highly popular with the Tories, from his own county of Warwickshire, and four months later was rumoured to have been persuaded by Bolingbroke to enter the ministry with other Tories when an opportunity offered so that 'by accepting anything now [they might] be in a capacity to turn out the remaining Whigs in a short time'. Bromley's course, in short, was very much that of the dominant powers in the University he represented; he accepted the dynasty, became disillusioned at the extent to which the king committed himself to the Whigs, but had hope of an ultimate return to office based on the differences within the royal family and the Whig ranks themselves.[1]

After the alarms of the latter years of the previous reign, Bromley and Whitelock were re-elected in 1715 without opposition, and when Whitelock died in November 1717 the precarious relations between the ministry and the University made a quiet election essential. A court Tory was required of prestige sufficient to prevent any candidate of other connexions being put up and to defeat any wild schemes of the younger and more rebellious members of the University. The requirements were so plain that all the prospective candidates were well known even before Whitelock's death. Delaune would champion young Simon Harcourt if he could; in July 1717, upon a rumour that Whitelock was dead, Dr. Dod, one of the medical fellows of All Souls, had begun to canvass on behalf of the younger and rabid Tories, and was known to be ready to stand again. At the same time Gardiner, Smalridge, Charlett, the other influential heads who affected statesmanship and a predilection for the middle of the road, and the Harleyites produced their trump card in George Clarke, fellow and benefactor of All Souls, virtuoso, formerly of Queen Anne's intimate

---

[1] *Wentworth Papers*, pp. 411, 423, 429; Boyer, *Political State*, ix. 24, 210, 216–18, 280, 397; Cobbett, *Parliamentary History*, vii. 330–4; *Hist. MSS. Comm. Stuart MSS.* ii. 93, 464, iii. 447, iv. 453 *et passim*; Coxe, *Walpole*, ii. 75.

circle and, still earlier, M.P. for the University in James II's parliament.

The election ran its predestined course. The Harcourt interest had no hope in competing for votes against Clarke and withdrew at once. Dod was known already as a trouble-maker in All Souls; he had supported the agitation against the requirement to enter holy orders, and Archbishop Tenison had allotted him to one of four medical fellowships tenable by laymen. Dod hoped for support among 'the young masters who are the warmest', and ill-assorted malcontents who, like Hearne, regarded Clarke as 'more fit for an Alderman than a Member of Parliament for the University'. His electoral problem was to secure at least one of the two great blocks of votes mobilized by Christ Church and Magdalen; the power of the Harleyites was sufficient to deny him the one, while Gardiner and Bromley successfully wooed the other for Clarke. The by no means entirely specious propaganda of the heads 'that Dr Dod is a down-right Jacobite, that he is too ingenious, and that his warmth will bring him into confinement, and that he will expose the University and draw the malice of the government upon it', the genuine merits of Dr. Clarke, and the fact, as Stratford admitted, that unlike other university elections the election of burgesses was not conducted by scrutiny, finally destroyed Dod's chances, and he withdrew leaving a clear field to Clarke. It was unlikely that circumstances would again favour the heads so powerfully, however, and upon rumours that Bromley was dead Dod continued his agitation. Dod was soon at blows with Gardiner again, but became reconciled with Clarke, supported him against King in 1721, and promised benefactions for his building schemes at All Souls.[2]

In his autobiography Clarke wrote as if his election were carried through without his knowledge, but he had been championed as a prospective university burgess as early as 1704 by Dean Aldrich before he had lost office for voting for Bromley to be Speaker. Gardiner, whose cause in college affairs he steadfastly promoted, was urging as early as 1710 that 'nothing but Dr. Clarke's modesty

---

[2] *Hearne's Collections*, vi. 67, 110–12, 120, 122–4, vii. 26; Nichols, *Illustrations*, iii. 282–3; Bodl. MS. Ballard 20, fo. 25; *Hist. MSS. Comm. Portland MSS.* vii. 231, 232, 235, 236, 341; *All Souls Archives*, pp. 292, 293, 320, 321, 333, 338. In London there was talk that Sir Constantine Phipps might stand, presumably in the Chancellor's interest, but he was not heard of in Oxford. Bodl. MS. Ballard 32, fo. 37.

continues people's inclination to Sr. Wm. [Whitelock]', and
Hearne was doubtless well informed in speaking at intervals of
an interest being made for him. Recommended to succeed Blathwaite in 1689, he was Secretary at War 1692–1704, held various
other offices, and sat at intervals in Parliament for different seats
until 1713, keeping closely in touch with university affairs through
Gardiner and Charlett. In Anne's later years he was friendly with
Atterbury, Ormonde, Bolingbroke, Harcourt, and Pope. He
attended Arran's election as Chancellor on his return from France,
and in his autobiography earnestly denied a story put about to
prevent his election in 1717 that on this journey he deliberately
avoided the Duke of Ormonde. In his day Clarke was besieged by
aspirants to fellowships at All Souls, but his greatest mark upon
that and other societies (such as Christ Church) was in the building programmes he promoted and the benefactions which he
made.

   In 1710 he had exerted all his influence to prevent a visitation
of All Souls, in 1718 he was scheming again to prevent a visitation
of the University, and became so embittered at the threats and
experiences of visitations that he transferred the greater part of
the benefactions in his will from All Souls to Worcester, on condition that 'there shall be no appeal to the Visitors, or anywhere
else, from the electors' choice of Fellows and Scholars . . . to avoid
the shameful and unnecessary expences which I have known some
visitors put Colleges to, upon such occasions, and to prevent their
arbitrary and partial proceedings'. Man of affairs, bibliophile,
amateur of the arts, and patron of learned societies, Clarke has
been aptly characterized as 'almost a late-born figure of the
Renaissance'. The University's entanglements with principalities
and powers might be more readily remedied by the more com-
monplace gifts and steadier political application of William
Bromley, yet no one could have been better conceived to silence
present disputes in the University than George Clarke.[3]

   'He yt now fills Sr. Wm. Whitlock's place this parliamt. does
in a manner take possession of it for ye future', remarked Lord
Aylesford in 1717, and so it proved—but not without some violent
alarms at the next general election. Ever since the election of
Delaune as Margaret professor in 1715 with the support of only
two heads, the Whig Warden of Wadham and Shippen of the

---

[3] See note H, p. 281.

Harcourt connexion, there had been the risk that fanatical Whig and Tory juniors might join in common revolt against the leading heads. The risk increased, as we have seen, as the former began to realize that the ministry would not win their battles for them, and as the latter saw that no dividends had accrued from the flirtation with the Prince of Wales. In the election for a Camden professor in May 1720 'all the Whigs voted for Harrison, . . . the most open and professed Turk of this place', and carried the day. Sedgwick Harrison, whose candidates were rebuffed in the next election of fellows at All Souls, replied by beginning an agitation against Clarke at the next parliamentary election, canvassing for Dr. King, Principal of St. Mary Hall.

King, Lord Arran's secretary, had had a grievance against George Clarke since 1716 for preventing Lord Arran from making him an assessor in the Vice-Chancellor's Court, it being 'a most ridiculous thing to make a man a judge, in order to teach him to be a lawyer', and resolved to stand several months before the election. King, whom the Chancellor installed Principal of St. Mary Hall at the end of 1719, had been of Arran's circle from the beginning of the reign, and listed Atterbury among the three persons of his acquaintance eminently possessed of presence of mind (one of the others being physician of Bethlehem Hospital!). His picture gallery included Lely's portraits of the Stuarts, he reckoned the Duke of Ormonde 'the best bred man of his age', and to friends displayed a silver medal of the queen of the titular James III. His circle of acquaintances in 1720 is illustrated by an account of a dinner-party with the Marquis of Caernarvon at Balliol, where he sat down with the two sons of the Earl of Dartmouth, Sir Walter Bagot, Sedgwick Harrison,[4] Lord Craven's brother, Dr. Hunt (then tutor to the marquis), Henry and Stephen Fox, Theophilus Leigh (who succeeded Hunt as Master), and Humphrey Lloyd, one of the Tory fellows of Jesus.

King's Toryism was always of the turbulent sort. In 1718 he was threatening to sue the Principal of Magdalen Hall for fees due to him as the Chancellor's register; championing Hearne against the Vice-Chancellor's censure of his book, he persuaded Lord Arran to put in Dr. Shippen as Vice-Chancellor at the begin-

---

[4] In some manuscript verses circulated against King after the election, and published a generation later, he was represented as being Harrison's tool throughout (*A Satire upon Physicians* (London, 1755), Appendix).

ning of the following year in the hope that he would be more lenient, and through him the affair was patched up. King, of course, approved Thomas Warton's equivocations in 1719, and in 1721 was at loggerheads with Gardiner, Charlett, and their friends, not only for supporting Hearne but because he accused them of ruling the University by fraudulently concealing the statutes. What was known to the government by letters pilfered from the post, but only suspected in the University, was that King had compromised himself with the Jacobites and was in correspondence with Captain Halstead, one of the handful of conspirators taken in Oxford by Pepper in 1715. When the truth leaked out in Oxford late in 1722 Stratford heard 'two of our Heads bless God that they have not drank a bottle with him for six months last past. You know that Act limits information for words to that time.'[5]

King, therefore, hoped to profit from the political and constitutional animosity against the heads who had retained their influence from Queen Anne's reign, and had the special prestige of a close connexion with the Chancellor. With Bromley still labouring to unite the Tories under Wyndham with the Harleyites, King's object was to direct the attack against Clarke, who was visibly the choice of the heads rather than the electors; the heads in their turn sought to deprive King of one of his chief assets, his connexion with the Chancellor. Six months before the election they were exerting pressure on Lord Arran, and it is an interesting comment on his alleged Jacobitism that he soon turned King out of his secretaryship.[6]

As in other times of stress, Oxford dons began to assail each other in the national press. A letter to Arran in *The Weekly Journal* began, according to Hearne, as a circular put out by the Provost of Queen's against King, who printed it in his own cause.

[5] Packington Hall MSS.: Ld. Aylesford to Ld. Guernsey, 14 Aug. 1717; *Hist. MSS. Comm. Portland MSS.* vii. 212, 274, 336; Bodl. MS. Ballard 20, fos. 87, 164; Christ Church MS. Arch. W. Epist. 16, no. 95; W. King, *Political and Literary Anecdotes of his Own Time* (London, 1818), pp. 6–9; *Hearne's Collections*, vi. 204, 210, 375, 400–1, vii. 3, 32, 185; J. P. Phillips, 'College Life at Oxford One Hundred Years Ago', *N. & Q.*, 2nd series, x. 366; P.R.O. SP 35/28, fo. 169, no. 89: /30, fo. 68.

[6] P.R.O. SP 35/28, no. 89; *Hist. MSS. Comm. Portland MSS.* vii. 312; *Hearne's Collections*, vii. 318; Christ Church MS. Arch. W. Epist. 16, no. 95. He was succeeded by Henry Watkins of Christ Church, former secretary to another Tory martyr, Lord Strafford, impeached by the Whigs, 1715–16.

The University, it was claimed, was a 'Sacred Place, where peace
and order ought to reign', but King's methods would make election '*Mobbish* and *Popular*'.

If once the *younger and unthinking part of the university* meet with
success against their *Governors*, they, like a furious horse, will too
soon feel their strength and throw off all *submission*, and, consequently, *opposition* and *rebellion* will be their first *principle*.

Still worse than 'the green understanding of youth' was the fact
that a close contest might give the balance of power to the Whigs,
who, though at present intending to vote 'each according to his
Personal Inclinations', might be organized by any 'great man'
and give the death-blow to Tory supremacy in Oxford.

How the Whigs would behave was a question which perplexed
all shades of Tory opinion, Stratford being scarcely able to credit,
but quite unable to deny, rumours that they would go over to
King in a body. To add to the uncertainty King began to rake up
'many votes, who have no names in any college books, and . . . left
the university many years ago'. The technical qualification for
the franchise was a matter of the greatest obscurity; a specially
prepared paper, still preserved in the university archives, labori-
ously argued that the franchise was confined to doctors and
masters *actualiter creati*, who had paid their fees and kept their
names in the buttery books for six months prior to the election.
But a record number of doubtful votes were cast at the election,
and prolonged litigation might well have followed.[7]

The heads, all but unanimous against King, struck out as many
names as they could from the buttery books, and slandered King
as mercilessly as he had attacked them. Their argument that the
sitting members were entitled to sit until they gave real offence
consorted ill with the precedents since the Revolution, or even
with Clarke's election as one of the wild youth in 1685. The claim
that Clarke was peculiarly acceptable to Bromley was countered
with the evidence that nearly twenty years earlier he had voted
against the Occasional Conformity Bill. A letter from Lord Arran
in favour of the sitting member had to be hastily withdrawn in

[7] *The Weekly Journal*, 10 Feb. 1721/2, reprinted in *Hearne's Collections*, vii.
328-9 (a pamphlet which has proved impossible to trace is discussed in Christ
Church MS. Arch. W. Epist. 16, no. 97); *Hist. MSS. Comm. Portland MSS.* vii.
314, 317; University Archives: MS. S.P.C. 6, 'Concerning the Qualifications of
an Elector in the Elections of Burgesses for the University of Oxford.'

face of the charge a peer ought not to interfere in the election of commoners. But the heads exerted the utmost pressure upon members of their houses, Dr. Morley, Rector of Lincoln, and Dr. Gibson, Provost of Queen's, being especially savage. According to Sedgwick Harrison no pains were spared to persuade the Earl of Abingdon to exclude Edward Bertie, student of Christ Church, from his will for promising to vote for King.[8] All this campaigning had its effect, and when the poll was completed on 21 March 1722 it read:

> W. King   159
> G. Clarke   278
> W. Bromley 338

Each candidate polled a large number of doubtful votes, but although King called for a scrutiny the following day, he was much too far in arrear to make it worth while to challenge them.

The poll nevertheless contained some surprises. Only Brasenose, Christ Church, New College, Oriel, Queen's, University, and Hart Hall voted with tolerable unanimity for Bromley and Clarke. Morley's efforts at Lincoln had failed to prevent the majority of second votes being cast for King. He had been the first choice of Balliol whose erratic Master, Dr. Hunt, suffered much abuse for allowing such favour to an old member of his society, and he rallied also the minority Tory faction of Jesus, a large minority of St. John's, Magdalen, and Trinity,[9] and, of course, the unanimous support of St. Mary Hall. The piquant feature of the poll, however, was the voting of the Whigs. 'It was pretty remarkable', commented Stratford, 'that Meadowcourt of Merton, who informed against Wharton, and Wharton himself, both voted singly for King', but it was still more remarkable that King should receive the unanimous testimony of Exeter, the votes of the leaders of the dissident interest at Merton, and half a dozen more from Wadham, all these voters being aggressive anti-

---

[8] There was also strong episcopal pressure which provoked a pamphlet entitled *Copy of a Letter to a Certain B[ishop] on Account of a Pragmatical Interposition in a Late Election for the U[niversity] of O[xford]* (n. pl. or d.). The offending prelate appears to be Gibson, though it is stated that he was not educated at Oxford.

[9] At Trinity King's supporters included scholars whom the President had recently held back from their degrees to prevent their election as fellows to the detriment of the court interest in the college (*Whitehall Evening Post*, 8–10 June 1721).

Jacobites. Court Whigs like Carter, Clavering, or Holland were plainly for the existing order in the interests of moderation and university discipline, but the factious were for an upheaval of any kind. Stratford's explanation was that through his friend Dr. Munro, later the astute physician of Bethlehem, King had applied to Lord Chancellor Macclesfield, who had dispatched his purse-bearer, Sir John Doyley, himself an Oxfordshire man, to the University accordingly. Nevertheless, King's relations with the Whigs remained a matter of controversy, and even a generation later he was reproached with having applied to Walpole for the Whig vote.[10]

The conflict did not end with the poll. The heads struck first by instructing 'that most egregious Coxcomb and Rascal, Joseph Bowles', Keeper of the Bodleian, and tool of the Provost of Oriel, who after repeatedly promising to vote for King had actually served as writer to the other side, to publish the poll. By this means they sought to discredit King by showing that he had polled badly among the foundation members (whom he described as less independent than the non-resident members), and by annotating votes as 'doubtful', and so forth, in a way King's friends considered libellous. Harrison alleged that the heads had resolved to attack King's main stronghold by ordering their 'Inspectors... to object to all Balliol votes except the Fellows'. A few months later Sedgwick Harrison produced the pamphlet already quoted in which he replied in great detail to all the charges made against King. This pamphlet was held back as a prelude to the next stage in the campaign, which opened in the autumn.

On 25 October 1722 King petitioned the House of Commons that Bromley and Clarke had been unduly returned by means of the illegal practices of the Vice-Chancellor as returning officer, and was supported by another petition from Sedgwick Harrison, Robert Brynker, a turbulent Tory of Jesus, Joseph Sanford of Balliol, and others, alleging the same illegalities and also that 'Mr. Bromley was not qualified to serve, as by the Charter he ought to be'. The point of this charge was that the charter under which the University chose its burgesses 'plainly directed [them]

[10] [S. Harrison], *An Account of the Late Election for the University of Oxford* (London, 1722); *A True Copy of the Poll for Members of Parliament for the University of Oxford taken March the 21st, 1721* (Oxford, 1722); *Hist. MSS. Comm. Portland MSS.* vii. 317–18.

to chuse out of [their] own body'. This was a normal requirement of borough charters, and was never enforced, but King's friends claimed that it should be strictly construed in the universities whose representatives were exempt from the property qualification.

King went up to London 'with a resolution as he told his cronies . . . , to call Walpole, Bromley and Clarke to account', while his enemies harked back to the mystery of the Whig votes and reported Walpole as affirming that King had solicited his interest to obtain a favourable hearing for his petition at the price of informing against members of the University who were disaffected to the government. This King denied in an eloquent advertisement in *The Evening Post* typical of those which characterized his later career. Stratford declared the advertisement irrelevant as he was sure the scheme was engineered by King's 'brother-in-law, one Withers, a hearty Whig'. The whole transaction ended in mystery, for although Stratford continued to relate the story as coming from Walpole and to expect 'that there will be a narrative of the plot laid before the House', there were no further proceedings on the plot or the petitions, and for King the whole enterprise proved an unrewarding failure. According to Hearne, however, the acrimony which followed the election had at least one significant consequence, that in July 1722, in the election of a new President of Magdalen, Robert Lydall the favoured candidate was defeated by the resentment of the junior fellows at his treachery towards King, and Edward Butler, himself a future university burgess, was elected.[11]

The confused decade which followed the Hanoverian accession marked the climax of a generation of political turmoil which deeply marked both the University and colleges. Domestic conflicts in which politics had been a principal ingredient had cost All Souls, Magdalen Hall, and Wadham large endowments, and, on the other hand, had contributed to the establishment of Gloucester Hall as Worcester College. All Souls was clamped more firmly than ever to the obligation of electing founders' kin

[11] *Hearne's Collections*, vii. 349, 388, viii. 21–22; *C.J.* xx. 43; *Hist. MSS. Comm. Portland MSS.* vii. 340, 341, 345. A satire of King's petition in verse, said to be contemporary, was published later in *A Satire upon Physicians* (London, 1755), pp. 60–63.

to fellowships, University College ended with a completely new (though hardly more satisfactory) set of statutes, and with Oriel had been pronounced by the courts to be a royal foundation subject to royal visitation. Violence had been done to the statutes of Balliol, and avoided only by a damaging contest in Christ Church and Oriel.

There had been extraordinary activity by local Visitors, and no one knew that there would be no future political threat from the ministers of like intensity. Nor had the professional standards of the University been improved by the faction struggles in Jesus, Exeter, Merton, Wadham, and elsewhere, or by the methods employed by heads such as Shippen to sustain their interest in their own House and University. None of the major political connexions, whether owing allegiance to Harcourt, Harley, or the Whigs, had scrupled to bring pressure to bear upon the University from the outside, and none reaped the full harvest for which they had hoped. No serious study of the reasons for the academic decline of Oxford in the middle of the eighteenth century has ever been attempted, but among them must be reckoned the sacrifices made to politics in these years, sacrifices which the University, as a school of the Church in a time when political and ecclesiastical disputes were not readily distinguished, could hardly avoid making. There were mistaken Whigs who thought that the Tory leaders had been plotting a Jacobite restoration on the eve of Anne's death and that serious conspiracy continued in Oxford: there were mistaken Tories who thought that the Whigs seriously intended to undermine the Church by encouraging occasional conformity and heterodox theology, and there were many prepared to exploit the illusions of both in a crude struggle for the profits of politics. Oxford paid heavily for the shortcomings of all three.

From a political viewpoint the Oxford battle proved inconclusive. Amhurst exaggerated Whig gains in his famous couplet:

> From our old track whole colleges depart
> And preach new doctrines with Hoadleian art.

The Whigs consolidated their hold in a number of colleges and steadily increased it in Christ Church, but the failure of the ministry either to carry out a visitation or to organize their ecclesiastical patronage ruthlessly for partisan ends prevented

anything like a general upheaval. Moreover, the early influence
of Wake, and the subsequent rise of Gibson, checked the spread
of Hoadleian arts even in the Whig ranks. The first quarter of
the eighteenth century, however, was sufficient to shatter any
truth there had ever been in the claim of the leading heads that
unanimity was the hall-mark of academic politics. Here Amhurst
wrote at his best:

> The spirit of unanimity continues amongst them still; Oxford is
> just the same in its ancient and in its present state; Whigs and Tories,
> Georgites and Jacobites, orthodox and unorthodox are not the only
> distinctions; but they have also their various divisions and sub-
> divisions; we see Whigs engaged against Whigs, Tories against Tories,
> masters against doctors and heads of colleges, senior fellows against
> junior fellows, one college against another college, and many colleges
> against themselves.

According to Amhurst such chaos must result when pedantic
dons pledged to an obsolete academic system began to play at
politics, but the truth was that at Oxford as at Westminster the
realignment of connexions had begun which in half a century was
to leave the political world divided unambiguously into Court and
Country. Already the Oxford Tories had lost Dr. Carter, the
Provost of Oriel, the archetype of the court politicians who
steadily deserted the connexion in less spectacular fashion over
the years; already there was a minority of Whigs who found
either that there was not pasture enough to feed the beasts or
that Whigs with a monopoly of power ill resembled their opposition forebears. In Oxford, as in the country as a whole, the Whig
ranks were losing their 'country' adherents, though Oxford had
never cultivated the confessing 'independent' or 'real' Whigs who
kept alive a Radical tradition down the century. Dr. King in some
respects justified the coalition of rebellious Whigs and Tories who
supported him, for in time he evolved from loyalty to the dispossessed court over the water to orthodox 'country' hostility to
court influence of any kind.[22]

[22] N. Amhurst, *Oculus Britanniae*, p. 40; *Terrae Filius*, i. 37.

PART III

OXFORD IN OPPOSITION
1725–51

That nursery of nonsense and bigotry, Oxford. . . .

Horace Walpole to George Montagu, 30 May 1751

O this sink of debauchery! O this school of sedition; . . . what sort of mortals must those gentry be, who send their sons to Oxford to be instructed in the principles of religion, morality, and government?

[George Coade], *A Blow at the Root* (1749)

CHAPTER IX

A New Whig Connexion

BEFORE Hanoverian rule had completed its first decade, the ministry had abandoned its hopes of a visitation at Oxford, and had little more to gain from exerting pressure on college elections. The sweeping victories obtained by court influence in the central administration, in local government, and in the House of Commons were not to be repeated in Oxford. Yet the ministers could afford to disregard neither the literary power of universities still mainly in the hands of their enemies, nor their influence in forming those potent propagandists, the parish priests. Edmund Gibson, Bishop of London and the most influential of Whig churchmen, suggested a policy of inducement rather than compulsion. In 1723 he launched a scheme for Whitehall preachers by which twelve dons from each University of approved scholarship and Whig principles should take a regular turn of service at the Royal Chapel. An adequate stipend was offered, as well as the prospect of subsequent appointment as chaplains to the king. By this means Gibson hoped to benefit court society, which never seemed to him totally beyond redemption, and to further the Whig cause in the universities by enabling the favoured preachers to 'answer objections against the administration, and confute the lies and misrepresentations of the enemy upon their own knowledge and observation'.[1] Stratford was right in supposing that this inexpensive scheme for confounding the devil in both court and academic dress would 'not increase the number of honest thorough Whigs; [and] rather unite and confirm, than break the perverse Tories',[2] but at least the ministers might now reward less inadequately some who had gone to great lengths for them.

In the following year Gibson and Townshend concerted a more substantial act of grace, the foundation at each university ('to reduce them to a better sense of their duty')[3] of a regius chair of modern history and languages. The character of this timely act of royal munificence owed much to the almost Fabian illusion of Whig intellectuals that Tory principles could not survive an historical education, and to the more accurate conviction, pressed on the ministry by David Gregory, the first holder of the Oxford chair, that

the methods of education in our universities have been in some measure defective, since we are obliged to adhere so much to the rules laid down by our forefathers . . . the old scholastic learning has been for some time despised, but not altogether exploded, because nothing else has been substituted in its place.[4]

By combining the study of modern languages with that of history a flow of trained recruits for the diplomatic service might be created, and new vigour imparted to the Whig cause in the University. The king's friends at Cambridge produced an effusive address of gratitude, but at Oxford, according to manuscript verses which circulated amongst the aristocracy, 'the present was near upon being refused'.[5] Neither the academic nor the political motives of the benefaction were such as to arouse enthusiasm, and a crowded Convocation passed a chilly letter of thanks, rejoicing that the hours for teaching modern languages would not interfere

---

[1] N. Sykes, *Edmund Gibson* (London, 1926), pp. 92–94. Gibson's further plan reminiscent of the days of Atterbury, to distribute prebends to the king's friends in the universities came to nothing.

[2] *Hist. MSS. Comm. Portland MSS.* vii. 377.

[3] W. Coxe, *Memoirs of Sir Robert Walpole*, ii. 299.

[4] P.R.O. SP 36/6, fo. 227.

[5] Lamport Hall: Westmorland MSS. W. (A) 4. IV. 4 (13).

with the traditional curriculum, and very cynically acknowledging his 'Majesty's gracious tenderness towards our ancient constitution'.[6]

This letter was naturally ill received at Court, and was denounced in the Whig press as 'too jejune, and the manner of sending it up by one of the Beadles, disrespectful'; when Townshend informed the University of the passing of the letters patent, he made it quite clear that the king expected a display of gratitude now, and the Dean of Christ Church was sent down to Oxford to produce it. As it transpired, although there was some precedent for sending just a letter on such an occasion, only the Vice-Chancellor, Gardiner, Shippen, and the Rector of Lincoln thought it worth while to defy the government again, and Delaune was enthusiastically in favour of an address. The efforts of the Whig heads to make assurances of political subservience were defeated, but the address was gracious enough, and the presentation was marred only by the dithering of the Vice-Chancellor, Dr. Mather, who 'was in a maze'.[7]

The Whigs, however, were at their most ineffective in ecclesiastical affairs, and did not persist even in the policy which had led to the foundation of the modern history chair. Townshend exercised great self-abnegation in passing over his two favourite candidates in the interest of an 'unexceptionable' appointment, that of David Gregory, who at the age of twenty-eight was no great historian. But despite Newcastle's solicitous attention to the interests of Old Westminsters,[8] the government made no attempt to keep up the number or safeguard the prospects of the king's scholars. One valuable Whig propagandist, Dr. Tottie of Worcester, was bred in this stable, but the chair was allowed to become a sinecure, and was resigned by Gregory in 1736. To guarantee the political fidelity of the professor the appointment was originally renewable every twelve months, but Gregory's successor, William Holmes, President of St. John's, orthodox theologian, and late Vice-Chancellor, not only protested that 'there were few less capable' of making a success of the benefaction than himself,[9] but

---

[6] University Archives: MS. Conv. Reg. Bd 31, fo. 208; *Hearne's Collections*, viii. 214.

[7] Boyer, *Political State*, xxviii. 479–80; University Archives: MS. Conv. Reg. Bd 31, fos. 214–17; *Hist. MSS. Comm. Portland MSS.* vii. 387–90.

[8] P.R.O. SP 35/64, fo. 335.

[9] On this and the whole question of the benefaction: Sykes, op. cit., pp. 94–107;

matched the action to the word by voting for a Tory burgess for
the University within a year. The difficulty of managing university Whigs like Holmes may be among the reasons why the ministers failed to persevere in their policies at Oxford, for as one of
the king's chaplains he had looked a safe candidate. Herein lay
the trouble, however, for the government regarded 'the removal
of Holmes . . . [as] certainly impracticable, on account of his
having been preferred by the Royal Family here, and having
since procured the Archbishop's friendship',[10] connexions which
enabled him to add the deanery of Exeter to his other preferments in 1742.

Nevertheless, the steady pull of court influence had its effect in
Oxford as elsewhere, and there were greater efforts to put on an
appearance of conformity. Hearne no longer attended at what he
regarded as an apostate church, but was constantly infuriated by
reports of 'vile, Whiggish stuff' from Oxford pulpits. The establishment of the modern history chair gave an obvious opening to
Streat of Merton,

who, as he is a most rank, vile Whig, so he extoll'd this Prince . . . in as
lofty colours as he could, telling them, in the usual manner, that he
was the most excellent that ever sat upon the Throne, and that his
goodness and virtues are universally seen and acknowledg'd, even in
all countries, that he is a most generous & kind Friend and Benefactor
to our two Universities, with abundance of other canting stuff.

Preachers took the ministerial cue more frequently than since the
earliest days of the new dynasty,[11] and if on the king's birthday
in 1727 'Jonathan Colley . . . Chantor of Xt Church . . . set a
penitential anthem', it was probably to spite the Dean more than
His Majesty.[12]

Moreover, there was immediate action against the Tory scandal
of George Coningsby's sermon commemorating King Charles the

Sir Charles Firth, 'Modern History in Oxford, 1724–1841', in *E.H.R.* xxxii. 3–12;
P.R.O. SP 35/50, fo. 14.
   [10] *Hist. MSS. Comm. R14, App. pt. ix, Buckinghamshire MSS.*, p. 10; Holmes
was regarded by the Whig gentry as 'a Gentell man & very ingenious' (*Verney
Letters of the 18th Century*, ii. 69), but was an object of scorn to the Tories
(*D.N.B.*). Ministerial circles had been aware of his political unreliability before
his appointment (Coxe, *Walpole*, iii. 136). For his theological views, *Hist. MSS.
Comm. Egmont Diary*, i. 402.
   [11] *Hearne's Collections*, viii. 387, 408, x. 65, xi. 69.
   [12] Ibid. ix. 310.

Martyr in 1727. Coningsby had originated from Wadham, but as
an admirer of Dr. King had migrated about 1720 to St. Mary Hall,
and had obtained some notice for a university sermon in 1722 in
which he violently denounced the anti-trinitarians and equated
them with libertines. Hearne regarded him as 'a good preacher
and . . . (as a Complyer) an honest man', and in this character in
1727 he commended Charles I as 'a Prince that was not alien by
birth, & that he preferred to dignities in the Church men of true
worth and learning'. For this offence to the king and bench of
bishops he was summoned before the Vice-Chancellor and a committee of heads and doctors. This committee was heavily weighted
in the Whig interest, presumably because, apart from Shippen,
the Tory heads either decided not to risk a conflict or were not
invited by the Vice-Chancellor. Coningsby fell back on the thread-
bare defence that he had lost his notes, was convicted of preaching
doctrines 'of a seditious tendency & highly reflecting on the
present government, the publishing of which . . . might prove
very prejudicial to the University and the governors of it', and
was sentenced to permanent suspension from preaching in the
University. This prompt action was doubtless stimulated by the
knowledge that Whig informers had already been in touch with
Gibson, through whom the matter was laid before the king. The
Vice-Chancellor and heads received a letter of commendation
from Townshend,[13] Coningsby was exempted from one of the
burdens of university life, and after transferring to Balliol as tutor
to the grandson of the eccentric Lord Peterborough, received preferment in his native county of Hereford. Stratford thought him
badly treated, but the matter blew over, and twelve years later
the censure was removed by two of the surviving judges.[14]

Not only the sermons but the bells too rang to the appropriate
official tune on most of the public celebrations, and the House of
Lords never resumed the discussion of Oxford bell-ringing it had
abandoned in 1717.[15] University addresses containing a fair show

[13] As usual on official occasions, Vice-Chancellor Mather broke down, thank-
ing the king for 'so favourably resenting [sic] what they did' (P.R.O. SP 35/64,
fo. 110).
[14] G. Coningsby, *The Folly of Opposing Natural Reason to the Doctrine of
the Trinity* (Oxford, 2nd edn. 1723); *Hearne's Collections*, ix. 65, 263, 266, 269;
University Archives: MS. Conv. Reg. Bd 31, fos. x, xi; *Hist. MSS. Comm. Portland MSS.* vii. 455.
[15] *Hearne's Collections*, viii. 217, ix. 310, 355, 363, 405, x. 88–89.

of loyalty were sent up to the king as regularly as in the golden days of yore. When in the act of attainder Atterbury reaped the ultimate reward of an unmanageable temper, he was repeatedly attacked from Oxford pulpits, and though he had his sympathizers, the University addressed loyally.[16] The University expressed its concern at the peril of His Majesty's person from the Pretender in March 1727 (though the address was only carried by a small majority),[17] and began the new reign of George II with temperate expressions of joy, looking forward to the day when, 'upon a nearer and more intimate experience', the king would 'more fully discover in her, the genuine character of an undissembled loyalty, a loyalty . . . arising from the pure fountains of reason and revelation'. On the marriage of the Prince of Wales the University enthusiastically addressed the king again, and annually for some years thereafter congratulated him upon each successive increase in the prince's family.[18]

Even in 1723 Townshend, who had a pathological fear of their politics, admitted that 'the universities . . . behaved themselves at least inoffensively', and the new reign offered the opportunity for an even brighter gloss. His Majesty was proclaimed 'with universal applause, and loud acclamations of *Long Live King George the Second*', and all the traditional celebrations. For the first time for many years a book of congratulatory verses was produced, displaying the skill and sentiments of all the Whig heads; according to Hearne, Warton the notorious poetry professor had a good English copy rejected 'under pretence of reflecting upon Q. Eliz., but . . . the true reason was that there were girds . . . on the present usurpers & their agents'.

Once in print the Oxford poetasters were not lightly to be restrained. At the end of 1733 the Prince of Orange came to England to be married to the Princess Anne, George II's eldest daughter; the marriage was postponed owing to his illness, and on the prince's return from his convalescence at Bath the following March he stayed for a few days at Christ Church to see the sights of Oxford. This visit aroused the greatest enthusiasm, the

[16] *Hearne's Collections*, viii. 81; C. Thornton and F. McLaughlin, *The Fothergills of Ravenstonedale* (London, 1905), p. 84; P.R.O. SP 35/54, fo. 327.

[17] *Hearne's Collections*, ix. 288, 292.

[18] University Archives: MS. Conv. Reg. Bd 31, fos. 242, 246: Be 32, fos. 58, 83, 95, 107; B.M. Add. MS. 29601, fo. 99; Queen's College MS. 473; *Hearne's Collections*, ix. 320, 326.

climax of which was reached when, like William III as Prince of Orange in 1670, the prince received a doctorate in the Theatre packed with a record concourse exceeding 4,000. This splendid homage to the representative of the usurper of 1688 was crowned on the occasion of the marriage by a book of fulsome praises in English, Welsh, Latin, Greek, and Hebrew verse. As usual the ministry had its observers, but (notwithstanding the jaundiced imagination of Hearne) the daily diary transmitted to Newcastle by David Gregory, the regius professor of modern history, could give nothing but satisfaction. On the original wedding day the foundation stone of the new cloister at Queen's had been officially laid, complete with loyal inscription in honour of the queen's special benefaction of £1,000, so that the whole matrimonial celebration had been a great success in Oxford. On the marriage of the Prince of Wales to Augusta of Saxe-Gotha in 1736 the ministry might suspect a double edge to the congratulatory verses poured forth, but the University was giving a public pledge of the loyalty to the dynasty which, with some discomfort, the majority of its members had borne from the beginning.[19]

After the disappointment over the modern history chair, Walpole's ministries had obtained sufficient pledges of conformity by respecting the independence of the University, and had prevented the prestige of Oxford from being conferred on any serious act of opposition. Moreover, what time and the influence of crown patronage did not accomplish might be achieved by a new generation of Whig leaders in Oxford. Outstanding among these was John Conybeare. Highly thought of when he first came up to Exeter in 1708, he was elected fellow in 1710, three years before proceeding to his B.A. degree. He early became known to the government as an energetic supporter of the Constitution Club in the attack on Warton, but his ultimate success and failure turned on two other connexions. Conybeare was both a popular preacher and an orthodox if somewhat unexciting theologian. In reply to the modernist writers he published a university sermon on

---

[19] *Hist. MSS. Comm. Weston Underwood MSS.*, p. 428; *Hearne's Collections*, ix. 321, 355–6, xi. 304, 309–10, 315, 318–20; B.M. Add. MS. 32689, fo. 168; *Epithalamia Oxoniensia* (Oxford, 1734); Queen's College MS. 474, press cutting dated Oxford, 14 Nov. [1733]; *Gratulatio Academiae Oxoniensis . . .* (Oxford, 1736). Hervey's cynicism about the University's enthusiasm for the Prince of Orange shows how difficult it was for Oxford men ever to give satisfaction to those in authority (Hervey, *Memoirs*, i. 224).

miracles in 1722 which went rapidly through four editions, and followed it up with another, *The Mysteries of the Christian Religion Credible*. In 1725 he justified subscription to the XXXIX Articles in another sermon which earned him even a posthumous notoriety. This combination of Whig and Anglican orthodoxy made Conybeare a man after Gibson's heart. Gibson had him appointed a Whitehall preacher, and in 1732 accepted the dedication of his attack upon Tindal's *Christianity as old as the Creation*, by which time Conybeare's theological reputation extended overseas. He had also been taken up by the Whig laity; Macclesfield presented him to the rectory of St. Clement's, Oxford, and Talbot, Solicitor General and son of the Bishop of Durham, made him tutor to his two sons. To the Talbots were dedicated sermons of 1727 and 1729, but expectations of preferment were extinguished by the death of the bishop, and Conybeare succeeded the parsimonious Matthew Hole as Rector of Exeter College.

His hopes were now pinned on Gibson, whose opportunity came with the death of the Dean of Christ Church at the end of 1732. It was pressed on the Court that 'the way is now open to fix and warn that College in duty and affection to their Majesties', and that 'the streams that flow from Westminster will mend those of Isis'. Conybeare, whose straitened finances might be eased by the Deanery, fitted the first requirement perfectly, and though it was admitted that he would 'not please the Christ Church men so well as if he had been a Westminster scholar . . . that is their only objection to him'. A lampoon on the Oxford heads excepted Conybeare from censure as

> a rev'rend Sage.
> Alma's chief Fav'rite! Glory of his Age,

and henceforth it was his responsibility to marshal the Whig interest, to accommodate the embarrassing flood of Westminster alumni sponsored by Newcastle, and bear the brunt of the Tory pamphleteers who ascribed the inspiration of 'his mercenary pen' to 'hopes of lawn sleeves'. Conybeare's aspirations to the bench were dimmed a second time, however, by Gibson's fall from political favour, and only in 1750 was he raised to the impoverished See of Bristol—even at which late date he still felt entitled to interfere in the management of his old society, Exeter College.[20]

[20] See note I, p. 281.

Besides Conybeare there were lesser lights, some of whom were
to be among the chief Whig propagandists in the great contests
of the next decade. Prominent among these was John Burton,
fellow of Corpus. 'He was intimately connected with many of the
bishops; and perhaps he was the more acceptable to them, as he
never asked anything for himself. A Hayter, a Lowth and a Secker
were in the number of his friends', besides Bishop Potter. Hearne,
despite a sneaking regard for his antiquarian interests, naturally
detested him as an 'indiscreet' pro-proctor, and because in 1728 he
had made a scene in Convocation against a letter from the Chancellor to confer the degree of M.D. by diploma upon a non-juror,
but was absent a few months later when the same privilege was
sought for one of his fellow collegians, who was a Latitudinarian
and a friend of the Duchess of Marlborough. In 1729 he dedicated
to the Provost of Eton two Latin sermons in which he advocated
some reforms in the University. In 1733 Burton sought new
pastures as a fellow of Eton, rector of Maple Durham (the best of
the Eton livings), and a Georgia trustee, but regularly preached
in the university pulpit, wrote on university affairs, and had
already instilled his notions on politics and university reform into
his cousin and pupil, Edward Bentham.[21] The latter was as yet
unknown; graduating from Corpus he became Vice-Principal of
Magdalen Hall in 1730 and fellow of Oriel in 1731. It was here, in
the next great crisis in the University, that he first gained his
reputation as a defender of the cause of the cousin who pushed
him forward. Gibbon wrote of him much later as 'still treading
in the footsteps of a Burton, whose maxims he had adopted, and
whose life he published'. Gibbon was prepared to think comparatively kindly of Burton, but was not alone in regarding
Bentham as an inferior copy of a not particularly outstanding
original.[22]

Apart from Holmes, President of St. John's,

[21] *Hearne's Collections*, ix. 72, x. 5, 40, 212–13, 253, xi. 263; *Biographia Britannica*, iii. 48. It was through him as a Georgia trustee that the Wesley brothers
went out to Georgia, *Journal of John Wesley*, ed. N. Curnock (London, 1916),
viii. 285–91; *Hist. MSS. Comm. Egmont Diary*, ii. 194, 196. See also H. B. Fant,
'John Burton D.D., one of the founders of the Colony of Georgia', in *Oxoniensia*,
vi. 70–83. Another Whig fellow of Corpus was Nathaniel Forster, whose correspondence is preserved in B.M. Add. MS. 11275.
[22] E. Gibbon, *Memoirs of my life and writings*, ed. G. B. Hill (London, 1900),
p. 80; cf. *D.N.B.* Boswell and Johnson formed a livelier impression: *Boswell's
Life of Johnson*, ed. G. B. Hill, revised L. F. Powell, ii. 445.

A fawning Flatterer, a holy cheat!
Cunning in mischief! practis'd in Deceit!

and Tottie of Worcester, both already mentioned, the old Whig
stronghold at Merton still held fast to the faith, while Exeter was
more Whiggish than ever. Outstanding among the younger
fellows was Francis Webber, already a friend of the influential
Conybeare, who resigned his living of St. Clement's, Oxford, to
him on succeeding to the Deanery. Among the first to resume
the publication of aggressive Whig propaganda in the next
decade, he was to prove a stormy petrel in later years.[23] Of an
older generation was Henry Felton, Principal of St. Edmund
Hall from 1722, a place he is said to have been given 'upon account
of a living that he is to secure from the Duke of Rutland to one
of Queen's Coll. Fellows, as soon as it falls'. He was chaplain to
successive Whig dukes of Rutland from 1709, and from them
received the livings of Whitwell and Barwick-in-Elmet. Though
on ill terms with his Whig predecessor Mill, Felton became a
Whig of the orthodox Gibson school. In his sermons, which were
anathema to Hearne, he condemned Atterbury's conspiracy, and
gave offence to the Tories in commemorating King Charles the
Martyr in 1732; he wrote against Papists and various Protestants
who deviated from the XXXIX Articles, and recommended himself to Smalbrook, the Whig Bishop of Lichfield, in the dedica-
tions. He was a member of the Whiggish deputation which
presented the University's address of thanks for the modern
history chair, and was unsuccessfully backed by Dr. Gibson,
Provost of Queen's and cousin of the Bishop of London, for the
Margaret professorship in 1728. Felton created something of an
upheaval in his own society and was good for a vote or other
service in the Whig cause till his death in 1740.[24]

A young Whig apostle was John Fanshawe, student of Christ
Church, who became regius professor of Greek in 1735 and proved
a sturdy supporter of Robert Trevor, the Whig parliamentary
candidate in 1737. So well did he serve the ministry in Convocation and elsewhere that in 1747 he was seriously considered by
the Pelhams for the sees of both Bristol and Oxford, but not

---

[23] *Alma Mater*, p. 28; *Biographia Britannica*, iv. 92.

[24] Bodl. MS. Top. Oxon. e 145, fo. 3; *Hearne's Collections*, viii. 24, 81, 293,
ix. 64, 309, x. 17, xi. 24, 254; *Hist. MSS. Comm. Portland MSS.* vii. 346, 462-3,
469-70.

being recommended by the archbishop he had to be content with the regius chair of divinity.[25] The rise of Fanshawe was symptomatic of developments in Christ Church as a whole. Uniquely exposed to the influence of crown patronage, the political complexion of the House altered more rapidly than that of any other society in the generation between King's forlorn hope in 1722 and the election of Newdigate in 1751. At the earlier date Christ Church was solidly behind the orthodox Toryism prevalent in the University, though still divided between the protégés of Harley and those of Atterbury and Bolingbroke. Stratford complained in 1726 that Dean Bradshaw's efforts 'to convert and new model the whole society' could not but divide it 'into distinct parties of Whig and Tory', a division which was almost equal at the election of 1737. The death of the old canons, however, the pressure of Conybeare, and a constant infusion of the pure streams of Westminster turned the House into an almost exclusive club of ministerial Whiggism by 1750. By this time Newcastle was of the opinion that a more active Dean than Conybeare (such as Fanshawe) was desirable, but the college was politically sound enough, suppressing isolated outbreaks of alcoholic Jacobitism among the undergraduate members with exemplary thoroughness. So jealously did the king guard senior appointments that even the Prince of Wales could hardly make a canon.[26]

The ministerial interest was thus consolidated in Wadham and Exeter, but Christ Church was their only major gain, and in a parliamentary election isolated Whig converts in other societies counted for little while the old Tory strongholds still held fast, and the loss of Christ Church was counterbalanced by the evolution of Magdalen under the rule of Edward Butler into a solidly Tory society. Moreover, the bitter feuds which had set Atterbury against the Harleyites, and King against Clarke, were gradually forgotten as the Tory connexions faced an apparently endless period in the wilderness. Oxford's reputed affection for lost causes had been little in evidence while the Tory factions had access to the spoils of politics, and the old loyalties could hardly have

[25] *Hist. MSS. Comm. R14, App. pt. ix, Buckinghamshire MSS.*, p. 10; B.M. Add. MSS. 32711, fo. 186: 32716, fos. 176, 379: 32887, fo. 69.
[26] *Hist. MSS. Comm. Portland MSS.* vii. 441; B.M. Add. MSS. 32689, fo. 202 (cf. Lord Fitzmaurice, *Life of Shelburne* (London, 1912), i. 14): 32716, fos. 176, 379: 32717, fos. 235, 300: 35409, fo. 317; Bodl. MS. Rawl. Lett. 96, fo. 435; H. L. Thompson, *Christ Church* (London, 1900), pp. 153-4.

become so deeply ingrained but for the character of Whig church policy. Gibson urged the government to use ecclesiastical patronage for the exclusive benefit of the Whig clergy, and thus to dragoon the Church into court politics as the ministry had hoped to dragoon the universities. The body of the clergy were treated as political outcasts, and Townshend and Walpole had no scruple in indiscriminately abusing their political opponents both lay and clerical as Jacobites. It was not only Oxford men who cherished old scores, for in 1728 it was rumoured in the University that 'it is still remembered who was and who was not chosen chancellor here in the beginning of the late reign, and that it has been declared that no visit shall be made to this place' by the royal family.[27]

In both University and Church this policy of proscription and abuse embittered the court Tories who had originally hoped to secure office under the new dynasty. Gibson himself admitted in 1727 that 'the body of Tory priests had stood entire for fourteen years last past, whereas the number of Whig presbyters was much narrowed by frequent removes to the bench';[28] the narrow basis of preferment had the same effects in Oxford of restricting the growth of the church Whig interest and uniting the Tories in frustrated and disillusioned opposition to the ministerial system in Church and State. Indeed, the one minister to be complimented by the University was Lord Chancellor Talbot who received a degree in 1735 for his unsuccessful contest with Gibson for the nomination to the See of Gloucester.[29]

Yet Gibson's failures were not solely due to the narrowness of his policy; he suffered from the perennial irresponsibility of the lay Whigs towards their ecclesiastical allies. Particularly where lesser preferments were concerned, the lay Whigs were all too ready to confer private favours, to the mortification of the martyrs of the party and the delight of its enemies. In Oxford, of the heroes of the Constitution Club only Conybeare attained any eminence, and even he was denied for twenty years the bishopric which everyone expected. The arch-conspirator Meadowcourt waited over fifteen years for a mere canonry, too long despite his unfortunate choice of patrons. Again, the party advantage ex-

---

[27] *Hist. MSS. Comm. Portland MSS.* vii. 461.
[28] For this quotation and the whole question see Sykes, *Gibson*, pp. 120–1.
[29] Earl of Ilchester, *Lord Hervey and his Friends* (London, 1950), p. 227.

pected from the foundation of the regius chair of modern history was never reaped, because Gibson's initiative was backed by no steadiness of ministerial policy. The government scarcely deserved to establish an influential court party in Oxford.

For the time being the ministers ceased to bully Oxford societies, but not all private Whigs followed suit. John Anstis, Garter Principal King of Arms, was a renegade Tory who had gone over to the Whigs and obtained the reversion of his place for his son of the same name, whom he entered at Corpus as a pupil of the Whig John Burton. In 1728 young Anstis was a candidate for a fellowship at All Souls, his father producing elaborate evidence that he was of the founder's kin. No election was made, and upon devolution to the Archbishop of Canterbury as college Visitor, Anstis appealed unsuccessfully. In the following year he stood again, but the college, thinking poorly both of founder's kin in general and his academic attainments in particular, elected another candidate. Anstis 'again appealed, but the Archbishop thinking him disqualified, dismissed his complaint. This behaviour so provoked the father that he did his utmost to wrest the visitatorial power out of the hands of the Archbishop and to vest it in those of the Crown.' He therefore petitioned the king to require the Attorney General to report whether the visitation of All Souls 'did not reside in his Majesty, and in case it did, that his Majesty would hear his complaint either in Privy Council or by his Chancellor or Delegates'. The legal basis for this case was so flimsy that no action was ever taken, but how distasteful it remained in the memory of the college was well illustrated in Wenman's History. Hearne, with characteristic perverseness, sympathized with Anstis, but on the whole the incident could only sharpen Tory animosity towards the Whigs.[30]

A further set-back to the Whig cause arose from the protracted conflict between Conybeare and Richard Newton, Principal of Hart Hall. Newton professed to have no party politics, though he has generally been reckoned as a Tory on the strength of Hearne's early admiration, a classification lately modified to that of a 'whimsical' Tory.[31] The overwhelming passion of Newton's life,

---

[30] MSS. of the Warden of All Souls College: Thomas Wenman's MS. History of the College I, fos. 84–87; C. T. Martin, *All Souls Archives*, pp. 362–4; *Hearne's Collections*, ix. 96, x. 66, xi. 42; B.M. Stowe MS. 799, fo. 23.

[31] R. J. Robson, *The Oxfordshire Election of 1754* (London, 1949), p. 173.

however, was to have Hart Hall incorporated as a college with statutes described by an ardent friend on his death as 'so wisely calculated for the good of the University that many of them have been already adopted by some other Colleges and will in time be followed by all'.[32] To secure the royal charter and the endowments the college required, Newton relied exclusively upon his two most distinguished pupils, the Pelham brothers; his chief backing at first came from the Whig heads (including the Rector of Exeter),[33] and as if this were not sufficient to tie him to the Whig cause, the plan to convert the hall into a college would deprive the Tory Chancellor of his patronage to the headship and cut across a scheme for the reversion already concerted between George Clarke, Charlett, and Lord Arran himself.[34] Newton accordingly began to ingratiate himself with the government, and in the University College case sought to prejudice them against Cockman even before an appeal was made.[35]

It was Newton's double misfortune, however, that hardly anyone in Oxford took him quite seriously and that he aroused the violent opposition of a faction in Exeter, led by the redoubtable Conybeare, who laid claim to a legal title to Hart Hall. Determined to prevent the incorporation of the Hall they persuaded Newcastle to stop all proceedings. This he did for another fifteen years while Conybeare and Newton assailed each other in pamphlets, the former complaining privately to Newcastle of his sense of unjust treatment.[36] In the parliamentary election of 1737 this recrimination resulted in Newton's leading the forces of Hart Hall 7 to 1 against the Whig candidate sponsored by Conybeare.[37]

So far was this from demonstrating his Toryism, 'whimsical' or otherwise, that Newton spent the rest of his life after the incorporation of the Hall in 1740 privately petitioning the Pelhams

---

[32] Bodl. MS. Rawlinson Letters 96, fos. 336–7.

[33] For the voting of the heads on 28 March 1723, Bodl. MS. Rawlinson D 912, fo. 308.

[34] Bodl. MS. Ballard 20, fo. 107, printed by S. G. Hamilton, 'Dr. Newton and Hertford College', in *Collectanea*, ed. M. Burrows (Oxford, 1896), iii. 285–6. This essay gives an excellent account of the whole affair.

[35] P.R.O. SP 35/42, fo. 166; *Hist. MSS. Comm. Portland MSS.* vii. 352–3; *Hearne's Collections*, viii. 57–58.

[36] B.M. Add. MS. 32689, fo. 531.

[37] University Archives: MS. Conv. Reg. Be 32, fos. 67–68: *An Exact Account of the Poll as it stood between Mr. Trevor and Mr. Bromley* (London, n.d. [1737]).

for preferment and miscellaneous favours, and pamphleteering against the University in the Whig cause. In 1749 Henry Pelham was 'confident that he would do more to set the University right than any man in the kingdom', and wished he 'were thought Whig enough'—that is, wished the soundness of his attachment had not been obscured by his squabbles with the Whig leaders in Oxford—for the Deanery of Christ Church. Finally, at Newton's earnest solicitation, poetic justice was done by his preferment to a canonry at Christ Church under Conybeare himself, but too near his death for the dramatic possibilities of the situation to unfold.[38] The loss of Hart Hall to the Whig ranks in the later twenties and thirties cost the Whigs the support of only one eccentric head and a handful of votes, but as a minority movement they could not afford divisions.

A final factor which told against the Whigs was their persistent connexion with religious heterodoxy, notwithstanding the efforts of Gibson at the highest level[39] and of Conybeare in Oxford. Throughout the twenties Oxford was agitated not only by the hares loosed by the Bishop of Bangor but by the persistent attacks upon the doctrine of the Trinity. The differences revealed by these controversies among theologians claiming to be orthodox also made it embarrassing to defend academic subscriptions to the XXXIX Articles, on whose precise sense there was no agreement. Oxford Tories tended to regard the disquieting doubts which had been raised as, in a measure, an unfair attempt of their political opponents to secure an advantage, not merely by making concessions to dissenters outside the Church but by undermining the specific character of the Church from within.

At the end of 1728 their suspicions seemed to be confirmed, and all the issues raised again in a highly coloured form. In May a young relative by marriage of the high-church Earl of Aylesford,

one Jennens ... cut his throat ... and threw himself out of his window at the Temple. He was of Trinity College, and a sober, ingenious,

[38] B.M. Add. MSS. 32700, fo. 146: 32701, fo. 312: 32704, fo. 188: 32719, fo. 338: 32724, fos. 425, 451: 32726, fo. 493: 32730, fo. 444.
[39] Gibson regarded the liberal theologians as 'semi-infidels, who under the title of Xns are destroying the whole work of our redemption by Christ, and making Christianity little more than a system of morality. But their design is so barefaced and shocking that they make little progress among serious people'. (B.M. Add. MS. 39311, fo. 32).

virtuous young man in all appearance while he was there. There were found in his *scrittoire* several letters from one Stevens of Trinity . . . now a regent master, in deacon's orders and designing for priest's orders, curate of a village near Oxford, and probationer fellow of Trinity. The letters were full of blasphemy against Christianity; he declares himself a deist, and that he made it his business to propagate deism, but through Bangorianism, that it is sufficient at first to bring them to Bangorianism; and a great deal more of such horrible stuff. The friends of the poor gentleman that destroyed himself imputed his end to such principles . . . ,

and on Stratford's advice put the letters in the hands of the Bishop of Oxford. On his initiative a prosecution was begun in the Vice-Chancellor's Court. Stevens, corrupted, as some thought, by excessive devotion to mathematics, fled, and so did Cater, another Trinity man who had already been held back by the bishop from priest's orders for Arian views.

In October the whole affair became public, Stevens was expelled, and the Vice-Chancellor, Dr. Butler of Magdalen, resolved that the University should make an official stand on the issue, which now became a party affair. The majority of the heads hesitated to commit themselves on a theological question which carried such immediate political implications, but the programma advocated by the Vice-Chancellor was opposed by the Whig heads of Christ Church, Jesus, and Wadham, and at first by Felton of St. Edmund Hall. He was said to be encouraged by Edmund Gibson who on this occasion would not surrender the party advantage to the cause of orthodoxy. As soon as it was clear that the Whigs were alone in opposition the Tory heads rallied, and passed a ferocious programma denouncing the 'ill designing persons' who had attempted to instil the poison of infidelity into 'the unguarded inexperience of less inform'd minds', called tutors to 'a double diligence' in instructing their pupils in the faith, and to forbid them books tending to 'the denying the authority of the scriptures, the subverting Christianity, and introducing in their stead deism, profaneness and Irreligion'. Nor was this the last case where colleges were 'infected with deists' and expulsions followed.[40]

[40] *Hist. MSS. Comm. Portland MSS.* vii. 468–70; J. Spence, *Anecdotes, Observations and Characters*, ed. S. W. Singer (London, 1820), pp. 387–8; *Vice Chancellor's Programma*, 2 Dec. 1728; *Hearne's Collections*, x. 71, 86, 305.

Nor did a subsequent Whig essay in orthodoxy improve the situation. Less than a year later, on 21 September 1729, Joseph Betty, fellow of Exeter, in a university sermon, plunged into a furious defence of episcopalian church government and the dignity of the clergy.

Must they be exposed to the capricious humours [he indignantly asked], the witty malice, and the raging insolence of Arians and Atheists, of Libertines and Latitudinarians, of Socinians and Deists? Must their offices be despised, their doctrines rejected, their persons vilify'd, and they themselves obliged to be men of sorrows, and acquainted with grief?

Betty proceeded to vindicate the orthodoxy of the Whigs at Exeter, as distinct from the older and more suspect 'Lollards' of Merton and Jesus, by proving firstly the divine and apostolic authority of the episcopalian ministry,

Secondly, That all opposition to this ministry really is, and must necessarily be look'd upon as sinful. Thirdly, That no excuse can be offer'd by man, which may plausibly be supposed to prevail with God, to pardon those that persevere in the guilt of this abominable sin,

and fourthly, *inter alia*, that there was no hope of salvation apart from the grace mediated by the episcopalian Church. This tirade went rapidly through several editions, but so did a spate of replies avidly consumed by a public scenting a new Sacheverell.

Inevitably the University as a whole was implicated in the controversy, and was attacked as a body in an anonymous pamphlet by John Warner, landwaiter. To him the unity of the Church consisted in its possession of one hope, one faith, and one baptism, and the only sign of schism in England consisted in 'a *factious, contentious* temper' incarnate in men like Betty who unhesitatingly consigned the greater part of the Protestant world to damnation. Warner preferred the liberalism, the anti-clericalism, and the facile explanations of the unpopularity of the clergy which so incensed Betty.

If the clergy . . . instead of preaching peace and charity and love, stir up envy strife and contention amongst Christians, then they are ministers of satan not preachers of the gospel of peace . . . it's no wonder that they meet with that scorn and contempt which their conduct so justly deserves. . . . The *English* clergy, have it no longer in their power, would to God none had an inclination, to abuse and deceive the people with their *pious frauds*, and *consecrated trumpery*.

In Betty's view, 'barely to recite such monstrous and shocking opinions is . . . an ample confutation of them', and he would condescend to no further argument until his opponent revealed his name. Another writer, one Jacob Gingle, attacked Betty's weakest point, his insufferable arrogance, and ridiculed him both in prose and verse. On reading the sermon 'I was seiz'd with such raptures of joy, that I could not forbear saying, Blessed be the womb of Oxford, the Alma Mater, that brought forth parson Betty, and the breasts of Exon. College, which gave him suck . . .'.

As if this were not bad enough, an official Bangorian skeleton was produced from the cupboard of the Constitution Club when Peter Maurice, 'as a proper antidote against Mr. Betty's sermon', brought out a second edition of *The True Causes of the Contempt of Christian Ministers*, the sermon which had brought upon him the censure of the University in 1718. (This particular scourge of the high church had a long life yet, for in 1837 it was again reprinted in a swashbuckling anti-tractarian collection entitled *The Popery of Oxford Confronted, Disavowed, & Repudiated*.) Pursued by both his political allies and his creditors, Betty ended his life on 1 January 1731 by taking laudanum, the college astutely circumventing the amens of the Tories by faking the date of his death in both the college register and the monument in the chapel.[41] The seamy side of Whig churchmanship could hardly have been more effectively displayed than by this hornets' nest aroused by the sermon of a Whig don dedicated to the Whig Bishop Potter. Everyone knew that Queen Caroline (who had already offended the Oxford medicals by her caustic wit),[42] favoured the liberal churchmen; before long the theological acumen of Peter Maurice was rewarded by a Lambeth D.D., and after his death Tindal the deist was discovered to have enjoyed a government pension of £200 a year.[43]

Conventional Oxford high churchmen might well prefer to stand by their banners than to risk the hazards of a Betty or the

---

[41] J. Betty, *The Divine Institution of the Ministry and the Absolute Necessity of Church Government* (3rd edn., Oxford, 1729); J(ohn) W(arner), L(andwaiter) *An Address to the University of Oxford . . .* (2nd edn., London, 1730), pp. 37–38 60–61; J. Gingle, *The Oxford Sermon Versified* (2nd edn., London, 1730), p. iv P. Maurice, *The True Causes . . .* (2nd edn., London, 1729); Boase, *Registrum Collegii Exonensis*, p. 134. Hearne, like everyone else, was deceived by the false date of death. *Collections*, x. 374–5.

[42] Ibid. ix. 331.

[43] *Hist. MSS. Comm. Egmont Diary*, i. 206, 408.

disappointments of a Conybeare. Always subject to the influence of the midland gentry, the University now followed them as they developed the 'country' line in politics. The alcoholic vapourings of the gentry at the High Borlace were a welcome feature of the Oxford summer; in 1732 the University conferred doctorates upon four of the stalwarts of the club, and in the following year Theophilus Leigh, Master of Balliol, became the first clerical member.[44] It was therefore hardly surprising that 1733, the great year of opposition effort, was chosen for the first Oxford Act for twenty years,[45] at which the great concourse should demonstrate the hold which Oxford still had upon the influential public. In many ways the Act was a great success, though marred in Hearne's view by the entertainment provided by 'Handel and his lowsy Crew . . . a parcel of Pickpockets'; no *Terrae Filius* was appointed, but political and personal satire was provided by a pamphleteer who assumed the role, and by those who replied to him. The main political accusation in these pamphlets was that the Dean of Christ Church had stickled hard in Oxford for the Excise Bill, and it was ironically commented that the writer of the pamphlet must be 'a Jacobite, or Tory', an equation which the ministry had worn very thin. At least the Whiggish Vice-Chancellor of 1734, Holmes of St. John's, would risk no further embarrassment, and contrived narrowly to defeat the proposal for a fresh Act.[46]

In Oxford, as elsewhere, the defeat of the Excise Bill had been the occasion of enthusiasm, bell-ringing, and bonfires. Meadow-court, again an informer to the government, gave his atrocious imagination free vent in describing the

return of that foul, malignant spirit, that I once resisted almost unto blood. . . . I [am] convinc'd from hence that the same measure of leaven is still fermenting in this learned lump, that the high ecclesias-ticks are not to be reclaim'd by generosity and indulgence, and that nothing will satisfy the tory-clergy but the recovery of those church-lands and that church-power of which they think themselves sacri-egiously robb'd.

[44] *Hearne's Collections*, xi. 99, 106, 246.
[45] In 1725 it seems to have been the Whigs who wanted to make a demonstra-ion by holding an Act (*Hist. MSS. Comm. Portland MSS.* vii. 397).
[46] *Hearne's Collections*, xi. 224–43, 332; *Terrae Filius 1733*; *The Oxford Toast's Answer*; *Alma Mater*. A Scots observer was totally unimpressed (*Hist. MSS. Comm. Laing MSS.* ii. 235–6).

His description of three days of disorder and treason was improved for posterity by Hervey and Coxe, but Delafaye, the Under-Secretary of State, took a soberer view, and stressed the fact that no sign of disloyalty had been given at the Act, despite the rendering of very Whiggish verse. Even in Oxford the Whigs did not stand together, for Conybeare 'willingly took the Employment of vindicating the University and assuring the world in his knowledge it was a groundless and malicious information of Meadowcourt'.[47]

Among Oxford as among other opposition politicians some reservations were felt on the score of the king, not least when, during the war of the Austrian Succession, he contrived to maintain his Hanoverian troops on British pay,[48] but this was far from justifying Walpole's wholesale classification of Tory and country politicians as Jacobites. The University not only produced all the ceremonial tributes to royalty with becoming effusiveness, but was ready to take up the cause of the Prince of Wales, who from the beginning aspired to add the big guns of Oxford to his armoury.[49] That there were Oxford men who, when out of the country, would drink the health of the Duke of Ormonde everyone, including the government, knew, but the University occupied no place in the Pretender's conspiratorial plans. What passed for Jacobitism now was the sort of sermon preached by John Wesley in 1734, for which he had obtained the approval of the Vice-Chancellor, that obsequious court politician, Dr. Holmes, before delivery, so as to 'bid Wadham, Merton, Exeter and Christ Church, do their worst'. In 1732 Swift, in disillusioned old age, thought court politics entirely triumphant in Oxford, which he found 'wholly changed, and entirely devoted to new principles . . . a most corrupt seminary'.[50] The truth was that the University was as always overwhelmingly loyal to the dynasty, and predominantly out of sympathy with the ministers. In the thirties and early forties the struggle between court and opposition forces in

[47] Coxe, *Walpole*, i. 404, iii. 136, 137; Lord Hervey, *Some Materials towards the Memoirs of the Reign of King George II*, ed. R. Sedgwick (London, 1931), i. 171; *Hearne's Collections*, xi. 185; *Letters of Spencer-Cowper, Dean of Durham 1746–74*, ed. E. Hughes, Surtees Soc. clxv (1950), p. 4.

[48] Or when his father over-spent on the civil list, *Hist. MSS. Comm. Leyborne Popham MSS.*, p. 288.

[49] *Hist. MSS. Comm. Egmont Diary*, i. 160.

[50] *Hist. MSS. Comm. Weston Underwood MSS.*, pp. 502, 517, 519; T. Jackson *Life of Charles Wesley* (London, 1841), i. 33; *Swift Corr.* iv. 294.

the University seemed to have ended in stalemate, either side acknowledging the strongholds of the other, and although, outside Christ Church, Whig strength was not increasing, it was a question how long the University would maintain its attitude of independence towards the Court once it was represented by a generation that knew not Anne, nor even George I.

CHAPTER X

A Quiet Interlude

THE stalemate in university politics was apparent in its parliamentary history. Only twice between 1722 and 1751 did an election contest reach a poll, and there were few of the alarums and excursions which had characterized the previous thirty years. At the elections held on George II's accession there was 'talk of an opposition in the University by one Mosely', probably Sir Oswald Mosely of Manchester and Staffordshire, but it soon evaporated.[1] In 1732 William Bromley died, 'a martyr in the service of the university', taken ill while attending a debate. At once Sir Thomas Dyke, a young Tory baronet, began to sound the ground, but withdrew before the overwhelming support received by the even younger candidate sponsored by George Clarke, Lord Cornbury, the 21-year old son of the Earl of Clarendon and Rochester, just returned from his travels.[2]

Cornbury possessed every possible advantage. By pedigree he laid claim to the ancient Hyde connexion, to the traditions of the great Lord Chancellor, and the practical advantages of his forebears' service as High Steward of the University, a place still occupied by his father. Though Lady Mary Wortley Montagu confessed 'he had certainly a very good heart', she thought little of his head, and discouraged his attentions to both her daughter and the muse of poetry; but in opposition literary circles he was extremely popular. A friend of Gay and Swift, he became intimate with Bolingbroke and Pope who praised his character and his verse. Just before the election he pledged his political reliability by refusing a pension from the ministry.[3]

Nevertheless, Cornbury's politics were not as unequivocal as

[1] *Hist. MSS. Comm. Portland MSS.* vii. 450.
[2] *Hearne's Collections*, xi. 29, 32–33; *Hist. MSS. Comm. Leyborne-Popham MSS.*, p. 289.
[3] *Hist. MSS. Comm. Egmont Diary*, ii. 187; *The Works of the Rt. Hon. Lady Mary Wortley Montagu* (5th edn., London, 1805), iv. 195–7; *Swift Corr.* iv. 138–9, 285–6, 294; *The Works of Alexander Pope*, ed. W. Elwin and W. J. Courthope, viii. 356, 372, 374, ix. 142–3, 157, 455.

was commonly thought. In the previous year he had been introduced into Jacobite schemes by the 'half-mad' Duchess of Buckingham. Their plan amounted to purchasing the parliamentary
opposition, Whig and Tory, for the Pretender by promises of
offices, pensions, and titles. Lord Cornbury was to be a lord of the
bedchamber, but if the report of his appointment to a similar
place in the household of the Prince of Wales in 1738 can be
accepted, he soon began not only to renounce a conspiracy so
absurd that he can hardly have taken it seriously, but also to
evolve via the Court of the exile, and the Court of the heir-
apparent, into a court politician of his true family type.[4]

The next election came with the death of George Clarke, full of
years and honour, on 22 October 1736. To the end of his days he
remained true to the Tory opposition; in Oxford he was reported
drinking healths with such apostles of the old interest as Lord
Noel Somerset, Tom Rowney, and William Shippen, and to
various academic purposes he bequeathed most of his wealth.[5]
For some reason the by-election did not take place for over three
months, an ample interval for the Whigs to choose and propose
a candidate. Their choice, sponsored by Conybeare, fell on Robert
Trevor, an alumnus of Queen's, elected fellow of All Souls in 1725.
He had entered the Secretary of State's office as a clerk in 1729,
and in 1734 became secretary to Horatio Walpole's legation at
The Hague, where in various capacities he was to serve for the
next twelve years. In many ways he was a good candidate, for his
intimate association with the Walpoles guaranteed full court
backing, while as the son of that Lord Trevor who had been one
of the last friends of Harley in the last Tory ministry, and the
appointed champion of the Harleyite canons at Christ Church
in their struggle with Atterbury, he might sway a number of
Harleyite and Christ Church votes.[6]

His opponent was the son of another supporter of Harley, still
more dear to Oxford, William Bromley, the namesake of a more
famous father. He had already sat for Fowey (1725) and the
county of Warwick (1727-34), and in 1734 had been entrusted by
the opposition with their most important effort of the year, the

[4] *Hist. MSS. Comm. Stuart MSS.* i. p. xvi; G. H. Jones, *The Main Stream of
Jacobitism* (Cambridge, Mass., 1954), pp. 150-4, 211.
[5] Lamport Hall: Isham MS. IC 2680; *A True Copy of the Last Will and
Testament of George Clarke* (London, 1737).
[6] Swift, *Prose Works*, v. 453; *Hist. MSS. Comm. Portland MSS.* vii. 129.

motion to repeal the Septennial Act. As a boy, in the great days of 1713, he had mixed with the Tory circle at Christ Church, even before his matriculation; his younger brother Francis, one of the writers of congratulatory verses at the coronation, was still prominent there. William himself had succeeded his father on the board of Radcliffe trustees, an influential body of benefactors, membership of which proved to be an advantage to a succession of parliamentary candidates, and had been created D.C.L. in 1732.[7]

In Horatio Walpole's view, Trevor's prospects turned largely on the imminent translation of Dr. Potter, Bishop of Oxford, to Canterbury. With his support, Trevor could win many who would 'be influenced by the disposition and weight of so much power and preferment in the hand of an Oxford man. He has promised fair and will be talked to in a very serious manner by good authority'. The difficulty with this approach was that the Oxford constituents with their pride in independence, their strict rules against candidates' canvassing,[8] might readily resent the intrusion of a peer, even of their own number, and despite the precedents created by former Tory bishops and peers. At Christmas the Whigs were pessimistic, ten days before the election the betting was 2 to 1 on Bromley, and at the poll Trevor was overwhelmed by an even greater margin, 329 to 126. Nothing could demonstrate more clearly how successfully Whig expansion had been checked. Despite the active partisanship of the bishop, the Dean of Christ Church, and men like David Gregory, Fanshawe (who was rewarded with the regius chairs of Greek and Divinity), and Shaw of Queen's (who eventually succeeded Fanshawe in the former chair), a small majority of Christ Church men, including Charles Wesley, voted for Bromley as 'our old member', and when the overwhelming defeat of Trevor became certain, there was no temptation for spineless Whigs such as Dr. Holmes to stand by the cause. Only Merton, Wadham, and Exeter voted solidly Whig; the Whig interest at Jesus had evidently made no advance, and that of St. John's crumbled away.[9] The Whigs seemed likely never to succeed unless the Tory interest became badly divided.

---

[7] Cobbett, *Parliamentary History*, ix. 394 seq.; J. Swift, *Journal to Stella*, ed. H. Williams, ii. 626; *Hearne's Collections*, ix. 370, 386, xi. 37, 60.

[8] B.M. Add. MS. 40266, fo. 136; T. H. B. Oldfield, *The Representative History of Great Britain and Ireland* (London, 1816), iv. 362.

[9] B.M. Add. MS. 32690, fo. 199; *Hist. MSS. Comm. R14 App. pt. ix, Buckinghamshire MSS.*, pp. 4, 10; *Hist. MSS. Comm. Weston Underwood MSS.*, pp. 458,

So decisive was Bromley's victory that when the Tory interest temporarily fell apart on the news of his sudden death five weeks later, the Whigs were too weak to exploit the opportunity. Some Whigs in Oxford were willing to go through the motions again, but Archbishop Potter would do nothing, and Horatio Walpole strongly counselled Trevor not to risk a second disgrace. There was still a possibility of a contest between Tories; Matthew Frampton, an Oxford physician and former fellow of Magdalen, was talked of; Edward Butler, President of Magdalen, and Peregrine Palmer, fellow of All Souls, actually stood. Butler, as a relative by marriage of Dr. Sacheverell, the head of the largest and wealthiest Tory house, and almost the only Tory head apart from Dr. King who was not in orders, had an obvious claim; Peregrine Palmer was the brother of Thomas, another Oxford man, well known as a Somerset squire, antiquarian, M.P. for Bridgwater, a benefactor of All Souls, and an intimate friend of George Clarke. Connected with both the Harleys and the Wyndhams, the Palmer brothers were of an acceptable Tory pedigree, and Peregrine, succeeding to the Fairfield estates on the early death of Thomas in 1735, seemed very much of the mould of Oxford members in an age when Toryism was synonymous with being out of office.[10]

But after 1722 the Oxford Tories abhorred internecine strife.

The contest in the University was a friendly one . . . the two candidates agreed to try their interest with ye Tories only and not to ask the vote of anyone who had voted in ye former election for Mr. Trevor . . . having applied to their several friends and comparing votes it was found that Dr. Butler had a great majority and therefore his competitor Mr. Palmer went at ye head of his own friends and voted for ye Doctor.[11]

Eventually Palmer reaped the reward of his solicitude for domestic peace. In the middle forties, when Cornbury's conduct in Parliament gave increasing dissatisfaction, Sir Thomas Hanmer, one of

471–2, 475, 482; *Journal of the Rev. Charles Wesley*, ed. T. Jackson (London, 1849), i. 68; *An Exact Account of the Poll as it stood between Mr. Trevor and Mr. Bromley.*

[10] *Hist. MSS. Comm. R14 App. pt. ix, Buckinghamshire MSS.*, p. 5; *Hist. MSS. Comm. Weston Underwood MSS.*, pp. 482, 483; J. Collinson, *History and Antiquities of the County of Somerset* (Bath, 1791), i. 255; *Hist. MSS. Comm. Portland MSS.* vii. 300; *Hearne's Collections*, viii. 292, ix. 360, xi. 46, 61; Lamport Hall: Isham MS. IC 2676.

[11] *Hist. MSS. Comm. Weston Underwood MSS.*, pp. 487, 490.

the last survivors of Queen Anne's Tory heroes, was thought of
as a prospective university member[12] on the strength doubtless of
the sumptuous edition of Shakespeare which Dr. Smith, Provost
of Queen's, and Dr. Shippen, Principal of Brasenose, persuaded
him to present to the University Press, and which provoked a
celebrated passage of arms with Warburton;[13] but when the
vacancy arose by the death of Edward Butler in 1745, it was
Peregrine Palmer who was unanimously elected to fill it.

Butler's sole mark upon the political history of the age seems
to have been to vote against the government in half a dozen
recorded divisions; Palmer was even less active, and the political
stalemate which took the fire out of Oxford elections was matched
by the comparative passiveness of the university members in Parliament. After the Bill to facilitate the building of the Radcliffe
Camera, and the petition against the London waterworks scheme
in 1721, there was little university business to put through, and
though Bromley spoke on a technical point in the debate for sus-
pending habeas corpus on 12 October 1722, and backed the
Pension Bill of 1731, he was no longer the crusader of yore.[14]
Clarke also was inactive, and neither member voted on the motion
to make good the civil list arrears on 23 April 1729. Cornbury and
Clarke both voted against the Excise Bill in 1733,[15] the former
advocated the reduction of the land forces in 1737 and 1738,
opposed the ministers' Bill for the punishment of Edinburgh
after the Porteous riots, and lived up to his connexion with
Bolingbroke and the opposition.[16] The University, usually fortunate in having its interests safeguarded in special legislation,
obtained inclusion in a Bill 'for the more effectual preventing the
unlawful playing of interludes within the precincts of the University of Cambridge' in 1737, and concessions in the Acts on the

[12] Lamport Hall: Isham MS. IC 2508.

[13] A curious sidelight on this is cast by P. Nichols, *The Castrated Sheet in the
Sixth Volume of Biographia Britannica* (London, 1763). One copy is filed in
Queen's College MS. 464.

[14] *C.J.* xix. 483, 500, 602; University Archives: MS. Conv. Reg. Bd 31, fos.
171–3; 7 Geo. I, c. 13; Cobbett, *Parliamentary History*, viii. 38; *Hist. MSS. Comm.
Egmont Diary*, i. 138.

[15] Cobbett, op. cit. viii. 1308. 'Godfrey Clarke' is presumably a mistake for
George Clarke.

[16] *Hist. MSS. Comm. Carlisle MSS.*, p. 193 (the report of his moving an
address for a reduction of the forces in 1730 is clearly a mistake, presumably for
Morpeth: ibid., p. 66; *Hist. MSS. Comm. Egmont Diary*, i. 12); ibid. ii. 350;
Cobbett, op. cit. x. 295–302.

patronage of Papists (1738) and wine licences (1740),[17] but the only serious issues affecting it arose from the noisy anti-clericalism of the thirties.

Anti-clerical opinion supported repeated attempts of the dissenters to secure repeal of the Test and Corporation Acts (a move opposed by Cornbury in 1739)[18] and was the chief power behind the introduction of the Mortmain Bill in 1736. This Bill proposed to make it unlawful to give lands, or money for purchasing lands, to 'charitable uses' unless the conveyance should be executed twelve months before the donor's death, thus making benefactions such as Oxford had received from Radcliffe and Clarke impossible for the future, and being partly occasioned by talk of Michel's benefaction to Queen's. The Bill also proposed to limit the number of advowsons purchased by colleges, thus restricting the prospects of preferment of the fellows of at least the wealthier colleges.[19] The Vice-Chancellor, Stephen Niblett, went down to London for several weeks to pull wires, and the papers he deposited in the archives at All Souls provide a fascinating study in the techniques by which sectional interests influenced the legislature at this time.

Before the middle of March, Cornbury and Clarke were concerting plans with Sir William Wyndham, Watkin Williams-Wynne, William Shippen, Lord Noel Somerset, Sir John St. Aubin, Baptist Leveson, and Dr. Lee, who strongly recommended the University not to petition to be heard by counsel, there being no legal obscurities in the Bill and no prospect of the petition being granted. All the political friends of the University could hope to gain was a clause permitting colleges to fill up whatever licences were still outstanding, and to receive bequests of money or stock. If Sir Joseph Jekyll, the Master of the Rolls, who introduced the Bill would not yield upon their representations, they must try their fortune in the House. The University might take hope from the known sympathies of some of the court party for

[17] University Archives: MS. Conv. Reg. Be 32, fo. 71; 10 Geo. II, c. 19; *Oxford Council Acts 1701–52*, p. 209; 11 Geo. II, c. 17; 17 Geo. II, c. 40.

[18] *Hist. MSS. Comm. Egmont Diary*, iii. 47.

[19] For some years it had been held that the systematic purchase of livings by colleges had been 'to the great discouragement of study' (ibid. i. 108–9), and in 1725 a proposal was defeated to tack a clause preventing colleges from purchasing advowsons to the Bill 'for better effecting' the proposal to build fifty London churches (*C.J.* xx. 451).

the poverty of many colleges, an advantage offset by 'this hott man', the Vice-Chancellor of Cambridge, 'who attacked Mr. Shippen in a very warm and angry manner' and proved unwilling to concert measures with Oxford. In consequence Cambridge not only petitioned against the Bill but petitioned ahead of the sister university, where Convocation had to revise their original petition on humbler lines.[20]

The Cambridge grievance was that the friends of Oxford had not only armed themselves with fourteen draft amendments to the Bill, to introduce according to whatever turn the debate took, but produced two printed papers for distribution among members.[21] In these papers it was urged that as recently as the Act of 7 & 8 William III, c. 37, Parliament had provided for the enlargement of academic endowments by means of royal licence, and that the purchase of advowsons did not deprive lay proprietors of the enjoyment of any property in the usual sense of the word. Of all charitable ends, those of the universities most deserved endowment, and it could not be fairly alleged that charitable bequests were upsetting the balance of property in the country.

Inveigled by the audacity of the sister university into petitioning, and into going with the Cambridge Vice-Chancellor to a meeting of ministerial supporters at the Cockpit, Niblett sought anxiously to anticipate the presentation of the petition by soliciting favours at Sir Robert Walpole's levee. Cornbury not only refused to be drawn into such a proceeding but lectured him that 'a formall application to a minister by way of address to solicit a matter to be determined in Parliament is what I have never yet thought of', and doubted whether it was consistent with the dignity of the University or himself as a member of the House. Meanwhile the Vice-Chancellor had been strenuously collecting ammunition for his parliamentary friends in the shape of information about college endowments and livings. Theophilus Leigh, Master of Balliol, who was only slightly less informative than most heads, declared:

I find most of us are very heavily brought to answer any of your

[20] University Archives: MS. Conv. Reg. Be 32, fos. 56–57.
[21] *Reasons Humbly offered to the House of Commons against the Bill now depending for restraining the Disposition of Lands . . . as far as Relates to the University of Oxford* (1736); *Some Plain Reasons humbly offer'd against the Bill now Depending in Parliament &c.* (1736), All Souls College MSS. Appeals and Visitors' Injunctions, nos. 530, 532.

interrogatorys. However lest they should prove ugly leading questions the less our answers are publish'd or made use of the better.
Our License of Mortmain is almost fill'd up. Our annual revenue is
very low.

From such grudging answers it transpired that the colleges were
very poor, supported over 530 fellows, possessed 290 livings (of
which only 48 were worth more than £100 p.a.), and that only
Jesus, Exeter, and St. John's had any considerable licences in
mortmain still unfilled.

In the Commons these plans met with a mixed reception. The
Speaker was 'employ'd in the service of the Universities', and, on
the major point, they were exempted from the restrictions on
endowment; it now became an argument for the Bill that the
universities ought to benefit from being the only outlet for death-
bed charity. On the score of the advowsons they fared less successfully. It was argued 'that numbers of livings in the University
only made the Fellows lazy, whereas when pinched in their circumstances, and without prospect of College livings, they would
study hard to go out in the world'. None, however, suggested
such a radical interference with private property as to reduce the
redundant intellectual proletariat by cutting off college advowsons, and the Bill merely provided that no college henceforth
might purchase livings exceeding in number half the total of its
fellowships, a concession which enabled the less happily provided
colleges to purchase a few more livings. In view of the fact that
Cornbury had expected a motion forbidding colleges to expel
fellows who refused to take orders, this was very satisfactory.

Dr. Holmes now consulted the heads of Queen's, Merton,
Balliol, Hart Hall, Magdalen Hall, New Inn Hall, and the proctors, and recommended the Vice-Chancellor to petition the Lords
to allow colleges to exchange poor for better livings without
exceeding the moiety, while the President of Corpus advocated
'private applications' with a view to getting all foundationers
included in the number of fellows. The Duke of Beaufort was
chosen to champion the University's cause in the Upper House,
but the duchess being ill, Lord Gower took over the lead.[22] His
amendment to enable colleges to exchange livings was defeated,

[22] Both Watkin Williams-Wynne and Lord Abingdon had recommended the
Duke of Leeds or Lord Foley if they were willing to act. Ibid., nos. 558, 561. Lord
Gower was one of the members of the High Borlace created D.C.L. in 1732.

and the debate returned to familiar ground. The opposition condemned the restriction of charitable activities by legislation of a
type originally designed to curb the iniquities of popery; those in
favour of the Bill deplored the prospect of the growth of over-
mighty corporations which might prove fatal to every noble
family in the land, the tendency of the clerical governors of
charities to pester property owners on their death-beds to the
impoverishment of the natural heirs, and the notorious fact that
lay gentlemen who became governors of hospitals did so not to
promote charity but to extend their patronage. But when the Bill
became law, despite all the hard words about idle dons and im-
perious bishops, the universities emerged in a highly privileged
position compared with, for example, Queen Anne's Bounty.[23]
The one busy episode in a quiet interlude had ended satisfactorily.

[23] All Souls College MSS. Appeals and Visitors' Injunctions, nos. 509–61; *Hist.
MSS. Comm. Egmont Diary*, ii. 242, 255–6, 267, 269, 271; Cobbett, *Parliamentary
History*, ix. 1110–56; Nichols, *Illustrations*, iv. 689–70; Lamport Hall: Isham
MS. IC 2491. George Fothergill, fellow of Queen's, denounced the pretentions
of the anti-clericals to promote social welfare in a university sermon, *Sermons
on Several Subjects and Occasions* (Oxford, 1761), p. 275.

CHAPTER XI

The Crisis Renewed: a Tory Triumph

THE sudden flurry of activity aroused by the Mortmain Bill threw into relief the tranquillity of the thirties as a whole, a tranquillity soon destroyed in the next decade. The victories of 1741 were indeed duly celebrated in Oxford with the encouragement of a town-and-gown mob;[1] but, on the one hand, the parliamentary conduct of Lord Cornbury began to give increasing dissatisfaction to his former supporters,[2] and, on the other, political tension grew up between the supporters of the ministers and their opponents in the University; inevitably they branded each other as Whigs and Tories, though the evolution of Lord Cornbury was to show how little of their traditional meaning the terms now conveyed.

Cornbury was not of the stuff of unbending opposition. In 1739 he refused to follow Wyndham's Tories into secession, and when the opposition to Walpole got the bit between its teeth, he stood aside. In February 1741 he spoke against Sandys's motion for the removal of Sir Robert Walpole on much the same grounds as he had opposed Walpole's Bill against Edinburgh four years earlier, that penalties justified only by a successful criminal prosecution were being imposed upon wholly inadequate evidence. In the following year he supported the House of Lords in their rejection of the Bill to indemnify informers against Walpole, now Earl of Orford, on the grounds that the Commons were threatening the balance of the Constitution by seeking to overawe the Upper House. In April 1742 he was on the court list for the committee of secrecy on Walpole's activities, and in the following December he failed to accompany Dr. Butler to vote against Hanoverian troops being taken into British pay. In 1743 he refused to speak against the Hanoverian troops, and defended Carteret's foreign

---

[1] Bodl. MS. Rawlinson Letters 96, fo. 50.

[2] Cornbury's manœuvres can now be followed in their parliamentary context in J. B. Owen, *The Rise of the Pelhams* (London, 1957). Mr. Owen stresses Cornbury's independence even of opposition connexions, an independence which came to look rather sinister to his constituents.

policy—small wonder that that inoffensive Euseby Isham, Rector of Lincoln, should begin to growl that he would have no chance of re-election if he accepted an office 'without being called up to the Lords', while Dr. King had long since given him over as a traitor.

In 1735 Cornbury raised a protest against the employment of Hessian troops—a standing army having always been one of his aversions—and received the dedication of Bolingbroke's letters on *The Spirit of Patriotism*, but he was now a patriot only in the provisional sense understood by the Grenville clan, with whom he had been intimate for some years. Even in 1742 he had flattered the ego of Lord Hardwicke, and by 1748, his health failing, he paid obsequious court to the king and the Duke of Newcastle to obtain permission to visit the spas abroad.

Family attachments [he explained to His Majesty], the habits and prejudices of first connexions, and the consequences of these in several parts of my life, have depriv'd me of all the satisfaction I could have felt, and of all the advantages I might have found, in being most particularly attached to your Majesty's service.

He had merely mistaken, not neglected, his duty to the king; he abhorred 'those unintelligible factions' with which he had been so long connected. Truly it was no great step to the peerage with which the king ended his parliamentary association with the University in 1751.[3]

Though the Man of Sin, Sir Robert Walpole himself, had been removed from office, it was evident to the old school at Oxford that the constitutional system had not been regenerated; the strange manœuvres which preceded the formation of a new court party under Henry Pelham, in which even such a die-hard as Sir Watkin Williams-Wynne was offered a peerage, increased the uncertainty in the University; Oxford Tories were already anxious that Lord Cornbury might confront them with the dilemma of dividing their interest or returning a placeman. These circumstances and the misfortunes of the war bred a violence of opposition language in Oxford not heard for many years, and provided a climate in which there blossomed a new Tory leader, Dr. King, Principal of St. Mary Hall, who, defeated in his youth, despised in his middle years, became a hero in his prolonged latter days.

[3] See note J, p. 282.

After his breach with the official heads of Oxford Toryism and his fiasco in the election of 1722, King virtually disappeared from university affairs for twenty years. Much of this time was spent in Ireland where he became involved in a long series of lawsuits with his uncle, Sir Thomas Smyth, one of Ormonde's protégés in the Irish administration. King attributed his troubles to his uncle's wife, a lady of unsavoury reputation, and savagely attacked their whole circle, including one of Swift's former friends, Captain John Pratt, another fallen creature of Ormonde, in a satire which he regarded as his literary masterpiece, *The Toast* (1732 and 1736). King tried to hold back the publication of this work in England for fear that it might prejudice his lawsuits, and alleged that it put him in extreme ill-odour with the ministry. King's correspondence with Swift, with whom he became intimate in the thirties and who assisted him with the later versions of *The Toast*, was indeed frequently pilfered by the Post Office for political reasons.[4] King and Swift were united by both political and literary interests, and from the autumn of 1735 the former was entrusted with the publication of Swift's tract on *The History of the Last Four Years of the Queen*, written in 1713. Disagreements followed, for Lord Oxford and other friends advised that publication be postponed and the text altered, and King himself thought the ministry would never allow the pamphlet to appear as it stood. King arranged the publication of Swift's poem 'On his own Death', but omitted certain lines in the interests of prudence.[5]

Even amongst the bright lights of the opposition men of letters, King sustained a reputation for both wit and scholarship, qualities which were to make him the idol of the old interest at Oxford, and which, on at least one occasion, he put at the service of the opposition journal, *Common Sense*. His connexion with the Jacobites in this period, however, remains obscure. An intercepted Jacobite letter of 1736 suggests that King was still connected with them, though he was not of the inner circle. He wrote several Latin poems on stale patriot topics, and in his *Anecdotes* he appears as a conventional Tory, shocked at the defections first of Gower and then of Pitt to the court party, but sensitive enough to the charms of office to scold Pulteney for failing to save the Constitution by forming a patriot ministry on the fall of Walpole. Yet he claimed

---

[4] *Swift Corr.* vi. 26, 28, 74, 111. On the question of *The Toast*, ibid. v. 458 seq.
[5] Ibid. v. and vi, *passim*.

to have had a surprise interview with the Pretender in the apartments of Lady Primrose in September 1750, to have dissuaded him from making another attempt, and to have kept in touch with him by messenger for some years subsequently, until finally disgusted by his degeneracy and submission to his Scottish mistress Walkenshaw. It is unlikely that King had been in any sense a serious conspirator for many years, but his equivocal politics won him a reputation for honesty amongst the increasingly sentimental old interest in the University and county, and provided a release for the intemperance for which, as a teetotaller in a hard-drinking society, he denied himself the usual outlet.[6]

In the forties the University still delighted in conferring degrees upon leaders of the opposition in both Houses; King gave vent to the political frustration of the Oxford Tories and flattered his own academic vanity when he presented the graduands by making violent speeches against the ministers in Latin so ambiguous as to provide him with a loophole for escape. He ingenuously described his speech on the graduation of the Duke of Hamilton in April 1743 as 'only intended . . . as a lesson for his Grace', but dared not 'venture it by the post'. The following August he recommended the young Earl of Lichfield as the embodiment of all the patriot virtues. A month later, on presenting the Earl of Orrery, he attacked the miserly creatures 'who use their rhetorical ability, such as it is, and their parliamentary power, which is very great, to the destruction of their country', and presented Sir Edward Turner 'in a very polite, tho' severe speech, on modern patriotism and the times'. These speeches involved King in his first exchange of pamphlets; he was accused of abusing the whole order in Church and State for Jacobite ends, and the University was urged to expel him. 'Leaden' Gilbert, Bishop of Salisbury, also called for his expulsion, which King declared himself ready to suffer if the bishop could propose it in Latin in person.[7]

[6] Jones, *The Main Stream of Jacobitism*, p. 198; *Hist. MSS. Comm. Weston Underwood MSS.*, p. 466; W. King, *Political and Literary Anecdotes of his own Times*, pp. 42–47, 96, 196–8; *Opera Gulielmi King* (n. pl. or d.).

[7] L. Dickens and M. Stanton, *An Eighteenth Century Correspondence* (London, 1910), p. 95; three speeches are collected in *Wm. King's Speeches* (Bodl. Gough Oxford 144); *London Evening Post*, 1–4 Sept. 1744; *Epistola Objurgatoria ad Gulielmum King cui accessit epistola canonici in reverendum admodum ad archidiaconum reverendum admodum* (London, 1744); Bodl. MS. Eng. Hist. d 103, fos. 80, 82, 84; H. Walpole, *Memoirs of the Last Ten Years of the Reign of George II* (London, 1822), ii. 194.

For the moment the incident blew over; even a quiet man like Euseby Isham praised King for the coolness of his speeches in Convocation, and a serious threat of French invasion and then the rebellion of 1745 turned attention to greater things. Most of the evidence for Oxford history in the next two years is difficult to interpret, but it is clear that, consistently with its conduct throughout the reign, the University was determined to give bold and ample evidence of its loyalty. On the news of the threatened French invasion in February 1744 the University assured the king that 'the solid and disinterested principles of piety and loyalty, [which] have ever engag'd your University of Oxford in the defence of their sovereigns upon all important emergencies' would not fail now; indeed, no Englishman would expose his property to the designs of 'an arbitrary, enterprising Prince'. Again, in September 1745, after the outbreak in Scotland, an address was sent up to the king, abhorring the schemes of a Popish Pretender acting as a lackey of France and Spain. Ligonier's horse were regally entertained in Oxford on their way north, and in the following spring Convocation burst into paeans of enthusiasm for the king and duke who had suppressed the rebellion; they noted the exemplary loyalty of the clergy which had become 'as seasonable and useful now in defence of our present happy constitution, as it was at first in the establishment of it', and applauded the security which His Majesty conferred on his great seminaries of religion and learning. More than this the ministers could hardly ask, nor could the implication that the place-hunting principles of the other university, that especial darling of the Duke of Newcastle, were not 'solid and disinterested', be construed as treason. The suppression of the revolt was celebrated at Oxford with sermons, 'extraordinary illuminations, fireworks etc. and many loyal healths went cheerfully round'. Nevertheless, the events of 1745 aroused savage controversy for the next decade.[8]

As the Tories harboured the dark suspicion that the Whigs were at heart little more than free-thinkers, so in the recesses of the Whig mind lurked the notion that Tory opposition to the ministers implied treason, a notion newly strengthened by Tory susceptibility to the eloquence of Dr. King. In times of peace even

[8] Lamport Hall: Isham MS. IC 2696; University Archives: MS. Conv. Reg. Bf 33, fos. 75–76, 140, 260–1; Bodl. MS. Top. Oxon. e 145, fo. 6; *London Evening Post*, 21–23 Nov. 1745; *Gent. Mag.* 1744, p. 161.

Whig propaganda would allow that not politics but 'good cheer, especially good liquor is the very life and support of Jacobitism in this kingdom', but in a time of actual rebellion such a concession was less easy. Harcourt, a household official, feared treason in the county; the Archbishop of York heard 'a discouraging account of Oxford', no doubt from Whig sources (though such good place-hunters as the Grenvilles first thought of sending their valuables to Oxford for safety). More important than Whig fears, however, was the determination of a section of the party to profit from the crisis.

The Whig peers of the county led the way in forming an association to preserve the constitution in Church and State on terms which did not commit them to immediate action. This partisan profession of loyalty made the word 'association', as one Whig confessed, 'odious and ridiculous enough in Oxford', quite apart from its unhappy suggestions of Whig manœuvres in the 1690's, and of the armed might of Cromwell beyond that. In consequence the association was signed by none of the squires or peers most closely linked with the Oxford Tories, not even by Lord Cornbury, now within the orbit of the Court, and by no one in the University other than the Whig heads of Jesus, Christ Church, Exeter, and Queen's, a couple of Whig dons (such as the former regius professor of modern history, David Gregory, and the aggressive Francis Webber of Exeter), George Huddesford, the Tory President of Trinity, the spineless John Mather, President of Corpus, and the peace-loving Vice-Chancellor, Euseby Isham, Rector of Lincoln, who could hardly refuse to sign after the University had pledged its utmost in its address to the king. It would have been prudent for the Tory dons to have swallowed their prejudices and joined the association, but they did not, and from an early stage their failure to sign was made a reproach, and when the great electoral campaign in the county was beginning in 1752 it was claimed that the association had 'unmasked the traitors in disguise'.[9]

Still worse, the Whigs took advantage of the Oxford pulpit. A violent opponent of Jacobitism and Popery, Francis Potter, at

[9] E. Bentham, *Letter to a Fellow* (London, 1749), p. 53; *Original Letters Illustrative of English History*, ed. Sir Henry Ellis, 3rd series (London, 1846), iv. 345-9; *Letters from Thomas Herring, Archbishop of Canterbury, to William Duncombe* (London, 1777), p. 84; *Verney Letters*, ii. 200; press cutting of 22 Oct. 1745 in Queen's College MS. 474.

this time vicar of Burford, preached at St. Mary's on 24 November 1745 on Jer. xxii. 30—'For the children of Israel have only provoked me to anger with the work of their hands saith the Lord'— the erring Israel in this case being the University. 'Persecution and popery are, and must be, ever inseparable . . . our only security against falling into their hands is a steady adherence to the present government.' Any prince raised under the influence of France and Rome must indelibly bear the mark of the beast, a fact which furnished 'many seasonable arguments against what hath been long and much insisted on, Unalterable Hereditary Right', and, of course, against the University's official principles of loyalty.

The ultimate truth of Potter's sermon, that security in Church and State depended on the defeat of the Pretender, was not to be denied, however unpalatably it might be conveyed, but exception was possible to an equally rabid discourse on 5 November by John Free, vicar of Runcorn and Vice-Principal of Alban Hall, on *The Bloody Methods of Propagating the Popish Religion a Plain Proof that it is not of Divine Original*. From the Levitical law of retribution, Free argued that where any antagonist, such as the Papist, contravened the law of nature by 'cruel and bloody purposes', it was proper to resist, 'breach for breach, eye for eye, tooth for tooth &c.' So far, no doubt, Free carried his congregation with him, but he continued without apparent logic to demolish the characteristic charges of Tories against the ministry. Were there those who complained of the weight of taxes? They were 'profligate wretches, [who] by their expensive follies, and more expensive vices, have ruined themselves and their dependents, and laid that to the charge of the government which ought to be charged on their debaucheries'. Were there those who held that Britain's main war effort should be at sea instead of on land? They were blind to a truth 'obvious . . . to the meanest understanding . . . *That the increase of French territory is the increase of French Power*', and a threat to everything sacred. Free forbore 'to say by what particular persons or parties among us these delusions have been propagated', but openly declared that their 'ambition and avarice, the wantonness of some, and the folly and ignorance of others, nay the very fashion of the times, have conspired with the enemies of church and state'.

Scarcely had Free thus consigned the greater part of the

University to perdition than he was pressed by Francis Webber of Exeter, representing 'the King's Friends in the University', to publish the sermon. Free professed surprise that the Vice-Chancellor refused him access to the University Press, though the sermon sold well in Oxford after publication in London. He did not dissemble that the object of the sermon had been as much to obtain preferment as to expound the gospel, but the 'vulgar academics' who maintained 'that tho' . . . I had in my own opinion performed gloriously, yet they were well assured, that the preaching of this sermon was the worst day's work I had ever done in my life', proved right. Though Potter progressed through prebends to archdeaconries in the west of England, Free (whose father had suffered unrewarded for his loyalty in the Oxford riots of 1715) languished in the vicarage at Runcorn. 'Horrid times', he declaimed in 1750, 'horrid times indeed! when a government is so weak and dastardly . . . [when a] ministry, pretending to be their master's friends could . . . sacrifice . . . his MAJESTY's most faithfull and distinguished good subjects.' Inscribed on the long roll of Whig martyrs forgotten by the ministers, Free continued for years to rave against the existing order in the character of an independent Whig; and, disappointed by the prince whose church 'ought to have afforded me better bread', he paid ineffectual court to the Duke of Cumberland.[10]

Torn by a strenuous election for a public orator in which Lisle, a Magdalen Tory, had defeated Hind of Christ Church, the senior proctor, inflamed by provocative Whig preaching, confused by animosity among the heads and perplexity at changes in the ministry, Oxford opinion was further distracted by outbreaks of undergraduate indiscipline. In 1745 George Augustus Selwyn, placeman, wit, and *bon viveur*, was expelled from Oxford on a charge that he had bought wine from an unlicensed seller, and at a party of fashionable young men did 'impiously affect to personate our Blessed Saviour, in his institution of the Holy Sacrament, and heinously and profanely apply . . . [His] words . . . to the intemperate purposes of the . . . club'. He had the support of the Whig Dr. Brooke, the regius professor of civil law, talked of appealing to the ministry, and was said to have bought up a debt so as to have it in his power to arrest a proctor.

Two years later there were three serious cases which led directly

[10] See note K, p. 282.

into the political maelstrom of 1748. Charles Slingsby Duncombe of Lincoln showed what Whigs thought of Dr. King by assaulting his maidservant, 'and, forcing himself after her into the lodgings of the said Dr. King, did there behave in a rude and indecent manner'. Refusing to make a public apology, he too was expelled. In midsummer there was serious disorder in Exeter, probably with the Jacobite tinge of the troubles in the following year. Dr. Holmes, President of St. John's, dealt severely with one of his undergraduates and a fellow who were involved, and the Vice-Chancellor gave ample satisfaction to the Whig authorities of the college by binding the others over to the Assizes, where the Grand Jury found no true bill.[11]

Lastly there was a tragic incident at Christ Church, where a drunken college servant was found dead with a fractured skull at the bottom of a staircase;[12] at the coroner's inquest a verdict of wilful murder by persons unknown was returned, but the culprits were popularly supposed to be two intimate friends of George Selwyn, Lord Abergavenny and Lord Charles Scott, second son to the Duke of Buccleugh, and horrifying stories appeared in print alleging that, themselves in liquor, they had tortured the poor fellow to death. Again the Vice-Chancellor collected evidence for the Assizes, but Scott died in college within a few weeks. Some comic but embarrassing relief to all this was provided by the public offer of John Pointer of St. John's to die at the block in place of Lord Lovat, one of the traitors of the '45.[13]

There was material here for misrepresentation, and still worse, at a time when there were mounting Tory fears that 'there seldom wants hungry courtiers in any reign, who hope, by misrepresenting these seats of learning, to get their Houses dissolved, in order to share the plunder among themselves',[14] friends of the ministry

[11] This verdict was 'much blamed by all the friends of the Govt. but . . . the great triumph of its enemies' (*Letters of Spencer Cowper, Dean of Durham*, Surtees Soc. clxv. 84).

[12] A similar scandal occurred at Cambridge a year earlier (*London Evening Post*, 1–3 April 1741.

[13] *London Evening Post*, 31 Jan.–2 Feb., 7–9 Feb. 1745; Bodl. MS. Rawlinson Letters 96, fos. 187, 273; J. H. Jesse, *George Selwyn & his Contemporaries* (London, 1843), i. 68–69; University Archives: MS. Conv. Reg. Bf 33, fos. 129 seq., 187–8; Lamport Hall: Isham MS. IC 2700; B.M. Add. MSS. 29601, fo. 229: 32713, fo. 616; Walpole's *Letters*, ii. 268; *A Letter to the Heads of Oxford on a Late Very Remarkable Affair* (London, 1747); *Gent. Mag.* 1747, p. 184.

[14] *The Gentleman and Lady's Pocket Companion for Oxford* (London, 1747), pp. 20–21.

who had failed to convict the University of treason could now
pose as champions of academic discipline and reform. This new
crusade began in the Exeter and Christ Church cases, and (as in
the hey-day of Nicolas Amhurst) became firmly grafted upon the
older stock of political agitation during the disorders of February
1748.

The Tories began the year indignantly repudiating the name
of Jacobite, and arguing that the late rebellion proved that loyalty
was abundant in the south, and 'particularly distinguished in
those whom calmer times had justified in their opposition to bad
ministries'.[15] The edge of this argument was soon blunted by
treasonable cries from Oxford undergraduates in their cups. On
23 February (the birthday of the Pretender's youngest son) Dawes
of St. Mary Hall was challenged and made the celebrated declaration: 'I am the man that dare say God bless King James the 3d
and tell you my name is Dawes of St. Mary Hall. I am a man of
independent fortune and therefore am afraid of *no one* or *no
man.*' Whitmore of Balliol was even more explicit: 'God Damn
King George and all his assistants. God Bless King James the
Third of England, Prince Charles and Prince Henry, Duke of
York.' This episode was intrinsically less serious than some of the
previous year, but the Whigs were now on their toes. Three days
later the rioters were reported by Richard Blacow, an irascible
M.A. of Brasenose, who collected witnesses of the treasonable
utterances and demanded condign punishment from the Vice-
Chancellor, Dr. Purnell, Warden of New College. The Vice-
Chancellor refused to accept Blacow's depositions, at first because
Blacow who was unco-operative throughout apparently wished to
submit written depositions concocted privately and refused to be
examined, and subsequently because he thought he could not
legally accept depositions more than three days after the offence.
The Vice-Chancellor was abused by the adherents of the court
party as a 'Jack' and reported to the ministry by Blacow. In March
he was summoned to London to render an account of his conduct,
and soon afterwards a programma was issued expressing both
the University's 'abhorrence & detestation of such factious and
seditious practices' and its determination to punish all offenders.
Since much of the trouble originated in lavish private entertain-

[15] *Westminster Journal*, 23 Jan. 1748, reprinted in *Gent. Mag.* 1748, p. 27.

ments, deans and tutors were to press their pupils to dine in hall, and the proctors were to inspect coffee-houses.[16]

The issue, however, was out of the hands of the Oxford authorities already; on the 6th of May Dawes, Whitmore, and Luxmore (a Balliol man) were brought down to London in the custody of a messenger, charged with uttering treason, and given bail. Contrary to the advice of the Attorney General, who was convinced neither of the soundness of Blacow's evidence nor of the commission of an offence against the law, the ministry resolved to prosecute the Vice-Chancellor also. Both in these proceedings and in their ecclesiastical patronage they resolved anew to avoid giving 'encouragement to the Tory clergy', and, as at the beginning of the Hanoverian era, their literary hacks followed their lead. To drive home the parallel, an anonymous *Life of Humphrey Prideaux* was published containing his plan for depriving the universities of their independence, and the Whig sheet, *The Jacobite's Journal*, tuned up with scurrilous charges that the principles of that wine-bibber, Aristotle, were evidently still esteemed in Oxford, and that the intellectual mediocrity of the University was a consequence of its Jacobitism.

Their nonsensical principles are the fruit only of that shallow learning (I had almost said ignorance) which is taught in seminaries half reformed from popery, and which are ready, on the first occasion to return to the bosom of that Alma Mater. Doctrines hoarded up in the repositories of luxury, laziness, bigotry and error, whose learning consists in words, wit in quibble, religion in grimace and superstition, and the most refined policy centers in the dark interests of priestcraft.

A visitation was the only hope. Thus were the old weapons of political abuse and theological modernism refurbished in the cause of Whig politics and educational reform.[17]

Within the University, Edward Bentham (who used the opportunity to ingratiate himself with the Bishop of Oxford and Lord Hardwicke) came forward with a plea for the young 'to reverence

[16] B.M. Add. MSS. 35887, fos. 21–26: 32717, fos. 427, 562; *Memoirs of a Royal Chaplain 1729–63*, p. 147; *Gent. Mag.* 1748, p. 214; Bodl. MS. Top. Oxon. e 145, fo. 7; MS. Dep. b 48, fo. 34. A most valuable account of this episode from the Attorney General's viewpoint is given in a typescript copy of the manuscript Legal and Political Diary of Sir Dudley Ryder in the Ryder Papers at Sandon Hall, see pp. 33–38.
[17] *Gent. Mag.* 1748, pp. 222, 234; *The Jacobite's Journal*, 2, 30 April, 7 May, 4 June 1748. Richard Newton also petitioned the government to take action (P.R.O. SP 36/106, no. 71: cf. SP 36/109, no. 6).

authority in whatever hands you find it', an argument once dear
to the Tories, and ridiculed undergraduate pretensions to opinions
on serious issues. He suggested that the theory of indefeasible
hereditary right should lead its supporters to trace the true heir
among the descendants of kings prior to the Conquest, and that
pupils who found tutors who recommended treasonable notions
to them should assess their honesty by the fact that they had all
taken the oath of abjuration. This barely veiled attack upon King
was followed even more explicitly in a pamphlet in which a 'loyal
Oxonian' defended the principles of Hoadlianism against a non-
juror, argued that Oxford had always been in the van of reform
since the day of Wycliffe, and that

> when some of the junior students shall be better informed, when *his*
> EMINENCE *the very learned C[ardina]l* KING, *the* CICERO *of the present
> age, shall have published his eloquent orations in defence of the Pro-
> testant Royal Family: and his Phillipicks* (divinae famae) *against a
> Popish pretender* . . . that learned Society will make full amends for
> the temerity and indiscretion of some of their rash and inconsiderate
> members, and no longer suffer themselves to be misled by some per-
> sons of *anti-revolutional* and *anti-constitutional principles.*[18]

King was, of course, in unrepentant mood, and in 1749 replied
to Bentham in a series of lampoons in verse, proposing to publish
a poetical translation of Bentham's pamphlet, and ridiculing him
both as a scholar and Whitehall preacher.

> Men of Oxford, I tell you, (and faith! it is true)
> Not a page of this work did I write with a view
> To inflame our great folk, or to hurt one of you.
> But howe'er, to cajole my good friends at Whitehall,
> And to find out the way to some pretty neat stall,[19]
> Let me roundly declare ye are Jacobites all.
>
> . . . .
>
> There are seasons for all things; and I a logician,
> A Divine, and a preacher, and Metaphysician,
> Am obliged on a sudden to turn politician.

---

[18] B.M. Add. MSS. 35590, fo. 75: 39311, fo. 58; E. Bentham, *A Letter to a
Young Gentleman* (n. pl., 1748); *An Epistolary Conference between a Reverend
Non-juror and a Loyal Oxonian* (London, n.d.).

[19] In 1752 Bentham was canvassed for a stall at Durham as 'a Tory, but a man
of extraordinary good character, and very moderate, and who has served the
Govt very much at Oxford in opposition to his more violent Brethren' (*Letters
of Spencer Cowper, Dean of Durham*, Surtees Soc. clxv. 157).

When the poetical abridgement appeared, Bentham was characterized as

> Half a casuist, half lawyer, half Courtier, half Cit,
> Half a Tory, half Whig (may I add, half a Wit?)

Another lampoon in the King manner represented Bentham as arguing

> For that is right I must aver,
> Which G[eorge] approves, or's M[inister]
> And that is *wrong* which they condemn;
> We're but Machines, t'act under them.
> And thus two arts, you plainly see,
> *Ethics* and *Politics* agree.

King was right to defend sentimental politics by ridicule rather than by reason, but some more solid support was needed urgently.[20]

This support, it was hoped, would come from the Prince of Wales, with whom the predominant party in Oxford and their friends at Westminster began an active flirtation. In June 1747 the prince had authorized negotiations between his connexion and the Tories for an agreement on the basis of country-party doctrines, overtures which were welcomed by such well-known friends of Oxford as the Duke of Beaufort, the earls of Westmorland and Lichfield, Lord Foley, and Nicholas Fazakerly. Negotiations were still being pursued to the satisfaction of Oxford opinion at the time of the indiscretions of Dawes and Whitmore, and contributed to the maintenance of the University's independence. When at loggerheads with the king and the king's favourites at Cambridge in 1749, Oxford offered verses to the prince, and Theophilus Leigh, Master of Balliol, affirmed that the University's gratitude to him was such as to guarantee her political support whenever it might be needed. According to Horace Walpole, Oxford Tories differed with the prince over the university by-election in 1751, but they rendered every honour on his premature death soon afterwards. The Vice-Chancellor spoke of him as the University's patron despite the embarrassment caused by ministerial resentment at their mutual relations. This brief honeymoon with the Prince of Wales also illuminates the king's determination not to allow His Royal Highness to offer himself

[20] See note L, p. 282.

as a candidate for the Chancellorship of Cambridge, and to contest his patronage at Christ Church.[21]

The prince, however, could not arrest the course of justice. In October Dawes and Whitmore, with the aid of a band, created fresh disturbances outside Balliol gate, and were expelled, Theophilus Leigh acting in the Vice-Chancellor's place in accordance with instructions transmitted from the Lords Justices by the Duke of Bedford. During the following month, with both trial and jury carefully watched by the ministry, Whitmore and Dawes were found guilty, fined, and sentenced to two years' imprisonment, and to providing substantial security for good behaviour for the next seven years, and to being carried round 'all the Courts in Westminster Hall with a paper affixed to their foreheads, inscribed with the words laid in the information, and the judgement of the Court'. The next few weeks were wretched in Oxford. The Vice-Chancellor was due to face trial (the *London Evening Post* remarking gloomily that the last such case had been brought by the High Commission in the reign of James II), and the University of Cambridge was reported to be scheming to complete the picture of Oxford disloyalty by breaking all precedent and addressing the king on the conclusion of peace ahead of Parliament, on whose lead the politicians of Oxford were waiting. In the event the Vice-Chancellor's trial was postponed, for Luxmore, the third of the undergraduate defendants, was acquitted, 'the evidence (most of which was due also to appear against the V. Chr.) having lost all credit with the jury (most of which jury, too, are upon the V. Chr.'s pannel)', and it was assumed that the Attorney General would either not risk the loss of another decision, or 'try for another jury'. In fact, new charges were substituted for the old.[22]

The Vice-Chancellor was nevertheless still under an official cloud; Dr. Leigh was advised by the friends of the University that Oxford should not fall behind Cambridge in loyal appearances,

---

[21] See note M, p. 282.

[22] Balliol College MS. 403, fos. 76, 78, 80; B.M. Add. MSS. 32717, fo. 355: 35887, fos. 21–26; *London Evening Post*, 10–12 Nov. 1748; Thornton and McLaughlin, *The Fothergills of Ravenstonedale*, p. 199. A few years later it was implausibly alleged that Luxmore's acquittal was due to the fact that his father's powerful electoral interest at Okehampton was devoted to the support of ministerial candidates (*An Answer to Mr. B——w's Apology* (London, 1755), p. 14); Sandon Hall, MS. Ryder Diary (typescript), pp. 42, 45–46, 59; Bodl. MS. Dep. 648, fos. 21–30, 40.

and the king 'signified to Lord Arran, by the D. of Grafton, yt
he would receive the University Address, [but] from other hands
than the V. Chr.'s'. After a hot debate whether the time for such
felicitations had come, an adequate address was passed by Convocation which not only gave thanks for the return of peace, but
promised to enforce peace within the University 'by example, by
exhortation, by discipline, by severity . . . and to give a right and
loyal direction to the warmth of youth'. Two heads only wished
to include some reference to the recent trials, and to that of Dr.
Purnell still pending. One of these, Conybeare, Dean of Christ
Church, sensed that his favour with Newcastle was ebbing, and
that a great effort for the party was required lest his hopes of
preferment melt finally away. He now persuaded Secker, Bishop
of Oxford (himself performing a lengthy atonement for an ill-
advised act of opposition a dozen years before), to present the
whole discussion in a bad light to the ministry, with the result
that the Duke of Newcastle concluded that the address itself was
'indecent and improper', and animosities 'found so early admit-
tance, and took so deep root, that it was resolv'd by some great
men (to which purpose a select number of bishops were made
subservient) that the Address should not be receiv'd'. The king
declared the address improper, and of course it leaked somewhat
inaccurately into print, to the accompaniment of glycerine tears
from the Tory press:[23]

> Oxford! I grieve at heart your hapless lot;
>   Your virtue, steady Loyalty forgot!
> In this a strange absurdity there seems;
>   G[eorg]e cant be angry, that you turn'd out J[ame]s.

More serious than this official affront to the University were
well-founded rumours that the ministry was again planning a
'grand visitation', or at least the assumption of powers to nominate the Chancellor. The great protagonists of the plan were
Hardwicke, who suspected that 'many of the fellows have not
taken the oaths, [and] might be turned out immediately', the

---

[23] Balliol College MS. 403, fos. 82, 85, 86, 90; *Bedford Correspondence* (London, 1842–6), i. 594–5; B.M. Add. MS. 35590, fo. 230; *London Evening Post*,
17–19 Jan. 1748/9. The address was printed in *Gent. Mag.* 1749, pp. 20–21.
Manuscript copies in University Archives: MS. Conv. Reg. Bf 33, fo. 260; B.M.
Add. MS. 32717, fo. 554.

Duke of Bedford, and Lord Gower, the former high Tory, and they were resisted by the Attorney General who had already failed once to procure satisfactory evidence of alleged delinquencies at Oxford. Moreover Sherlock, the new Bishop of London, who had been 'spoken to plainly' on appointment about the need to keep down the Tory clergy, collected support in the House of Lords for an inquiry and political intervention at Oxford with the zealous support of both Chesterfield and Granville. Newcastle, always readily convinced 'of the necessity of doing something, and that soon', was also in favour of a visitation provided that Cambridge, which had lately made him Chancellor and Hardwicke High Steward and 'whose behaviour is as meritorious as the other is to be censured', were exempt. In the Commons 'one reason given for the necessity of keeping up a larger body [of troops] was, the disaffection of our University . . . in the same debate some bitter things were spoken against the University'.[24] Oxford must look to its defences, and for the first quarter of 1749 the *London Evening Post* assumed major responsibility for the protection of the University. Almost every other number contained some feature on lines as hackneyed as the charges which were rebutted. Old references were revived to the sufferings of the University during the civil wars and under James II; even Allibone's poem on the visitation of 1648 was revived. An anonymous correspondent cruelly quoted from a Cambridge sermon preached at the time of the Revolution which perfectly represented the present situation of Oxford, speaking of [25]

some rejoicing at our failings, and watching cautiously for any miscarriages; some causelessly complaining of our want of zeal and true devotion, (one may guess what they mean), some of our sheltering Ignorance and harbouring Idleness; some of our uselessness and insignificancy to the commonwealth.

Oxford propaganda was also characterized by a sour hostility to Cambridge and to the egregious courtier she had elected as Chancellor.

See Granta's Senate by Inducements led,
Elects wise Newcastle for their Head:

[24] B.M. Add. MSS. 29601, fo. 245: 29602, fo. 1: 32718, fos. 29, 31; H. Walpole's *Letters*, ii. 356; Balliol College MS. 403, fo. 90.
[25] *London Evening Post*, 7–10 Jan., 21–23 Feb., 14–16 March 1749.

> All, or in Church or State, they now may claim,
> Lawn, Furs, Posts, Pensions wait the happy Cam.

Lord Arran would soon die, and would it not be then

the most effectual way for the Gentlemen in disgrace to *recover favour* . . . to chuse the yet undignified Br[othe]r [Henry Pelham], or some other great man who may at that time preside over the Tr[easur]y, for his successor, without any regard to *Learning, personal qualities* or *education?*

Finally, the old cry was raised of the defence of charters and corporations. The sins of a few undergraduates, and the errors of judgement of the Vice-Chancellor, could not justify such 'a notorious invasion of private property'. If the Crown assumed the nomination of the Vice-Chancellor it might well nominate the Lord Mayor of London.

> Whether guilty or not, the Vice-Can let 'em quarter,
> But beware of encroachments on Freedom and Charter.[26]

In April the University staged a great demonstration of the public support it enjoyed in the opening of the Radcliffe Camera. The political significance of the celebration was duly noted in the press. The University would 'receive all strangers with more courtesy than they have met with themselves': afterwards it was reported that 'the decency with which the whole ceremony was conducted . . . convinced many [that] calumnies [were] vented against that learned body'. Honorary degrees would be conferred and there would be

many seekers to qualify themselves for pluralities, Chancellorships etc., but it is not doubted, but that the University will be parsimonious in her favours, and . . . pay the compliment of a slight to such who have slighted her, and foreign to what they were about, unjustly abused her. . . .

The assembled throng was to prove that, though in trouble, Oxford was not friendless, 'many noblemen and eminent persons testifying their regard and affection to that learned body'. In this respect the celebrations were a tremendous success. On the day the Radcliffe Camera was opened—'the Grand Hurly-Burly' as the Whigs described the solemnity—a glittering company of 3,000 packed the Sheldonian, and in the course of the week tradesmen

---

[26] Ibid., 28–31 Jan., 2–4 Feb., 31 Jan.–2 Feb., 7–9, 14–16 Feb. 1749.

and musicians took their fill of the £20,000 that was spent. Though Cambridge representatives were conspicuous by their absence, they were alive to the moral of the performance, and urged Newcastle to come to Cambridge for his installation as Chancellor as 'a means of drawing to ye university a concourse of people of fashion not inferior in number to what appeared at Oxford upon ye opening of ye Radcliffe Library'.[27]

Prominent among the celebrities were the benefactors themselves, the Radcliffe trustees, the Duke of Beaufort, the Earl of Oxford, Sir Walter Wagstaffe Bagot, Sir Watkin Williams-Wynne, and Edward Smith, stout apostles of Toryism all. Even as trustees they were at loggerheads with the ministers, being under prosecution by the Attorney General for the management of the trust, and they confirmed both their politics and their affection for the University by electing Lord Arran as a trustee, and commencing plans to meet a long-felt Oxford need by establishing a teaching hospital. The enormous wealth of the trust gave the trustees a great influence in the University for many years, an influence which they now used to nominate whom they would to degrees. It was here that the first political embarrassment arose. It had been understood in the University that no assistance of the sort demanded by Newcastle in Cambridge would be given to professional advancement by conferring degrees in divinity and medicine. Finally, it was agreed to honour the divines favoured by the trustees on a subsequent occasion, and to confer medical degrees upon three Scottish doctors.

Doctor Taylor of All Souls in a most audacious speech, called the candidates medicasters, empyricks, & what nots. Doctor King was unprepared, yet after much internal conflict, he hammer'd out three pretty severe sentences against Dr. Taylor which touch'd him to the quick....[28]

This was an unhappy augury for the speeches at the opening of the Camera by which the celebrations are remembered. The high

[27] London Evening Post, 16–18 March, 4–6, 22–25 April 1749; Gent. Mag. 1749, p. 165; Bodleian Quarterly Record, i. 171; B.M. Add. MS. 32718, fo. 193. Sir Roger Newdigate gave a lively account of the preliminaries to his wife (Warwick C.R.O. B 1999).
[28] B.M. Add. MS. 33061, fos. 445–55; Balliol College MS. 403, fos. 105, 126, 137; Lamport Hall: Isham MS. IC 2902; Warwick C.R.O. Newdigate MS. B 1999; Bodleian Quarterly Record, i. 165. The Tory press denied that the Radcliffe trustees asked for the medical degrees (London Evening Post, 8–11 April 1749).

moment of this overcrowded day came when 'Dr. King arose in all
the majesty of ancient eloquence' (though, according to malicious
Whigs, with his son 'behind him to prompt him, & to hold his
lemon'). 'The Doctor had been previously desired to be decent in
his political reflections. But—he was resolved to go off gloriously,
& to speak, this once, with all the spirit of a dying patriot.' He
lamented the days of Queen Anne, 'when no Briton need blush
for our national honour; when our senate was uncorrupt', when
every constituency followed the lead of Oxford in choosing candidates well affected to the Constitution. His severest animadversions were reserved for

> those detestable informers, who have so embroiled our affairs of late,
> that they hoped to eclipse the lustre of the university and extinguish
> it in their own infamy . . . [who] have accused our glorious vice-
> chancellor, and in such an extraordinary manner, that no kind of
> punishment can be heavier than the accusation itself . . . who (pests
> of society!) contrive that the congratulations and addresses we offer
> . . . should be rejected, nay looked upon as criminal.

With a manifold *Redeat*, he concluded by praying for the restoration of a patriot kingdom in which the University might flourish.

To these aspersions the Whigs contrived an immediate reply.
The next day Henry Brooke, fellow of All Souls and regius
professor of civil law, who a few years earlier had appealed to
Parliament against his college Visitor,[29] 'behaved like an angel'.
Somewhat speciously

> he hop'd that such a concourse of venerable persons had been now
> assembled, not *from a political principle but the love of learning* . . .
> the man who endeavour'd to rouse the spirit of discontent by insinua-
> tions against the peace of his country, (& by the Country must be
> meant the Laws, the Constitution & the King of it) took the ready
> way to undermine those laws & that constitution, which alone coud
> support the University & Great Britain. And . . . he woudn't scruple
> to pronounce such a man the greatest enemy to his Country.[30]

---

[29] H. Brooke, *An Appeal to the Publick from an Unappellate Tribunal, or an Impartial Inquiry into the Rise, Progress and Extent of Visitatorial Power, in a Letter to a Member of the House of Commons* (London, 1740).

[30] *Bodleian Quarterly Record*, i. 165–72; W. King, *Oratio in Theatro Sheldoniano . . .* (London and Oxford, n.d.); *Translation of a Late Celebrated Oration . . .* (London, 1750).

Ill endowed for the purchase of books, the Radcliffe Library, like the Infirmary later, proved something of a white elephant, and Kennicott, the Hebrew scholar, sought the sinecure librarianship in order to stack his manuscripts upon the unused tables,[31] but the passage-of-arms at the opening touched off the fiercest paper warfare in which the University had been involved since 1717, and redoubled the animosity of the ministers. Circumstantial reports of the proceedings were at once sent up by the Whigs, and the government was pressed to take immediate action, for not only was every political omen favourable but they could make

vice & immorality . . . the great point to be insisted on, in which no party distinctions have anything to do . . . & how sensible soever the Jacobites may be of the real design, yet it will confound & baffle 'em . . . under this colour the extirpation of disrespect and disaffection to the King & his Government may be happily effected.

Several privy councils seem to have been held, but although Hardwicke, Newcastle, and the Archbishop of Canterbury urged legislation against Oxford, the Speaker denounced a draft bill as tyrannical, the Attorney General doubted if it was technically satisfactory, and the Solicitor General was sure it would cement the alliance between Oxford and the prince. The decision to drop the Bill was taken at a meeting of parliamentary supporters of the court in Lincoln's Inn Fields at the end of April, at which it was urged that there was insufficient parliamentary time left for the necessary legislation (although three bishops and a judge had already been appointed to the visitatorial commission), and that the University had already whipped up a dangerous amount of support.

Three days later, with this withdrawal still generally unknown, an Oxford counterblast was organized at the St. Albans Tavern near Pall Mall, in a meeting attended by 13 peers and 103 M.P.s of Tory and Leicester House connexions. This open union of the two factions was addressed by Beaufort and Wynne, both Radcliffe trustees, and resolved, 'heart and hand', to be ready for any similar emergency in future, and to meet again at the beginning of 'the next session to observe and oppose not only measures

---

[31] *London Evening Post*, 27–29 June, 12–14 Nov. 1751; B.M. Add. MS. 38201, fo. 373. Cf. a circular paper by William Scott, later Lord Stowell, in Bodl. Bliss B 417, no. 1.

directly threatening the universitys, but also any other points which should appear to them destructive of the public good'. However, neither this reprieve nor the final abandonment in June of the prosecution of the Vice-Chancellor aroused much jubilation in Oxford. It was felt that he would have been better served by an acquittal, and the campaign in pulpit and press occasioned considerable nervousness.[32]

The thunders of the court preachers had begun at St. Mary's in March 1748, when John Tottie, fellow of Worcester College, archdeacon of Worcester, and chaplain to the king, had attacked revellers like Whitmore and Dawes in a heavy discourse on *The pernicious effects of an intemperate indulgence in sensual pleasures*. A year later an official opportunity arose for reply to the opposition on the day of thanksgiving for the peace. Appointed to preach before the Commons, Conybeare expounded the burning issue of the nature of true patriotism. This subject enabled him to introduce a glowing panegyric of the king, and to turn the opposition slogans against their makers. 'A spirit of party hath prevailed, which according to its own little interests, breaks in upon the great duties owing to the public', questioning both men and measures. Such criticism, claimed the Dean, belonged to Parliament alone. On the same day Kennicott, a zealous Whig of Exeter College, whose hopes were at this moment placed in the Earl of Sandwich, was using the text Jer. xxxiii. 10, 11 to introduce an analysis of the diplomatic situation in a sermon before the Mayor and Corporation of Oxford. The peace, he insisted, was a great deal better than might have been expected. Now was the time for party distinctions to subside and for all men to give loyal support to the best of kings. That 'certain little tutor', Edward Bentham, was appointed to preach the next sermon on King Charles the Martyr before the House of Commons, and after characteristically feeble argument concluded that 'whoever tempers his mind with the true spirit of religion, will be far better pleased to find occasion of applauding his rulers than blaming them'.[33]

[32] Bodl. MS. Top. Oxon. b 43, fos. 23–25; Balliol College MS. 403, fos. 98–99, 102–3; Walpole's *Letters*, ii. 372–3; B.M. Add. MS. 35590, fo. 301; Sandon Hall: MS. Ryder Diary (typescript), pp. 63–66, 70.
[33] J. Tottie, *The Pernicious Effects of an Intemperate Indulgence in Sensual Pleasures* (Oxford, n.d. [1748]); J. Conybeare, *True Patriotism* (London, 1749); B. Kennicott, *The Duty of Thanksgiving . . .* (London, 1749); E. Bentham,

Pamphleteers were freer than preachers to attack personalities, and a cloud of hornets descended upon Dr. King, who published in London the speech delivered at the opening of the Camera when the Vice-Chancellor refused publication in Oxford. John Burton of Corpus and Eton attacked him in detail, and made the most of his attachment to the Stuarts. 'Whence comes his attachment to a family who have been expelled for being the most notorious violators of [liberty]? Whence his unreasonable aversion and seditious invectives against a family, who are and only can be the support of it?' Equally absurd was his pretence that 'there was no bribery or corruption under a Tory administration, and . . . nothing else under every other'. In family pride Burton noted that though Bentham's *Letters* were 'stiled by our speech maker with his usual obloquy, epistolae famosae', he did not attempt to answer them. King's reply to this was to produce a fly-sheet purporting to have been written by Burton himself, in which were listed all the abusive adjectives he had coined for the Principal of St. Mary Hall. The *London Evening Post* came loyally to his defence, declaring that had King's speech 'been publish'd 120 years ago, it would have been reputed a *Republican Libel*', and thus, according to Burton, 'what were republican principles in the last century are Jacobite principles in this'. But this, like all King's controversies, ended in facetious abuse, and more serious issues were raised elsewhere.[34]

The attack on Oxford institutions was developed on two very different lines in 1749. In a pamphlet entitled *A Blow at the Root*, the traditions of Nicolas Amhurst were revived. This tract proposed to 'demonstrate beyond all possible contradiction, that the rebellion [of 1715] was entirely occasioned by the wicked principles taught in our universities and schools . . . but the seeds of rebellion were permitted to remain', and the complete reformation in the universities and schools shunned by George I and Walpole must now be undertaken to root up the evil growth. Moreover, the present age was fundamentally wiser than the past.

The experience of all ages has convinc'd that few corruptions of a

Sermon preached before the House of Commons . . . on Jan. 30, 1749/50 (Oxford, 1750).
[34] J. Burton, *Remarks on Dr. K[ing]'s Speech at the Dedication of Dr. R[adcliffe]'s Library* (London, 1750); *An Answer to Dr. King's Speech. By the Rev. Mr. John Burton* (n.pl. or d.); *London Evening Post*, 11–13 Jan. 1750: 13–16 Jan. 1750.

public nature, can withstand the power of a free enquiry. . . . To this we owe our Reformation from Popery, and our happy deliverance from the wicked tyranny and usurpation of the See of Rome. To this inestimable privilege are we also indebted for the present disgrace of superstition, enthusiasm, persecution, and the eternal overthrow of those stupid and slavish doctrines of passive obedience, non-resistance and the absolute, indefeasible hereditary right of Princes.

An upheaval in Oxford was more than a political necessity, it was an acknowledgement of the progressive spirit of the times, and the later battles of the University cast their shadows before as the writer demanded the same acknowledgement in the Church which 'still retain'd in its doctrines, worship and discipline, a good deal of absurdity and contradiction, which was introduc'd by the weakness and wickedness of ecclesiasticks of former ages.'

Edward Bentham, who burst into print again, could not enliven his pages by even so shallow a general idea as that of the innate superiority of modern knowledge, arguing that though things were bad they might be worse, and probably would be if the Pretender returned. He was on stronger ground in showing that, unlike dons who played with Jacobitism,[35] the government had not contravened the law, but foolishly undertook to demonstrate the undemonstrable, that the financial burdens of state which so grieved the opposition would have been incurred whether the Revolution had taken place or not, and so exposed himself to King's well-aimed ridicule.[36]

As so often before, Oxford writers harked back to 1648, and republished the reasons of Convocation against the reforming ordinances of that day, with Clarendon's commendation of them as 'a monument of the learning, courage and loyalty of that excellent place, against the highest malice and tyranny', and exhibited their scholarship in witty rhyming Latin verse.

[35] The writer of *Oxford Honesty, or a Case of Conscience* (London, n.d.) put it more tersely: 'A SWEARING JACOBITE PARSON! What man of common morals can think of him without indignation?'

[36] *A Blow at the Root, or an Attempt to Prove, that no Time ever was, or very probably ever will be, so Proper and Convenient as the Present, for Introducing a Further Reformation into our National Church, Universities and Schools* (London, 1749). This pamphlet is ascribed by Halkett and Laing to Aaron Tozer, but is shown by Bodl. MS. Top. Oxon. b 23, fos. 24–25, to be by George Coade; E. Bentham, *A Letter to a Fellow of a College* (London, 1749); King, *Poetical Abridgement*, pp. 44–50.

At quid fecit *Alma*,
Quae gloriae palma
    Per secula porta ornata 'st?
Quam, quaeso, obmendam
Clamare *delendam*,
    Ecclesia et aula parata 'st?

King, as well as the rhymer, noted the universal cry *delenda est Oxonia*, and this was the title of one of the best pamphlets of the year, by Horace Walpole. This tract was designed 'to pass . . . for an Oxford performance: tho the intention was very Whig; to preserve the Liberties of the University, & to show that the scheme of the Ministry was parallel to the behaviour of K. James 2d, which had given rise to the Revolution'. In all this there was nothing very original, but the pamphlet is of interest as showing how discontented court Whigs could be brought to the defence even of Oxford, and for the skilful use of paradox which led to the pamphlet's being seized at the printers 'before publication, by the Secretary of State's messengers, who were sent thither after some of the Remembrancers'. Oxford men, he declared,

wish to have it reconciled to their apprehensions, how affection to the eldest son of the Elector of Hanover should be a mark of Jacobitism; how attachment to the House of Pelham is whiggism & loyalty. They think they have seen, that to forswear the interests of Hanover is the way to introduction into the closet; & they say they have known the head of the Jacobites [Gower] preferred to one of the first posts in the government.

So backward-looking were eighteenth-century political writers that it was rare on either side for an argument to be drawn from the political confusion of the day.

It required no great acumen in the *London Evening Post* to rejoice in an outbreak of drunken Jacobitism at Cambridge just before the great duke's installation, but another pamphlet skilfully surveyed the Hanoverian era, showing how at the outset the Whig ministers were supported by 'a party at Oxford [who] were to rise and be preferr'd among the rest, purely by merit of aspersing the characters of such gentlemen there' as preferred the ministers of Queen Anne to those of George I. The present propaganda against the University was as malicious as that of Amhurst who served every faction in turn. The crisis was an incident in the contest for local influence between the Duke of Marlborough and the Earl of Abingdon, a doubtful but interesting assertion in view of the great county election campaign which began soon afterwards.[37]

The academic year 1749–50 began with the Vice-Chancellor breathing resentment at the informer who had caused him the expense and trouble of being cited in the courts three times without having an opportunity of vindicating his innocence.[38] But by now the government were contemplating gentler means of influence; the Archbishop of Canterbury humorously told Newcastle that 'your Grace needs no prompter in the favour of the Cambridge men', but thought it advantageous if preferments were more often given to 'the most distinguished Heads & others in both our universities', and in particular to Dean Conybeare whose continued neglect reflected ill upon Whig principles. In April 1750 Hardwicke was likewise commending Blacow, whose persistence had touched off the whole crisis. 'As all further thoughts about the Universities seem to be laid aside, it seems to be the only thing left to give some encourgemt. and spirit to the well affected . . . it is my real opinion that if nothing should be done, it would be a matter of objection.' But although he had the support of Archbishop and Lord Chancellor, and had been petitioning for two years, Blacow found, as so many others, that the way of the Whig martyr was hard, and much more informing was required of him yet.[39]

The government's withdrawal before the threat of disturbances in the country and a combined opposition in the Commons did not end the controversy in the press, but helped to change its

[37] *Reasons of the Present Judgement of the University of Oxford concerning the Solemn League and Covenant* . . . (London, 1749); *Carmen Rhymicum, Monachicum, Momo dicatum* . . . (London, 1749); P. Toynbee, 'Horace Walpole's *Delenda est Oxonia*', *E.H.R.* xlii. 95 seq.; *London Evening Post*, 17–20 June 1749. There were also disturbances on constitutional issues at Cambridge not unlike those fomented at Oxford by Dr. King in his youth (Nichols, *Literary Anecdotes*, vi. 472–3); *Laws and Arguments in Vindication of the University of Oxford* (London, n.d.).

[38] Dr. Purnell had not heard the last of this affair, for in 1758 the Bishop of Winchester, who had earlier confirmed the election of the sixth successive Warden of New College as Warden of Winchester, quashed the election of Purnell on the grounds that the Warden of New College was debarred by the statutes. He appointed Golding, a fellow of New College, 'a friend to King George [who] no more dreamt of this advancement than he did of being Pope [and] was frightened out of his wits' (*Memoirs of a Royal Chaplain*, pp. 300–3).

[39] B.M. Add. MSS. 32719, fos. 210, 337–8, 345–6: 32720, fos. 29, 217, 221: 32722, fos. 8, 67: 32717, fos. 427, 562.

character. King's personal duels continued, and Dr. Brooke, the Whig 'angel' of the opening of the Radcliffe Camera, smote him again in defence of Bentham and Burton. Brooke now willingly avowed that the number of genuine Jacobites among the Oxford Tories was inconsiderable, and 'men so absurd, so very impious place[d] themselves much below the dignity of reason and argument'. Nevertheless, did not those who admittedly were not Jacobites invite the innuendoes of the world outside? What minister for a generation past had earned their approval? Was it not true that except in two or three colleges elections were always rigged in the Tory interest, and that 'in certain public elections, made by the whole body of the University, the first point resolved by the ruling party hath been, *that the vote of every Whig Elector should be fruitless?*' With the state a generous benefactor of the University, with the Church flourishing and the dissenters declining, 'the modern Tories of Oxford must not only be destitute of Faith and Honour, but they must be blind to their *own interest*, design their own destruction, and be esteemed Idiots as well as Transgressors . . .'. Nor could they complain at the rejection of their address, for it was absurd 'to afford the soft and tender appellation of *intemperate sallies of youth* to *crimes* of a *treasonable* tendency'.

King, in the character of an Eton schoolboy, replied to this argument with fresh scurrility, written ironically against himself, and devoted a whole appendix to destroying Brooke's character of Burton. The latter, it appeared, had always been a disturber of college and Convocation, and the society 'which suckled him rejoiced at his removal from it'.[40] Small wonder that Dr. Hunt, professor of Hebrew, preached a university sermon against defamation.

As the prospect of political intervention faded, discussion turned increasingly towards the need for disciplinary changes. A number of articles and the correspondence they evoked were published in the *General Evening Post* and some other papers in the early months of 1750, and subsequently printed in pamphlet form by that diehard reformer Richard Newton, Principal of Hertford College, the 'Well-wisher to the University of Oxford',

---

[40] [H. Brooke], *A Letter to the Oxford Tories* (London, 1750); [W. King], *The Old Lady in her Tantrums or Mother Oxford Ranting at her Eldest Son K[I]NG* . . . (Eton, 1950); *London Evening Post*, 26–29 Oct. 1751.

who originated the series and brought it to Newcastle's notice. He urged that if discipline were not reformed the University would soon become a place improper for the education of youth. The reformation could only be carried through by Parliament, as responsibility for the present situation, in which elections were swayed by family and fortune, could be laid upon no single academic authority. Only in Christ Church and Hertford was the head not chosen by the fellows, and college discipline was undermined by disreputable intrigues for the succession to the headship.

In reply it was urged that the University could not be helped by a revival of the clamour, that it was hazardous to encourage governments to 'break in upon ancient establishments', and, a familiar cry in later years, that it was doubtful if the legislature could absolve men from their oaths. No statutes could bind Oxford electors more closely to the choice of merit than those in force; if the electors broke through them they would break through any others. The remedy proposed was the very worst, to 'vest the appointment of our governors in other hands', and, unkindest cut of all, 'there is one college here, [Hertford] where not only the governor was not chose by his fellows, but has had the making of his own statutes: can it be said, that even this distinguished society flourishes more than any other?'

Soon afterwards charges of homosexual delinquencies were made against members of the University, and denied by William Lewis of Christ Church. With discussions of new regulations taking place at Cambridge, and the first stirrings of the controversy which led to the great attack on the university test, the issue of university reform gradually took a different turn. Now even Oxford heads could not afford not to be reformers, and at the end of 1750 Dr. Browne, Master of University College, the new Vice-Chancellor, entered 'upon the plan of reformation which his predecessor had begun, . . . [hoping] to make such a progress therein, by the meeting of Parliament, as what may reasonably stop the mouths of our enemys, and open those of our friends'. Other heads followed him in putting their houses to rights, but it was after Dr. Browne's time that his own college rose in revolt against an attempt to make undergraduates pass their time in academic pursuits.[41]

[41] See note N, p. 282.

The final squibs in the agitation ostensibly for university reform coincided with a more normal political conflict in the election of a new university burgess. The leaders of the old interest in Oxford had got wind of Cornbury's expected elevation to the House of Lords in November 1750, and had begun their campaign long before his resignation about a week before the election on 31 January 1751.[42] Their choice of candidate fell on Sir Roger Newdigate, a Warwickshire baronet, who had succeeded Pulteney unopposed as knight of the shire for Middlesex 1742–7, another county where he possessed extensive property and many friends. Elected as a stout opponent of the Walpoles,[43] he was defeated at the next general election, but his supporter, James Clitherow of Boston House, himself a Queen's man, put him forward at Oxford through his son-in-law, William Blackstone.[44] A progressive landlord who poured money into the development of coal-mines, canals, and turnpikes, Newdigate commended himself as the reverse of progressive in politics. Proud of his independence, imbued already with a distaste for public life which deepened gradually into disgust, professing with complete sincerity that nothing less than the honour of representing such a bulwark of political purity as the University, and preserving the old interest against its enemies, could have persuaded him to return to parliament, Newdigate embodied all the ideals of the country politicians, and believed in a kind of political anarchy in which the less of central government there was, the better. Blackstone was quite candid that it was the old interest that mattered, not merely to procure a suitable M.P. at this juncture, 'but also because we plainly forsee that ye choice of a Chancellor, whenever we have the misfortune to lose the present, depends upon the fate of this election'; could they 'have pitched upon any person, who in our opinions would better have discharged this trust, Sir Roger Newdigate's name would never have been mentioned here'.

It was a mark of the confusion of party at this date, however, that not only Sir John Phillips a Welsh, and Sir Willoughby Aston a Derbyshire baronet, were also favoured, but that there were other candidates proclaiming similar allegiances before

[42] Cornbury publicly excused the delay attending his elevation by his 'desire to give time to the University to agree' (B.M. Add. MS. 32724, fos. 81, 89).
[43] H. Walpole's *Letters*, i. 268–9.
[44] Warwick C.R.O. Newdigate MS. B 1573.

whom Newdigate thought he should withdraw in the interests of 'that impregnable unanimity wh[ich] has hitherto distinguished the University upon these occasions'. The first of these was Sir Edward Turner, an Oxfordshire baronet also defeated in 1747. He was a freeman of the City of Oxford, and at the time of Lord Wenman's election for that borough in 1749 he had canvassed for the succession when Wenman should transfer to the county at the next general election. He was expected to run Newdigate close, though Blackstone considered preventing a division in the old interest by arranging a compromise with him. Intimate with his brother-in-law Theophilus Leigh, Master of Balliol, created an honorary doctor of the University in 1744, Turner might well attract old-interest voters; yet within a couple of years he was leading the violent campaign of the New Interest in the county against Wenman.

This fall from grace was as yet unsuspected, but about three weeks before the poll Blackstone and his friends concluded that he was ineligible because he had received the freedom of the city of Oxford in 1742. This, it was claimed, terminated his member-ship of the University, for the statutes absolutely forbade the admission of freemen. As the charter which conferred representa-tion required burgesses to be members of the University, Turner could never sit for this constituency. Counsel's opinion was at once sought, and given in favour of Turner, on the grounds that mem-bership of the University could be terminated only by an official act, and the requirement of the charter was of no more signifi-cance than the universally evaded obligation of boroughs to send up a member out of their own number.

This opinion was circulated to all the common rooms except that in which Newdigate's champions foregathered at All Souls. The latter issued a reply consisting more of politics than law, to which it was answered that both Clarges in 1688 and Glynne in 1698 had been elected by the University while freemen of the city.[45]

Meanwhile the Christ Church interest had proposed a third candidate, Robert Harley, the second son of the third Earl of Oxford. Lord Oxford had been the pupil and correspondent of old Canon Stratford; even more than his cousin the second earl, the great Maecenas of scholarship, he had kept closely in touch

---

[45] On these legal questions: *A True Copy of the Poll taken at Oxford Jan. 31, 1750* (London, n.d.), pp. 3-8.

with university affairs, and was more than merely the bearer of one of the great names of the past. In 1743, when Arran seemed to be in decline, he had been thought of as Chancellor, with the ulterior hope that some of the family manuscripts might be acquired for the Bodleian. A Radcliffe Trustee, and one of the Tories who negotiated with the Prince of Wales in 1748, he had every claim to the loyalty of the old interest in the University. When, however, he found that his son would cause a contest, he ordered him to desist on the grounds 'that it wd be more honor to him to acquiesce under ye sense of the University than even to succeed upon a contested elecōn'. With this news arriving at the very moment when Blackstone's friends thought they had made Turner's candidature impossible, it looked as though Newdigate would have a smooth passage.[46]

However, 'some of Sir Edw. T.'s leaders, being angry at [their] disappointment, did in conjunction with my Ld. Oxfd's agent here, immediately repropose Mr. Harley', and got him his father's backing. Blackstone declared 'that ye University must for ever lose its weight & reputation if represented by a younger brother, a youth of 22, of no independent fortune, & one that some time hence is to be engaged in a profession [the law] ye most liable of any to temptacons', and a desperate race to the poll was forecast. Blackstone reckoned upon 'above 200 sure votes, besides neuters, & ye number of ye whole does not much exceed 400, including above 100 ministerial men'. It was nevertheless still felt that the political complexion of the candidates was sufficiently alike to justify the old interest joining the following of either Harley or Turner if their canvass showed them to be in the lead. Turner's friends, however, would listen to no compromise, and Harley's agents could not promise the Christ Church vote to Newdigate, should he be found stronger than Harley. From Newdigate's point of view this was crucial, for while he would probably triumph as long as his opponents were divided, it might be a close fight if all the minority factions supported one candidate. In one respect Blackstone's calculations proved too optimistic. Henry Pelham was trying to win Lord Oxford for the ministry, and this was sufficient to bring almost the entire Whig vote behind Robert Harley.

[46] *London Evening Post*, 8–10, 15–17 Jan. 1751; Warwick C.R.O. Newdigate MS. B 1482; Bodl. MS. Ballard 2, fo. 134; Balliol College MS. 403, fo. 59.

As the poll drew near Newdigate was on tenterhooks, but he finally cantered home safely with 184 votes to 126 of Harley's and 67 of Turner's. Although Blackstone had taken the precaution to whip in a considerable number of non-residents it was impossible to raise the passions of 1722, and the poll was even smaller than in 1737. The backbone of Turner's vote came from a large party in Queen's led by the Provost, and a small group in Magdalen. Harley's support was in its way equally disappointing. As the Whigs' candidate and a member of the society, he received almost the whole of the Christ Church vote; the old Whig strongholds of Merton, Exeter, and Wadham stood firm; there was still a Whig clique in Jesus, and the Whig faction at Trinity revived. But the only surprise sprung by Harley was to take the Principal and almost half the Brasenose vote from Sir Roger; on the whole it was an unhappy performance for an attractive Tory candidate with secret Whig support. His total poll barely exceeded that of Trevor fifteen years before, and Newdigate wrote his opponent's epitaph in the remark that 'ye Whigs in this experiment have shown themselves if possible of less consequence than in their last struggle & . . . their treachery has availed them no more than their open force'. Thus firmly had the old interest been bound together by Whig threats to university endowments in the thirties, and to academic patronage in the forties.

Sir Roger Newdigate might now pay a ceremonial visit to the constituency he had been forbidden to canvass, and the old interest might await the Chancellor's demise with confidence. Yet the ministerial interest was very far from downcast, and followed up the election by a pamphlet addressed to Lord Cornbury in which they ascribed the escape of the University from visitation to his lordship's influence, and begged his continued protection. Though paying tribute to Cornbury's 'independence', the writers warned Newdigate against 'caballings' through which 'the important interests of an university [would] be most preposterously tack'd to those of a faction' and would revive the hostility to the University recently evident in the Commons. Within two years it proved impossible to keep the ministerial interest in Oxford to platitudes as polite as this.[47]

[47] Warwick C.R.O. Newdigate MSS. B 1483, 1483a, 1485, 1486, 1487, 1518, 1519, 1530, 1531, 1574, 1873, 1874, 2403: 1575, 2395; B.M. Add. MS. 33061, fos. 365–6; H. Walpole, *Memoirs of George II*, i. 41; *A True Copy of the Poll: A Letter to Lord Viscount Cornbury* (London, 1751).

PART IV

THE COURT TRIES AGAIN
1751–68

And being thus listed in opposite parties, they fix odious names & distinctions on one another and hate and abuse one another though they know not the meaning of such names, nor what distinguishes them from one another. . . . One set of principles shall suit a man out of power and another when in power. . . .

> T. Randolph, *Party Zeal Censur'd in a Sermon preach'd before the University of Oxford at St. Mary's*, 1752

The Palladians [the Oxford Tories] defend themselves with great skill and resolution; and in all attacks which have been made hitherto, they have repulsed the enemy. But . . . as they are not in a condition to recruit their forces, and the Onocentaurs [the Whigs] receive continued supplies from the present governors of the Papyrolitan empire [the ministry], 'tis scarce possible that Pallantis should hold out much longer.

> W. King, *The Dreamer*, 1754

CHAPTER XII

The University and the County Election, 1754

SCARCELY had the threat to academic independence and to the supremacy of the Old Interest been overcome than the dons became involved in the great election contest brewing in the county and in internecine warfare among themselves. The long story of the struggle between the Old Interest led by Wenman and Dashwood, and the New Interest candidates, Parker and Turner, supported by the three new Oxfordshire peers, Marlborough, Macclesfield, and Harcourt, needs no re-telling for its own sake,[1] but forms an important chapter in the history of the University. From the beginning Harcourt had hopes not only of success in the county but 'perhaps of laying a foundation for attempting

[1] See R. J. Robson, *The Oxfordshire Election of 1754* (London, 1949).

something hereafter even in the University',[2] and the university Whigs, defeated in their character of academical reformers, or of supporters of a Harley, laboured with a will for the New Interest in the county, well knowing that the University had always been influenced by the politics of the neighbouring magnates and gentry. As the campaign was about to open, Dr. Randolph, President of Corpus, who had nominated Turner in 1751, strongly condemned the unhappy colleges 'in all of which Parties and Distinctions are too often apt to prevail',[3] but Turner's friends showed even less respect than his enemies for the President's conventional fulminations against party zeal.

To the organizers of the New Interest, who must mobilize every vote, the electoral interest of the colleges was by no means negligible. The dons' vote was small, and totally ineffective from being divided almost equally between the two sides,[4] but the Earl of Macclesfield derived great hope from 'the weight of Christ Church upon their tradesmen' when a friend became under-treasurer at the House; the proctors might be brought to give favours to voters employed as gardeners in the Physick Garden; and in October 1753 that optimistic amazon, Susan Keck, even hoped to win the Vice-Chancellor, Dr. Huddesford, President of Trinity.[5] Colleges might also sway the votes and the interest of many of the parish clergy.[6] Yet in an electorate of some 4,000 the votes influenced by the University and colleges could be of no more than marginal significance, and the chief value of dons was in propaganda and organization.

The first and most telling cry had been presented to the Old Interest from the outside, for the crescendo of the election campaign coincided with the tremendous opposition agitation which culminated in the repeal of the Jew Bill. In the autumn of 1753 the *London Evening Post* clamoured for the University to instruct its members to vote for repeal of the Bill, thereby vindicating her independence from the 'ostentatious *Praemia,* and the side of

---

[2] B.M. Add. MS. 32728, fo. 364 (quoted in Robson, p. 19).
[3] T. Randolph, *Party Zeal Censur'd* (Oxford, 1752), p. 4. This sermon provoked a reply from a Quaker, Ephraim Harman, in *A Letter to Thomas Randolph* . . . (London, 1752).
[4] Robson, op. cit., p. 76.
[5] Exeter College MSS.: letters to Thomas Bray from Thomas Blackall, 8 Feb. 1753; Susan Keck, 21 Oct. 1753; Lord Macclesfield, 23 Oct. 1753.
[6] Robson, op. cit., p. 85.

preferment', which were the ruination of Cambridge. Newdigate, indeed, demanded not only repeal but the omission of the phrase in the preamble of the repealing Act in which the ministers referred to the 'discontents and disquiets' which the opposition had raised. Meanwhile *Jackson's Oxford Journal* had been flooding the county with anti-semitism in the Old Interest; 'New Interest' and 'Jewish' had become synonymous in the political parlance of Oxfordshire Tories; and the inhabitants of Bicester intoxicated themselves with toasts to the Tory leaders and slogans of 'No Jews! No Naturalization! Wenman and Dashwood for ever!' Turner and his university friends were assailed in a characteristic squib entitled *The Christian's New Warning Piece or . . . the Circumcision of Sir E[dward] T[urner] Bart.*[7]

Rival cries became indispensable to the New Interest, propaganda more telling than the sermon of Dr. John Free who, infallible in saying the right thing at the wrong time, preached at St. Mary's in favour of the Jews. As early as May 1753 the New Interest accused Dr. King of pamphleteering for the other side,[8] and the mock report alleged to have emanated from Geneva that 'our Brethren the Dissenters of all Denominations in Oxfordshire, inform us with inexpressible pleasure, that every step is taken by the Low Party in that county to pull down the High Church, in order to pave the way for overturning the established Church of England', bears all the marks of his handiwork.[9] This recourse to ancient shibboleths may well have given the New Interest propagandists their cue. They retorted with equal anachronism that their opponents were Jacobites and Papists, a charge fabricated by Thomas Bray, fellow of Exeter, who was congratulated by Lord Harcourt in a splendid piece of self-persuasion:

The charge of perjury is a home thrust, & is for a weapon in our hands, as the clamour raised against the Jews was in their's. It has already done us infinite service, and will be a lasting advantage to us.

[7] *London Evening Post*, 23–25 Oct., 3–6 Nov. 1753; Cobbett, xv. 131–4; J[ackson's] O[xford] J[ournal], 9 June, 27 Oct., 3 Nov. 1753.

[8] It was King who made the only public comment on the Jew Bill to issue from the side of the academic Tories: 'God did not permit the Jews to eat swine because this would have been a kind of fratricide' (*The Dreamer* (London, 1754), p. 141).

[9] *J.O.J.*, 5, 12 May 1753. The dissenters were also alleged to think that the test 'should be dispensed with to them, as well as those outcasts of Heaven, the Jews' (ibid., 14 July 1753).

In short there is a great deal of truth in it, & therefore it is the more powerful. . . .

'Popery', declared Bray in the press, 'is a millstone which, hung about the neck of the old interest, will absolutely sink it'; the Radcliffe trustees were accused of absconding to Rome with their funds; Hardwicke was plagued with the story of a picture of the Pretender in the J.C.R. at Corpus which had occasioned the forcible intervention of Whigs from Christ Church and Merton; and eventually in July 1754, when the Oxfordshire return was before the House of Commons, the New Interest resurrected the charge again in its absurdest form in the Rag Plot. Now Mary Carnall, the wife of a Carfax grocer, claimed to have found treasonable verses in a bundle of rags left outside her husband's shop, an undoubted New Interest forgery which was at once presented as a 'false, malicious, infamous and treasonable libel' by a grand jury packed by Parker, Turner, Keck, and their friends.[10]

Bray, who at this point became a public, not to say notorious figure, has already appeared as one of the informers at the opening of the Radcliffe Camera, and was known as a turbulent character within his society. In 1745 he had been in a minority of one on the question of the sale of part of the college garden to the Radcliffe trustees, and having acquired the livings of Harnhill and Driffield in Gloucestershire, neither of which was consistent with his fellowship, fought a protracted battle with Rector Edgecumbe in the years 1748–9, and with the aid of the Visitor kept both fellowship and livings. Bray's election correspondence in the Exeter College archives reveals that by 1753 he was on familiar terms with all the pillars of the New Interest—Parker, Turner, Harcourt, Marlborough, Macclesfield, and Susan Keck alike— and was their chief organizer in Oxford. The latter's instruction to Bray was that 'should Sir James [Dashwood] come into Oxford or any of the Gang, they must always be faced, out eat, out drank . . . let the expense be what it will', and Harcourt, on whom he also drew for cash, was 'quite astonished that you have been able to do so much with so few materials'.[11]

[10] Exeter College MSS.: Lord Harcourt to Thomas Bray, 22 Jan. 1754; *J.O.J.*, 19, 26 Jan., 2 Feb. 1754; B.M. Add. MS. 35593, fo. 81. On the Corpus Case cf. Warwick C.R.O. Newdigate MSS. B 2209–11.

[11] MS. Register of Exeter College 1737–1827, pp. 54–69 *passim*; Exeter College MSS.: letters to Thomas Bray from Lady Susan Keck, n.d.; Lord Harcourt, 21 Jan. 1753.

The New Interest voters in Oxford mobilized with the aid of bribes, loans, and treats, and the county prepared by the packing of the assessors of the land tax, Bray's main duties lay in concerting the press campaign. He saw to the local publication of pamphlets, wrote in *Jackson's Oxford Journal* as long as Jackson would accept his effusions, in the *Gentleman's Magazine*, and elsewhere. It was Bray's duty also to keep the principals of the New Interest in touch with events in Oxford and to manage the London organizer of the campaign, none other than Richard Blacow, the still unpreferred informer of 1748. Long before Blacow became editor of *The Evening Advertiser* in the autumn of 1754, he was fussily inserting notices in the London papers, keeping his finger on the public pulse, and exerting what Kennicott regarded as his grossly overrated influence upon the ministers for the preferment of himself and his friends at Exeter. Kennicott, a great Hebrew scholar with a sharp pen in both political and ecclesiastical controversy, and the staunch Whig Rector Webber, formed with Bray an active triumvirate abused by King as 'the Bray of the three mouths'.[12]

Personalities had already begun to loom large in the University. The death of Richard Newton in 1753 had opened a contest between the university factions for the headship of Hertford. As in the days when the society was a hall, Lord Arran (who had been canvassed by the Tory Duke of Beaufort) made a nomination, one Fowler Cummings, while Christ Church, by virtue (as they claimed) of Newton's statutes, presented one of their own students, William Sharp, who had voted for Harley in 1751. Christ Church carried the day, and while Sharp pronounced a Latin panegyric upon Newton in the college hall, Fowler Cummings made a futile protest to a notary public.[13] The friends of the Old Interest in Oxford received a further set-back when Blackstone was disappointed of his hopes of the regius chair of civil law by his refusal to give Newcastle the expected pledges of political reliability. Murray encouraged him to read lectures in Oxford nevertheless, a design on which Blackstone declared himself already resolved. His deficiencies in public speaking, 'his temper, constitution, inclinations, & a thing called principle', had all con-

[12] Exeter College MSS. *passim*; *London Evening Post*, 9–11 July 1754.
[13] B.M. Eg. MS. 2618, fo. 231; *J.O.J.*, 2, 16 June 1753; *London Evening Post*, 29–31 May 1753.

vinced him that he could expect no great future in Westminster Hall, and that he should accept the advice of the many professional colleagues who urged him to return to academic pursuits. The county election of 1754 revealed to the full Blackstone's double character as academic lawyer and Tory politician, for he produced not only a celebrated signed treatise denying the right of copyholders to a freehold vote, but also considerable pseudonymous ammunition for the daily mud-slinging. From an early date the Whigs had no doubt that he and his flamboyant All Souls friend, Buckler, were writing against them, and Blacow considered him to be 'Coryphaeus' in the *London Evening Post*.[14]

The disappointments of Cummings and Blackstone, and the furious activity of the New Interest ant-hill in Exeter College, convinced the Oxford Tories that it was high time to discredit their leading opponents. Theophilus Leigh, Master of Balliol, Turner's brother-in-law, and a politician much changed since his election as Master, was an obvious target as 'the Rev. Dr. Twister', while an even more active stickler for the New Interest, Charles Jenkinson, bred of University College and unimpeachable Oxfordshire Old Interest stock, was slandered as 'Squire Lick-Spittle' and the 'Tall-Boy'.[15] Whatever respect the old interest retained for the character of Edward Bentham was destroyed when he was rewarded by a canonry at Christ Church for a little decorous journalism in the New Interest.

The key man, however, was Thomas Bray, and it was he who suffered the most unscrupulous attacks. On 18 July 1753 he received a letter from Theodosia Cornell, alias Cornill, alias Cornwell, a pregnant pauper from the Oxford workhouse, soliciting money on the grounds that he had fathered her expected child in Shotover woods on the previous Easter Sunday, and simultaneously the letter was published. The circumstantial detail arose from the fact that the Bishop of Oxford, an unblushing partisan of the New Interest, had appointed Bray (in succession to two

[14] J. Holliday, *Life of William, Earl of Mansfield* (London, 1797), pp. 88–89; Warwick C.R.O. Newdigate MS. B 1488; W. Blackstone, *Considerations on Copyholders* (London, 1758); *J.O.J.*, 12 May 1753; Exeter College MSS.: R. Blacow to T. Bray, 23 Aug. 1754.

[15] *J.O.J.*, 27 Oct. 1753, 2 Mar. 1754. Dr. Leigh's evolution from a patriot into one who put even his celebrated talents as a punster at the disposal of the Court is well described in verse in *The Election Magazine* (Oxford, 1753), pp. 41–42.

other Whigs) perpetual curate of Wheatley, a hamlet in the parish of Cuddesdon. The symbolic allegation was that in the circum- stances even spiritual ministrations to the (solidly Old Interest) parishioners of Wheatley must be involved in iniquity, and for factual verisimilitude it was alleged that one Sarah Walker had received a shilling from Bray to mind his horse during the inci- dent.

At the next Assizes Bray indicted Theodosia Cornell for defamation of character, and the political factions began a dis- creditable contest to keep a grip upon the only two witnesses, Cornell and Walker. Theodosia Cornell was kept in close custody by the Old Interest, though even a year later the Earl of Maccles- field hoped that 'if she could once be got from under the power of your enemies and her present supporters she might be prevailed upon by proper means and persons of address to unravel and lay open the whole of that villainous design'. Sarah Walker was cap- tured by the Bray faction, who found her a most difficult witness. Bray's intention was to keep her cool at Witney till the Assizes, but he found 'she wants to have money to spend in London in debauchery, where she would be liable to be decoyed away when I should want her'. Walker, indeed, reckoned upon unlimited blackmail, which she described as money to enable her to go into service, and Bray remained on tenterhooks lest the sums which passed should be revealed in cross-examination at the trial, or lest the witness herself escape. However, with the aid of Blacow and others Sarah Walker 'lived extremely well' and proved 'in high spirits' and ready 'to serve [her] friend without fail' at the trial. She deposed before three J.P.s, one of whom was Anthony Keck, that she had refused an offer of four and twenty guineas to sup- port Theodosia Cornell's testimony, and, no doubt to Bray's relief, helped to secure the conviction of her quondam friend in March 1754. Officially Bray's character was clear, though not to the satis- faction of the Old Interest hack-writers.[16]

The poll supervened closely upon this judicial testimony to the

[16] B. Porteus, *A Review of the Life and Character of Archbishop Secker* (Lon- don, 1773), p. 27; *J.O.J.*, 4 Aug. 1753, 9 March 1754; *London Evening Post*, 19–21 Sept. 1754; Exeter College MSS.: The King agst. Theodosia Cornhill; T. Bray to R. Blacow, 6 Dec. 1753; Sarah Walker to Thomas Bray, 7, 16 Nov. 1753; James Leverett to Thomas Bray, 18, 22 Feb. 1754; Sarah Walker to W. Wells, 3 Dec. 1753; The Deposition of Sarah Walker, 7 March 1754; Lord Macclesfield to T. Bray, 11 June 1754.

morals of Dr. Bray. With memories of the last threat of visitation still green, the Old Interest leaders in the University had been doubly cautious about the accusation of Jacobitism. The *London Evening Post* had hailed the accession of Dr. Huddesford as Vice-Chancellor as the death-blow to all calumnies—he being one of the Associators of 1745—while Blackstone, King, Buckler, and the other Old Interest propagandists had covered their tracks so well as to convince Mr. Robson that there was a serious lack of sympathy between the leaders of the Old Interest in county and University.

That the danger feared by the academic Tories was not illusory was proved in November 1754 when Pitt, seeking like Sunderland a generation before to rally the Whig corps to his leadership on the basis of their traditional faction cries, launched into a highly coloured account of the drowning of loyal songs at a party of his at the Angel Inn by a treasonable chorus from undergraduates drinking in a college across the street. This story was presented so as to convince all reporters of the debate, and Pitt's biographer, that the incident had occurred the previous summer. In fact, as everyone in Oxford remembered, Pitt's last visit had been five and a half years earlier, the undergraduates had been celebrating not in a college but in a coffee-house on the corner of Queen's College Lane, a calculated 36 yards from Pitt's room at the Angel, and in the very different circumstances of the University and himself at that time he had jovially encouraged indiscretion during the visit. Blacow improved the opportunity by regaling readers of *The Evening Advertiser* with a well-spiced account of the Pretender's picture at Corpus, but Kennicott wondered in bewilderment 'how are we to be managed now, if the Pitts & Grenvilles & Lytteltons unite against the University, & Fox &c. &c. [be] for it?'[17] It was with well-founded apprehensions of political episodes of this kind that the Tory heads had walked warily, and on the eve of the poll issued a strict programma, appointing wardens of the streets, confining undergraduates without votes to college, and ordering college gates to remain closed. No occasion

[17] H. Walpole, *George II*, i. 357–8; B. Williams, *The Life of William Pitt, Earl of Chatham* (London, 1913), i. 257–8; Warwick C.R.O. Newdigate MSS. B 1490, 2205–11; Exeter College MSS.: B. Kennicott to T. Bray, 28 Nov. 1754. Peregrine Palmer reported his speech to an Oxford correspondent '. . . to shew you what a spirit there is against you and . . . we may expect more of the same in the course of the county election . . .' (Bodl. MS. Top. Oxon. c 209, fo. 25).

of scandal should be given to aspiring Whigs, and the expected numerical superiority of the Old Interest would be safeguarded by a friendly mob barring their opponents' access to the polling booths in the Broad.

As is well known, Exeter College contravened the programma by opening their front gate to a party of New Interest voters who, after refreshment within, were admitted to the poll in the rear of the Old Interest mob by the back gate in the Broad, 'such instance of zeal and loyalty', in the view of Lord Harcourt, as 'no other Society can pretend to'. At last the university Whigs had committed a breach of academic discipline which the Tories could assail with a good conscience; moreover, since the returning officer had made an invalid return of all four candidates, and the issue of the election was in the hands of the House of Commons, both sides must assume an appearance of strength, especially as during the summer there was a real chance that Newcastle might ally himself with the Tories.

Blacow's ultimate preferment to a canonry at Windsor, his constant assurances of good things for his Exeter friends, and Kennicott's appointment as a Whitehall preacher in May 1754, were some evidence of New Interest strength. The strength of the Oxford Tories and of Dr. King in particular was exemplified when, on the death of the Earl of Clarendon and Rochester, Lord Arran presented the Earl of Westmorland as High Steward. This appointment aroused some surprise in both the University and the county, for Lord Lichfield had been publicly tipped for the honour, and the Duke of Beaufort, who inherited a long tradition of intimacy in university affairs, also had his hopes. Whether or not the passing over of the Earl of Lichfield indicates, as Mr. Robson thinks, some coolness between King and the Old Interest in the county,[18] it was a testimony to the healing of the ancient breach between the Chancellor and his former secretary (for the appointment was ascribed to King's influence) and to Lord Arran's continued support for the Old Interest in the University. At the Encaenia held for Westmorland's installation, the new High Steward complimented the University upon its politics while King presented a bevy of stout Tory honorary graduands

[18] Though Westmorland had been 'violent for the repeal of the Jew Bill' (*Bedford Correspondence*, ii. 139–40) and was uncle of Sir Francis Dashwood, a connexion of Sir James, the Oxfordshire candidate.

and improved the occasion with a prolonged onslaught upon the New Interest and Exeter College in particular.[19]

After the excitement of the Encaenia there was comparative quiet as the two sides awaited the issue of the next parliamentary session, but in August the first of two violent attacks by the Old Interest began, upon that prodigal son of the University, second only to Bray in his importance to the New Interest, Richard Blacow. In April 1754 Blacow had been the target of a verse in the *London Evening Post* in his capacity as an informer, but the Oxford Tories seem to have had little idea, or at least little evidence, of his activities in the underworld of the London press. Quite apart from his unwearied labours for the Oxfordshire New Interest, Blacow had discovered on Newcastle's behalf the editor and financial backers of the new opposition journal *The Protester* even before publication. When once he had become editor of *The Evening Advertiser*, however, Blacow could no longer cover his tracks, and suffered a violent blast of Old Interest spleen. Moreover, Blacow was found to have published an account of the absurd 'Rag Plot' in the London press two days before anything was known of it in Oxford.[20] After this discovery nothing could be too bad for the new canon, and he was flayed mercilessly in the *London Evening Post* without respite from August 1754 till the following January. Moreover, with the University collecting information of its own about the 'Rag Plot', Blacow began to fear legal proceedings, and endeavoured to extract advance information from the Vice-Chancellor, information which that worthy professed himself ready to provide in return for a list of those 'loyal subjects' who authorized Blacow to slander the University by publishing the notice of the 'Rag Plot'. Finally, King jovially classified Blacow with his Exeter friends as a 'Society of Informers', and the wretched canon, so long a butt to the Principal of St. Mary Hall, was stung into reply. He gave an elaborate vindication of his proceedings against Dawes, Whitmore, and the others, embellished by recent additions from Dr. Leigh, Master of Balliol, and wounded King at his tenderest spot by the libellous allegation that he was an inflammatory Irishman. Blacow's narra-

---

[19] See note O, p. 282.
[20] See p. 195 *supra*. Blacow also sent back to Exeter the congratulations of the king and Lord Holdernesse, the Secretary of State, upon the plot (Exeter College MSS.: Richard Blacow to Thomas Bray, 27 July 1754).

tive was soon controverted in another pamphlet, but his efforts to exalt himself at the expense of the University were of less interest than a furious conflict in Oxford itself.[21]

In September the Bishop of Oxford had suspected the Vice-Chancellor, Dr. Huddesford, of awaiting an opportunity of 'showing himself an honest man', an opportunity which came on 8 October when he was reappointed to his office by the Chancellor. Reviewing the events of his previous years of office, the Vice-Chancellor (who is variously described as 'restless', 'roguish', and 'a divine of the highest respectability')[22] complimented the young men of the University on their behaviour during the poll and scrutiny, and animadverted 'with a becoming zeal and sincerity, on the infamous behaviour of one College, which despight of all decency, opened its gates, and its cellars to the Refuse of Mankind, to be the shop of Corruption, and the factory of perjury'. In case the Exeter College delegation, which waited on the Vice-Chancellor, were disposed to believe his assurances that he had not intended to reflect upon their society, the charges were at once repeated and elaborated in the *London Evening Post* and *Jackson's Oxford Journal*. Thomas Bray immediately dispatched an abstract of the Vice-Chancellor's speech to the Earl of Macclesfield for transmission to Blacow and the Secretary of State, but, with the rest of his society, began to take fright at pressure from Blacow and his ministerial friends to do them a good turn by bringing an action against the *London Evening Post*.

In the end Rector Webber struck his first blow for the cause since 1745 by producing an anonymous *Defence*, a pamphlet which 'no one cares to own . . . , tho' there are several who will take it kindly, if the world will father it upon them'. In this pamphlet the rector denied the Vice-Chancellor's implicit claim to authority within the walls of his house, questioned the evidence on which he had concluded that 'not only the Hall and Courts of the Society had been conspurcated and defiled with Filth and Nastiness, Drunkenness and Gluttony; but even the very bed-chambers likewise made the scenes of riot and debauchery', and asserted that many of the voters had spent their time in reverent attendance at prayers. Though fearing that such altercations were beneath his dignity Dr. Huddesford replied in his turn. The con-

---

[21] See note P, p. 283.
[22] *Hearne's Collections*, xi. 31; Nichols, *Illustrations*, vi. 472 n.

troversy threatened to become interminable as the Old Interest rallied to his support in the fictitious person of 'a Cambridge Soph' and as Blacow obtained possession of parts of King's poem, *The Toast*, which he had never dared to publish. Subsequent pamphlets, however, could hardly add spice to the dish, and with Buckler of All Souls interpreting the imagery of the figures in the Oxford Almanack as Folly, Stupidity, and Debauchery, alias Bray, Theodosia Cornell, and Kennicott, the controversy dragged to a wearisome close.[23]

The misdeeds of Exeter College also brought to a head the battle of personalities. Despite the difficulty of attributing some of the pamphlets, it seems certain that a private war developed between King and the apostles of Exeter. King's equivocal history made him an inevitable target for New Interest abuse, and early in 1755 he published a comprehensive defence at the University Press (from which the Vice-Chancellor excluded all M.A.s during publication). Many of the charges made against his unsavoury past were readily disposed of, and he once again thundered out the accusations that Exeter College were trying to disgrace the University with the government, delivered a paean upon Lord Westmorland, and a vicious personal attack upon Kennicott as a parvenu, educated upon charity, now reviling his benefactors.

'A friend to Mr. Kennicott', who King had no doubt was Kennicott himself, replied with a vindication of the academic labours on account of which the University had allowed him to proceed B.A. ahead of the usual time, and struck at the darkest episode in King's political past. Was it not base ingratitude for a parliamentary candidate for the university seat to turn upon the one college which had given him unanimous support? 'And yet, EXETER, Sir, EXETER is that College; and YOU, Sir, YOU are that candidate.' Had he not applied for ministerial support to the Earl of Macclesfield? A similar argument was presented in a witty paraphrase in verse of King's speech at the opening of the Camera, which was accompanied by another contemporary rhyming paraphrase of King's petition to the Commons in 1722.

But the Principal was not readily to be driven from the field. Another pamphlet was directed against Bray and the High Sheriff; then a posthumous fragment of that laborious Whig Richard Newton, attacking Exeter for resisting the incorporation

[23] See note Q, p. 283.

of Hart Hall, was brought out with a certainly spurious preface commending its wisdom regarding loyalty to the State and University to the attention of the 'society of informers'. It was doubtless King himself who came back with *The Last Blow*, an ironical vindication of the Exeter men, satirizing their campaign 'in the *Evening Advertiser* . . . to convince the world that [they] are the only well-affected persons in the University', and their undoubted hopes that 'the notice which has been taken of us by the Vice-Chancellor, Doctor King, and other principal people of the university, as certainly insures to us the reversions of Bishopricks, Canonries, and Prebendaries, as a hearty squeeze by the hand from the Prime Minister'. *The Last Blow* proved to be only penultimate, for in 1756 in Convocation King crossed political swords with Jenner, the new regius professor of civil law, accusing him of behaving like a *Terrae Filius* and frothing at the mouth, and was skilfully bantered in return under the title of 'The old Trumpeter of Liberty Hall'. Yet for the moment the county election of 1754, even in its adopted guise as a university contest, was a spent issue, and it was some time before the rival factions found a fresh occasion of conflict.[24]

Thus the great Oxfordshire contest, in which the University had no official concern, left an unhappy backwash of hostility amongst the dons. The Rector and fellows of Exeter had appeared in the guise of a fifth column like the Constitutioners of Merton a generation earlier, and King probably did not exaggerate wildly when he spoke of them as generally ostracized. It was all the more important that they should make their fortunes outside the University and enjoy the unequivocal support of the ministers. Certainly the New Interest peers applied faithfully enough on their behalf. Rector Webber, after being promised a canonry at Christ Church, received the deanery at Hereford, but the old corps of Christ Church Whigs, with whom Newcastle had been in touch for so long, had precedence over the long-suffering Thomas Bray, who was kept waiting like Meadowcourt and Blacow. Kennicott became only a Whitehall preacher, and formed a literary connexion with the second Lord Hardwicke which lasted for many years but never yielded profit in terms of preferment. Once again the university Whigs had spent all and looked foolish for receiving so little in return.

[24] See note R, p. 283.

In the House of Commons the New Interest gained their way
by unseating Wenman and Dashwood who had headed the poll,
but they proved unable to maintain the whole of their gain. That
rising star of University College, Charles Jenkinson, received a
profitable introduction to Lord Holdernesse for his pains, but the
evil reputation he left among the Old Interest in the University
cost him dear fourteen years later. There were acrimonious repercussions over the establishment of the Viner bequest, which ultimately provided Blackstone with a chair, a settlement opposed
'by those very persons who, about two years since conducted an
opposition against the chief magistrate of this place'.[25]

As on so many other occasions academic theology was caught
up in politics. An influential movement among some of the
younger men was that of Hutchinsonianism. The Hutchinsonians
reacted strongly against the rationalism of the day, and sought to
justify an orthodox position by some odd scientific investigations
by which geological evidence for primitive Biblical history might
be produced, and by very eccentric treatment of the Hebrew
scriptures, in support of quite new conclusions favourable to the
present state of knowledge. The Oxford Hutchinsonians' stress
on the Christian's dependence upon a special revelation aroused
unfavourable comment from outside the University, and their
Hebrew scholarship offered an obvious target to the great Kennicott. Yet when in 1756 he came to reply to Patten (of Corpus),
Wetherell (of University College), and Horne (of Magdalen), the
young Oxford apostles of the movement, the immediate ground
of his attack was not academic but political.

Wetherell's sermon on King Charles the Martyr's day, he
declared, maintained 'the justly exploded doctrine of *absolute
passive obedience*, and this in terms so extremely gross as even to
have out-Filmer'd Filmer'. It was a scandal that the governors of
the University advanced such Jacobites to the pulpit. Patten was
certainly no Jacobite, having taken the lead in removing the Jacobite picture at Corpus, and all three were among the Old Interest

---

[25] Robson, op. cit., pp. 164–5; Exeter College MSS.: Lord Harcourt to T. Bray,
30 April, 4 Aug. 1754; Lord Macclesfield to T. Bray, 13 Aug., 14 Oct. 1754; B.M.
Add. MS. 35596, fo. 65. This correspondence was still alive in 1775, e.g. Add.
MS. 35509, fos. 76, 132; *Correspondence and Diaries of J. W. Croker*, ed. L. J.
Jennings (London, 1884), iii. 177; Papers on the Vinerian Bequest in *University
Notices 1662–1821* (Bodl. G. A. Oxon. b 19); cf. Warwick C.R.O. Newdigate MS.
B 1493.

politicians who most readily transferred their loyalty to the Court
in the next reign. Kennicott doubtless considered that bad politics
meant more to the ministry than bad Hebrew, but had to contend
with the disapproval of the University when he next preached at
St. Mary's on 25 January 1757 on Rom. viii. 35, 37. In an animated
discourse on Christian fortitude he besought the clergy to learn
from the succession of national misfortunes and warn their flocks
against transgression. The truth of Christianity was evidenced in
its power to support men under adversity, and this very fortitude
had been the great contribution of Oxford to the success of the
Glorious Revolution, 'an event ever to be mentioned by *true*
Englishmen and *true* Protestants with transports of gratitude'.
Should popery (the alleged crime of the Old Interest) or persecution reappear, 'I am persuaded, there would stand forth, in this
Place, many of the disciples of Jesus, unshaken by torture, and
faithful unto death'. As if the sentiment were not unpalatable
enough, some of the congregation were sure Kennicott had said
'*even* in this Place'. Small wonder that the sermon aroused vigorous opposition, and that the Vice-Chancellor refused his im-
primatur.[26]

Yet there was no occasion for triumph on the part of the Old
Interest, for already Dr. Huddesford the Vice-Chancellor was at
loggerheads with the Tories of All Souls over the affairs of the
University Press, and it was a question whether Exeter College
and the present court connexion would not be strong enough to
defeat a divided Tory body.[27]

[26] See note S, p. 283.
[27] G. Huddesford, *Observations relating to Delegates of the Press* (Oxford,
1756); [B. Buckler], *A Reply to Dr. Huddesford's Observations relating to Delegates of the Press* (Oxford, 1756).

CHAPTER XIII

Two New Chancellors and a new King

LORD ARRAN's greatest service to the University consisted in surviving to the age of 88, and thus depriving the ministry of any opportunity of placing the University under favourable govern- ance without parliamentary intervention until the sands of the administration were running out with the life of the king. The Chancellor's death in December 1758, however, reopened the political contest in Oxford at a time when the days of the present political system were known to be numbered. No serious contest for the office of Chancellor could be remembered, but it was vital for supporters of the present Court to make an effort while the influence of their friends subsisted, and the general confusion of Old Interest politics was worse confounded by the obscurity of a future in which the only certainty was the ultimate triumph of the present reversionary interest.

Three candidates were at once named, the earls of Westmor- land and Lichfield and the Bishop of Durham. Westmorland, the late Chancellor's choice as High Steward in 1754, was an obvious candidate for the succession, and was at once championed by a number of colleges, including All Souls, where the Tory phalanx led by Blackstone and Buckler had done much to elect Sir Roger Newdigate as university burgess. According to Horace Walpole, Westmorland had 'commanded the very body of troops which King George I had been obliged to send to Oxford to teach the University the only kind of passive obedience which they did not approve', but being deprived of his command in 1733 for opposi- tion to Walpole's Excise Bill he had entered upon a steady course of opposition. In this he still persevered, notwithstanding rumours in December 1756 that he was to be taken into the government. Among his other attractions was conviviality, the spirit of which in him burned all too bright; so resolute an enemy as Kennicott spoke highly of the unscripted Latin oration he had delivered at his installation in 1754, while to King he was 'learned himself . . .

a lover of learned men, and a steady asserter of the liberties of his country'.[1]

The friends of the Old Interest who had been disappointed of the pleasure of installing Lord Lichfield in 1754 now championed him afresh. Fourth in descent from Charles II,[2] Lichfield was of non-juring, even Jacobite stock; he himself boasted a long record of opposition to the Court in both Houses of Parliament, and like his ancestors had kept in touch with university affairs from his nearby seat at Ditchley. Lichfield's future was less unequivocal than his past, and already there was reason to suspect that he was casting an eye towards the ministry. But Newdigate regarded Lichfield as 'the same boy in his robes, Drs. gown or anything else, always jolly & good humour'd', and he was bound to appeal strongly to many Old Interest voters.[3]

The court candidate, equally well chosen, was Richard Trevor, Bishop of Durham. Like his elder brother Robert, who had upheld the ministerial flag in the parliamentary election of 1737, Richard enjoyed the now diminishing advantages of a Tory background combined with government support. He had been a canon of Christ Church, had held a prebend in that cathedral until his translation to Durham in 1752, and to Dr. King embodied all the failings of the Hanoverian bench. An aspiring patron of literary merit, he had been prudently appreciative of Oxford talents, and had preferred Joseph Spence, the regius professor of modern history, to a fat stall at Durham in the vexed year 1754. According to his biographer, Trevor was pressed into standing as a candidate by the importunity of hopeful friends, and he offered the voters the opportunity to resume a medieval tradition in electing a prince of the Church.[4]

Trevor's hopes, depended, however, less upon his merits than upon the divisions among his opponents. At the poll Charles

---

[1] *London Evening Post*, 21–23 Dec. 1758; H. Walpole, *George II*, ii. 341; *Letters of Lord Chesterfield*, ed. B. Dobrée (London, 1932), i. 71; *J.O.J.*, 11 Dec. 1756; *Correspondence of Samuel Richardson*, ii. 188; *Dr. King's Apology*, pp. 36–37.

[2] As his wife was fourth in descent from Oliver Cromwell.

[3] *The Post-Boy*, 14–17 July 1716; *Dawks's News Letter*, 21 July 1716; *Weekly General Post*, 14–21 July 1716; H. Walpole, *George II*, i. 164 n., ii. 340; Lamport Hall: Isham MS. IC 2486; Warwick C.R.O. Newdigate MS. B 1999.

[4] H. Rashdall and R. S. Rait, *New College* (London, 1901), p. 206; [G. Allan], *A Sketch of the Life . . . of Richard Trevor, Lord Bishop of Durham* (Darlington, 1776); King, *Anecdotes*, p. 183.

Jenkinson 'found the University in much better temper than [he] expected; the friends of Lord Lichfield and Lord Westmorland had so much exhausted their rancour upon one another that they had very little left for anyone else'. Tory animosity was sharpened by the early discovery that their two candidates divided the vote so evenly as to put Bishop Trevor clearly in the lead. Westmorland's friends desperately tried to get Lichfield disqualified on grounds similar to those urged against Turner in 1751. As always when the peace of the University was acutely threatened, doubts were raised as to the qualification for the franchise, both parties appealing for the opinion of Charles Yorke, the Solicitor General. It is clear also from the bishop's queries that he feared the Vice-Chancellor might destroy the poll-book immediately after declaring the result in order to prevent any inquiry into objections to particular votes. The campaign continued with the issue thus in doubt until the eve of the poll, when Lichfield withdrew, pooling his interest with that of Westmorland, who accordingly triumphed easily by 321 votes to 200.[5]

Whatever the machinations of the Vice-Chancellor, no poll-book survives, but from a list of the voters for the Bishop of Durham obtained by Newcastle, and an incomplete canvass book in the university archives, which tallies closely with it, it is possible to reconstruct the main tenor of the voting. The poll must have been as distressing to the Whigs as the coalition of the two Tory candidates on the previous day, for it proved that neither the uncertainties of the political system as a whole, nor such evidence of ministerial favour as the Exeter College men had been able to procure, had affected the political stalemate in Oxford. The great ministerial strongholds of Exeter, Merton, Wadham, and Christ Church held firm, and Hertford was more unequivocally Whig than ever; but the ravages of time were barely visible in the Tory bastions at All Souls, Balliol, Magdalen, Oriel, and Pembroke. True, that 'famous Wight yclep'd Pimp L[eigh]' had taken a handful of Balliol voters over to the Court, and through Charles Jenkinson a foothold had been obtained in University College, but the Tories had swept the board in Lincoln, a badly divided, and in Queen's, a Whig, society, at the last parliamentary

---

[5] *Grenville Papers*, i. 286–7, 288; *Hist. MSS. Comm. R14, App. pt. ix; Round MSS.*, p. 296; B.M. Add. MS. 35635, fos. 195–7; *Letters of Richard Radcliffe and John James 1755–83*, ed. M. Evans (Oxford, 1888), pp. xxxi, 13, 17.

election, notwithstanding that Bishop Trevor was an old Queen's man.[6] The Whig enthusiasm of 1754 had clearly hardened the hearts of the Old Interest.

Once raised, the question of the legal qualification of candidates and voters did not lightly subside, and called forth various contributions from the weighty pen of Dr. Blackstone.[7] Francis Basset, a former Queen's man and future M.P. for Penryn, replied with indignation. He had voted without question in previous elections, but had now been deprived of his vote on the grounds that he had accepted the freedom of the city of Oxford a decade before. Blackstone might now be 'a strenuous advocate for the silent operation of the statute of *semel fruition*, as he is pleased to entitle it', but he had infringed the statute himself by his applications to various Oxford freemen (including Wenman and Dashwood) for the 'Registership of the County', and had further contravened the statutes by threatening to prosecute Basset in a superior court in a case undoubtedly determinable in the University. The truth was that the reigning opinion in the University, disturbed at the arrival of numerous 'foreign' voters with only a nominal membership of the University, like Beckford and George Hay of the Admiralty Board, had resolved to delimit the franchise in the interest of their undoubted supremacy among the foundationers and other active members. Counsel's opinion having been obtained that in certain circumstances the University had the right to amend or repeal the Laudian statutes, the Hebdomadal Board concurred by a substantial majority on 15 June 1759, and unanimously three days later, with the Vice-Chancellor's draft of a statute explaining the present statutes defining the membership of Convocation.

The minutes of these two meetings conceal a bitter struggle on the part of the court politicians. It happened that the proctors for the year, William Wright of Merton and George Austen of St. John's, had both voted for Trevor, and they led the campaign against the proposed legislation. They claimed that the case submitted for counsel's opinion had been faulty, that the Laudian statutes had been designed to end the chaos arising from the unhampered legislative authority of Convocation, and that no

[6] B.M. Add. MS. 33061, fos. 369–72; University Archives: Canvass Book for the election of Chancellor 1759, W.P. γ 3 (4); *Letters of Radcliffe and James*, p. 13.   [7] See note T, p. 283.

change could be made in them, as distinct from the ancient statutes, without royal licence. Furthermore, the ruling party had taken their course in the knowledge that no licence would be forthcoming for a statute patently 'made to answer private schemes', providing, for example, that all voters whose names were in the college books before the previous Easter should have their rights preserved. The majority of the Hebdomadal Board roughly attempted to suppress discussion of the proctors' case 'saying, "We do not want your reasons, but your votes"'.

The Whig heads therefore withdrew from the Hebdomadal Board, the proctors published their opinions along with a flurry of papers,[8] and at the next Convocation called to consider the draft statutes were abused by the Vice-Chancellor, Dr. Randolph, President of Corpus, and hissed by the junior members. The proctors now went out of office, and the Vice-Chancellor himself retired the following October, but not 'till he had uttered what it did not become him to speak nor that venerable Assembly to hear'. His violence was matched by another published tirade from the proctors in which they resurrected the old Whig bogey of a royal visitation. In July 1760 the new statutes went through, the first deliberate modification of the Laudian code; and, denied the opportunity of protesting in Convocation against measures which they regarded as 'invalid and inauthentic', the entire body of the Whig heads of Balliol, St. John's, Christ Church, Wadham, Exeter, and Hertford trooped off to declare themselves before a notary public. If anything was more ironical than this Whig glorification of Stuart prerogative it was the fact that in less than a dozen years each of the factions had reversed its attitude.[9]

Meanwhile, Westmorland had been installed Chancellor with a magnificence which set a standard for all subsequent entertainments. It was an hour of glory, too, for Dr. King, who, having piloted his candidate home, declaimed 'admirably' for fifty minutes, making Dr. Johnson clap his hands till they were sore. A brilliant company were further entertained by verses spoken by young gentlemen specially (and according to King, very clumsily) coached by Sheridan himself. Benjamin Buckler preached at St. Mary's on the intimate association of religion and learning, an association which rendered the preservation of

[8] Many of these papers are preserved in Bodl. Gough Oxford 96.
[9] See note U, p. 284.

religion and the Constitution dependent upon the preservation of the University, an association incarnate not in that amateur of letters Bishop Trevor but in the notoriously tipsy new Chancellor.[10] Yet not all the celebrations could disguise the one disadvantage to the Old Interest in the election of Westmorland, that another High Steward must be found. Here the Tory divisions still rankled, and Lord Westmorland made a private offer of the place to Lord Bruce before taking the honourable course of appointing Lord Lichfield, whose supporters had carried him to the head of the poll.[11]

The coolness between Westmorland and Lichfield, the apprehensions for the independence of the University aroused in Tory breasts by Blackstone's plans to leave the University,[12] and the fact that a court candidate had polled two-fifths of the votes in the last contest, all indicated the tantalizing possibilities which the situation still contained. Moreover, the political situation in Oxford was not as static as the voting in 1759 suggested. Prompted by the knowledge that Cambridge was about to address, the University had hailed the outbreak of war with a chauvinistic enthusiasm for the king's 'most sacred person' reminiscent of the days of Anne. Dr. King displayed an unexpected susceptibility to the lure of military glory and was reported to have spoken favourably even of Sir Robert Walpole. As the tide of victory set in in 1758 there were great celebrations in Oxford, and in February 1759 even *Jackson's Oxford Journal* published a verse describing how the Tories

> Their old fashion'd tenets quit,
> And step by step at last submit
> To Reason, Eloquence, and P[I]TT.

A continental war was now in full vogue, and the wonderful year of triumph in 1759 swept all inhibitions away. In November the Oxford heads agreed unanimously upon an immediate address, and prayed fervently that His Majesty might be succeeded

---

[10] J. C. Jeaffreson, *Annals of Oxford* (London, 1871), ii. 287; Warwick C.R.O. MS. Newdigate Diary, 5 July 1759; *Letters of Samuel Johnson*, ed. R. W. Chapman (Oxford, 1952), i. 123; *Harcourt Papers*, vii. 223; King, *Anecdotes*; *London Evening Post*, 9-12 Dec. 1758; *J.O.J.*, 7, 14 July 1759; H. Walpole, *Letters*, iv. 281; B. Buckler, *The Alliance of Religion and Learning considered* (Oxford, 1759).

[11] Bodl. MSS. d.d. Dashwood (Bucks.) a 4, Folder 2, Lady Westmorland to Sir Francis Dashwood, 23 Jan. [1760].

[12] Warwick C.R.O. Newdigate MS. B 2379.

by a line of princes inheriting his virtues as well as his crown, and reigning like him in the hearts of his people. At once the University celebrated with sermons, bell-ringing, and bonfires. Vain was it for John Burton to discourse politically at St. Mary's on a most impertinent text for an academic Whig—'That ye study to be quiet and to do your own business'—for the University was proclaiming its enthusiasm for king and war from the housetops.[13]

As the new reign commenced on 25 October 1760, with its prospects of a political new deal, all parties in Oxford clamoured for a speedy pledge of loyalty, and harassed the ailing Vice-Chancellor, Dr. Browne, Provost of Queen's, into pushing through an address assuring the young George III that his accession alone could compensate 'for the otherwise irretrievable loss . . . [of] a prince who was called from a people at a time when he had filled their hearts with the utmost joy'. Old Westmorland yielded to none in his admiration of the young prince 'acting upon such solid principles of reason and of virtue', but could not stomach the consummate hypocrisy about his grandfather, and exploded in a version of the 'King's Friend' theory like that later popularized by Burke. Was not the late Administration, he demanded of Dr. Browne, 'form'd to subvert the foundations of legal mix'd monarchy, by fraud and violence, by absorbing the powers of two parts of the legislative into the hands of a few administrators for the Crown'? What of its 'settled flagrant practices upon Countys and Boroughs, in their election of members, to constitute one part of the legislature'? What of the visible extinction of freedom of debate which had enervated the whole Constitution? Had they forgotten the taxes and debt incurred for foreign interests, the 'tyrannical vexations set on foot against the University', and the oppression of the young prince himself? The Chancellor, in short, refused to present the address, but the university delegation led by the 'High Steward, 2 Archbishops & 7 Bishops, 3 Dukes, 7 Earls, 2 Viscounts, one Baron, 4 Elder sons of Peers with Titles', not to mention such quondam enemies as Pitt, could fairly congratulate themselves on 'the fine show Oxford made at court',

[13] Warwick C.R.O. MS. Newdigate Diary, 14 April 1756; University Archives: MS. Conv. Reg. Bg 34, fo. 226: Bh 35, fos. 133 seq.; *A New Speech from the Old Trumpeter of Liberty Hall*, p. 25; H. Walpole, *Letters*, iv. 134; *J.O.J.*, 24 April, 8 May 1756, 1 Dec. 1759; B.M. Add. MS. 32898, fo. 315; J. Burton, *University Politicks or the Study of a Christian, Gentleman, Scholar* . . . (Oxford, 1760).

which according to Horace Walpole caused the list of household appointments to be extended.[14]

The next testimony to Oxford's newly revived zeal for the royal person was a book of verses 'of condolance and congratulation' so fulsome in their adulation that Thomas Warton the poetry professor (whose father had created such havoc during his tenure of the same chair in 1719) wrote a bantering parody about a don who declared

> With hourly pleasure I can sit
> And talk of Granby, Hawk and Pitt:
>
> . . . . .
>
> At growth of Taxes others fret,
> And shudder at the Nation's Debt;
> I ne'er the fancied ills bemoan
> No debts disturb me but my own.

Chancellor, dons, and members of Parliament joined the chorus; Newdigate was informed that 'the good things of this world are coming amongst us', and urged to enlarge the civil list and 'to take some of it to your own share'. The University offered its official congratulations on the king's marriage, and pious Hutchinsonians derived great satisfaction from the 'very devout behaviour at divine service' of both king and queen. On the birth of the Prince of Wales in the following year the University discerned that 'the interests of Prince and people are so intimately and inseparably connected with each other' that the prosperity of all must be enhanced by the king's happiness, and dropped the broadest of hints in their joy at 'the pleasing prospect of a numerous royal progeny'.[15]

The pulpit resounded to the same gospel. In 1761 George Horne, fellow of Magdalen and a bishop to be, called at St. Mary's for the 'utmost endeavours to eradicate out of the minds of men those diabolical principles of *resistance to government in church and state*', for the imitation of King Charles's 'god-like virtues', and,

[14] Bodl. MSS. d.d. Dashwood (Bucks.) a 4, Folder, 2, *passim*, especially Lord Westmorland to J. Browne, 9 Nov. 1760; University Archives: MS. Conv. Reg. Bh 35, pp. 209 seq.; Warwick C.R.O. MS. Newdigate Diary, 13, 14 Nov. 1760; B.M. Add. MS. 39311, fo. 95; H. Walpole, *Memoirs of the Reign of George III*, ed. J. F. R. Barker (London, 1894), i. 18–19.

[15] *Gent. Mag.* 1761, p. 90; [T. Warton], *The Oxford Sausage* (Oxford, n.d.), p. 130; Warwick C.R.O. Newdigate MS. B 1839a; B.M. Add. MS. 39312, fo. 297; University Archives: MS. Conv. Reg. Bh 35, fos. 330 seq., 393 seq.

Hutchinsonian though he was, not an Exeter voice was raised in protest. Two years later, indeed, Thomas Bray, in preaching before the House of Commons on 31 January, made it clear that the royal martyr had invited trouble by offering the nation a choice of using strong measures or 'embracing slavery without contest or contradiction'; yet it remained apostolic doctrine 'that men are not the servants of God if they oppose and disturb the established government'. Most striking of all was the political evolution of Dr. King. He complained bitterly of 'a most infamous advertisement published . . . in a newspaper, on purpose to defame me . . . because as a member of the University I attended my brethren . . . with an address of congratulation on His Majesty's marriage'. How hard it was to 'have been reviled hitherto as a jacobite, and now . . . censured for going to court'. Knowing nothing 'of *public spirit* and the *amor patriae*', the Jacobite was fundamentally immoral; for the great end of a Stuart restoration he surrendered 'every principle of humanity'. At the election of a new university Chancellor in 1762, 'old King . . . wonder'd what people meant by opposing the Court when such fair advances had been made to us, and said with a grave face that he could account for it no otherwise, than by supposing they were *Jacobites*'.[16]

How much more successfully Oxford was now trimming its sails to the prevailing wind than Cambridge was apparent in 1763. On the conclusion of peace Convocation passed an address against which only 'three or four non placets were imperfectly muttered', affirming that 'Your Majesty, on your accession . . . found the nation involved in a necessary but expensive and destructive war; but your first care hath been to ease your subjects from this burthen', and delivered it with a magnificent retinue of 200; Cambridge, to whom their Chancellor, the fallen Duke of Newcastle, was now a liability, must praise his past politics by a reference to 'an expensive though successful war'. A fresh book of laudatory verses was produced, and splendid celebrations were put on at the Encaenia in July. King, who in his 79th year was still prominent, 'enlarged on the salutary effect arising from a general peace; [and] complimented his Majesty for his particular regard to Arts, to

---

[16] G. Horne, *The Christian King* (Oxford, 1761); T. Bray, *Sermon Preached before the House of Commons . . . on Jan. 31, 1763* (London, 1763); King, *Anecdotes*, pp. 190, 193–5; B.M. Add. MS. 39311, fo. 121b; cf. Lord Fitzmaurice, *Life of Shelburne* (London, 1912), i. 27.

Literature, and to the University of Oxford'. There could be no reply to the self-styled *Terrae Filius* who asserted that 'now the old True-Blue is faced according to Court-fashion with Green', and that 'the University borrows its complexion from its patron, as the Moon has light from the Sun'.[17]

It was characteristic of the situation, however, that not only did the old Tory Dr. King sing the praises of the new system, but the old Whig Dr. Burton also celebrated the end of the war. Politicians as far apart as the dukes of Beaufort and Marlborough, as the king's favourite George Scott and the double-dyed Tory John Hynde Cotton, received degrees. Dr. King looked eagerly for the extinction of party, encouraged by the flood of preferment which opened to Oxford men. Court politicians of the late reign were still promoted. Amongst the last of the recommendations which Newcastle had carried with George II (to the chagrin of Dr. Bray) had been the preferment of Burton and Tottie to canonries at Christ Church, and in 1763, on the death of John Fanshawe, their old ally and fellow canon Edward Bentham became regius professor of divinity; his vacant canonry went to John Moore, now chaplain to the Duke of Marlborough and twenty years later Archbishop of Canterbury. In 1761 that glory of Exeter College, Benjamin Kennicott, received a royal bounty of £200 p.a. completing a public subscription of £800 p.a. to forward his collation of the Hebrew MSS. of the Old Testament. Hoare of Jesus, Lord Harcourt's chaplain, obtained a prebend at Westminster. On the other hand, Blackstone was appointed Principal of New Inn Hall, became a K.C. and Solicitor General to the queen, and was publicly tipped for the Irish bench.[18]

Witnesses as various as Horace Walpole and Dr. King testified alike to a new glow of royal favour towards the University in the warmth of which rumours blossomed that George III was to end the long official ostracism by a visit to his learned and loyal subjects. In the spring of 1762 the University incurred 'prodigious expence' to render the Sheldonian Theatre 'the most superb room

---

[17] B.M. Add. MS. 38200, fo. 282; University Archives: MS. Conv. Reg. Bh 35, pp. 430 seq.; *Gent. Mag.* 1763, pp. 40, 181–2; *Jenkinson Papers*, p. 105; Warwick C.R.O. MS. Newdigate Diary, 6 April 1763; *J.O.J.*, 9 July 1763; [G. Colman], *Terrae Filius* (London, 1763).

[18] B.M. Add. MSS. 39316, fos. 36–37: 32906, fo. 435: 32907, fos. 237–8; *J.O.J.*, 8 Aug. 1761, 16 Jan. 1762, 21 May 1763; University Archives: MS. Conv. Reg. Bh 35, pp. 456, 459; [G. Colman], *Terrae Filius*, pp. 55–56.

in Europe'. The much-defaced ceiling paintings were taken down and restored, 'the Pillars, Galleries, and Area, ornamented by an exquisite variety of curious imitations of different kinds of marble, mahogany, &c., and the whole superbly enriched by gildings'. The labours of Messrs. Kettle and Son hereupon were assumed to be in preparation for a royal visit. When the summer passed without the king appearing. Oxford poetasters got their patriotic ballads cut and dried for the Act in the summer of 1763 when the king should outshine even the splendours of the Sheldonian. In April 1763 the London press confidently announced that the visit would take place at the rising of parliament, though *Jackson's Oxford Journal* and the Christ Church Whigs were still cautious. Similar reports were published and again unfulfilled six months later, and Oxford had to wait twenty years before George III revived the old tradition of royal condescension.

Nevertheless, the reports themselves were ample evidence of the new political standing of the University, and meanwhile Oxford loyalty could expand in the delighted patronage of the queen's German brothers and the King of Denmark, whom 'puffed up' Oxford doctors familiarly referred to as 'their Royal Brother'. No longer did a market for prints of the Pretender flourish on political frustration; Queen's welcomed the gift of Moreland's portrait of Her Majesty, and the Chancellor presented a full-length portrait of the king to be hung in the university picture gallery.[19]

The genuine country politicians of the University did not change their colour overnight. King still would not trust the elder Pitt, and Newdigate replied candidly:

I cant. answer your Qu. what my party is? I am only sure it is neither C[um]b[erlan]d nor Pelham, landed men must love peace, men proscribed and abus'd for 50 years together [should] be presented with foolscaps if they make ladders for tyrant Whigs to mount by, I like the King and shall be with his ministers as long as I think an honest man ought, and believe it best not to lose the Country Gentleman in the Courtier.

But even apart from the 'Whig' friends of the ministers of the

[19] B.M. Add. MSS. 39311, fo. 121 b: 38200, fo. 282: 38206, fo. 78; H. Walpole, *George III*, i. 13; *J.O.J.*, 13 March, 2 Oct. 1762: 9 April, 18 June, 17 Sept. 1763: 5 May 1764: 8, 15 June 1765: 17 Sept. 1768; *Hist. MSS. Comm. Weston Underwood MSS.*, p. 345.

217

last two reigns, the University as a whole had never quite lived down its past as a pillar of court politics, and the majority rejoiced in the new order. Oxford might still be a butt of the political propagandists; Robert Lloyd in *The North Briton* in 1762 teased the

> Fellows! who've soak'd away their knowledge
> In sleepy residence at College;
>
> . . . . .
>
> Mere drinking, eating; eating, drinking;
> With no impertinence of thinking.

Wilkes, who in the same journal was trying to prove that the Tories were 'those old enemies of liberty, those abettors of arbitrary power, those sworn foes of our constitution', flayed the University, its chancellors past and present, its elections, its loyal verses, and most of all its history. He revived all the ancient charges to show that the University had been Jacobite and authoritarian from the decrees of 1683 and the riots of 1715 even to the present time. The cry was hackneyed, but not for forty years had Oxford been attacked by such a rank political outsider, the leader of the very city Radicals with whom the friends of the University in the previous reign had often been pleased to act. Now the 'Oxford politicians' clamoured for a halter for Wilkes, and in December 1763 *Jackson's Oxford Journal* assailed the Rev. Mr. Kidgell's *Genuine and succinct account of an exceedingly profane libel, entitled 'An Essay on Woman'* for promoting the sales of Wilkes's obscenity by superfluous publicity.[20]

Meanwhile Chancellor Westmorland, like the rest of the Oxford pundits, had returned to Court, attempting to kiss the hand of Lady Sarah Lennox in mistake for the queen, but seeing his way clearly enough to the preferment of his nephew, Sir Francis Dashwood. Should he die, Oxford must be the theatre of a confusion far worse than at his own election, reflecting both the uncertainties in the political system as a whole and the ambiguous developments within the University. A month before the Chancellor died on 26 August 1762 the canvass had already begun.[21]

[20] King, *Anecdotes*, p. 96; Warwick C.R.O. Newdigate MSS. B 2311; *The North Briton* (London, 1769), pp. 36, 68, 70, 73, 80–83, 92–95, 104–7, 122, 126; *Hist. MSS. Comm. Various MSS.* vi. 302; *J.O.J.*, 3 Dec. 1763.
[21] H. Walpole, *Letters*, v. 36, 109; H. Walpole, *George III*, i. 52.

Lichfield, who had been disappointed in 1759, would certainly stand again, but the friends of Lord Westmorland still disliked him, and it was uncertain whether those who in 1759 had supported him because of his record of opposition would vote for him as a bedchamber official and Captain of the Gentleman Pensioners. Moreover, he had gone back on his promises to fight to the end for the Old Interest in the county. Wilkes, with whom Lord Lichfield preserved his usual easy relations, laughed at him for soaking away an originally promising future in good cheer; Archbishop Secker believed 'he sometimes drinks too much: but [I] have been assured that he doth it not habitually; and have never heard, that he delights in tempting others to excess; nor do imagine, that his House will be open to Oxonians for that purpose'. It was obvious that 'undoubtedly fitter persons' could be found, but Lichfield's geniality and local connexions had won him a considerable following.[22]

A bevy of other candidates were talked of—the Bishop of Durham who had been beaten at the post in 1759, John Thomas, Bishop of Winchester, Lord Oxford, heir to the old Harley interest, Lord Foley, Lord Suffolk, and Lord Aylesford. Of these, the last three became serious candidates. Lord Aylesford, the latest Finch to contest a university honour, laid claim to a tradition older even than that of Oxford and Foley, but although he had some support in University and New colleges, his was a forlorn hope, and he was the first candidate to drop out of the running.[23] Foley and Suffolk were the two candidates sponsored by the remnants of the Oxford Old Interest. Though accused of meanness, Foley, as a Tory peer of the last reign[24] and descendant of the Foleys who worked with Harley in the great days of Queen Anne, attracted so many of the former opposition votes that he was finally their champion at the poll. As a former member of Christ Church, he might divide that interest which in this election was among the last to be pledged.

Lord Suffolk, a curious young candidate of 22, was the chosen champion of Newdigate's friends, Winchester of Magdalen, Blackstone and Buckler of All Souls. At the end of the previous

[22] Ibid. i. 22; B.M. Add. MSS. 36796, fo. 149: 39311, fo. 119; *Grenville Papers*, ii. 5, 7; *North Briton*, no. xxix, pp. 92–95.
[23] *Jenkinson Papers*, pp. 47, 53, 55.
[24] e.g. *Hist. MSS. Comm. Hastings MSS.* iii. 113.

year Blackstone had been negotiating with Shelburne and Fox
(who brought him into the House for Hindon) with a view to
recruiting Tory support for the administration; his opponents in
Oxford could not understand his determination to annoy the
Court at this juncture, and considered that his now equivocal
reputation was a liability for his candidate.[25] Suffolk had always
enjoyed special consideration in the University; he had spoken
English verses at the installation of Westmorland, and made
another speech on his presentation for the degree of D.C.L. in
1761, less than four years from matriculation. However, the Vice-
Chancellor, Dr. Browne, Provost of Queen's, who led his whole
society in strenuous support of Lichfield, insisted that Lord Suffolk was too young to be chancellor, and when the canvass began
it became obvious that Suffolk not only could not succeed but
could not poll as well as Foley. It had already been agreed that
the weaker of the two should pool his interest with the stronger,
and two days before the poll Suffolk withdrew, glorying in his
nomination, and declaring he 'had rather have ten voices from
disinterested personal attachment, than a hundred from the
obsequious tribe of ministerial devotees'.[26]

From the poll in 1759 it was obvious that this obsequious tribe
could probably carry a candidate of their own against a divided
Tory interest, and could give certain victory to any candidate of
any other considerable interest whom they chose to adopt. Indeed,
the New Interest of 1754, Harcourt, Marlborough, Thomas Bray,
Charles Jenkinson, and their young friend Shute Barrington,
canon of Christ Church, had been the first to stir as soon as Westmorland began visibly to decline. In the present temper of the
University a really attractive court candidate must win, and
might effect a revolution in the place. Lord Harcourt, who had
no official standing in this matter, went straight to the point: 'I
wish Lord Bute was Chancellor', he wrote to Jenkinson, 'because
I think he is in every respect the properest person, and the most

[25] According to Wilkes, the Vice-Chancellor opposed Suffolk partly from
resentment at Blackstone's former investigations of the scandals surrounding
the University Press (*North Briton*, p. 94).
[26] MSS. of President of Magdalen College: Dr. J. R. Bloxam's MS. Collections, vol. ii, fos. 171, 173, 175, 181, 183, 185; *J.O.J.*, 7 July 1759: 25 Sept. 1762;
Magrath, *The Flemings in Oxford*, iii. 443; *Jenkinson Papers*, pp. 53–56, 58, 60;
B.M. Add. MS. 38469, fos. 56, 60, 62, 68; Bute MSS., Lord Shelburne to Lord
Bute, 18, 19 Nov., 11 Dec. 1762; *Correspondence of Radcliffe and James*, p. 20.

220

likely to be serviceable to the Crown and to the public in this important station.' Bute had recently become Chancellor of the University of Aberdeen, and though he had no connexion with Oxford he must, as the known darling of George III, attract every wavering vote, and might prove as liberal a benefactor to his friends at Oxford as Newcastle had been at Cambridge. Barrington (who like Fox and Shelburne considered Blackstone devoted to Bute) thought he would attract the interest of the Vinerian professor, and compel Lichfield to give up the contest; Dr. King might also lend the diminished weight of his popularity. And in Bute Dr. Bray had also conceived a sudden passion for a Stuart. Unhappily for the hopes of the old Oxford Whigs and their new allies their chosen horse would not run, and Bute's absolute refusal compelled the reconsideration of tactics.

Whatever his past, Lichfield was now in substance a court candidate who would poll many former Tory votes by virtue of old connexions;[27] strongly backed from the beginning by Queen's, Brasenose, and Trinity, he was gaining ground in New College, All Souls, and Lincoln. His main disadvantages to the New Interest were his geniality to both friend and foe, and the fact that he would never occupy a political position of real influence. It would, nevertheless, be a great stroke if, as the price of victory, the friend of so many true-blue societies could be brought to make concessions to the Whigs. 'Would it not be reasonable', argued Bray, 'that his Lordship should give some assurance to the great men who apply to the Whiggs, that he will nominate Vice-Chancellors out of their Heads of Houses, in their turns?' Barrington thought he should 'be prevailed upon to promise the nomination of the High Stewardship to the Duke of Marlborough, Lord Harcourt, or some other unexceptionable Whig'. Jenkinson set to work to secure the agreement, and Barrington sighed with relief 'upon the moral certainty of an event which [if] Lord B[ute] had engaged in, we both should have been mortified had he been vanquished'.[28]

The agreement concluded, Bray worked with a will to organize the Whig interest. Dr. Hay, one of the Admiralty Lords, could

[27] Cf. Henry Fox to Lord Shelburne, 4 Sept. 1762. (Bowood MSS.): 'If Lord Litchfield do's not succeed Lord Westmorland it will be another bad symptom. Had his Lordship continued a Jacobite he had been sure. But I hope he will carry it.'
[28] *Jenkinson Papers*, pp. 47–60; B.M. Add. MS. 38469, fos. 38–76.

bring out St. John's; the Dean and canons would organize the
Christ Church vote. Merton, lately a society of 'four and twenty
wardens and one fellow', no longer formed a solid phalanx, 'but
the List for making interest for Fellows, will show how they may
be applied to'.[29] The support of the Whig interest in these societies,
and in Exeter, Wadham, and Jesus, was promised, and when the
poll was ultimately closed Lord Lichfield had not only vanquished Lord Foley by 321 to 168 but still had voters in hand
should they have been needed. It was only in the old Whig
societies—Exeter, Merton, Wadham, and Christ Church—that
Lichfield carried the day by an overwhelming margin, but although Foley was widely supported, he could carry only two
heads, Dr. Musgrave, Provost of Oriel, and Dr. Blackstone, now
Principal of New Inn Hall, and a majority only in New College,
Pembroke, Oriel, Balliol, and Worcester. Lichfield himself regarded his election as a blow at

those [party] Distinctions which have been so happily abolished elsewhere. The countenance of such a Prince appear'd to me as a higher
recommendation than any personal interest of my own, & the suf-
frages of those who objected to me upon this acct. were by no means
desirable: they seem to have been ambitious of distinguishing themselves, & by persevering to a poll they have succedeed.

Certainly as Horne, the Hutchinsonian, remarked, 'such a tumble
of parties was never known before! Only imagine to yourself
Bilstone and Jenkinson, Allen and Bray united together in the
support of the same interest!'—and with King abusing Foley's
friends as Jacobites the comedy was complete.[30]

Lichfield's aspirations to live above party, and his resolutions
'to execute my office for ye general good' boded ill for the partisan
hopes of the New Interest, and less than a year after the election
Shute Barrington perceptively forecast 'that Lord L[ichfield] will
pursue measures which must hurt his own character and interests,
and prove detrimental to the Whigs of this place'. As the next

[29] See note V, p. 284.
[30] *Jenkinson Papers*, pp. 58–60; University Archives: MS. Conv. Reg. Bh 35,
p. 396 (the figures for the poll are taken from the Acta Convocationis and differ
slightly from those given in current correspondence and widely from those
adopted by the editor of the *Jenkinson Papers*); Warwick C.R.O. Newdigate MS.
B 1798; B.M. Add. MSS. 32942, fo. 368: 39311, fo. 121b, 123; *North Briton*,
no. xxix, pp. 92–95.

Vice-Chancellor Lichfield appointed David Durell, Principal of
Hertford, the least important of the Whig heads of the last reign,
and the Whig heads did not come into their own for another
thirty years, nor the Rector of Exeter for nearly fifty. His first
patronage went to the Tory Niblett, Warden of All Souls,[31] who
became chaplain to the Band of Gentleman Pensioners. The new
High Steward was not an unexceptionable Whig peer but the Irish
Earl of Cork, recently M.P. for Warwick, in the heart of the
territory which had produced such apostles of old ways in Oxford
as the Bromleys and Newdigate. Moreover, Lichfield remained
faithful to Lord Bute longer than prudence dictated, and his
small political influence declined still farther. He remained a
favourite with the king, but in 1765, 'a good deal in liquor', he
hastily left a meeting of ministerial peers, having proposed an
amendment to the Address, and in the following year turned
down Lord Chatham's offer of a place.

If Lichfield was thus of small avail to the Whigs, he 'excited a
general disgust against him' in the traditionally Tory societies
by a dispute with New College in 1767 over the fine assessed on
the land he leased from them in the Vale of Aylesbury. The
Chancellor began by 'intimating yt ye exorbitant fines of Colleges
had long been the subject of complaint, and would at last provoke
a Parliamentary interposition. Such a declaration from a Tory,
from an academic, from an University Chancellor, was thought
very remarkable', and though Lord Lichfield withdrew before
the general furor, 'his friends [could] only excuse him by supposing him when writing to have been—drunk'. The result of
this unfortunate episode was that Lichfield became generally
unpopular, and before the next great conflict in the University
a few months later his interest had crumbled away almost completely.[32]

While these developments were still in the future, however,
while Lichfield's triumph was still untarnished and the new reign
still seemed to have decisively altered the constitutional situation
by the abolition of party, the University was confronted by a new

[31] 'Commonly called Puff Niblett from his puffing and blowing whenever he
speaks' (North Briton, p. 94).
[32] Warwick C.R.O. Newdigate MS. B 1798; Jenkinson Papers, p. 164; London
Evening Post, 14, 16 Sept. 1762; Grenville Papers, iii. 114, 390; B.M. Add. MSS.
39311, fo. 194: 38457, fos. 43, 12; H. Walpole, Last Journals, ed. A. F. Steuart
(London, 1890), i. 139.

election with the death on 30 November 1762 of Peregrine Palmer. He atoned for seventeen totally undistinguished years as university burgess by a legacy of £500 to his old society, All Souls. Shute Barrington wished to find 'a whig of character, moderation & attachment to a minister', but confessed that 'such a person . . . does not at present occur to me', while the young men he eventually thought of were impossible from being under age or born in Scotland. Nor could Bray suggest anything better than a consultation with Lichfield. For long enough there had been a threat of opposition to the Old Interest at just such a juncture, but it now collapsed for lack of a suitable candidate.

Meanwhile a group of former Old Interest heads including the Vice-Chancellor (Provost of Queen's), and the heads of Magdalen, All Souls, Brasenose, and Oriel, acted promptly by sending an invitation to Sir Walter Wagstaffe Bagot, of Blithfield, Staffordshire. Sir Walter, who had represented Newcastle-under-Lyme 1724–7, and the county of Stafford 1727–54, had already retired from public life on the grounds of being, as he put it, 'an old fellow with one foot in ye grave, what at best was never expert in Parliamentary business, & now unfit for it', but his past record, combined with early nomination, gave him a decisive lead. On his return from the parliamentary session of 1753 he had been met in his home county 'by upwards of 700 freeholders . . . expressing their approbation of his conduct in Parliament in so zealously opposing the bill for naturalizing the Jews', and he had been one of the Tory graduands at the memorable Convocation of July 1754. A country politician of the same type as Newdigate, he was already a hero with the old opposition connexions, while the apostles of the New Interest took comfort in the expectation that he would vote with the ministers at what both he and Lichfield regarded as 'a ticklish crisis' for the constitution, and in the certainty that any other court candidate would have been overwhelmed. So long-standing a courtier as David Gregory, Dean of Christ Church, as well as former Tories, were relieved that a contest was avoided, for 'the younger part of the University . . . are made of very combustible stuff'. Thus it came about that less than three months after the triumph of the court interest in the election of Lichfield the University returned unopposed a new burgess of the type that might have been elected at any time in the last reign. The aristocratic Barrington might sneer at the choice of a 'Staffordshire baronet' but he could do no worse.[33] The Old Interest seemed as safe as ever.

[33] *J.O.J.*, 29 Jan. 1763, 21 July 1753, 6 July 1754; B.M. Add. MS. 38458, fos. 10, 12, 14; *Jenkinson Papers*, pp. 100, 101, 105; Warwick C.R.O. Newdigate MSS. B 1451, 1526, 1859, 2231; William, Lord Bagot, *Memorials of the Bagot Family* (Blithfield, 1824), pp. 86–88.

CHAPTER XIV

Another Placeman Defeated

THE years which followed the peace of 1763 were gradually to drive home in Oxford the truth that the new reign had effected no fundamental alteration in the constitutional situation. The University retained its place of favour, and some of the reviled Tories of the last reign, such as Blackstone, continued to make their way in the new. But the psychology of the independent country gentlemen did not change, and the circle of those to whom politics was largely a struggle for place and profit remained much what it had been. Old connexions in Oxford persisted longer than anyone thought possible in 1761 or 1762, and the main difference was that the confessing 'Whigs' who under George II had been the apostles of party purity against a majority alleged to be Jacobites now besought the University to end 'that attachment to party names which their enemies charged them with . . . those distinctions were worn out everywhere else, and are in fact found to be only nominal . . . we were called upon to follow that example which his Majesty had so graciously set us'. To none of their number was such a doctrine dearer than to Charles Jenkinson, who was now fairly launched in the political world, and who in the middle sixties was finding it desirable to dissociate himself from the declining fortunes of Lord Bute with whom, at the beginning of the reign, he had been 'absolutely in love'. A secure independent political status could be obtained by a candidate of Jenkinson's straitened resources in only one seat, that of his old University.[1]

That his thoughts were moving in this direction Jenkinson confessed to Shute Barrington in May 1766. He had some nominal encouragement from Lord Lichfield, but depended chiefly upon Barrington and the organizers of the New Interest of 1754—Harcourt, Macclesfield (who offered to provide him with a freehold qualification in Oxfordshire), Bray, Kennicott, and Theophilus Leigh. They considered that Bagot might well resign for

[1] B.M. Add. MS. 38457, fo. 40; *Jenkinson Papers*, p. xxi; *Grenville Papers*, i. 359.

'a seat in Parliament is a matter of much more indifference to him than to his family, who consider it as an amusement, & as the means of employing his time', but before the end of 1767 it was clear that he would probably not survive till the general election the following March. Jenkinson's friends urged him to get in touch with the influential—the Bishop of Durham, Lord Mansfield, Blackstone, and the Duke of Grafton to whom Lord Abingdon was under obligations for recent assistance in the appointment of Kennicott at Radcliffe Librarian. His hopes, however, rested not merely upon backing of the king and his own political promise but upon the fact that 'tho' a Whig, [he] might by means of connexions with some Tory families, draw off a sufficient number of that party to carry [his] election'. The younger son of a cadet branch of the Oxfordshire Jenkinsons, he hoped through them, the Dashwoods, and other local families of the second rank, to win fifty or more Old Interest votes which with a Whig strength of some 200 should be sufficient. Moreover, on 27 January 1768 the election of his old friend George Horne as President of Magdalen, on an interest organized by Phipps Weston, one of the fellows who 'was employed in cataloguing the King's books at the Queen's House', opened the prospect of a large poll from that numerous society.[2]

The difficulties were firstly that Jenkinson had not yet lived down his labours on behalf of the New Interest in 1754, and secondly that he could afford neither to give other candidates a start nor to be caught canvassing before a vacancy actually arose. Furthermore, in view of the present hardening of Oxford opinion, it would be calamitous to appear as the Chancellor's man or to be nominated by the Whigs like Trevor in 1759; the ground must be so prepared that, like Lichfield in 1762, he might be nominated by some of the Old Interest and then triumphantly adopted by the New. By Christmas Eve 1767 the son of Sir James Dashwood, the Old Interest hero of 1754, was being talked of—a skilful ruse to divide Charles from the 'country' Jenkinsons in Oxfordshire. Two other stalking-horses in Lord Beauchamp and Lord Robert Spencer were also set up, and three serious candidates in Thomas Fitzmaurice, Dr. Hay, and Francis Page.

Thomas Fitzmaurice was the brother of the wealthy young

[2] B.M. Add. MSS. 38305, fos. 20–21, 31, 37, 41, 46: 38457, fos. 1–4, 17, 19–20, 21, 29, 38, 67, 69: 38205, fos. 276–7, 285; *Jenkinson Papers*, p. 411.

Earl of Shelburne, who combined a predilection for opposition
with an early political apprenticeship to that inveterate placeman, Henry Fox. Even at Christ Church in the fifties Shelburne
attached himself to the minority who contested the overwhelming dominance of the Old Westminsters, and became intimate
with Dr. King, under whom Fitzmaurice was later entered at St.
Mary Hall. Thus not only had Shelburne (in whose wake Fitzmaurice necessarily followed) Tory connexions in Oxford from
his younger days but he had already drifted into a policy of con-
ciliation towards America favoured by the Rockinghams and
many country politicians which was shortly to lead to his resignation. Shelburne's candidate therefore might attract Radical votes
whether of nominally Tory or Whig origin and, if elected, would
free the family borough at Calne for another candidate to support
the earl at the new turn in his politics.

Dr. Hay was a Grenvillite who had lost his place at the Admiralty Board with the fall of his connexion in 1765 and his seat at
Calne when it had been bought by Shelburne in 1761. Influential
at St. John's, he had been talking of standing for the University
since 1759, and was the more dangerous to Jenkinson as he could
not fail to win some Whig support. Francis Page was the totally
undistinguished local and 'country' candidate. He had taken the
name and inherited the property of his great-uncle Sir Francis
Page, and in 1750 had, by purchase, become squire of Steeple
Aston. A graduate of New College, he had been honoured with
a doctorate at the opening of the Camera, and had no other
qualities to recommend him than the independence of 'an honest
country gentleman, hospitable, good-natured'. Jenkinson's Christ
Church friends regarded him as a forlorn hope.[3]

The emergence of serious opposition and the fact that Jenkinson's plans leaked out in a coffee-house conversation early in
January brought on the campaign in earnest, notwithstanding
that Bagot was still alive. The news of his death reached Oxford
on 21 January 1768, and it was at once evident that the leaders
of the Old Interest had not been idle, for through Dr. Hallifax of
Lincoln they immediately dispatched an invitation to Sir William

[3] B.M. Add. MSS. 38457, fos. 5, 7, 12, 75: 38305, fos. 35, 37, 39, 41–45; Fitzmaurice, *Life of Shelburne*, i. 13–15; *Grenville Papers*, i. 288, iii. 332; C. C.
Brookes, *A History of Steeple Aston and Middle Aston* (Shipston-on-Stour, 1929),
pp. 228, 235–7; *London Evening Post*, 13–15 April 1749.

Dolben of Finedon, Northamptonshire. From a tactical viewpoint no better candidate could have been found, for not only was Dolben extremely popular in the University at large but he would divide the large poll of Christ Church, his old society, on the solid backing of which Jenkinson was heavily dependent. The son of a former Visitor of Balliol, and descended from archbishops both of Canterbury and York, Dolben embodied in a high degree the political and religious sympathies of the country gentry; he was a good scholar 'and a determined opposer of the Catholick pretensions'. The practical token of his religion which at present rejoiced the hearts of Oxford dons was his generosity, as a lay impropriator, in returning the tithes to two churches; no one doubted his reliability at a time when both the beliefs and the possessions of the Church were stridently attacked; and in later years he steadily supported the anti-slavery campaigns of that other devout country gentleman, William Wilberforce. The day after the invitation had gone to Dolben, one of Jenkinson's chief supporters, Dr. Markham, Dean of Christ Church, despaired of success should Sir William stand, and refused to endanger his interest in his society by exerting pressure in a hopeless cause. Not even the applications of both archbishops were of any avail.[4]

It was not certain, however, that Dolben would stand, despite the pressure of the Old Interest to 'preserve the peace of the university'. He was known to have undertaken to represent Northamptonshire at the general election in March, and at first he could only offer to go back to the county to consult his friends. Jenkinson's allies urged

that a mere country gentleman, to represent such a body as ours could never be a dignified choice. That we ought always to have one of our representatives an active and efficient man . . . whose attendance would be more constant than that of country gentlemen usually is

so as to defeat the 'wild propositions' which threatened the interests of the University in such times. Meanwhile, Fitzmaurice's campaign was well under way, and revealed that he had the support of the remaining friends of the Chancellor (who had been

---

[4] B.M. Add. MSS. 38305, fos. 36, 38–39: 38457, fos. 7, 9, 15, 19, 21, 25, 27, 34, 40–41; Lamport Hall: Dolben MSS. D(F) 39, 42, 52, 53, 58, 59. Sir John Dolben's papers as Visitor of Balliol are also at Lamport Hall; *Records of the Cust Family*, iii, ed. L. Cust (London, 1927), pp. 273, 278.

expected to support the court candidate) including Dr. Nowell, his secretary, Public Orator and Principal of St. Mary Hall, Dr. Chambers, Principal of New Inn Hall, and Weston's force at Magdalen on which Jenkinson had counted. On 25 January Dolben informed the University that his friends had no objection to his obliging the University at the moment, though they would not release him for the general election, and 'Mr. Blackstone serv'd the University writ . . . to put a stop to the cabals & intriguing'.[5]

With only nine days to the poll, the Old Interest were delighted at Dolben's decision, but Dean Markham was justifiably annoyed, and lectured the Warden of All Souls that it was not for Dolben's

dignity, or the dignity of the university to lend himself to stop a gap merely to disappoint the fair pretensions of another gentleman, that it was too much in the system of a Borough Jobb. That it must be particularly resented at Ch[rist] Ch[urch] where Sir W. had many friends as it looks as if he meant to abuse their friendship and turn it to their embarrassment . . . that this step of his wou'd probably keep the university in hot water till the Gen[eral] Election.

Still worse, Fitzmaurice gave up a hopeless contest and transferred his interest to Dolben. No appeal to the latter's honour was of any avail, since he regarded himself as a third party chosen by the University to avoid a contest. It was now clear even to the reluctant Dr. Markham that Jenkinson's only course was to decline a contest at the moment, and though a bad second to Fitzmaurice, to hope that his genteel acceptance of the will of the University would win him some of Dolben's votes at the general election.[6]

There were more alarums yet. The Warden of All Souls and Dr. Buckler were found canvassing for Fitzmaurice, which seemed proof positive of Blackstone's treachery to Jenkinson. An anonymous paper directed against this conspiracy of the All Souls leaders and the Provost of Oriel was put up summoning members of Convocation to a meeting in the Theatre 'to consider of a proper person to represent the University, in order to prevent an affair of so public a nature from being privately conducted by a self-appointed Junto', but no one appeared except the Vice-

[5] B.M. Add. MS. 38457, fos. 34, 36, 40–43, 44, 49; Warwick C.R.O. Newdigate MS. B 1841.
[6] B.M. Add. MSS. 38457, fos. 44, 53, 55, 63, 65, 67: 38305, fos. 45–50.

Chancellor and a handful of onlookers. Worst of all was the shocking end of the Provost, Dr. Musgrave. He was 'a vain ambitious silly illiterate man who had trimmed from side to side in ye electn. of members for ye univy., been made to believe Sr. Wm. Dolben wd. not stand, had appeared agst. him, then sollicited [for] him'. A violent and unbalanced man, the Provost 'had so heated his brain with election matters' that after calling up the Warden of All Souls 'in the night, to take pen in hand instantly', he took to his bed for two days, and then 'plunged a knife into his throat in the presence of his wife & died within 6 minutes'; Leigh, who revelled in the catastrophe, declared that Mrs. Musgrave 'saw blood plentifully gush from the Bed'. For the moment a horrified fascination superseded even the election excitement, and altogether overshadowed the labours of Dr. Wetherell, Master of University College, upon the election register which the University now possessed by virtue of its new statutes. But not even the chances of mortality in Oriel College could prevent the unopposed election of Sir William Dolben on 3 February, a triumph which he gracefully acknowledged to commit him 'to make Religion, Loyalty, and regard for the Publick Weal the principles of all my actions'.[7]

Seven weeks now remained to the poll in the general election. During this time Fitzmaurice and Jenkinson could complete the canvass they had begun under such difficulties during Bagot's decline, and the Old Interest must find a new candidate to replace Dolben. The management of Jenkinson's campaign now passed from the Dean of Christ Church, who had proved unable to control a society which he confessed was aloof. 'Our people in general do not cultivate much acquaintance abroad.' The new agent was Dr. Wetherell, Master of Jenkinson's old society, University College, a Hutchinsonian, full of oily obsequiousness to the great but invaluable in the present juncture for the daily screeds of voters' connexions which he compiled after conning the electoral list; though too optimistic in his assessment of the canvass he did better than the pundits of Christ Church. Wetherell's labours not only enabled him to work a secure passage into the court interest but for a few years made him the most important politician in the

---

[7] B.M. Add. MS. 38457, fos. 71, 74, 79, 82–88, 93, 103; Bodl. MS. Gough Top. 29, fo. 208; Browne MS. T.C.C. R4, 57/28; University Archives: MS. Conv. Reg. Bi 36, fos. 44, 46–47.

University; so violent a former enemy as Benjamin Kennicott was now glad to act with him. Unhappily for Wetherell, who spared no effort in a cause which might win political security for Jenkinson and lawn sleeves for himself, the applications made on his recommendation, which fill hundreds of folios in the Jenkinson papers, did as much harm as good; the corporate sense of the colleges remained as always the most important single electoral factor, and the innumerable applications from politicians, churchmen, and even bankers like Glyn and Hallifax, brothers of two fellows of Lincoln, only encouraged the ancient cry of independence which grew stronger as polling day approached. 'Every engine is at work against us', cried his enemies, 'even down to the Bps.'[8]

The election campaign proved as great a disappointment for Jenkinson as for Wetherell. The desperate expedient of the Old Interest in electing Dolben for seven weeks only, suggested that they would not be able to find a candidate; and in a straight fight with Fitzmaurice, Jenkinson expected to win. However, the friends of Francis Page had not let his candidacy drop, and others favoured another squire, Mr. Drake of Amersham. Wetherell was delighted at the news, as he was convinced that either candidate must '*divide*, what for distinction sake we must call the Tory interest'; but within a week of the election of Dolben the friends of the two candidates had met twice at the King's Head and determined to combine in support of Page. He, reported Kennicott gloomily, 'will be powerfully supported by New College, St. John's, Trinity, Oriel, Corpus, Braz-Nose, Queen's, and by part of Jesus, Balliol, All Souls, Magdalen &c.' Thus Jenkinson was confronted with an Old Interest candidate who, though undistinguished, could rely on many of the old strongholds of Tory power, and who, as a relative of Robert Lowth, Bishop of Oxford, had the novel asset of episcopal backing.[9]

Nor did the canvass in the colleges go as well as expected. The election of George Horne, for many years an intimate of both Jenkinson and Wetherell, as President of Magdalen did not fulfil its promise of securing a large poll for the court candidate. Fitzmaurice had long had an interest in Magdalen and a powerful

---

[8] B.M. Add. MS. 38457, fos. 24, 246, 259; Warwick C.R.O. Newdigate MS. B 2379.

[9] B.M. Add. MSS. 38457, fos. 115, 117, 119, 121, 127, 144, 170: 38305, fo. 51.

friend in Phipps Weston who had contrived the election of the new President. Horne acquitted Weston of any attempt to force his hand, but declared that the peace of his society would be wrecked for ever if he tried to change their allegiance.[10] Both Wetherell and Theophilus Leigh had hopes of breaking up the Tory interest at Queen's, where the fellows were 'not violent men', but in spite of pressure from the college Visitor, the Archbishop of York, and John Robinson, the political agent of the great northern magnate, James Lowther, the Provost would do no more than equivocate.[11] Jenkinson was still hopeful of the prospects at All Souls, where his kinsman Sir Banks had a vote and where he could not doubt that Blackstone's court connexions must bear fruit. But Banks reported that they were thinking of setting up Blackstone as a candidate, and all messages indicated that they would take the steps most likely to defeat Jenkinson's hopes. To the Oxford Whigs 'Dr Blackstone's duplicity is too clear to admit of doubt', though his manœuvres were shrouded in mystery. Dean Markham confessed 'his books shew he is not a Tory in principle, and what the object is to which he thinks it worth his while to sacrifice truth and honour, I am at a loss to conceive'. Though his interest was now confined to All Souls, it was still tantalizingly important. Jenkinson sought to improve his reputation in the University by assisting the city corporation when they were disgraced before the House of Commons for endeavouring to auction their seats to pay off the municipal debt—but the Master of Balliol darkly suspected that the advantage would accrue to Blackstone who would stand for the city.[12]

If the doors which had seemed about to open to Jenkinson in the Tory societies now closed successively, the situation amongst the Whigs was also disquieting. Dr. Tottie considered that not only had there been no decisive change of sentiment in the University but that it was 'absolutely necessary that *the Whigs shd. be united in your support by every method of persuasion & influence*'. Tottie's premiss that the old Whig solidarity had been eroded by the confusing circumstances of the new reign was borne out by the canvass. It was common ground among the parties

[10] Ibid., fos. 105, 116, 137, 160. Weston was subject to very considerable pressure from the Court, and upon Fitzmaurice's withdrawal voted for Hay and Jenkinson.   [11] B.M. Add. MS. 38457, fos. 103, 119, 169.
[12] Ibid., fos. 101, 116, 122, 148; *Cust Records*, iii. 278; Warwick C.R.O. Newdigate MS. B 1841.

that Newdigate, though the object of some criticism, should be continued in his seat; the other candidates were competing for second votes. It was thus a serious circumstance for Jenkinson that Henry Barton, Warden of Merton, was a first cousin of Francis Page, and was expected to divert a fair proportion of the college from the Whig interest into his family cause.[13]

The situation at St. John's was much worse, for the college was launching a candidate of its own, the Grenvillite lawyer Dr. Hay.[14] Mr. Feiling's bald assertion that Hay and Jenkinson were two candidates sent down by the government is belied by the complete mystification of the latter's friends as to Hay's objects. The whole enterprise was the more bizarre since Hay (a friend of Bute who was regarded by the Tory Suffolk as a worthy independent candidate) had steadily supported the Grenville ministry on the issues thrown up by the turbulent Wilkes, while his sponsor, Thomas Fry, President of St. John's, was an eccentric supporter of Wilkes and liberty. 'On what bottom . . . Dr Hay can possibly stand', confessed Wetherell, 'is to me utterly inexplicable.' As a comparative late-comer to the contest, Hay found most of the votes outside St. John's already pledged, and he was not helped by the well-founded rumour that he was being supported by the enigmatic Dr. Blackstone.

To make confusion worse confounded, a fortnight before the poll Blackstone privately commended Hay to Newdigate as his prospective companion in the representation with an estimate of his strength which exceeded his performance at the poll by more than three times. The preposterous reason given out in the University for Hay's nomination was that Jenkinson's 'friends had made overtures of a coalition with Page's in order to throw out Sr. Roger Newdigate. Upon which Dr Blackstone advised Dr Hay to be a candidate to join Sir Roger.' In fact a coalition between any of the other new candidates was more likely than an alliance between Page and Jenkinson, but it was small comfort to the latter that Dean Markham still expected to secure some votes from St. John's for him. And his friends still feared that Hay had been set up as a stalking-horse for Page.[15]

---

[13] B.M. Add. MSS. 38457, fos. 121, 205: 38578, fo. 42.

[14] A letter from George Hay to Charles Yorke (endorsed '1768, Dr. Hay sans date') conveys the impression that the initiative was taken by Dr. Fry, President of St. John's (B.M. Add. MS. 35638, fo. 404).

[15] See note W, p. 284.

With four candidates competing for the second seat, any one of whom might decline the poll and transfer his interest to another, forecasts of the voting became unusually hazardous. A week before the election estimates from different sources put Page ahead of Jenkinson, the former having rather more than 200 votes, the latter about 180. Fitzmaurice's strength was reckoned between 100 and 150 including 8 or 9 heads, with Hay far behind with some unknown but small number. The main threat to Page was the possibility of a coalition of Jenkinson and Fitzmaurice, rumours of which the agents of both factions hastened to deny. At the last Jenkinson seems to have urged Wetherell to try the prospects of such an alliance, only to learn that there was no hope of support from Fitzmaurice's votes. Fitzmaurice had pledged himself to the cause of independence, of which the only other champion could be Page. It became Wetherell's chief labour to keep Fitzmaurice in the contest to the end, in the sure knowledge that he was drawing votes from the opposition faction. On the eve of the poll, however, Fitzmaurice instructed his manager, Nowell, Principal of St. Mary Hall, to transfer all his interest to Page, whose friends undertook to support Fitzmaurice in return at the next vacancy. 'The cry of independence was so general that all persons were to be proscribed who did not vote for Page', and the doom of Jenkinson's cause was sealed.[16]

On 23 March the University polled very nearly its estimated full strength of 500, and gave a resounding victory to Old Interest and independence.

Sir Roger Newdigate	.	.	352
Francis Page .	.	.	296
Charles Jenkinson .	.	.	198
Dr. George Hay	.	.	62

On Newdigate's native heath there was 'nothing . . . but singing and hallowing Newdigate & Page for ever', while Dr. Winchester rejoiced that 'the dark cloud that hung over us we happily broke through, and have dispelled it, we hope for another half-century. Applications, the most strenuous, from the great, both temporal and spiritual, cannot yet break our Phalanx.' Dr. Johnson also remarked acidly upon the pressure of outside influence, the bringing

---

[16] B.M. Add. MSS. 38457, fo. 170, 231, 264, 270, 285, 307, 320–1: 38305, fo. 52; Warwick C.R.O. Newdigate MSS. B 1498, 2304.

up of the enfranchised slaves of power, and rejoiced in the election of 'an Oxfordshire Gentleman of no name, no great interest, nor perhaps any other merit, than that of being on the right side'. Wetherell wept 'to think that a poor fox-hunting squire is preferred before one of the greatest political characters in the kingdom', and Jenkinson's whole corps could not but be depressed at the magnitude of his defeat. Clearly the Old Interest estimates of the poll were near the mark; all but a handful of Fitzmaurice's votes had gone to Page, and, as voters openly confessed, once Newdigate was safe, Jenkinson's enemies of whatever connexion poured into Page's interest. Even had Hay never started his red herring from St. John's, Jenkinson still could not have got in.[17]

Not only was the court candidate defeated but the old court Whig interest had received a set-back. Exeter, Hertford, Wadham, and Merton stood firm, but although the latter gave all their first votes for Jenkinson they reduced the value of their support by giving most of their second votes to the Warden's cousin, Page. Jenkinson had attracted a useful number of the votes surrendered by Fitzmaurice at Magdalen, but Christ Church was solid for the Court no longer. In spite of the efforts of Harcourt's chaplain Hoare, the Whigs at Jesus polled no more heavily than of old; collegiate connexions at University and the Master's interest at Balliol had produced a few votes, but otherwise the old Tory colleges seemed stronger than before. In so far as any change was visible in the political stalemate, it was in favour of the Old rather than the New Interest. Well might the ministerial connexion be downcast and the enthusiasts rejoice that 'the University is still superior to ministerial influence, its independency is sacred'.[18]

Time, however, would not stand still even for the Oxford independents. The ruin of party even amongst politicians with memories as long as those of Oxford dons was attested in the elections of 1768 by the extreme difficulty of the faction leaders in attributing either political labels or motives to their opponents. On the whole the connexions of former years had been held to-

[17] University Archives: MS. Conv. Reg. Bi 36, fo. 50; Warwick C.R.O. Newdigate MSS. B 1839, 2045, 2051, 2212, 2264, 2338, 2379, 2380, 2443A; B.M. Add. MS. 38457, fos. 317, 320-1, 324-5; *Letters of Samuel Johnson*, ed. R. W. Chapman (Oxford, 1952), i. 208-9.
[18] The Poll Book, Bodl. MS. Gough Oxon. 4, was subsequently printed (Oxford, 1768); Portland MS. (University of Nottingham), no. 340.

gether more by force of habit and the pressure of senior members
of the various common rooms than by any real conviction on
political or academic issues. The court politicians were pledged
to the ministry, and already powerful influences were at work
rallying the independents to the administration, a process later
consummated by the blandishments of the Younger Pitt and fears
of the French Revolution. Even Sir Roger Newdigate, whose disgust with court politics abated nothing with the years, was
reckoned a government supporter by 1774, his reliability (though
not his zeal in attending the House) steadily increased with time,
and before long Vicesimus Knox, a former fellow of the Whig
society at St. John's, could unblushingly adopt his opponents' old
slogans, and 'venture to pronounce George the Third a Patriot
King'.[19]

Independent sentiments were first influenced by the notorious
Wilkes, who once again sought to re-animate the Whig connexions who were now out of office by raising in the House the
old cries against Oxford Jacobites. Rehearsing the old bogeys
from the Duke of Ormonde onwards, Wilkes affected still to 'hear
the seditious shouts of applause given to the pestilent harangues
of the late Dr King'. Notwithstanding his apostle in President
Fry at St. John's,[20] Wilkes was cordially detested in the University, which now had the pleasant experience of being able to appeal
for ministerial protection against its detractors. After the elections of 1768, Wetherell, who as Master of University College had
been able to support in Newdigate and Jenkinson candidates of
diametrically opposed political tendencies, became Vice-Chancellor, resolving to secure his future by energetically supporting the
ministerial interest. The firstfruits of his office were an address to
the king voted by Convocation attacking Wilkes and the Radicals
by whom 'the sacred name of liberty is converted into an engine
of party rage, to destroy that glorious fabric [of the constitution]
of which it is the ornament and support', a perfect statement of
the former ministerial case against Dr. King. Nor in subsequent
years was there any more sympathy for Brass Crosby and Oliver;
and though in 1770 'two or three leading societies' had still not

[19] *The Correspondence of King George III*, ed. Sir J. Fortescue (London,
1927–8), iii. 74; V. Knox, *Essays Moral and Literary* (9th edn., London, 1787),
i. 29.
[20] See note X, p. 284.

'shaken off their long ingrafted aversion of court influence', the Radical issue had produced an unwonted unanimity in political matters. Wilkes had soured the taste of independence. Moreover, another cause adopted but not created by Wilkes was already being agitated—that of religious liberalism. Well might Oxford high churchmen rejoice that under the best of kings the administration in 1770 fell to their friend and neighbour, Lord North.[21]

[21] *Debrett's Parliamentary Debates*, iv. 516 n.; *North Briton*, pp. lxxiii–lxxiv. The address was apparently drawn up by Dr. Nowell and subsequently purged in Convocation 'of some exceptionable passages, such as "Men of abandoned principles and desperate fortunes", Blasphemy &c....' (Haythorne, op. cit., p. 33); Dr. Fry claimed that this address was passed by a majority of only 9 (B.M. Add. MS. 30870, fo. 124); *J.O.J.*, 25 March 1769; B.M. Add. MS. 38206, fos. 69, 102, 208, 213, 268; Warwick C.R.O. Newdigate MSS. B 2351, 2370.

PART V

THE RECONCILIATION OF COURT AND UNIVERSITY, 1768–80

London must be the seat of divinity, as the mart of politics; a tavern the place of debate, as though the most memorable revolution in the English church should take its rise over a bottle.

London Evening Post, 1 Feb. 1772

Associate yourselves, O ye people, and ye shall be broken in pieces.

Isa. viii. 9

There is none righteous, no, not one.

Rom. iii. 10

CHAPTER XV

Religious Liberalism and the Crisis of 1772

THE expulsion of the six calvinistic methodists from St. Edmund Hall in 1768 has been immortalized by Dr. Johnson. 'Sir,' he declared of them, 'I believe they might be good beings; but they were not fit to be in the University of Oxford. A cow is a very good animal in a field, but we turn her out of a garden.'[1] Accused before the Vice-Chancellor by Higson, the Vice-Principal of the Hall, a man whose sanity was soon to give way altogether, the six evangelicals were found guilty of praying and preaching in private houses which were regarded as conventicles. Their theological views on the dark questions of predestination and reprobation were also strongly condemned, and they were turned out to seek fresh pastures under the guidance of men like John Newton. This famous story has often been recounted,[2] and concerns the political

---

[1] *Boswell's Life of Johnson*, ed. G. B. Hill, revised L. F. Powell, ii. 187.

[2] See, for example, S. L. Ollard, *The Six Students of St. Edmund Hall* (London, 1911); J. S. Reynolds, *The Evangelicals at Oxford 1735–1871* (Oxford, 1953), pp. 37–40.

fortunes of the University only in its repercussions. 'Oxford has begun with these rascals, and I hope Cambridge will wake', commented Horace Walpole; in the evangelical camp, John Wesley rejoiced at the public condemnation of the doctrines he abominated; and 'ye Abp & Bps approved of ye rigourous proceedings'. Such a chorus of praise, however, gave no inkling of the ultimate consequences of this unusual exercise of academic jurisdiction.[3]

The verdict was pronounced by four influential heads—Vice-Chancellor Durell, Principal of Hertford, Thomas Randolph, President of Corpus and Margaret professor, Thomas Fothergill, Provost of Queen's (and brother to George, the late Principal of St. Edmund Hall, who had preached against predestination ten years before), and Thomas Nowell, Principal of St. Mary Hall, opponent of Wilkes and now the chief defender of the official act of discipline. Their influence in committing the University to a particular theological line was strengthened by the ministerial countenance they enjoyed. Durell had just obtained a prebend at Canterbury and a valuable chapter living in Sussex; Randolph had recently become archdeacon of Oxford and now acquired a canonry at Worcester; while Nowell's standing in ministerial favour was acknowledged by his appointment to the modern history chair in 1771. Atterbury, the senior proctor and grandson of the turbulent bishop, who was an assessor in the case, was also rapidly preferred in the Irish Church despite an incautious attack on Lord Chancellor Camden in December 1768, which brought on him the wrath of Dean Markham. In fact, apart from the Vice-Chancellor, those who condemned the evangelicals were leading lights in the growing body of courtiers of Tory origin.[4] Whether this public opposition to the principles of the evangelical revival would conform to the interests of either the University or the Court was a question soon to be explored.

That the expulsion was an unreasonable exercise of discipline was widely recognized, not least because for more than a generation undergraduates had worshipped with impunity in the Quaker meeting-house.[5] Such severity compared ill with lenience towards

[3] H. Walpole, *Letters*, vii. 183; John Wesley, *Journal*, v. 293; Haythorne, op. cit., p. 32.   [4] Ollard, op. cit., pp. 28–29.
[5] *The Journal of the Life of Thomas Story*, *passim*. The last occasion when Story encountered undergraduates assembled in the meeting-house for rowdyism rather than worship was in 1735: p. 716.

the excesses of the gilded youth in the University. Men of liberal inclinations were angry. Dr. Fry, the Wilkesite President of St. John's, though no Methodist, did not disguise from the Vice-Chancellor his conviction that the proceedings 'seemed rather a Star-Chamber method. [He] told him so, & thought such Statutes ought not to be inforced, they savour'd too much of Laud the Lawgiver'. Bentham, regius professor of divinity and an old court Whig, refused to have anything to do with the case.[6]

Serious theological controversy followed. The friends of the evangelicals did not let their case go by default, and in a pamphlet dedicated to the Chancellor accused the university authorities not merely of injustice but of denying the teaching of the Church they professed to represent, and of the Reformation in which that Church had been reborn. The doctrines of election and predestination were the doctrines of the XXXIX Articles; nor could the University validly convict the evangelicals of antinomianism in view of the XIth Article that justification was by faith alone, and the XIIIth that good works done before justification had the nature of sin. Sir Richard Hill could find no words too strong for a recent sermon at St. Mary's, published at the Vice-Chancellor's request, 'with this bare-faced title, NO ACCEPTANCE WITH GOD BY FAITH ONLY', and concluded that if the teaching of the Church of England were indeed that of the Oxford Arminians, then the Apostles themselves were heretics.[7]

This attack called forth two replies from Oxford.[8] Thomas Randolph published an old sermon as a high-church antidote to the evangelicals' enthusiastic assurance of salvation. From Rom. viii. 1–6 he argued that sinful Christians 'grieve the Holy Spirit of God, and forfeit the earnest of their inheritance. It is vain therefore to expect from the Spirit any absolute assurance of our final salvation: for that must depend on our own behaviour.' The Spirit indeed bears witness with our spirit, but in so doing 'must partake of the fallibility, and weakness of our spirit'; moreover,

[6] Haythorne, op. cit., p. 32.
[7] [Sir Richard Hill], *Pietas Oxoniensis* . . . (London, 1768). This pamphlet was at the time ascribed to George Whitfield, and it is clear that some of the works aroused by this controversy were circulated among the evangelical leaders before publication. *Hist. MSS. Comm. R15, App. i, Dartmouth MSS.* iii. 188.
[8] There was also *A Vindication of the Proceedings against the Six Members of Edmund Hall* (London, 1768) [by William Browne], which claimed that the students had broken the statutes, that they were academically inadequate, and that their contempt of good works was contrary to the XIIth Article.

'the spirit of God does not infuse into us virtue, and religion, without our own concurrence'. The same issue formed the core of Thomas Nowell's official apology for the Vice-Chancellor and his assessors. He rebutted accusations that the Court had proceeded unjustly, but devoted himself mainly to arguing that the doctrine of universal redemption was not only that of the Oxford martyrs but an essential of Christian orthodoxy. It was, indeed, through the antinomian implications of the doctrine of election that 'Cromwell ... waded thro' slaughter to a throne, and imbrued his hands in his sovereign's blood'.[9] Quite apart from this specific issue, there seemed to be only two possible consequences of rejecting the rationalist basis of Nowell's creed, the blind faith of authoritarian Popery (after which some suspected the Methodists hankered), or the blind faith of enthusiastic sectarianism, of which he now accused them.

This pamphlet brought out Augustus Montague Toplady 'to vindicate the best of visible churches, from the false charge of Arminianism fastened on her', and to ask

1st, not so much whether the Calvinistic doctrines are right or wrong *in themselves*, as whether they are, or are not, the doctrines of the church of England: and 2. whether, on proof of their actually being the doctrines of our church, Arminians can, with a safe conscience, and *bona fide*, SUBSCRIBE to those doctrines. ...

To Toplady the XVIIth Article on Predestination was sufficient to establish that doctrine in its Calvinistic form as the standard of the Church of England, while the doctrine of reprobation, though not taught explicitly in the official formularies, was 'plainly *implied* in our articles, and expressly *asserted* in the scriptures'. On the further question of the latitude to be allowed in subscription to the articles, Toplady poured scorn on

one of the most furious Arminians now living ... Mr. John Wesley who, like many others, endeavouring to leap over the 17th article of the Church of England, very gravely tells us, that that article ... 'only defines the term', but does not affirm the doctrine.

Nor at the beginning of the Hanoverian era had Waterland solved the dilemma

---

[9] T. Randolph, *The Witness of the Spirit* (Oxford, 1768); T. Nowell, *An Answer to a pamphlet entitled, Pietas Oxoniensis* (Oxford, 1768 and subsequent editions).

that if ARIAN subscription to TRINITARIAN articles is palpably dishonest; then by all the rules of argument in the world, ARMINIAN subscription to articles, that are CALVINISTIC, must and can be no less criminal.

In thus brutally arraigning the Oxford high churchmen for selling the pass, the evangelicals were not merely trying to score a debating point, nor merely infuriated at what they regarded as Arminian efforts to minimize the power of grace. John Newton was worried that

the revival on the side of the Established Church . . . does not yet balance the defection that has obtained among the Dissenters within the past 50 years, in which the Presbyterians have so generally renounced the truths which were dear to their forefathers, and the most deliberate contemptuous and malignant opposition to the Gospel of Christ arises now from that quarter, which once gloried in it.

The revival, indeed, had not yet counterbalanced 'the defection' within the Church itself, and the evangelicals were convinced that the Arminian attitude towards doctrine and subscription rendered it impossible to defend sound doctrine against liberal encroachments. It transpired that the same view was held by the liberals themselves.[10]

Only two years before, the great controversy between the liberal and the orthodox theologians, which had never completely died away since its first great eruption at the beginning of the century, had broken out with fresh violence upon the publication of Blackburne's *Confessional*. The orthodox took their stand on the ground that the articles of the Church were in no sense contrary to reason (by which was meant mainly the mathematical sort of reason which had won great triumphs in the seventeenth century), and that Protestantism was the religion of the Bible, which could itself be rationally demonstrated to be the Word of God. Unhappily for the orthodox, even in Queen Anne's time, the liberals were able to establish firstly that from an arithmetical point of view the doctrine that the Godhead was a unity of three persons was not a mystery above reason but a patent absurdity, and secondly (in the work of Dr. Clarke) that the doctrine was not contained in the Bible at all. Blackburne not only re-stated these

[10] A. M. Toplady, *The Church of England Vindicated from the Charge of Arminianism* . . . (London, 1769), pp. 3, 16, 18–19, 92; *Hist. MSS. Comm. R15, App. i, Dartmouth MSS.* iii. 200.

arguments with great vigour, but brought another old argument into the forefront of the debate. He claimed that Arians and liberals asked for no more latitude in subscribing trinitarian articles than orthodox Arminians habitually obtained in subscribing articles which he as vehemently as the evangelicals asserted were Calvinistic in tendency.

Blackburne concluded that the Church should recognize that the articles had been outdated by the progress of knowledge, and that the present generation should complete the work of the reformers in purging idolatry and leaving the scriptures themselves as the sole rule of faith. Such an advance would have the additional merit of easing the tender consciences of men like himself and his son-in-law, Theophilus Lindsey, rector of Catterick, of winning for the ministry men of goodwill who could not swallow even a first subscription, and of promoting that other favourite scheme of the enlightenment, the reconciliation of Protestants estranged by ancient shibboleths.

Thus the articles to which the University of Oxford required subscription at both matriculation and graduation were assailed as relics of a barbarous past; and the whole Anglican ascendancy was questioned as the liberal dissenters exploited the controversy to demand exemption from their subscription to articles the bearing of which was so evidently disputed in the Church. Worse still, the liberals argued that if Oxford rationalism had led to the expulsion of the evangelicals it should logically lead to the abolition of the present subscription, so strained by rationalists, Arminian or Arian. William Hopkins, who had been at All Souls in Tindal's time, and as vicar of Bolney had made alterations in the liturgy, asserted that

the present alarming run of Methodism is an immediate dispensation of Providence, intended to punish rational believers, who have shown so little zeal in the cause of genuine Christianity. These enthusiastic people believe the most obnoxious articles in the strict and literal sense, and thereby confound the subscribing clergy with their own weapons; and consequently the only reasonable way to stop the progress of this prevailing sect, is to abolish subscription to the Thirty-Nine Articles; whereby the clergy will be enabled to confute their arrogant pretensions by Scripture, rationally interpreted, without incurring the censure of prevarication in the case of subscription.[11]

[11] W. Hopkins, *Queries Recommended to the Consideration of the Public*

Certainly the one party to the controversy with an easy conscience was that of the Calvinistic evangelicals. Possessed by a
vivid sense of being caught up in the sovereign purposes of God,
they were impervious to the intellectual questionings of the
liberals; they championed the articles as the truth rather than
the arbitrary requirement of State or Church; and they possessed
an experimental conviction that the articles were the truth ab-
jured by high-and-dry orthodoxy, and unknown to the liberals.
Liberal arguments that the doctrine of original sin was an impos-
ture of unscrupulous priests had no effect upon men overwhelmed
by the sense that by grace they had been delivered from nothing
less. Moreover, on the grand article of predestination, which increasingly occupied the forefront of controversy, they had stood
zealously firm from the beginning, secure in the knowledge that
in some shape this doctrine was at the core of the biblical testimony, however hard it might be to demonstrate all the Calvinistic
refinements to which they were attached. To complete the dis-
comfiture of the University, Toplady strengthened his case for
strict clerical subscription by recommending the abolition of
academic subscriptions which bore hardly upon the young and
the laity.[12]

For long enough Oxford writers maintained an uneasy silence
before this invitation to choose between orthodoxy and rationalism, the twin pillars of their creed. It was easier for them to point
out the failings of the liberals than to find a positive defence of
subscription as then required. They were extremely chary of the
only reputable defence, that the articles were a fair summary of
the truth, and perhaps already darkly suspected what is now clear,
that the intellectual premises which they shared with their
liberal opponents made a convincing defence of the Trinity and
other doctrines practically impossible, and that on the ground
chosen the liberal case was bound to appear the stronger, whatever the defects of individual writers.[13]

with Regard to the Thirty-Nine Articles (London, 1772). Cf. St. James's
Chronicle, 30 Jan. 1772: 'The crazy structure of Methodism will never fall while
it is underprop'd by the 39 Articles of the Church of England.' Disney Papers,
i. 171. The same doctrine was propounded by the leaders of rational dissent,
A. Kippis, A Vindication of the Protestant Dissenting Ministers (London, 1772);
Israel Mauduit, The Case of the Dissenting Ministers (London, 1772).

[12] A. M. Toplady, Free Thoughts on the Projected Application to Parliament
for the Abolition of Ecclesiastical Subscriptions (London, 1771).

[13] For recent discussions of this from different points of view: L. Hodgson,

In the spring and summer of 1771, however, events compelled the Oxford leaders to come off the fence, for the Feathers Tavern Association was formed to petition Parliament for relief from clerical subscription,[14] and the 'general body' of the dissenters also began to agitate for further relief.[15] A lively agitation against academic subscriptions was begun at Cambridge, the whole question was thoroughly aired in the press, and the news leaked out that there were no religious tests at Trinity College, Dublin. On 31 December 1771 it was even alleged that the Vice-Chancellor of Oxford was to be petitioned for relief from academic subscriptions, though Wetherell reported that 'we have nothing of that sort here, & I will venture to say that Government cou'd not do a more acceptable thing to this place than to quash it [at Cambridge] with a high hand'.[16] In the violent press campaign George Horne, President of Magdalen, took a pseudonymous hand on the orthodox side,[17] and Thomas Randolph, Margaret professor, who had published his sermon against the evangelicals in 1768, now gave a public lead against the liberals. In a charge he insisted upon the New Testament requirement that those who taught should be sound in the faith, a requirement met by subscription to the articles. No subscription was required of laymen; there was no compulsion to enter the ministry; and although there was much clamour about the hardship suffered by those whose views changed after they had taken orders, he believed that 'instances of these *starving, conscientious non-subscribers* [were] . . . very rare'. Not only was there nothing Popish about the requirement of uniformity from ministers, there was nothing Calvinistic about the articles themselves, for the framers had been influenced by the moderate standpoint of the Confession of Augsburg.[18]

The Doctrine of the Trinity (London, 1943), App. vi; R. N. Stromberg, *Religious Liberalism in Eighteenth Century England* (Oxford, 1954).

[14] T. Belsham, *Memoirs of the Late Rev. Theophilus Lindsey* (London, 1812), pp. 47–48.

[15] A. Kippis, *A Vindication of the Protestant Dissenting Ministers.*

[16] *London Chronicle*, 5 March, 8 June 1771; *St. James's Chronicle*, 31 Aug. 1771; *General Evening Post*, 26 Nov. 1771; *London Evening Post*, 10, 31 Dec. 1771; *London Chronicle*, 9 Jan. 1772; Dr. Williams's Library: Disney Papers, i. 6, 9, 28, 69, 91, 123, 135; B.M. Add. MS. 38207, fo. 76.

[17] He wrote as 'Clericus' in the *General Evening Post*, 19 Sept. 1771; Dr. Williams's Library: Disney Papers, i. 36.

[18] T. Randolph, *The Reasonableness of Requiring Subscription* . . . (Oxford, n.d. [1771]). Cf. Archdeacon Balguy, *Discourses upon Various Subjects* (Winchester, 1785); *Remarks upon Certain Proposals* . . . (London, 1771).

In all this there was nothing new, nor any serious effort to meet the anti-trinitarian position, but by the beginning of 1772 the main centre of interest had shifted from the press to the House of Commons. Despite some distinguished academic support at Cambridge, the promoters of the Feathers Tavern petition encountered a prudential reluctance to sign on the part of the liberal clergy, and in the end mustered only about 250 signatures, including those of a considerable number of laymen. A committee which waited on Lord North in January 1772 found him courteous but unhelpful; nevertheless, the petition was brought into the House on 6 February 1772.[19] Lord John Cavendish and Sir George Savile declining at the last moment on the grounds of insufficient mastery of the subject, the motion for leave to bring up the petition was made by Sir William Meredith, an old radical Tory who had been created D.C.L. at the opening of the Radcliffe Camera in 1749, and who was still in opposition, supporting Wilkes and the Rockinghams in the new reign.[20] Meredith, who had been abused as 'the tool and a very ignorant one, of an impious wretch, one Priestley, a dissenting minister',[21] pleaded for the recognition that 'the 39 Articles of the Church of England were framed when the spirit of free inquiry, when liberal and enlarged notions, were yet in their infancy'.

The next speaker, on whom the House waited expectantly as at no other time in his career, was Sir Roger Newdigate, and he launched one of the most eloquent debates of the whole century. The public reports represent him in violent mood, which he protested to his wife was 'most infamous'. 'I was in no passion, my Ba, never abus'd the persons who sign'd the petition nor said the Church wd never forget, but only that it must have a short memory if it forgot & that I quoted as not my own.' He appears, however, to have made a personal attack upon the petitioners for still taking the bread of the Church while trying to withdraw from every undertaking they had made. A strenuous application to the works of Clarendon and Blackstone bore fruit in the arguments that to countenance the petition would be contrary to both the coronation oath and the Act of Union.[22]

[19] Dr. Williams's Library: manuscript letters of T. Lindsey to W. Turner, 1 Nov. 1771; T. Belsham, *Memoirs of Lindsey*, p. 52.   [20] See note Y, p. 284.
[21] Bancroft Transcripts, vol. ii: Rev. Dr. Berkeley to W. S. Johnson, Canterbury, 14 March 1772.
[22] This debate was widely and fully reported, e.g. Cobbett, xvii. 246 seq. See

The original intention of Lord North and the archbishops had been 'to see it upon the table out of civility to [the] Petrs. but not to have done [anything] upon it', and Newdigate congratulated himself on preventing such a temporizing course. The general attitude of the conservatives was summed up tersely by Hans Stanley.

I have in my creed a fortieth article; and that is public peace. This essential purpose I never found in all my reading or experience greatly promoted by theological controversy. . . . Consider the fury of religious mobs and drop the idea. Political mobs are in comparison of them harmless as doves.

Burke, as so often, injured the cause he sought to defend by claiming that 'in their closets they [the clergy] may embrace what tenets they please, but for the sake of peace and order, they must inculcate from the pulpit only the religion of the state', a view of subscription contrary to the best Anglican opinion throughout the century. There being no Toplady or Madan in the House to claim the virtue of truth for the articles, the only defensive arguments left were those of expediency. The also-rans of the last Oxford election—Hay, Jenkinson, and Fitzmaurice—also rallied to the cause of *alma mater*, the latter adding to the academic character of the debate by reading passages of *The Confessional* and Blackstone's *Commentaries*.

On the other side there was quotation also from Alderman Sawbridge who said 'the Articles were so strikingly absurd, that he wished them to be read, and would read them himself; but having gone through a few of them he declared he would not attempt to expose them further than they did themselves'. There were others, too, in favour of the petition with no other weapon than ridicule, but the debate was distinguished by a speech in the best vein from that man of strong convictions, Sir George Savile:

Some gentlemen [he said], talk of raising barriers about the church of God and protecting His honour. . . . What! man, a poor contemp-

also Warwick C.R.O. Newdigate MSS. B 2516, 4046, fos. A, C, O. There is an interesting account of the debate by Theophilus Lindsey which not only confirms the reports of Newdigate's violence but ascribes to it the failure of North's plans to avoid a debate. Dr. Williams's Library: manuscript letters of T. Lindsey to W. Turner, 7 Feb. 1772.

tible reptile talk of raising barriers about the church of God! He might as well talk of guarding omnipotence. . . . The church of God, Sir, can protect itself. Truth must, if a fair trial be but allowed it, prove victorious . . . if the things which are necessary to salvation are not plainly revealed, then there is no way of salvation revealed to the bulk of mankind at all. Whatever is obscurely revealed, will always be obscure, notwithstanding our decisions. . . . We should not there-fore set bars in the way of those who are willing to enter and labour in the church of God. . . . Did [Christ] ask . . . whether they were Athanasians, or Arians, or Arminians? No—he delivered that admir-able and comprehensive maxim: 'He that is not against me is for me: go ye and say likewise.'

This was 'enlightenment' at its best and most generous, but it was not sufficient to carry the day. In the division the friends of the petitioners were defeated by 217 to 71, the tellers for the two sides being Meredith and Sir Henry Hoghton, a Lancashire baronet of ancient lineage and dissenting connexions, and New-digate and Charles Jenkinson. A full meeting of heads of houses at Oxford voted enthusiastic thanks to Newdigate and Page for their 'noble defence of our ecclesiastical establishment', and Wetherell, the Vice-Chancellor, also congratulated Jenkinson. Yet the liberals were well pleased with the debate, and, in a sense, the whole high-church party and the University of Oxford as a corporate body were now deeper in trouble. The petitioners' defeat in the House was said to have been 'decided by the firm retainers to the Treasury who seem'd to care but little about the merits of it', and in any case they had attracted wider support among the influential laymen than among the clergy. Furthermore, 'all parties in the debate agreed that the imposition upon Intrants and Graduates in our Universities was a shameful and glaring evil', even such Oxford stalwarts as Jenkinson and Hay, and it had been urged against the petitioners that they should have applied first to the universities for relief. The political world plainly cared not a fig for the arguments by which Dr. Randolph had lately justified subscription by budding doctors and lawyers, and Meredith at once promised to 'bring a Bill to compel the Universities if they would not remedy themselves'. Oxford was the chief villain of the piece, since the sister University went through the motions of instructing her alumni before requiring subscription, and it was soon known that Francis Page, the new university burgess, had promised on his own authority that Oxford would bow before the storm.[23]

This was by no means the only threat to the *status quo* in Oxford during the alarming February of 1772. Dr. Horne, President of Magdalen, wrote to Newdigate with the distressing news that a county meeting at Morpeth, 'said to have been occasioned by the claim of *agistment tythe*', and 'supposed to have the patronage of the Duke of Northumberland', had resolved on an application to Parliament to end the *Nullum Tempus* advantages of the Church. The right of the Crown, without limit of time, to resume property which had been in private hands, had lately been ended, and Henry Seymour, the promoter of the Bill, 'said that the *Nullum Tempus* of the King and Church were twins; that the first was buried, and the other he hoped would share the same fate'. To Newdigate, however, the parallel was by no means obvious, and in 1768, when the first (which he supported) was on foot, he had taken fright at Barrington's threat to introduce the second. The heads of houses now besought him to oppose any measure which might obstruct the flow of clerical or academic stipends, and sent circular letters to all former Oxford men in the House asking them to attend. Seymour had sent Archbishop Cornwallis a copy of the Bill, and suspected on the day of the debate that his confidence had been abused to provide Dean Tucker with material for a hostile pamphlet which was distributed to members at the door of the House; certainly Newdigate had a copy in advance, and before the debate the heads ordered 500 copies for distribution through the University. On the crucial day, 17 February, Page 'left the sick bed of a parent to attend the interests of the Church', the Bill was defeated by the narrow margin of 141 votes to 117, and the Hebdomadal Board 'with one heart and voice' sent their 'sincerest thanks for your second triumph in your House'.[24]

But barely had the doctrinal and material interests of the Uni-

---

[23] Warwick C.R.O. Newdigate MSS. B 2356, 4046, fos. I, O; B.M. Add. MS. 38207, fo. 85; *Letters of George Dempster to Sir Adam Fergusson*, ed. J. Fergusson, p. 76; *Letters of Theophilus Lindsey*, ed. H. McLachlan (Manchester, 1920), p. 45; MSS. M. J. Routh: P. Routh to M. J. Routh, 10 March 1772, printed in R. D. Middleton, *Dr. Routh* (Oxford 1938), p. 14; Dr. Williams's Library: manuscript letters of T. Lindsey to W. Turner, Catterick, 2 April 1772.

[24] *The Last Journals of Horace Walpole*. ed. A. F. Steuart (London, 1910), i. 19–22; Warwick C.R.O. Newdigate MSS. B 1760, 2009, 2356–9, 2361: MS. Newdigate Diary, 15 Nov. 1768, 24 Feb. 1769; Cobbett, xvii. 413–14; B.M. Add. MS. 38207, fos. 85–88.

versity been preserved than its political reputation was assailed by much the same combination of forces. On 30 January Thomas Nowell, the new regius professor of modern history in Oxford and the official apologist for the expulsion of the evangelicals, had preached the annual sermon on the martyrdom of King Charles before the House of Commons, the House consisting in this case of the Speaker and a handful of members. The usual vote of thanks and request to publish was subsequently made, and Nowell printed 700 copies fully expecting to make nothing from the proceeds. The sermon was old stock, having been preached at St. Mary's some six years before, and compared the civil war to the opposition of Korah and his company to Moses and Aaron. The war was due to no grievances or stretch of prerogative but to men who, he implied, were like the evangelicals, to 'the factious zeal, and turbulent spirit of men devoted to enthusiasm, frenzy and madness'. The princely virtues of the martyr also adorned George III, and he earnestly prayed 'that the guilt of an ungrateful abandoned people may not cause this sun to be withdrawn from us'.[25]

Well knowing the current fever of anti-clericalism, the Speaker at dinner following the sermon assured Nowell that he would be in trouble with the reviewers but, according to the latter, said that there was no need to make any alterations. On 21 February, however, the members having received their copies, it was moved that in future the thanks of the House be reserved until the sermon had been printed; Thomas Townshend, who had been strident against the Articles, declared the sermon should be burnt by the common hangman, and the Speaker now claimed that he had told Nowell to revise it. Four days later Boyle Walsingham initiated a disorderly debate by moving that the vote of thanks be expunged from the journals. Challenged by Newdigate to produce the exceptionable passages, he

> pulled the printed sermon out of his pocket; and, in his hurry, not readily finding the passages he alluded to, turned over several leaves: some of the members who sat near him, endeavoured to save time by pointing out to him the passages: this produced some conversation and joking.

Nowell's sentiments of divine right were defended by Dolben and

[25] Warwick C.R.O. Newdigate MS. B 2028; T. Nowell, *Sermon Preached Before the House of Commons on . . . January 30, 1772* (London, 1772).

Popham who had originally conveyed the thanks of the House, and by Newdigate 'with extreme violence and heat', but the sympathies of the House were all against them and eventually the vote of thanks was expunged without a division.[26]

In the course of the debate Frederick Montague pointed out that

the clergy of this country are in a very disagreeable situation when they are obliged to preach on the 30th of January. . . . If they follow the service of the church for that day, they must be condemned by reason, truth and justice; if they contradict the terms and spirit of the service, they will not find themselves without reproach and censure on that account.

On 2 March, therefore, he moved for a Bill to repeal the observance of that day. He branded the service with 'the name of impiety, particularly in those parts where Charles the first was likened to our Saviour', and declared that no time for abolishing it 'was so prosperous as the present, when the spirit of the doctrines preached by Dr. Nowell, were [sic] still tinkling in the ears of members'. Once again Sir Roger Newdigate stepped into the breach and 'opposed any the least alteration in any part of the Common Prayer Book. . . . He applied himself to the Scotch members, and intreated them to support the Act of Union on which their national religion depended.' And in the end, with the support of the king, the indignity of having one of the nation's historical memorials abolished because of the indiscretions of the regius professor of modern history at Oxford was avoided by the narrow margin of 97 votes to 125. Nowell was in the utmost distress at the notoriety he had earned, declaring that the offending passages were based on Clarendon's *History* and the Whig Bishop Ellys's tracts, which 'expressed his sentiments almost in the very same words'. The first impression of the sermon having sold out almost overnight, Nowell proposed to include these references in a new edition, but finally accepted 'the advice of [his] friends in not *reviving* [the trouble] by a republication under any form'. The public, however, was not altogether starved of a best-seller, for a pirated edition came out 'with the approbation of the Speaker, at the expense of a Member', prefaced by *Critical Remarks*, which according to the reviewer in *The Gentleman's Magazine* were 'not

---

[26] A proposal to inflict a similar censure upon the sermons of a Cambridge don in 1730 had been defeated (*C.J.* xxi. 429).

calculated to explode the doctrines advanced by Dr. Nowell . . . but to fix them upon the government'.[27]

The University had barely breathed grateful thanks 'to those noble champions who have stood forth to fight her battles', and to defend the 'Article, Liturgy & revenues' of the Church, than Newdigate was transmitting 'early intelligence of the motion of Sir H. Houghton [sic] in favour of the Dissenters'. Shelburne and his friends had always been more interested in relieving the dissenters from some of their present obligations under the Toleration Act than in altering the domestic arrangements of the Church of England, and through their connexion with Dr. Price had been drawn into the movement for this end, which had been launched even before the formation of the Feathers Tavern Association. The intention was to raise the matter in the session of 1772-3 'if some of their brethren who receive[d] the royal bounty money had not thought it their duty to acquaint the Treasury of it'. The London dissenters therefore resolved to hazard their cause at the very end of the present session, circularized the provincial dissenting ministers for their support, and endeavoured to obviate the resistance of the bishops by including a subscription acknowledging the scriptures of the Old and New Testaments to be of divine authority and to be the rule of faith.[28]

The dissenting ministers endeavoured to break away from the disputed ground of the Feathers Tavern petition and base their case on Locke's general argument for toleration. They disposed of the arguments that they were disloyal, or enthusiastic, and assured their own orthodox brethren that Calvinists would have nothing to fear from the abolition of the dissenters' subscription. They urged that the Toleration Act had exempted the dissenters from subscribing the articles on which they had differed from the Church in 1689; had there been a body of liberal dissenters then, they also would have received concessions. There were, of course, orthodox dissenters who wished to maintain subscription as a check upon the progress of arianism in their ranks, but the liberals claimed with some plausibility that the latter were a small minority, and that many even of those who had voted against subscription to the trinitarian articles in the famous

---

[27] See note Z, p. 285.
[28] Warwick C.R.O. Newdigate MSS. B 2361-2; Fitzmaurice, *Shelburne*, i. 440-2; *Gent. Mag.* 1772, p. 128.

division at the Salters Hall in 1719 had been orthodox ministers who had felt obliged to put considerations of liberty before those of orthodoxy. At all events, members of the House were well canvassed by the organizing group in London, and, with Lord North believed to be favourable, the omens looked good.[29]

George III, however, resolved to stand firm. While instructing North 'not to press those gentlemen who are brought on [the dissenting] interest into parliament to oppose this measure', he insisted that it was 'the duty of ministers as much as possible to prevent any alterations in so essential a part of the Constitution as everything that relates to religion'. But the First Lord, after conferring for hours with the court party, reported

not merely a possibility but a certainty that he will be beat if he opposes this measure in the House of Commons: The Opposition are all united in favour of it, and one half of the friends of Government will either stay away or vote with Opposition. The greater number of the gentlemen, who were with Ld. North last night strongly dissuaded him from attempting to throw it out in the House of Commons: Those, whose elections principally depend upon Presbyterians, must vote for this petition; Those who have a few dissenting constituents would avoid voting at all, as they are sure their dissenting friends would resent it, and that their Church of England would not thank them: Upon the whole, they look'd upon it as one of those bills, which ought to be thrown out by the House of Peers and not by the Commons, and conceiving that they had given evident proofs of their attachment to the Church in two instances during the present sessions, think it hard to be press'd a third time in a case, where their conduct may endanger their own seats, but where the Lords may act with perfect freedom without the least apprehension.

Events transpired as the court party had planned. When Sir Henry Hoghton moved for leave to bring in the Bill on 3 April, only those Oxford diehards Newdigate and Dolben opposed, the former raising the spectre of subversive presbyterianism, the latter fearing the Bill meant to 'root out the Christian religion entirely from the nation'. On the second reading Newdigate diversified the proceedings by an irrelevant justification of his friend Dr. Nowell, but court abstention had taken the heart out of the debate, and it was in any case difficult to justify legislation which, with the connivance of the authorities, was daily evaded.

[29] See note Aa, p. 285.

254

In the division the high-church faction led by Newdigate and Bagot could muster only 9 votes against 70.[30]

In the Lords, Shelburne brought Chatham out of retirement, and Richmond urged the Rockinghams to support the dissenters on grounds both of ethics and policy; Mansfield threw off his enigmatic attitude, and with the other great law lord, Camden, came out for the Bill. But the king had dispatched the court peers to the debate with the instruction that 'the question is a very short one, at the Revolution the Toleration Act was established, the Dissenters have not been molested, therefore why must now an alteration be made'. The Bishop of London cast doubt on the dissenters' enthusiasm for the Bill, alleging that

at a meeting lately of 90 persons, when it was proposed to return thanks to the committee for soliciting the Dissenters Bill which had passed the lower house, six were against it, twelve were for it, but far the greater part were silent, and said nothing one way or the other.

The defeat of the Bill was as inevitable and overwhelming as had been its success in the Commons, and it was rejected by 102 votes to 29 (including proxies).[31]

Thus in the early months of 1772 four resounding blows were delivered at the ecclesiastical causes dear to Oxford, and the University itself became an object of strenuous public criticism. Once again the lesson taught by Wilkes was underlined, that there might be worse things in a wicked world than the government, and that it might be necessary for all those privileged interests which constituted 'the establishment' in the broad sense to stand together. How well this lesson was learned in Oxford was to be strikingly illustrated in the course of the next summer.

[30] *Corr. Geo. III*, ii. 334–6; Cobbett, xvii. 432–40.
[31] Fitzmaurice, *Shelburne*, i. 440–2; Lord Albemarle, *Memoirs of Rockingham*, ii. 224; Bodl. MS. North d 24, fo. 151; *Corr. Geo. III*, ii. 341–2; Cobbett, xvii. 440–2.

CHAPTER XVI

Lord North and the University Test

In the summer of 1772 Lord Lichfield, the university Chancellor, began visibly to decline. The responsibility for preserving the peace of the University at this juncture was eagerly assumed by the Vice-Chancellor, Nathan Wetherell, Master of University College, who was now nearing the close of his fourth year of office. In 1764 Wetherell had defeated Joseph Betts, a friend of Jenkinson, in a hotly contested election for the college headship, by means of Old Interest votes and 'his powerful connexions'. As Master he had been able to serve both Newdigate and Jenkinson in 1768, and becoming Vice-Chancellor in the same year put his patronage at Jenkinson's disposal. From that time he had applied steadily for ecclesiastical preferment. 'It is not for me to chalk out a line of preferment for myself', he declared, '. . . yet I dare not from principle of conscience engage in the care of a parish to the duties of which I cannot in the present situation give any reasonable degree of attention.' He therefore applied for preferment in various cathedrals every time what he called 'the ecclesiastical wheel' was set in motion, alleging very plausibly that his notorious circumambulation into the court interest, sealed by the production of the address against Wilkes, had made some public recognition necessary to the maintenance of his self-respect. Finally, the ministry arranged to expose Lichfield and Wetherell to 'obloquy and outrage' by keeping the Vice-Chancellor in office for a fourth year until something should turn up, and he must have been very relieved in October 1771 to succeed that other courtier, Dr. Webber, Rector of Exeter, as dean of Hereford. A few months later, therefore, Wetherell was committed by every consideration of gratitude and self-defence to seek a court candidate for the chancellorship; a candidate far better than Bute was now to hand, a neighbour and alumnus of the University, the non-partisan son of the most moderate of the New Interest magnates, spoken of respectfully in the University as 'prime minister', Lord North himself. He could be held, despite some characteristic shuffling, to have defended the interests of Church and University in the previous session, and to him Wetherell applied on 14 August 1772.[1]

Wetherell advised North

> to address a letter to the President of Trinity [his old society] . . . saying that as he had always been a *friend to the Church & Universities* it was his firm resolution to continue to be so. This letter will be immediately communicated by the President to the Heads of Colleges &c., & will undoubtedly have the best effect.

Thus Trinity College might '*appear* at least to be . . . sollicitous for the object we have in view'. Wetherell then began diligently to prepare a copy of the electoral register as in 1768, and to make his applications. Two worries remained. Wetherell's term of office expired on 10 October, and should the Chancellor survive till then without appointing another Vice-Chancellor, an awkward constitutional situation would arise. However, on 19 September, via Dr. Tottie and the dinner table at Blenheim, it was discovered that Lord Lichfield had at last succumbed, and two days later Wetherell persuaded the heads to fix the date of the election for 3 October, notwithstanding 'that precipitating matters would look like a Cabal'. The support of the heads of 'Trinity, Jesus, Exeter,[2] All Souls, Queen's, Merton, &c. &c.' for this course augured well for Lord North's prospects.

There were still the manoeuvres of the self-styled 'Independent' interest to be dealt with. Wetherell recommended that the heart of this interest should be broken by applications to the heads of Brasenose and All Souls from the Radcliffe trustees, whose influence had been consummated by their recent munificence in opening the Infirmary and the Observatory. It proved that neither of these heads needed much persuasion to join the cause of Lord North, but Wetherell's suspicions that the independents had 'their eye chiefly on Lord Radnor' were well founded. Lord

---

[1] B.M. Add. MSS. 38304, fo. 54: 38469, fos. 111–12: 38206, fos. 69, 304, 315, 319, 343, 384, 394, 397: 38207, fos. 26, 27, 36, 41, 47, 55–56: 38470, fo. 43; Bodl. MS. North d 14, fo. 226.

[2] The present Rector of Exeter was the Whig veteran, Dr. Bray. He did not receive the recognition from the Court for which he had laboured so long till 1776, when he was appointed dean of Raphoe; in the same year he obtained leave to exchange this preferment for a canonry at Windsor and the rectory of Dunsfold (*Wood's History and Antiquities of Oxford*, ed. Gutch (Oxford, 1786), i. 109).

Radnor's[3] chief friend was William Scott, fellow of University College, a great lawyer and tutor of one of the Bouverie sons. Scott had withstood pressure from Lord Strathmore to vote for Jenkinson in 1768,[4] and still stood out for a 'patriot' line. However, he was not sanguine of success, and privately assured Wetherell that if the cause proved hopeless he would endeavour to persuade his candidate to withdraw in the interests of an unopposed return. It appeared that 'Ld. Radnor's chief interest is at New College—seven or eight at University & a few straglers in other societies'.

From the time the election date was fixed the patriots met almost nightly, only to reveal insuperable divisions among themselves.

Three candidates were proposed; first the Duke of Beaufort, who was pretty strongly objected to, as being supposed to have some particles of *Dependance* still hanging about him. Next Lord Radnor, & then our good neighbour Ld. Abingdon. Much altercation ensued, and they broke up without coming to any determination. . . .

Abingdon's cause was the first to collapse, 'people [being] . . . inclined to smile at the very mention of his name'; as if it were not enough for a family so long influential in the city to seek a hold in the University, the present earl had become a supporter of Wilkes. The dukes of Beaufort had been intimately connected with university affairs since their Jacobite days. The third duke had been created LL.D. in 1730 'in consideration of his distinguished zeal for both Universities', had been thought of as Chancellor in 1743 when a vacancy was expected, and the fourth had been interested in the High Stewardship in 1754.[5] The fifth and present duke had the disadvantages of having been Master of the Horse to the Queen 1768–70 and accepting the Lord-Lieutenancy of Monmouthshire in 1771, but enjoyed support from 'Oriel, part of Jesus, & some individuals in other colleges', and had no intention of abandoning the family claims. The bickering between the opposition groups grew worse as the poll approached, neither party being willing to pool its interest with the other, nor to compromise by the nomination of the present head of the old Finch connexion, Lord Aylesford.

---

[3] In 1767–8 Radnor had been a 'Tory' supporter of the ministry of Chatham and Grafton (*Corr. Geo. III*, i. 483–4; *Chatham Corr.* iii. 330).
[4] B.M. Add. MS. 38457, fos. 82, 171, 180.
[5] *J.O.J.*, 26 Jan. 1754, 6 Nov. 1756; Bodl. MS. Ballard 2, fo. 134.

Their desperation was reflected in their time-honoured but very dreadful apprehensions of a prime minister for a Chancellor. His Lordship is to send down two members at the next election, to force Mr. Jenkinson down our throats, to put a stop to all University business if every arbitrary mandate is not complied with, &c. &c. &c.

Wetherell reckoned that the two connexions together could not muster more than 130 or 140 votes, but they refused absolutely to come to terms. When Parson Woodforde came up to vote with the New College interest for Lord Radnor, he found the total strength of his candidate amounted to only 73 votes; Scott accordingly withdrew Radnor's name. The Duke of Beaufort was even weaker and his candidacy was also withdrawn at the last moment. To make quite certain an anonymous friend of Lord North inserted in *Jackson's Oxford Journal* on the morning of the expected poll, documents convicting Radnor of gross malpractices in the last Wiltshire county election, an indiscretion for which Jackson had later to make a grovelling public apology.

Thus it was that Lord North was elected Chancellor of the University of Oxford without opposition, and to the applause of most of the academic political connexions which had been influential in the past. Militant independency which had triumphed as recently as 1768 was not only defeated but unable even to agree upon a candidate. It remained to be seen whether upon the next vacancy for a university burgess this defeat could be reversed. But to all appearance the political wheel had turned the full circle. Once again, as at the Restoration, the Chancellor of Oxford was the king's especial favourite[6] and the leading minister. Moreover, although Newdigate and Page had been elected in the cause of independence, so strong was the tide now drawing independents towards the ministry, that they too could be reckoned supporters of the Court. And although the Church and University might once again be in danger it was not, as in 1710 or 1717 or even 1749, from the government but from the opposition that the threat now came.[7]

[6] George III was delighted with the result, considering 'the choise is a compliment to me'; true to his character as 'a conscientious bull in a china shop' he informed North: 'I am certain this will stimulate you to recommend on vacancies none but men of character and abilities for the Regius Professorships, and I can assure you that I shall expect all those I appoint to perform such duties as the heads of houses shall require of them' (*Corr. Geo. III*, ii. 398, 400).

[7] B.M. Add. MS. 38470, fos. 43–96 *passim*; Bodl. MS. Eng. misc. c 75, fo. 44:

On receiving the delegates of Convocation for his installation at Downing Street, North 'gave great satisfaction' by an unscripted Latin oration,[8] but of more immediate importance in effecting his utter rout of opposition than scholarship, or even the patronage attaching to his political eminence,[9] was the urgent need of the University for protection in the subscription controversy. None needed protection more than Dr. John Clarke, Provost of Oriel, who became a whipping-boy to the liberal press for months on end for dismissing the Rev. Mr. Phillips 'from his curacy of Purleigh in Essex because he presumed to sign the Petition for relief in the matter of subscription to the 39 Articles'.[10]

Sermons like that of John Allen, Vice-Principal of Magdalen Hall, who preached at St. Mary's under the inflammatory title, *Associations against the Established Church Indefensible*,[11] only made things worse. A much more intelligent contribution came from Thomas Winchester, fellow of Magdalen, a political friend of Newdigate, and an apparently worthy clergyman whose reputation was destroyed for ever by his misfortune in being tutor to Gibbon. By tracing carefully the history of the XVIIth Article on predestination, he endeavoured to show that it was deliberately designed to exclude the peculiarly Calvinistic interpretation of the doctrine by omitting all mention either of reprobation or of absolute and unconditional predestination to life. This pamphlet had the additional merit of strengthening the weakest point in the Arminian case. Dr. Tottie, the old Whig, laboured on the same point to prove that the compilers had intended a large latitude.[12] Toplady returned again 'to drive a nail in the ark', however, with a catena of scripture proofs of the articles, and

MSS. North d 14, fos. 217, 223–4, 226–7, 229, 232, 237, 240: d 15, fo. 5: d 24, fos. 170, 175, 177; J.O.J., 3 Oct. 1772; *The Diary of a Country Parson: The Rev. James Woodeford 1758–81*, ed. J. Beresford (London, 1924), i. 115.

[8] Warwick C.R.O. Newdigate MS. B 2366.

[9] '"For", saith the Psalmist, "promotion cometh neither from the East, nor from the West, nor yet from the South". "From whence then," said the Heads of Houses in Golgotha assembled, *"but from the North."*' (*General Evening Post*, 10 Oct. 1772; Dr. Williams's Library: Disney Papers, ii. 142).

[10] *General Evening Post*, 29 Sept., 6, 17 Oct., 5, 28 Nov., 3, 5 Dec. 1772; Dr. Williams's Library: Disney Papers, ii. 132, 138, 160, 172, 180, 194, 196: iii. 2.

[11] Published at Oxford, 1773.

[12] [T. Winchester], *A Dissertation on the XVIIth Article of the Church of England* (London, 1773); J. Tottie, *Sermons and Three Charges* (Oxford, 1775), p. 372. This charge was attacked in the *General Evening Post* on 25 June and 9, 28 July 1772. Dr. Williams's Library: Disney Papers, ii. 70, 80, 89.

Ambrose Serle, a Calvinist civil servant, went to the essential issue that, despite their professions of belief in the sufficiency of the scriptures, the liberals were substituting the rationalism of the enlightenment for the Word of God as the criterion in religion.[13]

From the time of the Feathers Tavern Petition academic subscriptions had been hotly debated, but Cambridge was the immediate object of attack. Richard Watson, regius professor of divinity there, ridiculed academic subscriptions, and did not doubt that relief would soon come.[14] The university burgesses also wrote to the Cambridge Vice-Chancellor, informing him of Meredith's intention to move for a Bill to abolish academic subscriptions if the universities took no steps themselves. 'Two dark and confused meetings were held, in which it is difficult to say whether fear, or ignorance, or servility, were most conspicuous in certain of the Heads', the outcome of which was that on 19 February 1772 the Vice-Chancellor of Oxford was officially informed that the Cambridge heads considered they had no authority to alter the statutes, though they saw no danger in abolishing subscription for those graduating bachelor in arts. In June, after the best legal opinion had ruled that the University was competent to alter the statutes, the Senate nevertheless decided, to the disgust of liberals and petitioning undergraduates, to concede only that graduates in arts, instead of subscribing the Articles, should declare themselves *bona fide* members of the Church of England as by law established. At Cambridge, where the liberal movement was strong and led with more ability than scruple, the die was now cast; if there was to be any radical academic initiative in the matter of subscription, it must come from Oxford.[15]

That the monolithic solidarity of Oxford opinion of which Wetherell had boasted early in 1772 no longer existed, was already

---

[13] A. M. Toplady, *The Doctrines of the Church of England proved to be the Doctrines of Christ* (London, n.d.); A. Serle, *An Address to the Serious and Candid Professors of Christianity* (2nd edn., London, 1773).

[14] [R. Watson], *A Second Letter to the . . . House of Commons relating to the Subscription required of Graduates in the Universities* (London, 1772).

[15] Warwick C.R.O. Newdigate MSS. B 1524, 2360; D. A. Winstanley, *Unreformed Cambridge* (Cambridge, 1935), pp. 301–16; *London Chronicle*, 27 Feb. 1772; *St. James's Chronicle*, 28 March 1772; *London Evening Post*, 16 June, 14 July 1772; *Whitehall Evening Post*, 18 June 1772; Dr. Williams's Library: Disney Papers, i. 203, 234, ii. 61, 62, 82; McLachlan, *Letters of Theophilus Lindsey*, p. 46; manuscript letters of T. Lindsey to W. Turner, Catterick, 2 June 1772.

public knowledge. A pamphlet[16] attacking lay subscription was published in the University confessing 'that our practice herein hath long been objected as a reproach to us by our enemies, and that our friends have frequently confessed they knew not what apology to make for it'. The academic subscriptions had originally been imposed without due care in times of panic, and it was a cardinal difference between the churches of England and Rome that the former did not require, as did the latter, the assent of laymen to articles of religion as distinct from articles of faith. It was therefore preposterous to impose this special burden upon undergraduates when a simple declaration of conformity to Anglican worship would answer the end in view. To this argument Thomas Randolph replied that the times were still perilous, and that there was no object in risking the admission of the descendants of the original Papists and Puritans, while Lewis Bagot developed the interesting idea of which little was heard in this debate, that religious instruction was an essential part of the education of all scholars at a Christian university.[17]

The original *Reflections* had been occasioned by fly-sheets which it was the custom to circulate among the common rooms when important issues were under debate, and which poured forth in a flood upon the appearance of the Feathers Tavern Petition. From these papers, which unfortunately are all anonymous, it is clear that there were some very vocal liberals in Oxford, and others who considered it prudent to compromise with opposition on their own terms rather than be compelled to accept terms imposed by parliament. One writer was

credibly informed that when all the Bishops, who were in London, (nineteen in number) met on the 9th [March, 1772] . . . and conferred together on the present question, they were all unanimous that something effectual ought to be done, and that soon, by each university. They were of opinion that the best line that could be drawn was that which the Act of Uniformity prescribed.

[16] *Reflections on the Impropriety and Inexpediency of Lay Subscription to the XXXIX Articles in the University of Oxford* (Oxford, n.d. [1772]). This pamphlet is attributed by Halkett and Laing to Blackstone's friend Benjamin Buckler; the Bodleian copy (Godw. Pamph. 2704) is inscribed in manuscript 'Tho. Fry, St. John's, Oxford', of whom the contents seem much more characteristic.

[17] [T. Randolph], *An Answer to a Pamphlet entitled, Reflections on the Impropriety and Inexpediency of Lay Subscription* . . . (Oxford, n.d. [1772]); [L. Bagot], *A Defence of the Subscription to the XXXIX Articles required in the University of Oxford* (Oxford, n.d. [1772]).

Subscription to the XXXIX Articles should be required only of those who might be admitted to Convocation. The same writer claimed 'authority to add' that the Chancellor and burgesses were also in favour of a change. It was also urged that the subscriptions were absurd when foreigners of other religions, such as Russian Greek Orthodox, had frequently been admitted. The conservatives protested that 'the attack upon University Subscription is an attack . . . upon the outworks of the Fortress' of the religious establishment, that it was no 'season for tampering with the fences while the waters rage', that the subscription at matriculation only implied acquiescence in as distinct from assent to the doctrines, and, of course, that the University had no power to repeal the statutes. This latter argument was not without force, for the validity of the opinions of Morton and Wilbraham obtained in 1759 had always been disputed. In 1770 there had been a ferocious dispute concerning the statute on academic dress touched off by 'the Servitors of Christ Church, [who] contrary to express statute and immemorial usage appeared in the academical habit of the Foundationers'; and amongst the arguments used to defeat the bulk of the reforms proposed by a party of heads who favoured the ministry had been the assertion that the University had no power to alter statutes confirmed by royal authority.[18]

About the end of April 1772 the papers which had been circulating in the University were published in pamphlet form,[19] and were commented on as a collection in another pamphlet. This writer was entirely in favour of maintaining Oxford as an Anglican preserve, but since the papers proved there were 'scarce two persons in the University or out, who understand your Subscription precisely in the same sense', it would be better to require matriculants to declare that they were members of the Church of England and would conform to its liturgy and worship, the very solution, in short, which was adopted at Cambridge.[20] While the

---

[18] For the dispute over the Statute De Vestitu et Habitu Scholastico: Bodl. Gough Oxford 73; *Remarks on some Strictures Lately Published* . . . (Oxford, 1770); *Remarks on Observations* . . . (Oxford, 1770) [copies of both these pamphlets are bound in Bodl. Gough Oxford 80]; B.M. Add. MS. 38206, fo. 268.

[19] *A Complete Collection of the Several Papers which have been Published in Oxford on the Subject of Subscription to the XXXIX Articles* (Oxford, 1772); *A Collection of Papers designed to Explain and Vindicate the Present Mode of Subscription Required by the University of Oxford* (Oxford, 1772).

[20] *A Letter to the Rev. *** M.A., Fellow of *** College, Oxford, on the Case of Subscription at Matriculation* (Oxford, 1772).

statutes were being altered in Cambridge, controversy appears to have subsided in Oxford, but it revived again in the autumn, and it was then apparent that under the stress of prolonged religious controversy the bulk of the high-church party had for the time being lost its confidence and that having been impeached by both Calvinists and liberals of being unfaithful to the articles which they claimed to defend, felt no longer able to justify them as an academic test. In William Scott's view the University was divided into three parties on this issue,

one desirous of abolishing the present subscription without providing any substitute; the heads of this party are Dr. Tracy [Warden of All Souls], and Dr. Hoare, Principal of Jesus; another willing to admit a moderate test, amongst whom are our Master [Dr. Wetherell], Dr. Huddesford [President of Trinity], and I apprehend a majority of the University; a third party headed by the President of Corpus [Dr. Randolph, Margaret Professor], Provosts of Worcester and Oriel, and the Warden of New College, declare against all alteration.

These divisions were to occasion many embarrassments and an unexpected end to the controversy.[21]

The first embarrassment was suffered at the end of October when with Thomas Randolph, Margaret professor of divinity, still rigid against any concession, Edward Bentham, regius professor of divinity, the old court Whig, urged total repeal of the subscription in favour of a declaration, the only significant point of which was a repudiation of the authority of the Pope of Rome. Another paper, possibly by Randolph, asserted that the present statute 'cannot be altered without casting a reproach upon the piety and prudence of the governors of the University for two hundred years past; nor without the suspicion that there is something wrong and indefensible in the Articles of the Church of England'. The most that could be conceded was an explanation in English that the matriculant was a sincere member of the Church of England and believer in the truth of the articles.[22] By the middle of November the Vice-Chancellor, Thomas Fothergill, Provost of Queen's, had persuaded a meeting of heads by 11 votes to 5 to repeal the present statute; the following week Dr. Randolph, who had bowed to the will of the majority, presented a new form of

[21] Warwick C.R.O. Newdigate MS. B 2239.
[22] *Oxford Papers For and Against Subscription to the 39 Articles at Matriculation* (Bodl. Oxon. b 17), nos. 11-13.

subscription which was accepted as a motion for Convocation by
11 votes to 9. The matriculant, he proposed, should subscribe a
declaration professing himself a son (*filium*) of the Church of
England, promising to conform to its liturgy and worship, to keep
out of illicit conventicles while he was in the University, and to
submit himself to instruction in church doctrine.

The Vice-Chancellor sought the advice of the Chancellor
and burgesses before approaching Convocation. Newdigate perforce declared his 'wish Stare super vias antiquas', and declared
Meredith would 'sneer at this and cry, we have owned ourselves
to be wrong but are too perverse to get right'. Moreover, the proposed 'subscript[ion] to the Ch. of E. as by law established is still
more comprehens[ive] than that to the articles; that you now
require an assent to your discipline as well as your doctrines, both
equally above the capacity of the young students'. Defects in the
drafting also alienated support in the University, especially 'the
obvious impropriety of employing a metaphorical term of in-
determinate signification (*filium*) in a legal test'.[23]

At the turn of the year Newdigate got Meredith to postpone
the motion for his Bill while members of Convocation assembled
from far and wide to discuss the proposed alteration. As finally
moved, the new draft statute seems to have taken a completely
different form from that originally adopted by the heads, requiring the acknowledgement of the royal supremacy and the statutes
of the University, and a declaration in English of membership of
the Church of England. Two things were now obvious: first, that
the University could not abandon subscription entirely without
publicly confessing it had taken the wrong part in a decade of
controversy, and second, that there seemed no possibility of agreement on any satisfactory alternative to the present test. In Convocation on 4 February 1773 Dr. Tottie, the old Whig, and Dr.
Bagot, the son of the late Tory burgess, eloquently opposed any
change; the Vice-Chancellor was compelled to read Newdigate's
letter, which made a great impression; and for the second time in
three years the leading heads were defeated in an effort to change

[23] Warwick C.R.O. Newdigate MSS. B. 1673, 1674, 2239, 1675, 1676, 2040, Sir
Roger Newdigate to the Vice-Chancellor, Arbury, 18 Nov. 1772. The drafting
of the proposed subscription was also violently attacked in the press, and
members of Convocation were exhorted to vindicate the cause of 'independency'
against 'the artful and wary Nathan' Wetherell, by rejecting it. *St. James's
Chronicle*, 9, 28 Jan. 1773; Dr. Williams's Library: Disney Papers, iii. 10, 29.

the statutes, this time by a majority of 2 to 1.[24] A majority for reform had been converted into a majority against by the impossibility of agreeing upon any alternative and by the demagogy of Newdigate.[25] George Horne, President of Magdalen, made quite clear to the Chancellor what was required: 'we stand in need of some powerful protection, and we therefore fly to him, who is, under God, the most able to protect us, . . . To you my Lord, your orthodox university looks up . . . to preserve her dignity and her utility inviolate.'[26]

The Vice-Chancellor, however, would not lightly give way, and on 15 February he published a proposal to be moved on 3 March consisting of an explanation of the statute, interpreting the act of subscription to imply that the matriculant adhered to the Church and its worship, and, so far as he knew, held no doctrines contrary to those received in it. This explanation was unanimously accepted at a meeting of the heads but naturally provoked a storm of opposition in the University. It appeared to go back on the recent vote of Convocation; it was as abhorrent as a new statute to those who believed the University had no right to legislate in these matters; furthermore, it not only narrowed the existing subscription but denied its object, which was to secure assent to the truth of the articles. The fact that the motion appeared to be in response to North's indecisive expressions of desire for a change only made it worse. The result was that when he came to put the matter in Convocation the Vice-Chancellor was in abject terror, and upon the objection being raised that the motion was *ultra vires* he dissolved the assembly without putting the business. William Scott was sure that the motion would have been heavily defeated in any case. With scant regard for their dignity the heads issued a further document trying to show that the statute requiring subscription at matriculation was not among those enacted by royal authority. But it was of no avail; on 30 March their motion was rejected again, and all that remained was a legacy of recrimination in which the divinity professors had taken an unhappy part.[27]

---

[24] See note Bb, p. 285.

[25] Warwick C.R.O. Newdigate MS. B 2213.

[26] [G. Horne], *A Letter to the Right Hon. the Lord North, Chancellor of the University of Oxford, concerning Subscription to the XXXIX Articles* (Oxford, 1773).

[27] *Oxford Subscription Papers* (Bodl. Oxon. b 17), nos. 16–24; Bodl. Gough Oxford 96, pp. 1–3; Warwick C.R.O. Newdigate MSS. B 2367, 1681, 2241, 2244,

Confusion reigned not only among the reforming heads at Oxford but in the camp of Sir William Meredith. On 9 February 1773 he moved for leave a week hence to bring in a Bill confining the obligation to subscribe to the XXXIX Articles to those on whom it was laid by Act of Parliament. On the following day this motion was discharged in favour of another for the House to go into committee to consider academic subscriptions. This motion was deferred for a fortnight, and when he ultimately introduced it on 23 February Meredith was induced by opposition to try to change the motion again. He rested his case on the approval expressed in the House the previous year for a removal of academic subscriptions, supported by the writings of men like Dean Tucker who distinguished between academic and clerical subscription. Newdigate at once replied that the object of this motion was the same as that rejected last year, 'to set open the doors of the church, and to admit within her pale, dissenters of every denomination . . . to wound our ecclesiastical establishment, to overturn her fences, and lay her bulwarks in ruins'. Welbore Ellis urged that it was improper for the House to interfere with the domestic affairs of the universities.

On the other side there was the usual rhetoric that the articles were 'the offspring of monkish enthusiasm, begot by ignorance upon superstition', and were in any case inappropriate now that the universities had ceased to be chiefly seminaries of the Church. Charles James Fox, who had opposed the Feathers Tavern Petition in the previous year but spoken against the university test, now alleged his own early scruples against subscribing. In a reactionary tirade, Dolben even included among the signs of the depravity of the times his old political enemy 'Dr. Kennicott of Oxford, [who] tells the public that we have a spurious Bible, to which no credit should be given; he has therefore received 10,000£ for collecting manuscripts, and will not, I suppose, have finished before he receives another 10,000£'. What support the secure preferment of such a man at Oxford could afford to the university test was not clear, and Lord North further confused the issue, and betrayed his influence with the Vice-Chancellor and his friends, by insisting that 'the subscription required of youth at their matriculation implies nothing about their assent to the 39 Articles; they

1420, 2368; *General Evening Post*, 23 Feb. 1773; *London Evening Post*, 2 March 1773; Dr. Williams's Library: Disney Papers, iii. 48, 52.

barely subscribe their names in token of being members of a church which maintains such and such doctrines'.[28] A debate so aimlessly begun could hardly be very fruitful, and in the end the House was probably glad to bury the whole issue by defeating the motion by 159 votes to 67.[29]

Once again the cause of the dissenters came up in Parliament at the same time as business directly concerning the University. In February leave was given to bring in a Bill for the relief of dissenters, and on 2 March Sir Henry Hoghton presented the Bill itself. Once again the opposition to change was led by Newdigate and Page with that other loyal friend of Oxford, Sir William Bagot, son and heir to the late burgess. The course of this debate was more exciting, as the church party exploited to the full divisions among the dissenters. A number of dissenting congregations petitioned against the Bill and employed as counsel to plead their cause Robert Chambers, Vinerian professor of law at Oxford and Principal of New Inn Hall. But the heart was taken out of the debate by the fact that, as the small divisions testify, North had decided to put the onus of rejecting the Bill upon the Lords. Though only fourteen members could be brought to vote against the Bill, its fate in the Upper House was sealed. Once more Church and University were saved.[30]

---

[28] Lord North's letter read at the Convocation of 4 Feb. had been characteristically equivocal, but it appeared to William Scott 'to recommend strongly, tho' with great delicacy an alteration as a measure, if not absolutely necessary, yet highly expedient' (Warwick C.R.O. Newdigate MS. B 2244). The view he was now expressing was identical with that of the explanation proposed at the same time by the Vice-Chancellor and heads, and North's pressure may well account for the humiliating course they pursued in Feb. and March 1773.

[29] Cobbett, xvii. 742-58; Warwick C.R.O. Newdigate MSS. B 2041-3, 1828, 1424, 2432, 1681.

[30] Cobbett, xvii. 759-90; Warwick C.R.O. Newdigate MSS. B 2043, 2301, 1420, 2368, 4046, fos. D, E, F, K, M; S. Wilton, *An Apology for the Renewal of an Application to Parliament by the Protestant Dissenting Ministers* (London, 1773).

EPILOGUE

The Reconciliation Confirmed

WITH the defences of the establishment secured on both fronts, Oxford men could enjoy to the full the 'extraordinary temptations to riot and licentiousness' created by the 'unprecedented magnificence' of the Encaenia in July at which Lord North made his first appearance as Chancellor.[1] Even during the celebrations, however, there were signs of unhappiness ahead. Benjamin Wheeler, the poetry professor,[2] wrote a high-flown patriotic ode prophesying the day when

> distant tribes with haste consign
> Their wavering homage to a guardian King.[3]

The homage of the 'distant tribes' in the American colonies was wavering indeed. Challenged abroad, the political organism of which Oxford men regarded the Church and University as inseparable members, was to be attacked by radicals at home. Even at this Encaenia William Jones, fellow of University College and a superb scholar in many fields, prepared to vindicate the cause of independence and liberty, the great end of learning.

> Our Academical Liberty may be considered as a chaste virgin, whom we have educated in these bowers with a jealous care; we have now intrusted her to a guardian [Lord North], whose resolution it will be, not only to view her himself with a modest eye, but to preserve her with incessant vigilance from every presumptuous suitor.

This oration was not delivered, but published later; however, Jones would not always be silent, and it was evident that in Oxford, as elsewhere, country traditions could develop into some strange kinds of radicalism.[4]

---

[1] MSS. M. J. Routh: P. Routh to M. J. Routh, 9 June 1773, printed in Middleton, *Dr. Routh*, p. 15; Jeaffreson, *Annals of Oxford*, ii. 291.

[2] He subsequently held chairs in natural philosophy and divinity.

[3] B. Wheeler, *Ode at the Encaenia held at Oxford, July 1773, for the reception of . . . Lord North, Chancellor of the University* (Oxford, 1773).

[4] Sir William Jones, *An Oration Intended to have been Spoken in the Theatre*

Moreover, the degree conferred upon Dr. James Beattie, the author of an *Essay on the Nature and Immutability of Truth in Opposition to Sophistry and Scepticism* was a testimony to the fact that religious controversy was very far from ended.[5] Successive liberal defeats had barely diminished the flood of propaganda in the press, and although Theophilus Lindsey was early discouraged, and to the disgust of Blackburne became a Unitarian in November 1773, the Feathers Tavern Association continued its agitation, and some dissenters at least professed to be encouraged by the prospects of securing further relief.[6] Early in 1774 Oxford became once more the target of abuse, and criticisms published by John Napleton, fellow of Brasenose, of Oxford examinations served as ammunition to the liberals to discredit the Oxford system altogether.[7]

Once again it fell to Dr. Randolph to champion the cause of orthodoxy. Once again he fell back upon the distinction between articles of faith and articles of religion; though the Church bound no man's conscience, she had the right to prevent congregations being confused by ensuring that candidates for the teaching office measured up to her standard. He confessed frankly that there were some changes he would like to see in the articles and liturgy, but it was impossible to compromise with men who ran constant press campaigns against the whole establishment. Lindsey had resigned his benefice, and he had acted the honest part. To William Paley 'this sort of reasoning [came] . . . as well from the mouth of the Pope's Professor of Divinity in the University of Bologna, as from the Clarendon Press'. The only test which could be justified was that 'which could adapt itself to the opinions, and

at *Oxford on 9 July 1773* (London, 1783); Lord Teignmouth, *Memoirs of the Life and Correspondence of Sir William Jones* (London, 1804), pp. 110–11.

[5] *Hist. MSS. Comm. R15, App. i, Dartmouth MSS.* iii. 204. The conferring of the degree was itself attacked in the press. *St. James's Chronicle*, 31 July 1773; Dr. Williams's Library: Disney Papers, iii. 113.

[6] McLachlan, *Letters of Theophilus Lindsey*, p. 48; Dr. Williams's Library: manuscript letters of Francis Blackburne to Theophilus Lindsey, 13 Oct. 1775; B. Fawcett, *The Encouraging Prospect that Religious Liberty will be Enlarged, Considered, and Applied to the Case of the Protestant Dissenters* . . . (Shrewsbury, 1773).

[7] [J. Williamson], *Opinions concerning the University of Oxford, and Subscription to the 39 Articles* (London, 1774); *Whitehall Evening Post*, 3, 24 Feb., 2 April 1774; *London Chronicle*, 12, 22 Feb., 5, 22 March; Dr. Williams's Library: Disney Papers, iv. 21, 28–29, 55, 23, 25, 38. See also *Gent. Mag.* 1774, pp. 358–9, 503–4.

keep pace with the improvements of each succeeding age', a view of religious knowledge which Randolph deplored.[8]

In 1774 the representatives of Oxford contrived to block a fresh motion for relief in the matter of clerical subscription,[9] but the American war, with its plain lesson that all was not well with the established order so lavishly praised in the early seventies, indirectly assisted the cause of liberalism, at least outside the Church. In 1778 the passing of a Bill for Catholic relief[10] was made easier by the need for Catholic recruits, and in its turn made the refusal of further concession to Protestant dissenters more difficult. In January 1779 representatives of the dissenters began negotiations with the Primate and bishops, a Bill for their relief was drawn up and revised by Blackstone, and in his sermon on 30 January the Bishop of Exeter declared himself openly in their favour. He was supported by the bishops of St. Asaph, Lichfield, and Carlisle. For the moment the Archbishop of York and the Bishop of Oxford held up the attempt, so the dissenters resolved to apply directly to Parliament through Sir Henry Hoghton.[11]

The Vice-Chancellor at Oxford, Dr. Horne, President of Magdalen, was thoroughly alarmed at the scope of the proposed relief. '. . . An unbounded licence for preaching and teaching, without so much as a general declaration of belief in the scriptures as a Revelation of God's will, is more than a Christian government ought to grant.' If the motion succeeded, the university test would be repealed and there would 'be no end of motions in this way while any establishment shall remain'. Lewis Bagot,

---

[8] [T. Randolph], *An Answer to a Pamphlet Entitled, Considerations on the Propriety of Requiring a Subscription to Articles of Faith* . . . (Oxford, 1774); [W. Paley], *A Defence of the Considerations on the Propriety of Requiring a Subscription to Articles of Faith* . . .; On Lindsey's resignation: T. Lindsey, *Apology on Resigning the Vicarage of Catterick* (London, 1774).

[9] Cobbett, xvii. 1325–7; Warwick C.R.O. Newdigate MS. B 1421; McLachlan, *Letters of T. Lindsey*, pp. 49–51, 54; J. Tucker, *Religious Intolerance no Part of the General Plan either of the Mosaic or the Christian Dispensation* . . . (Gloucester, 1774); [J. Fell], *The Justice and Utility of Penal Laws for the Direction of Conscience Examined* (London, 1774); [B. Thomas], *A Letter to Shute, Bishop of Llandaff* (London, 1774); J. Toulmin, *Two Letters on the Late Application to Parliament by the Protestant Dissenting Ministers* (London, 1774).

[10] McLachlan, *Letters of T. Lindsey*, pp. 55–56.

[11] Unitarian College, Manchester: manuscript letters of Theophilus Lindsey 1775–89, 30 Jan. 1779. For Wilkes's connexion with this negotiation, *Hist. MSS. Comm. R4, Macaulay MSS.*, p. 399.

who was now Dean of Christ Church, protested that those who sought relief seemed unwilling to give any guarantee that they were Protestant dissenters, and plainly doubted North's reliability.

> It was thought [he wrote] that the connection of a great man with this university would have proved a favourable circumstance to the establishment. The crisis is come—and whatever his own fears or his own policy may suggest—he ought to be apprized in a pretty firm tone of the sentiments of this place.

Horne's fears were shared by the heads, and a crowded Convocation approved a petition asking for some specifically Christian declaration to be required, Horne himself favouring the trinitarian affirmation made by the Quakers under the Toleration Act. Unhappily for Oxford high churchmanship, the soundness of the hierarchy was as suspect as that of North, and the University was reported as 'much dissatisfied with . . . [the] laxity' of the declaration submitted to the ministry by the Primate.[12]

The parliamentary debates proved equally disappointing. Sir Henry Hoghton urged the usual arguments, reinforced now by the claim that concessions could not be denied to Protestant dissenters when relief was given to Roman Catholics. Sir William Bagot, the brother of the Dean of Christ Church, who led the opposition to the Bill, urged that the times were too perilous to permit of an alteration in the constitution, for 'there wanted nothing but the implacable spirit of religious controversy to blow upon the very existence of this empire'. Wilkes tried to calm Bagot's fears for the future of Christianity by owning the dreadful truth. 'Deism . . . Sir, sound pure deism, has made rapid progress, not only in this island, but in every part of the continent. It is almost become the religion of Europe . . . every year adds to the number of disciples of deism.' So little incongruous did this argument appear to Wilkes that he immediately boasted of his membership of the Church of England, and quoted the text much canvassed by the liberals that 'in every nation, he that feareth God, and worketh righteousness is accepted by him'.[13] Newdigate gave a topical and personal bent to the opposition. It was not the Church but the dissenters that exemplified the spirit of persecu-

---

[12] Warwick C.R.O. Newdigate MSS. B 1759, 1425, 1753–7.
[13] Acts x. 35. Wilkes quotes the substance rather than the letter of the verse.

tion; did not every ship from America bring home stories of the outrages suffered by the laity and clergy of the Episcopalian Church at the hands of dissenters? Moreover,

> when this Bill for the relief of the dissenters was last in agitation, his levees were every morning crowded, not with divines of the Church of England trembling for their incomes ... but with honest worthy and respectable Protestant dissenters ... who came to complain of the measure in agitation ... because under the pretext of relieving them from subscription, it would let in the Anti-Trinitarians, the Anabaptists, and all manner of sects.

A week later Bagot and Newdigate divided on the motion for leave to bring in the Bill and could raise only 6 votes against 77. North supported the petition sent up by the University, and suffered another tirade from Wilkes. Declaring that the conduct of the University had been 'uniform, to abridge on every occasion, as far as they could, both religious and civil liberty', he harked back again to the Oxford decrees of 1683, and justified his innuendoes by the facts that Oxford had asked for no test upon Roman Catholics in the previous year and that the liberal University of Cambridge had made no petition now. Dunning asserted that opposition to the authority of the civil magistrate in matters spiritual was the distinguishing tenet of Protestant dissenters throughout Europe, but by a moderate margin the declaration proposed by North survived. This was Oxford's one success, for the Bill passed the Commons, and with support both in the ministry and on the bench the Bill could not now be thrown out in the Lords.[14]

However, consolation might be derived from the fact that although old pamphlets on the Test and Corporation Acts were still to be republished, and the old arguments rehashed, the articles were now safe until a time—then unforeseeable—when a movement from Oxford, hitherto their most powerful defender, should argue that without casuistry they were, not indeed irrational, but un-Catholic.

The impact upon Oxford of the conflict in the American colonies was not confined to the question of toleration. North's recommendation of Johnson for the degree of D.C.L. in 1774 was

---

[14] Unitarian College, Manchester: manuscript letters of Theophilus Lindsey 1775–89, 10, 17 March 1779; Cobbett, xx. 239–47, 305–22; Warwick C.R.O. MS. Newdigate Diary, March–April 1779.

probably intended as an inexpensive reward for his pamphlet *Taxation no Tyranny*.[15] In October 1775 the University gave vociferous support to its Chancellor's ministry in an address to the king which abhorred the 'artifices and seditious proceedings' in America, and deplored the way in which 'the liberty of the press ... has been prostituted to sedition, and most grossly abused by a faction'.[16] This provocation brought Burke to his feet in the House, accusing North of tampering with the address before it reached the king, and charging the University in almost the old Whig manner with 'interfering with politics, advising a civil war, and calling those that opposed it rebels and traitors'. But it was a measure of how far the times had changed that the man who undertook the defence of the University was that old court Whig who had formerly attacked her at the behest of the ministers, Edward Bentham. With the king Oxford needed no justification, for there were renewed rumours that 'his Majesty means to visit Oxford . . . [and] should he go there without paying the same attention to Cambridge, or in any instance manifest a predilection for the University of Oxford, it will shock the prejudices of many of his most respectable subjects'.[17]

The changed times were apparent also in the election of 1780. Throughout the spring the University was disturbed by rumours that Newdigate intended to resign his seat, an act for which no precedents (except where members were to be summoned to the Upper House) could be remembered. For this reason, and because Newdigate's low opinion of public life was well known, no one at first took heed. In 1767 Newdigate had 'seen enough of Parliaments, and of the miserable state of this country to be without concern whether I ever sit there again', and in 1772 there had been strong but unfounded rumours of his resignation.[18] In the middle years of the decade his enthusiasm for parliamentary attendance had been further diminished by continental tours in search of

[15] *Boswell's Life of Johnson*, ed. G. B. Hill, revised L. F. Powell, ii. 318 n. 1.

[16] University Archives: MS. Conv. Reg. Bi, fo. 363. John Scott, the future Earl of Eldon, declared of this address: 'I gave it neither support nor opposition, for I do not care sixpence about the matter' (H. Twiss, *Life of Lord Chancellor Eldon* (London, 1844), i. 97).

[17] Cobbett, xviii. 854; [E. Bentham], *The Honor of the University of Oxford Defended against the Illiberal Aspersions of E[dmun]d B[urke] Esq.* (London, n.d. [1776]); *Hist. MSS. Comm. Stopford-Sackville MSS.* i. 71–72).

[18] Warwick C.R.O. Newdigate MSS. B 2333, 2141; B.M. Add. MS. 38207, fo. 76.

objets d'art, by his gothic reconstruction of Arbury, his coal-mines and canals. Now the issue was brought to a head by a libellous paper circulated in the University asserting that he was about to resign because he had been taken to task by Nathan Wetherell for idleness in his public functions. His friends Thomas Monkhouse, fellow of Queen's, and Lewis Bagot wrote asking for a firm decision about the resignation and for the means to rebut the charges which were being made.[19]

No solicitations could shake Newdigate's resolution to withdraw from public life, and, in a long letter of resignation to the Vice-Chancellor, he sketched his own history and gave a remarkable exposition of the philosophy of an independent politician who had been drawn by the circumstances of the times and of the new reign to support the Court upon independent principles. He had entered Parliament for Middlesex

when ... chozen unanimously to supply a vacancy ... occasioned by the sudden retreat of a great patriot leader [William Pulteney] who in the moment of victory had disappointed his hopes of nation. In the wreck of Principle wch. followed, I joined the small remnant of real Patriots, independent themselves, & void of all ambition but that of serving their country.

In these early years he had seen 'the greatest abilities accompanied with the lowest baseness & the utmost efforts of united political virtue sufficient to overturn the ablest of ministers [Sir Robert Walpole] but not to break the system of influence which he had established'. After the collapse of the popular interest in Middlesex, only unsolicited election by the University could have brought him back to public life. The system of influence, which had early disgusted him, had led to a succession of disasters at home and abroad despite the efforts of a patriot prince and a minister bred of opposition stock. In every Parliament there had been

majorities implicitly following the dictates of the minister of the day, changing their opinions as the minister was changed, and in one of them enacting under one minister, repealing under another, and re-enacting under a third. In all of them oppositions conducted by

[19] Warwick C.R.O. Newdigate MSS. B 1834, 2141, 1835, 1837, 1427, 1836, 1838, 2371, 2011, 2372; Sir R. Newdigate to the dean of Hereford, Spring Gardens, 6 May 1780.

interested & factious leaders, for private ends fomenting civil discord. . . . The people at large more corrupt than even the representative body, & that more corrupt than even the minister himself. To this the general disregard and contempt of Parliament [is] unavoidably consequent. . . . From this source is derived such debility and relaxation that they are no longer able to support their own authority, nor the dignity of the Crown, even under a Prince of the most unsullied virtue & a minister most moderate & gentle in his assertions of power. From this fatal source are derived the too successful rebellion of one part of the Empire, the sullen discontent & kind of armed truce in another, and the ferment now raging under our feet and ready to burst out into flames. Were but elections conducted with the same spirit with which yours are conducted!

Would the nation but emulate the virtuous independence of the University of Oxford, the Constitution would regain its pristine vigour, and Parliament would once more be the object of veneration.[20]

The candidates who had already been launched to contest the expected vacancy all prided themselves upon their independence, though interpreting it in different ways. Wetherell early applied to Charles Jenkinson to stand again, but that most professional of politicians had already been twice bitten, and in the changed circumstances of 1780 declared 'they know the character and abilities of Sir William Dolben, & in my opinion they cannot chuse a better man'. Dolben, like Newdigate, had evolved into an independent supporter of the Court, and having failed to prevail on Sir Roger to remain at his post in the hour of trial, eagerly succeeded to his interest.[21] The University, however, still contained heirs to the tradition of die-hard opposition to whom independence still meant opposition to the Court.[22] Their leader in the last contested election—that of Lord North in 1772—had been William Scott. For some time he had been looking for a seat in Parliament which would not cost a great deal, and his friends in the University could not have had an abler candidate. They now required University College 'to propose him in justice to his

[20] There are copies of this letter in Warwick C.R.O. Newdigate MS. B 2012; and University Archives: MS. Conv. Reg. Bk 37, fo. 112.
[21] B.M. Add. MS. 38307, fos. 169, 170; Warwick C.R.O. Newdigate MSS. B 1635–6.
[22] On 20 July 1779 a vigorous circular had been sent to members of Convocation opposing a scheme of voluntary payments for the war effort (Bodl. G.A. Oxon. b 111 (no. 62)).

merit'.[23] The sponsorship of a third candidate from the same faculty was also pressed on the same rather reluctant society, that of William Jones. The college interest having already been given to Scott, Jones's friends, 'chiefly young men ... [who] have shown more zeal than conduct in the affair', published an address explaining that the failure of his society to support him was due to their impression that he was about to be appointed to the bench of judges in India and so would be unable to serve. His friends would not solicit votes in the University, but would state that 'for his University he entered the lists with a foul-mouthed and arrogant Frenchman, who attacked Oxford in three large volumes of misrepresentation and scurrility. . . . To Oxford he is known to be attached by the strongest possible ties.' Jones indeed had not only defended the scholarship of his *alma mater* against Anquetil du Perron nine years before, he had flattered her political independence. The University

choisit ses réprésentans parmi ceux qui ont le plus de talent et de vertu. . . . La moindre recommandation de la part du ministère; la moindre cabal de la part du candidat suffirait pour le faire rejetter. A-t-il des talens, de la vertu? Il peut espère d'atteindre à cette haute dignité. N'en a-t-il point? Il ne l'atteindra jamais.[24]

'This', remarked Charles Parker, 'sounds . . . like being one's own trumpeter, & approving yourself before you are approved of others', and Jones had an odd confidence in his own virtue, for he was prepared to seek ministerial favour so as

to have twenty thousand pounds in my pocket before I am eight-and-thirty years old; and then I might contribute in some little degree, towards the service of my country in parliament . . . without selling my liberty as too many of my profession are not ashamed of doing; and I might be a speaker in the house of commons in the full vigour and maturity of my age.

An advocate of independence attained through court influence, a tutor in the family of Spencers of Althorpe, and a friend of Cartwright and Wilkes, Jones regarded Radical independence as a Whig rather than a Tory cause, and thought the political

[23] Twiss, *Life of Eldon*, i. 114; Warwick C.R.O. Newdigate MS. B 2141.
[24] Ibid.; Jones's address, *To the University of Oxford, May 5, 1780* (Bodl. Gough Oxf. 90 (22)); [W. Jones], *Lettre à Monsieur A[nquetil] du P[erron]* (London, 1771).

principles of the other candidates the reverse of his own. He was certainly an adherent of the Radical party which they held guilty of faction and disorder, and their worst fears were confirmed in a pamphlet of his of 1782, in which Jones, in the person of a scholar, provided a peasant with a musket, and concluded a dialogue thus:

S[cholar]: But what if a few great lords, or wealthy men were to keep the King himself in subjection, yet exert his forces, lavish his treasure, and misuse his name, so as to domineer over the people and manage the Parliament?

P[easant]: We must fight for the King and for ourselves.

Yet this had been Oxford doctrine fifty years before, and had been urged in Parliament at the time of the excise crisis. Finally, though Jones would not canvass inside the University, he solicited votes of non-residents with abandon, optimistically approaching even Horace Walpole. But no election at Oxford had ever been won mainly by non-resident voters, and on 2 September 1780 Jones instructed Dr. Wheeler, who was now regius professor of divinity, to withdraw his name. Scott also found that his support was inadequate and also withdrew. Thus Dolben, still priding himself on independence of another kind, was returned unopposed. In his view,

if some spirited control is not soon exerted over the lawless rage of the multitude or rather the daring, democratic insolence of their leaders, they are likely to become perilous in the extreme. Yet so mighty are some of these leaders, and so much does the witchcraft of opposition fascinate almost all young Englishmen, that it requires a discreet head as well as a strong hand to subdue the one and convince the other.

With the emergence of serious political issues and mob disorder, the Tory was overshadowing the Radical in Dolben as in so many of his constituents.[25]

The shrill attempts of the candidates in the election of 1780 to exploit the traditional independence of the University were in a sense incongruous, for the result of the election confirmed that of

[25] *Letters of Sir William Jones* (London, 1821), i. 129, 143–59; W. Jones, *The Principles of Government in a Dialogue between a Scholar and a Peasant* (n. pl., 1782); Warwick C.R.O. Newdigate MS. B 1636. There are interesting character studies of Jones in J. Walker, *Oxoniana* (London, n.d. [1809]), iv. 136–7, and N. S. Marsh, 'Sir William Jones 1746–94', *University College Record*, 1954–5, pp. 79–95.

1772 in showing that Oxford had become reconciled with the Court, and that the estrangement which had begun in 1714 had at last been healed. The visits paid by the king in the next few years only confirmed a now well-known fact. Yet, in the terminology of the eighteenth century, the claims to independence were not without substance. Now, and long afterwards, candidates were forbidden to canvass in person;[26] candidates seeking to create an interest were under the compulsory disadvantage of posing as the spontaneous choice of one of the connexions among the resident members. Gratuities were expected for bedels, and benefactions for colleges, but election itself was gratis. Moreover, although most of the neighbouring magnates had a following, the University never became a pocket borough. Outside influence reached its peak under Queen Anne, but in the bitter strife of those years no faction ever approached supremacy over the others. Under the first two Hanoverians the friends of Oxford, deprived of ministerial patronage, had not the means to sway large numbers of votes. The University was perforce independent, and the poll-books are convincing evidence that by far the most important influence upon the voters was that of the corporate traditions and pressure of the colleges themselves, electioneering assets which even at Christ Church were never devoted wholly to the service of outside interests. Even when Oxford became reconciled with the Court again in the seventies her vaunted independence was not entirely fictitious, for the religious standpoint of the dominant school in the University was a potential embarrassment to ministers who had to heed influential opinion. As time passed the supremacy of protestant high churchmanship within the Church, and the privileges of the Church within society, were increasingly to be challenged. Even before 1780 the day had been foreshadowed when the ministry might purchase the survival of the unreformed political system at the expense of the ascendancy of the unreformed Church.

[26] Lamport Hall: Fitzwilliam MS. F(M) 197; R. Heber to Lord Fitzwilliam, 14 April 1814.

NOTES

Note A, p. 36. This was one of the reproaches already noted, made against university court politicians at the County election:

> Not weather-cock Kennet, such turnings can show,
> To bail Highchurch one Day, and Vote next for the Low.

The Oxfordshire Election (London, 1710). An interesting comment upon the situation of Vice-Chancellor Lancaster, and an illuminating example of the exploitation of the crisis by the arch-intriguer Robert Harley, is given in his letter to Dr. Stratford on 19 Dec. 1709 (Portland MSS. B.M. Loan 29/171): 'You may depend upon [it], there has been a settled scheme laid of a visitation on both universities & also of all the clergy to the old tune; this thing of Dr. Sacheverell sprung the mine before they were quite ready. . . . I hear the Vice Char. brought the Doctor in his coach to Westminster Hall: they who did this little think the Dr. was the tool to beat down Xt Church, & you wil[l] find the vice chacrs. patron [the] L[ord] Tr[easurer] wil[l] not own him & dare not let them know how far he countenanced that [one word illegible] wch. this wil[l] destroy & I hope it wil[l] serve to unite the university & clergy. . . .'

Note B, p. 55. Accounts of the riots differing only in the innuendoes are to be found in: *Hearne's Collections*, v. 62–63; N. Amhurst, *Terrae Filius* (London, 1726), ii. 120 seq. (misdated 1714); *Hist. MSS. Comm. Portland MSS.* vii. 222–3; *Hist. MSS. Comm. Various MSS.* viii. 99 (the last two references misdated 1717); R. Rawlinson, *A Full and Impartial Account of the Oxford Riots* (London, 1715). A Quaker account stresses the provocation of the Whigs: *The Journal of the Life of Thomas Story* (Newcastle upon Tyne, 1747), pp. 474–6. Much correspondence on this and subsequent troubles is published in Hobson, *Oxford Council Acts 1701–52*, App. V, pp. 324–60.

Note C, p. 65. Boyer, *Political State*, xiii. 233 seq.; *St. James's Evening Post*, 24–26 Jan. 1716–17; *The Weekly Journal*, 26 Jan. 1716–17; *The Flying Post*, 26–29 Jan. 1716–17; Christ Church MS. Arch. W. Epist. 20: Bp. of Bristol to Abp. Wake, 11 Jan. 1716–17: D. Wilkins to Wake, n.d.; University Archives: MS. Conv. Reg. Bd 31, fo. viii. Charlett now, as twenty years earlier, was abused by his enemies as a Jacobite. In 1696 he made the obvious defence: 'It is not easy to imagine why I should be in haste to make room for Mr. Obadiah Walker, who is known to wish very heartily a return to some lodgings, which he says I have much mended for him' (*Hist. MSS. Comm. Downshire MSS.*, I, pt. ii. 716). Now his defence was a lifetime's record as a court politician.

Note D, p. 94. In 1718 Tooley, along with Dry and Downes of St. John's, was accused by *The Flying Post* of supplying 'Jacobite Letters and other Trumpery' to Mist's *Weekly Journal*. Downes reacted fiercely with a pamphlet, *The Flying Post Posted* (London, 1718), under the pseudonym 'Mrs Anne Roberts' (*The Flying Post*, 8–10 May, 7–10, 12–14, 21–24

June 1718). According to Hearne, Downes resigned his fellowship as a non-juror, but the *Alumni Oxonienses* does not record him as ever being a fellow. *Hearne's Collections*, viii. 34.

Note E, p. 103. Christ Church MS. Arch. W. Epist. 16, nos. 164 [264]–191 [291]: 22, R. Meadowcourt to Abp. Wake, 18 May 1722: 23, same to same, 25 June, 1 July 1725; P.R.O. SP 35/18, fos. 91, 254: /21, fo. 342: /22, fo. 37: /25, fos. 10, 160, 273: /33, no. 193: /43, no. 163: /57, fo. 7; *D.N.B.*, article on 'Richard Meadowcourt': *Hearne's Collections*, viii. 154, ix. 404, xi. 361; R. Meadowcourt, *The Duty of Preachers Explained and Stated* (London, 1721); B.M. Add. MS. 32689, fo. 341: *Letters by Several Eminent Persons Deceased including the Correspondence of John Hughes Esq. . . .* (London, 1772), ii. 249; *Letters of Spencer Cowper, Dean of Durham 1746–74*, ed. E. Hughes, Surtees Soc. clxv (1956), 167.

Note F, p. 107. Boyer, *Political State*, xviii. 233–5; *Diary of Mary, Countess Cowper, Lady of the Bedchamber to the Princess of Wales*, ed. Spencer Cowper (London, 2nd edn., 1865), pp. 16–18 (cf. *Hist. MSS. Comm. Egmont Diary*, i. 233); Nicolson, *Letters*, ii. 440–6, 457; Christ Church MS. Arch. W. Epist. 15: ? to Abp. Wake, 30 Nov. 1715: Bp. of Bristol to Abp. Wake, 9 Jan. 1715/16: 20, same to same, 11 Jan. 1716/17; Bodl. MS. Ballard 6, fos. 41, 47; P.R.O. SP 35/17, fo. 159: /18, fo. 14; *Hist. MSS. Comm. Portland MSS.* vii. 220; *Muses Fountain Clear*, p. 19.

Note G, p. 110. 'The Oriel College Lawsuit, 1724–26' is discussed by F. J. Varley in *Oxoniensia*, vi. 54–69. There is material overlooked by him in: B.M. Add. MS. 36136, fos. 113–45; Christ Church MS. Arch. W. Epist. 15: G. Carter to Abp. Wake, 23 March [1716]: 16, nos. 192, 203, 228 [328]: 20, G. Carter to Abp. Wake, 19 Nov. [1716]: Earl of Sunderland to Abp. Wake, 7 Aug. 1717: G. Carter to Abp. Wake, 6 April [1718]; *Hist. MSS. Comm. Portland MSS.* v. 637, vii. 356, 378, 437; *Bolingbroke Corr.* iv. 465. For Carter's character: Oriel College MS. Memorandum Book of Provost Carter.

Note H, p. 122. *Hist. MSS. Comm. Leyborne–Popham MSS.*, pp. 285–7; Bodl. MSS. Ballard 20, fos. 22, 59 seq., 114–15: 21, fo. 198; B.M. Egerton MS. 2618, fo. 156; *Hist MSS. Comm. Portland MSS.* iv. 105, 269, vii. 67, 146; *Swift Corr.* ii. 178; *The Works of Alexander Pope*, ed. W. Elwin and W. J. Courthope, vi. 359, viii. 23; *Hearne's Collections*, vi. 98; Lamport Hall: Isham MSS. IC 2773, 3743, 3749, 3750; *All Souls Archives*, pp. 292 seq., *Hist MSS. Comm. R7, Ormonde MSS.*, p. 782; *A True Copy of the Last Will and Testament of George Clarke* (London, 1737), p. 58; *Victoria County History of Oxfordshire*, iii. 180.

Note I, p. 138. The article on Conybeare in *D.N.B.* is based mainly on that in *Biographia Britannica*, ed. A. Kippis (London, 1778–93), iv. 90–94; see also A. T. Thomson, *Memoirs of Viscountess Sundon* (London, 1847), ii. 181, 183; Packington Hall MSS.: Lord Guernsey to Earl of Aylesford, 12 Jan. 1732/3; *Alma Mater* (London, 1733), p. 19; *The Terrae Filius's Speech . . .* (London, 1733), p. 4; *The Oxford Toast's Answer to the Terrae Filius's Speech* (London, 1733), pp. 8–9; Nichols, *Illustrations*, iv. 293, 295; *Hearne's Collections*, xi. 61, 152; B.M. Add. MS. 32689, fo. 202; Exeter College MS. College Register 1737–1827, fos. 68–69.

Note J, p. 162. Coxe, *Walpole*, iii. 517, 519, 564; Cobbett, *Parliamentary History*, xi, 1372, xii. 728, 1053, xiii. 136–8 n., 144 n., xiv. 90; Lamport Hall: Isham MS. IC 2508; Bodl. MS. Eng. Hist. d 103, fos. 20, 22, 33; *The Letters of Horace Walpole*, ed. P. Toynbee (Oxford, 1903–18), i. 204, 206; ii. 164, 378; *Grenville Papers*, ed. W. J. Smith (London, 1852), i. 1–12 *passim*; B.M. Add. MSS. 35587, fo. 35: 32715, fos. 163–4: 32716, fo. 166. Cornbury's advice that the nation needed 'authority in government' later impressed the young George III. Feiling, *Second Tory Party*, pp. 38, 55; *Letters from George III to Lord Bute*, ed. R. Sedgwick (London, 1739), p. 82.

Note K, p. 168. F. Potter, *A Sermon preached before the University of Oxford ... on the Present Rebellion* (London, 1745); cf. his other sermons of 1745, *A Serious Address to the People of Great Britain* and *An Address to that Honest Part of the Nation call'd the Lower Sort of People*; J. Free, *A Volume of Sermons preached before the University of Oxford* (London, 1750); *The Speech of Dr. John Free containing a Concise and Clear Account of the English Constitution ...* (London, 1753); *The Sentiments of a True Anti-Gallican ...* (London, 1756). Free preached in favour of the New Interest in 1754. Apparently Potter was also refused access to the press. [G. Coade], *A Blow at the Root* (London, 1749), p. 60.

Note L, p. 173. W. King, *A Proposal for publishing a Poetical Translation of the Rev. Mr. Tutor Bentham's Letter to a Young Gentleman of Oxford* (London, 1749); *A Poetical Abridgement both in Latin and English of the Rev. Mr. Tutor Bentham's Letter to a Young Gentleman of Oxford ...* (London, 1749); *A Certain Proposal of a Certain Little Tutor for making Certain Reformations in a Certain Method of Education, most Certainly practis'd in a Certain University* (London, n.d.). The ascription of this pamphlet to Bentham by *Halkett & Laing* is clearly erroneous.

Note M, p. 174. B.M. Add. MSS. 32717, fos. 235, 300: 35870, fos. 128–30; Balliol College MS. 403, fos. 59, 104; *London Evening Post*, 8–10 June 1749, reprinted in *Gent. Mag.* 1749, p. 279; H. Walpole, *Memoirs of the Last Ten Years of the Reign of George II*, i. 41; Warwick C.R.O. Newdigate MSS. B 1521–3. Among the most popular verses sent up by the University on the prince's death were some pompous lines by Blackstone, *The Biographical History of Sir William Blackstone* (London, 1782), pp. 14 seq.; *London Evening Post*, 23–25 April, 6–8, 15–18 June 1751; H. Walpole, *Letters*, iii. 60.

Note N, p. 187. [R. Newton], *Wellwishers to the University of Oxford, and the Answers* (London, 1750). This collection was also published under the title *A Series of Papers on Subjects most interesting to the Nation in General and Oxford in Particular* (London, 1750); [George Wilmot], *A Serious Inquiry into some Late Proceedings in the University of Ox[for]d* (London, 1751); [W. Lewis], *An Answer to the 'Serious Inquiry ...'* (London, 1751); [George Wilmot], *A Letter to —— M.D., heretofore of —— —— College in the University of O—d* (London, 1752); *Free Thoughts on University Education ...* (London, 1751); Balliol College MS. 403, fo. 137; A. M. W. Stirling, *Annals of a Yorkshire House* (London, 1911), i. 204–7.

Note O, p. 201. Exeter College MSS.: Lord Harcourt to T. Bray, 30 April

1754: R. Blacow to T. Bray, 23, 27 Aug. 1754; *J.O.J.*, 5, 19, 26 Jan. 1754; *London Evening Post*, 15–17 Jan., 6–9, 9–11 July 1754; Lamport Hall: Isham MSS. IC 2185, 2705; *Correspondence of Samuel Richardson*, ed. A. L. Barbauld (London, 1804), ii. 186–98. Blacow soon received a candid opinion of himself by overhearing a conversation when walking in Windsor Park: 'a Canon, d—m him, a blunderbuss: if mounted on the wall there might be some danger of him' (Exeter College MSS.: R. Blacow to T. Bray, 22 Nov. 1754).

Note P, p. 202. *London Evening Post*, 18–20 April, 8–10 Aug. 1754– 9–11 Jan. 1755 *passim*; *J.O.J.*, 21 Sept. 1754; B.M. Add. MSS. 32731, fo. 533: 32732, fos. 80–81; Exeter College MSS.: George Huddesford to R. Blacow, 7 Oct. 1754: R. Blacow to Dr. G. Huddesford, 2 Nov. 1754; *Informations . . . Relating to the Treasonable Verses found in Oxford* (Oxford, 1755); *Dr King's Apology* (Oxford, 1755), Advertisement; R. Blacow, *A Letter to William King* (London, 1755); *An Answer to Mr B[laco]w's Apology* (London, 1755). It was Bray's duty to deliver copies of Blacow's *Letter* to all the right quarters in Oxford (Exeter College MSS.: R. Blacow to T. Bray, 7 March 1755).

Note Q, p. 203. B.M. Add. MS. 11275, fo. 122; *London Evening Post*, 8–10 Oct. 1754; *J.O.J.*, 12 Oct. 1754; Exeter College MSS.: Lord Maccles-field to T. Bray, 14 Oct. 1754: R. Blacow to T. Bray, 25 Feb. 1755; [F. Webber], *A Defence of the Rector and Fellows of Exeter College . . .* (London, 1754); Warwick C.R.O. Newdigate MS. B 2204; G. Huddesford, *A Proper Reply . . .* (Oxford, 1755); *The Conduct of —— College Consider'd . . . In a Letter from a Cambridge Soph . . .* (London, 1755); *A Letter to the Author of the Defence of Exeter College* (London, 1755); [B. Buckler], *A Proper Explanation of the Oxford Almanack . . .* (London, 1755).

Note R, p. 204. *Dr King's Apology* (Oxford, 1755); *A Letter to Dr King Occasion'd by his Late Apology* (London, 1755); *A Satire upon Physicians* (London, 1755); *Mr Boots's Apology for the Conduct of the Late H—h Sh—ff . . .* (London, 1755); [R. Newton], *The Principles of the University of Oxford* (London, 1755); *The Last Blow, or an Unanswerable Vindication of the Society of Exeter College . . .* (London, 1755); [W. King], *Oratiuncula Habita in Domo Convocationis Oxon . . .* (Oxford, 1757); *A New Speech from the Old Trumpeter of Liberty Hall* (London, 1756). See also *The Spy or Pasquin at Oxford* (London, 1755).

Note S, p. 206. R. Heathcote, *The Use of Reason Asserted in Matters of Religion . . .* (London, 1756) [Heathcote had previously attacked Thomas Fothergill's university sermon, *The Reasonableness and Uses of Commemorating King Charles's Martyrdom* (Oxford, 1753), in a *Letter to the Rev. T. Fothergill* (London, 1753)]; [B. Kennicott], *A Word to the Hutchinsonians . . .* (London, 1756); G. Horne, *An Apology for Certain Gentlemen in the University of Oxford . . .* (Oxford, 1756); B.M. Add. MS. 35593, fo. 81; B. Kennicott, *Christian Fortitude* (Oxford, 1757).

Note T, p. 210. *The Biographical History of Sir William Blackstone* (London, 1782) lists *Reflections on the Opinions of Messrs. Pratt, Morton and Wilbraham relating to Lord Lichfield's Disqualification* (1759) and

NOTES

A Case for the Opinion of Counsel on the Right of the University to make New Statutes, neither of which I have been able to trace but which are again referred to by Basset. Blackstone's strong opinion that the University had the power to alter the Laudian statutes could not be procured by the Oxford University Commission of 1852 (*Report*, p. 5) is now to be found in Blackstone's autograph in Bodl. MS. Top. Oxon. c 209, fos. 27 seq.

Note U, p. 211. F. Bassett, *The Case of a Gentleman Unjustly Deprived of his Vote at the Election of a Chancellor of the University of Oxford* (London, 1759); *Grenville Papers*, i. 288; *A Letter to a Late Member of the U—y of O—d with Respect to the Two Explanatory Statutes Proposed to the C—n* (n. pl. or d. [signed Oxford, 1759]); University Archives: W.P. Y 24 (i) MS. Minutes of the Hebdomadal Board, 1738–59. A manuscript copy of the protest of the Whig heads is preserved as a loose sheet in Balliol College MS. 403. The new statute was translated as if it were part of the Laudian code by G. R. M. Ward, *Oxford University Statutes* (London, 1845), i. 131–3.

Note V, p. 222. B.M. Add. MS. 39311, fo. 141; *Jenkinson Papers*, pp. 48–49. The solidarity of the Merton interest had probably crumbled during the long illness of Warden Robinson who died in 1759. 'The List' appears to have been a ministerial device for the continual manipulation of elections to fellowships at Merton. Two surviving lists for 1751 and 1758 contain detailed statements of the connexions and patrons of electing fellows. B.M. Add. MSS. 34740, fos. 311–12: 37682, fo. 216. There is a reference to a similar list in 1772 in B.M. Add. MS. 38470, fo. 82.

Note W, p. 234. B.M. Add. MSS. 38457, fos. 117, 122, 171, 184, 189, 227, 271, 285: 38578, fo. 40: 39311, fo. 223. On Hay: B.M. Add. MS. 38305, fo. 46; *Grenville Papers*, ii. 263, 266; MSS. of the President of Magdalen College: President Bloxam's MS. Collections II, p. 190. On Fry: W. Haythorne, 'The Twentieth President of St. John Baptist College', *Blackwood's Magazine*, ccxiii. 33. At the poll Blackstone voted for Hay, who was reported to have lost the votes of Dr. Buckler and Warden Tracy only because of his late start (Rashleigh MSS.: Jonathan Rashleigh to Philip Rashleigh, Oxford, 1 April 1768).

Note X, p. 237. B.M. Add. MSS. 30867, fo. 201: 30868, fo. 132: 30871, fo. 50. The inscription on the Bodleian copy G.P. 2705 (i) suggests that Fry was thought to be the author of the Wilkesite pamphlet *An Enquiry into the Doctrine lately Propagated concerning Libels, Warrants, and the Seizure of Papers . . .* (London, 1764). A strongly Wilkesite publication (London, 1768–74) was *The Oxford Magazine, or University Museum. Calculated for General Instruction and Amusement on a Plan Entirely New. By a Society of Gentlemen in the University of Oxford*. The truth about the connexion of this magazine with the University is totally obscure, but vol. x, pp. i–ii, replying to criticisms that the contents had changed character, claimed that many of the original Oxford contributors had fallen away, but that more were to be recruited.

Note Y, p. 247. Meredith had briefly supported the Grenville ministry, and sat on the Admiralty Board in the Rockingham administration. Yet he maintained his old 'independence' even in regard to the Rockinghams, and he was now, like so many old independent members, drifting towards the Court. In March 1774 he became Comptroller of the Household, but resigned because of disagreements on America in Dec. 1777. To the end he never fitted into the party scheme, and two of his favourite causes, religious toleration and reform of the criminal law, cut across party lines altogether.

Note Z, p. 253. Warwick C.R.O. Newdigate MSS. B 2027, 2029, 2361, 4046, fos. B, H; Cobbett, xvii. 312–21; *Gent. Mag.* 1772, pp. 134–5; *Corr. Geo. III*, ii. 514; B.M. Add. MS. 38207, fos. 90–91, 100; Cf. *A Letter to Dr. Nowell Occasioned by his very Extraordinary Sermon* . . . (London, 1772). Newdigate again protested to his wife that the press grossly misrepresented his attitude. 'I was in no heat nor warmth nor sd. any one of the absurd things imputed to me' (Newdigate MS. B 4046, fo. L). Another attempt to abolish the sermon celebrating King Charles the Martyr failed narrowly in 1774 (*Gent. Mag.* 1774, p. 97).

Note Aa, p. 254. [J. Fownes], *An Enquiry into the Principles of Toleration* (London, 1772); A. Kippis, *A Vindication of the Protestant Dissenting Ministers* (London, 1772); I. Mauduit, *The Case of the Dissenting Ministers* (London, 1772); S. Stennett, *A Free and Dispassionate Account of the Late Application of Protestant Dissenting Ministers to Parliament* (London, 1772); E. Radcliff, *A Sermon preached to a Congregation of Protestant Dissenters at Crutched Friars, Occasioned by a denial of Relief* (London, 1772); *London Evening Post*, 7 April 1772; Dr. Williams's Library: Disney Papers, ii. 6.

Note Bb, p. 266. *Oxford Subscription Papers* (Bodl. Oxon. b 17), no. 15; Warwick C.R.O. Newdigate MSS. B 2040, 1827, 1679, 2381, 1678, 2382, 1680, 2245. For the motion were the heads of Queen's, Magdalen, All Souls, Corpus, University, Balliol, Alban Hall, Exeter, Jesus, Wadham, St. Mary Hall, and New Inn Hall; against: Merton, Trinity, New College, Brasenose, Lincoln, Worcester, Magdalen Hall (Newdigate MSS. B 2367, 2244). For a liberal view of these proceedings [J. Disney], *A Short View of the Controversies Occasioned by the Confessional and the Petition to Parliament* . . . (London, 1773).

APPENDIX

Chancellors and Burgesses of the University of Oxford, 1688–1780

CHANCELLORS

1688 James Butler, second Duke of Ormonde
1715 Charles Butler, Earl of Arran
1759 John Fane, Earl of Westmorland
1762 George Henry Lee, Earl of Lichfield
1772 Frederick North, Lord North

BURGESSES

1688 Sir Thomas Clarges and Hon. Heneage Finch
1695 Sir William Trumbull and Hon. Heneage Finch
1698 Sir Christopher Musgrave and Sir William Glynne
1701 3 January, Sir Christopher Musgrave and Hon. Heneage Finch
    21 March, William Bromley *vice* Musgrave elected for Westmorland
1703 Sir William Whitelock *vice* Finch, now Lord Guernsey
1717 Dr. George Clarke, *vice* Whitelock deceased
1732 Viscount Cornbury, *vice* Bromley deceased
1737 9 February, Dr. William Bromley, *vice* Clarke deceased
    31 March, Dr. Edward Butler, *vice* Bromley deceased
1745 Peregrine Palmer, *vice* Butler deceased
1750 Sir Roger Newdigate, *vice* Viscount Cornbury, now Lord Hyde and a peer
1762 Sir Walter Wagstaffe Bagot, *vice* Palmer deceased
1768 3 February, Sir William Dolben, *vice* Bagot deceased
    23 March, Dr. Francis Page, *vice* Dolben who did not stand
1780 Sir William Dolben, *vice* Newdigate who retired

INDEX

Aberdeen, University of, 85, 221.
Abergavenny, Lord, 169.
Abingdon, earls of, 14, 18, 33, 62, 64, 98, 126, 159 n. 22, 185, 227, 258.
Adams, Fitzherbert, 12, 17.
Addison, John, 95.
Addresses to the Crown, 2, 11, 12, 13, 14, 24, 25, 32 n. 40, 36, 81, 107, 133, 135–6, 165, 175, 212, 215, 237, 274.
Aldrich, Henry, 19, 28, 30, 32, 39, 41, 42, 43, 121.
Alfred, King, 114.
Allen, —, 222.
Allen, John, fellow of Merton, 101.
Allen, John, Vice-Principal of Magdalen Hall, 260.
Allibond, John, 52, 80, 176.
All Souls College, 16, 17, 27, 28, 34, 39, 67, 72, 96, 101, 112–13, 120, 121, 122, 123, 128, 143, 153, 155, 157, 178, 179, 189, 197, 206, 207, 209, 219, 221, 222, 224, 230, 231, 232, 233, 244, 257, 264, 285 n. Bb.
Altham, Roger, 19.
Amhurst, Nicholas, 70, 79, 80, 91, 95, 105, 114, 115, 129, 130, 170, 182, 184.
Anatomy of State, 81.
Anhalt, Prince of, 53.
Anne, Princess, da. of George II, 136.
Anne, Queen, 2, 3, 11, 14, 21, 24, 26, 27, 29, 30, 34, 35, 36, 37, 38, 42, 49, 50, 52, 53, 55, 67, 70, 72, 81, 83, 97, 98, 108, 120, 122, 124, 129, 151, 156, 179, 184, 212, 219, 243, 279.
Anstis, John, 143.
Aristotle, 79.
Arran, Lord, 58, 59, 60, 62, 66 n. 24, 67, 71, 87, 115, 122, 123, 124, 125, 144, 175, 177, 178, 190, 196, 200, 207.
Aston, Sir Willoughby, 188.
Atterbury, Francis, I, Bishop of Rochester, 22, 28, 29, 32, 39, 43, 45, 46, 47, 49, 50, 52, 59, 64, 80, 97, 106, 107, 108, 109, 116, 119, 122, 123, 132 n. 1, 136, 140, 141, 153.
Atterbury, Francis, II, student of Christ Church, 240.
Augusta of Saxe-Gotha, 137.
Austen, George, 210.
Aylesford, earls of, 122, 145, 219, 258.
Ayliffe, John, 71, 72, 110, 111.
Ayscough, Francis, 118.

Bagot, Lewis, 262, 265, 271, 275.

Bagot, Sir Walter Wagstaffe, 123, 178, 224–5, 226, 228, 231.
Bagot, Sir William, 255, 268, 272, 273.
Baker, William, 104, 105.
Balliol College, 6, 17, 47, 48, 54, 116–17, 118, 123, 126, 127, 129, 135, 158, 159, 170, 173, 174, 197, 209, 211, 222, 229, 232, 233, 236, 285 n. Bb.
Baron, John, 47, 48, 116.
Barrington, Shute, 220, 221, 222, 224, 226, 250.
Bartlett, William, 106.
Barton, Henry, 234.
Basset, Francis, 210, 284 n. T.
Bateman, John, 40.
Bearcroft, Philip, 89, 100.
Beattie, James, 270.
Beauchamp, Lord, 227.
Beaufort, dukes of, 115, 159, 173, 178, 180, 196, 200, 216, 258, 259.
Beaumont, Sir George, 19, 20.
Beckford, William, 210.
Bedford, Duke of, 174, 176.
Bentham, Edward, 139, 171, 172, 173, 181, 182, 183, 186, 197, 216, 241, 264, 274.
Bentley, Richard, 13, 19, 29, 45, 65, 70, 74, 83, 92, 93.
Bernstorff, Baron von, 87.
Bertie, Edward, 126.
Best, William, 116, 117.
Betts, Joseph, 256.
Betty, Joseph, 147–8.
Bigg, Henry, 111.
Bilstone, William Powell (?), 222.
Blackburne, Francis, 243, 244, 270.
Blackstone, Sir William, 188, 189, 190, 191, 196, 197, 199, 205, 207, 210, 212, 216, 219, 220, 221, 222, 226, 227, 230, 233, 234, 247, 248, 262 n. 16, 271, 282 n. M, 284 nn. T, W.
Blacow, Richard, 170, 171, 185, 196, 197, 198, 199, 200, 201–2, 203, 204, 283 nn. O, P.
Blathwaite, William, 122.
Blechynden, Richard, 48.
Blencow, Sir John, 72.
Blencowe, William, 34, 35.
Bolingbroke, Viscount, see St. John, Henry.
Bouchier, James, 97.
Boulter, Hugh, 108.
Bounty, Queen Anne's, 25, 44, 160.
Bowles, Joseph, 109, 127.

287

INDEX

Boyer, Abel, 60, 71, 78, 80, 86.
Boyle, Charles, 19.
Bradshaw, William, I, Dean of Christ
 Church, 98, 108, 111, 141.
Bradshaw, William, II, fellow of Jesus,
 98.
Braithwaite, Thomas, 47, 110.
Bramston, Sir John, 11.
Brasenose College, 46, 55, 80, 96, 98, 99,
 106, 126, 156, 170, 191, 221, 224, 232,
 257, 270, 285 n. Bb.
Bray, Thomas, 194, 195, 196, 197–8,
 201, 202, 203, 204, 215, 216, 220, 221,
 222, 224, 226, 257 n. 2, 283 n. P.
Breton, Robert, 101, 102, 103.
Brickenden, Colwell, 47.
Bridgewater, Earl of, 107.
Bromfield, John, 111.
Bromley, Francis, 154.
Bromley, William, the Elder, 13, 19,
 20, 26, 27, 28, 29, 33, 34, 36, 38, 42,
 45, 47, 48, 50, 56, 58, 68, 96, 119, 120,
 121, 122, 124, 125, 126, 127, 128, 152,
 156, 223.
Bromley, William, the Younger, 153–
 5, 223.
Brooke, Henry, 168, 179, 186.
Browne, John, 187.
Browne, Joseph, 213, 220.
Bruce, Lord, 212.
Brydges, Henry, 116.
Brynker, Robert, 101, 127.
Buccleugh, Duke of, 169.
Buckingham, Duke of, 35.
Buckingham, Duchess of, 153.
Buckler, Benjamin, 197, 199, 203, 207,
 211, 219, 230, 262 n. 16, 284 n. W.
Burke, Edmund, 213, 248, 274.
Burnet, Gilbert, 28.
Burton, John, 139, 143, 182, 186, 213,
 216.
Burton, Thomas, 115.
Bury, Arthur, 21, 94, 105.
Bute, Lord, 220, 221, 223, 226, 234, 256.
Butler, Edward, 128, 141, 146, 155, 156,
 161.
Byne, Henry, 99.

Caernarvon, Marquis of, 123.
Cambridge, University of, 1, 3, 4, 13,
 29, 32 n. 40, 33, 35, 56, 58, 60, 65, 70,
 93, 132, 156, 158, 165, 173, 174, 176,
 178, 184, 185, 194, 212, 215, 246, 252
 n. 26, 261, 263, 264, 273, 274.
Camden, Lord, 240, 255.
Canterbury, archbishops of (see also
 under archbishop's names), 4, 40, 99,
 134, 143, 154, 180, 185, 216, 229, 248.
Carnall, Mary, 195.
Caroline, Queen, 148.

Carter, George, 48, 67, 108–10, 115, 127,
 130.
Carteret, Lord, 103, 161.
Cartwright, John, 277.
Carty, Bazil, 89.
Cater, John, 146.
Cato's Letters, 78.
Cavendish, Lord John, 247.
Chambers, Sir Robert, 230, 268.
Charles II, King, 91, 208.
Charles the Martyr, Commemoration
 of King, 25, 32, 135, 140, 181, 205,
 214, 215, 251–2, 285 n. Z.
Charlett, Arthur, 5, 13, 14, 17, 19, 20,
 22, 26, 29, 33, 42, 44, 47, 48, 56, 61,
 65, 67, 79, 87, 92, 93, 96, 101, 114,
 115, 120, 122, 124, 144, 280 n. C.
Chatham, Earl of, see Pitt, William,
 the Elder.
Cherry, Francis, 85.
Chesterfield, Lord, 176.
Christ Church, 4, 6, 8, 17, 18, 19, 22,
 25, 29, 30, 32, 34, 39, 42, 43, 45, 46,
 49, 53, 56, 59, 61, 68, 76, 89, 94, 96,
 105, 106–8, 115, 116, 121, 122, 124
 n. 6, 126, 129, 132, 134, 136, 138, 141,
 145, 146, 150, 151, 153, 154, 166, 169,
 170, 174, 187, 189, 190, 191, 193, 195,
 196, 197, 204, 208, 209, 211, 216, 217,
 219, 220, 222, 224, 228, 230, 231, 236,
 263, 272, 279, 280 n. A.
Clarendon, earls of, 16, 24, 41, 45, 57,
 152, 183, 200, 247, 252.
Clarges, Sir Thomas, 15, 16, 44, 189.
Clarke, Francis, 25.
Clarke, George, 16, 27, 28, 48, 93, 96,
 112, 120, 121, 122, 123, 124, 125, 126,
 127, 128, 141, 144, 152, 153, 156, 157.
Clarke, John, 260.
Clarke, Samuel, 79, 243.
Clavering, Robert, 68, 96, 102, 107, 108,
 115, 127.
Cleland, William, 91 n. 11.
Clitherow, James, 188.
Coade, George, 183 n. 36.
Cobb, John, 110, 111.
Cockman, Thomas, 114–16, 117, 144.
Code, Philip, 72.
Codrington, Christopher, 17.
College Statutes, 7, 8, 33, 70, 94, 114,
 186–7, 196.
Colley, Jonathan, 134.
Colston, Caleb, 60.
Common Sense, 163.
Commons, House of, 27, 35, 119, 176,
 181, 185, 195, 200, 215, 233, 247, 250,
 251, 267, 268, 273.
Compton, Henry, 12, 17, 32, 33, 34.
Conant, John, 40.
Coningsby, George, 134–5.

288

INDEX

Coningsby, Lord, 64, 88 n. 7.
Constitution Club, 55, 61, 62, 71, 72,
 81, 83, 88–92, 100, 111, 113, 137, 142,
 148, 204.
Convocation of the Church of England,
 22, 28, 30, 91.
Conybeare, John, 91, 106, 137–8, 139,
 141, 142, 143–5, 149, 150, 153, 154,
 175, 181, 185.
Cookes, Sir Thomas, 48.
Cork, Earl of, 223.
Cornbury, Lord, 116, 152–3, 155, 156,
 157, 158, 159, 161, 162, 166, 188, 191,
 282 n. J.
Cornell, Theodosia, 197, 198, 203.
Cornwallis, Frederick, 250.
Corpus Christi College, 26, 27, 42, 82,
 94, 116, 118, 139, 143, 159, 182, 193,
 195, 199, 205, 211, 232, 240, 264, 285
 n. Bb.
Costard, Henry, 89.
Cotterell family, 16.
Cotton, John Hynde, 216.
Cowper, John, 89, 100, 101, 102.
Cowper, Lady, 107.
Cowper, Lord, 87, 100, 102, 103.
Cox, Thomas, 101, 102.
Coxe, William, 150.
Craggs, James, 102, 103.
Craven, Lord, 98, 123.
Cromwell, Oliver, 91, 166, 208 n. 2.
Crosby, Brass, 237.
Crown, influence and patronage of the,
 4, 6, 7, 8, 15, 17, 29 seq., 72, 84, 99,
 111, 213.
Cumberland, Duke of, 168, 217.
Cummings, Fowler, 196, 197.

Dalton, Thomas, 34.
Dartmouth, Earl of, 35.
Dashwood family, 227.
Dashwood, Sir Francis, 200 n. 18, 218.
Dashwood, Sir James, 192, 194, 195,
 205, 210, 227.
Dawes, James, 170, 171, 173, 174, 181,
 201.
Defoe, Daniel, 43.
Delafaye, Charles, 102, 150.
Delaune, William, 30, 44–45, 46, 50, 79,
 90, 95, 96, 114, 115, 116, 117, 120,
 122, 133.
Denison, William, 114–16.
Devonshire, Duke of, 87.
Digby, Lord, 35.
Dobson, John, 111.
Dod, Pierce, 120, 121.
Dolben, Sir William, 229, 230, 231, 232,
 251, 254, 267, 276, 278.
Downes, Samuel, 280 n. D.
Doyley, Sir John, 107, 127.

Drake, William, 232.
Dry, John, 280 n. D.
Duncombe, Charles Slingsby, 169.
Dunning, John, 273.
Dunster, Thomas, 40, 65, 103, 122.
Durell, David, 223, 240.
Dyke, Sir Thomas, 20, 152.

Eastway, Richard, 106.
Edgecumbe, James, 195.
Edisbury, John, 20, 28.
Edwards, Jonathan, 46, 97.
Egerton, Henry, 107.
Ellis, John, fellow of Jesus, 97.
Ellis, John, Under-Secretary of State,
 17, 18.
Ellis, Welbore, 267.
Ellys, Anthony, 252.
Eton College, 139.
Evans, Abel, 54, 116.
Evans, John, 104.
Evans, Robert (?), 109.
Evening Advertiser, The, 196, 198, 204.
Evening Post, The, 56, 83, 128.
Eves, —, 66.
Ewelme, Rectory of, 25.
Excise Bill, 149, 156, 207.
Exeter College, 21, 34, 40, 94, 104, 105–
 6, 126, 129, 137, 138, 140, 141, 144,
 147, 148, 150, 154, 159, 166, 169, 170,
 181, 191, 194, 200, 201, 203, 204, 206,
 209, 211, 215, 216, 222, 223, 236, 256,
 257, 285 n. Bb.

Fanshawe, John, 140–1, 154, 216.
Fazakerly, Nicholas, 173.
Feathers Tavern Association, 246, 247,
 253, 261, 262, 267, 270.
Felton, Henry, 140, 146.
Filmer, Sir Robert, 205.
Finch family, 3, 16, 24, 219.
Finch, Heneage, 15, 16, 17, 18, 19, 25,
 26, 28.
Finch, Leopold William, 16, 19.
Fitzmaurice, Thomas, 227–35, 236, 248.
Fleming, Henry, 12.
Flying Post, The, 72, 73, 75, 100, 106,
 280 n. D.
Foley family, 20, 219.
Foley, Lords, 159 n. 22, 173, 219, 222.
Forster, Nathaniel, 139 n. 21.
Fothergill, George, 160 n. 23, 240.
Fothergill, Thomas, 240, 264.
Fox, Charles James, 267.
Fox, Henry, 123, 199, 220, 221, 228.
Fox, Stephen, 123.
Frampton, Matthew, 155.
Frederick, Prince of Wales, 118, 137,
 141, 150, 153, 173, 190.
Free, John, 167–8, 194, 282 n. K.

INDEX

INDEX

Nullum Tempus Bill, 250.

Occasional Conformity Act, 86, 87, 106.
Occasional Conformity, campaign against, 26–27, 50, 125.
Ockley, Simon, 68.
Oculus Britanniae, 80.
Oldisworth (Oldesworth), William, 98.
Orange, Prince of, 136–7.
Oriel College, 19, 25, 47, 48, 55, 66, 67, 108–10, 114, 115, 126, 127, 129, 130, 139, 209, 222, 224, 230, 231, 232, 258, 264.
Ormonde, Duke of, 11, 17, 18, 25, 31, 41, 48, 50, 55, 56, 57, 58, 59, 62, 64, 66, 70, 71, 81, 110, 115, 122, 123, 150, 163, 237.
Orrery, Earl of, 164.
Owen, Colonel, 59, 60, 70.
Oxford, city of, 14, 62, 63, 189, 233.
Oxford, 1st Earl of, *see* Harley, Robert, I.
Oxford, 2nd Earl of, *see* Harley, Edward, I.
Oxford, 3rd Earl of, *see* Harley, Edward, II.
Oxford Toasts, The, 95.
Oxford, University of:
bedels, 5, 72, 85, 279.
burgesses, election of (*see also under names of burgesses*), 5, 6, 15–20, 25, 28, 120, 121, 152, 154, 155–6, 173, 188–91, 224–5, 227–36, 277–8.
chancellors (*see also under names of chancellors*), 3, 4, 5, 11, 12, 25, 48, 57, 58, 67, 71, 81, 87, 97, 115, 116, 121 n. 2, 122, 123, 124, 139, 142, 144, 175, 188, 190, 191, 200, 202, 207, 212, 213, 214, 215, 217, 218, 220, 222, 223, 227, 229, 241, 256–9, 263, 266, 269, 274.
Convocation, 3, 4, 5, 8, 12, 18, 21, 29, 62, 90, 132, 139, 165, 183, 186, 204, 210, 211, 215, 224, 230, 237, 238 n. 21, 260, 263, 265, 266, 268 n. 28, 272, 276 n. 22.
Hebdomadal Board, 4, 5, 210–11, 250.
High Steward, 3, 41, 200, 207, 212, 213, 221, 223, 258.
proctors, 4, 62, 89, 101, 168, 193, 211, 240.
professors, 5, 6, 8, 14, 19, 21, 29 seq., 40, 68, 72–73, 89, 90, 97, 107, 113, 114, 122, 123, 132–3, 137, 140, 154, 166, 168, 186, 208, 214, 216, 240, 241, 251, 252, 259, 264, 268, 278.
statutes, 7, 210–11.
subscriptions, 7, 8, 80, 117, 145, 244, 249, 260–8.

Oxford, University of (*cont.*):
University Observatory, 25, 257.
University Press, 13, 156, 168, 203, 220.
verger, 5, 72.
Vice-Chancellor, 4, 12, 13, 14, 17, 20, 22, 29, 30, 34, 36, 39, 47, 49, 53, 54, 56, 57, 58, 59, 60, 62, 72, 73, 81, 85, 89, 90, 91, 92, 96, 106, 110, 112, 114–16, 117, 123, 127, 132, 133, 135, 146, 150, 157, 158, 159, 166, 168, 169, 170, 171, 174, 175, 177, 181, 182, 185, 193, 199, 201, 202, 203, 204, 206, 210, 211, 213, 220, 221, 223, 224, 229, 231, 237, 239, 240, 241, 242, 249, 256, 257, 261, 264, 265, 266, 267, 271.

Page, Francis, 227–36, 249, 250, 259, 268.
Page, Sir Francis, 228.
Paley, William, 270.
Palmer, Peregrine, 155, 156, 199 n. 17, 224.
Palmer, Samuel, 42.
Palmer, Thomas, 155.
Pardo, Thomas, 98–99.
Parker, Charles, 277.
Parker, George, 2nd Earl of Macclesfield, 192, 193, 195, 198, 202, 203.
Parker, Sir Thomas, 1st Earl of Macclesfield, 86, 107, 127, 138.
Parker, Thomas, Lord, 192, 195.
Parker's Academy, 27.
Patten, Thomas, 205.
Paynter, William, 105, 106.
Pearse, Robert, 92.
Pelham, Henry, 140, 144, 145, 162, 177, 190.
Pelling, John, 50, 68.
Pembroke College, 25, 47, 115, 209, 222.
Pembroke, Earl of, 29, 58, 97.
Peploe, Samuel, 93, 101.
Pepper, Colonel, 59, 60, 70, 71, 124.
Peterborough, Lord, 135.
Phillips, Sir John, 188.
Phillips, Rev. Mr., curate of Purleigh, 260.
Phipps, Sir Constantine, 57, 66, 69, 90, 121 n. 2.
Physick Garden, 193.
Pitt, William, the Elder, Earl of Chatham, 163, 199, 212, 213, 214, 217, 223, 255, 258 n. 3.
Pitt, William, the Younger, 237.
Pointer, John, 169.
Pope, Alexander, 122, 152.
Popham, Alexander, 252.
Portland, Earl of, 40.
Potter, Francis, 166–7, 168, 282 n. K.